BEYOND TH[E]

William Travis served in the RAF during the Second World War and after demobilization flew small planes round the world for commercial airlines. He became air advisor to the Sultan of Zanzibar and has since travelled the world, making his living by diving, shark fishing, rare shell collecting and nature conservation. He now makes his home in Samoa, where he runs a fishing business.

CENTURY TRAVELLERS

BEYOND THE REEFS & SHARK FOR SALE

Adventures in the Seychelles

William Travis

ARROW BOOKS

Century Travellers

Published by Arrow Books Limited
20 Vauxhall Bridge Road,
London SW1V 2SA

An imprint of Random Century Group

London Melbourne Sydney Auckland Johannesburg
and agencies throughout the world

BEYOND THE REEFS (©) William Travis 1959
First published in 1959 by George Allen & Unwin Ltd

SHARK FOR SALE (©) William Travis 1961
First published in 1961 by George Allen & Unwin Ltd

First published in one volume by Arrow Books Ltd 1990

The right of William Travis to be identified as the author of this work has been asserted by him in accordance with the Copyright, Designs and Patents Act, 1988.

This book is sold subject to the condition that it shall not, by way of trade or otherwise, be lent, resold, hired out, or otherwise circulated without the publisher's prior consent in any form of binding or cover other than that in which it is published and without a similar condition including this condition being imposed on the subsequent purchaser

Printed and bound in Great Britain by
The Guernsey Press Co. Ltd, Guernsey, C.I.

Phototypeset by Input Typesetting Ltd, London

ISBN 0 09 974990 4

TO POLLY AND JADE

Author's Preface to the Century Travellers Edition

> '... one should never go back'
> William Faulkner

The early morning air was chill and rain-squalls clustered the horizon when I came out of the wheelhouse onto the bridge. It was too cold for comfort and spats of rain stung my face – but a familiar outline on the radar-screen had stirred old thoughts and now I wanted to see if memory's image matched reality.

Then out of a break in the clouds loomed the clear lines of a tree-clad cone, rising in an unmistakable manner straight up out of the sea, and without thought I flung the old shark-fisherman's cry into the teeth of the wind:

> '*Silhouette dehors* ... !'

More than thirty years had passed since I had last glimpsed Silhouette – or indeed any of the islands of the Seychelles – and a sudden apprehension seized me. I was, as it were, trespassing on a portion of my life long since past ... In those far-off days I ranged over these same waters in a small sailing-craft of 9-tons burthen and now I was returning with a tuna-clipper of 750-tons. Just as my present surroundings had changed beyond any concept of a quarter-century ago, would not these islands have changed beyond all recognition? And Faulkner's words crept into my mind and I was uneasy and not altogether sure that what I had planned was wise. Thirty years was a long time in this fast-moving age. The Seychelles that I had known were a sleepy, back-of-beyond, British colony. Since then it had experienced independence, a social revolution followed by a second coup d'état, and was now a Republic under a Marxist form of government. In addition, it had become a major international tourist mecca and to its new airport winged jumbo-jets from all over the globe. What hope was there for me to unearth anything of that bygone era I had known and loved ... ?

Then Goethe's words, that he had Faust cry, came to my mind:

'Change is King . . . !'

– and I took comfort in this thought and went back inside the wheelhouse, resolved to wait and see what lay ahead before giving way to my fears.

Ten hours later I knew that Goethe was right and Faulkner wrong . . .

Certainly the Seychelles had changed – in many ways almost beyond physical recognition – but the past had somehow blended with the present to form an exciting new entity, and one with which I felt at ease. It was like going to see a woman one had once loved and finding in her place her daughter – modern and outgoing, with a different hairstyle and novel manners, but who still carried the lineage of her mother, made apparent in every gesture, every utterance and in her very bone structure – and I am again enchanted. But for all my enchantment I am also a 'fly-on-the-wall', an observer, a recorder of things-that-are, for such is my way.

These then are my findings . . .

In the 1950s there were three levels within the Seychelles social structure. At the top, a benign, slow and under-financed Colonial government. Below this a small core of wealthy land-owners and businessmen – and at the bottom a mass of poor, largely uneducated and prospectless rank and file. Now, in 1988, there exists an energetic 'Marxist' government whose controlled radio-broadcasts of a Saturday list a lengthy catalogue of those religious services that will be held throughout the islands the coming Sunday . . . Today there is a thriving tourist industry with half a dozen 'international-class' luxury hotels and all the attendant paraphernalia to cater for the 'wealthy capitalists' – and at the lowest level, once again, the bulk of the population. A population that is still 'poor', but nowadays a section with access to general education, socialized medicine, a plethora of sporting activities, and which is secured through state-controlled pension and insurance schemes. Certainly there is a compulsory youth-training programme covering political indoctrination together with basic paramilitary activities with which one may, or may not, agree.

But I note that which to my mind seems of more importance.

That there is no evidence of corruption and there is now pride in being Seychelloise – two complete turn-arounds from the past – as well as a rigorous conservation policy regarding natural resources and wildlife which is already showing significant results. Whole sections of coastline are now 'protected areas'. Offshore islands which I, for one, exploited, are now National Parks. The destruction of corals, witless collection of sea-shells, the importation or use of spearguns and the robbing of birds' nests are all activities totally proscribed.

There has been a total ban on any form of lobster-fishing now for almost five years, with the result that this resource is slowly recovering from past indiscriminate harvesting. Birds are protected and many endangered and unique species are now re-establishing themselves. The felling of rare timbers is outlawed; dangerous pesticides and herbicides are prohibited; firearms – sporting or otherwise – are banned; turtles are protected. The legislation is impressive and its results even more so.

And the end result is that now, after thirty years absence, I find these islands more exuberant in their wildlife and with more luxuriant plantlife than when I first came here.

Of course, perhaps I do not welcome all the changes that have taken place, for what was once dirt-cheap – accommodation, food and transportation – is now expensive. The same also is true of Antigua, of Hydra, of Tahiti. The Seychelles, a backwater in the 1950s, now parades its attractions on billboards and posters in travel agencies across the globe – what can you expect but costly 'souvenirs', amateur and overpriced 'artwork' and extravagant hotel bills?

But for those who would seek an essence of the Seychelles described in this book I would suggest that you do not wander aimlessly around the boutiques of Port Victoria, nor yet recline in your comfortable three-star hotel or lie on the beach at Beau-vallon. Get out, get away! Take an inter-island schooner to Praslin or La Digue, or venture still further afield.

WILLIAM TRAVIS

BOOK ONE
BEYOND THE REEFS

Contents

	Introduction	15
1.	Mahé	17
2.	Praslin	28
3.	Alphonse	45
4.	Farquhar	67
5.	On My Own	94
6.	Cosmoledo	109
7.	Turtle Hunt	139
8.	Aldabra	154
9.	Goats and Groupers	174
10.	Assumption	190
11.	Astove	206
	Epilogue	215

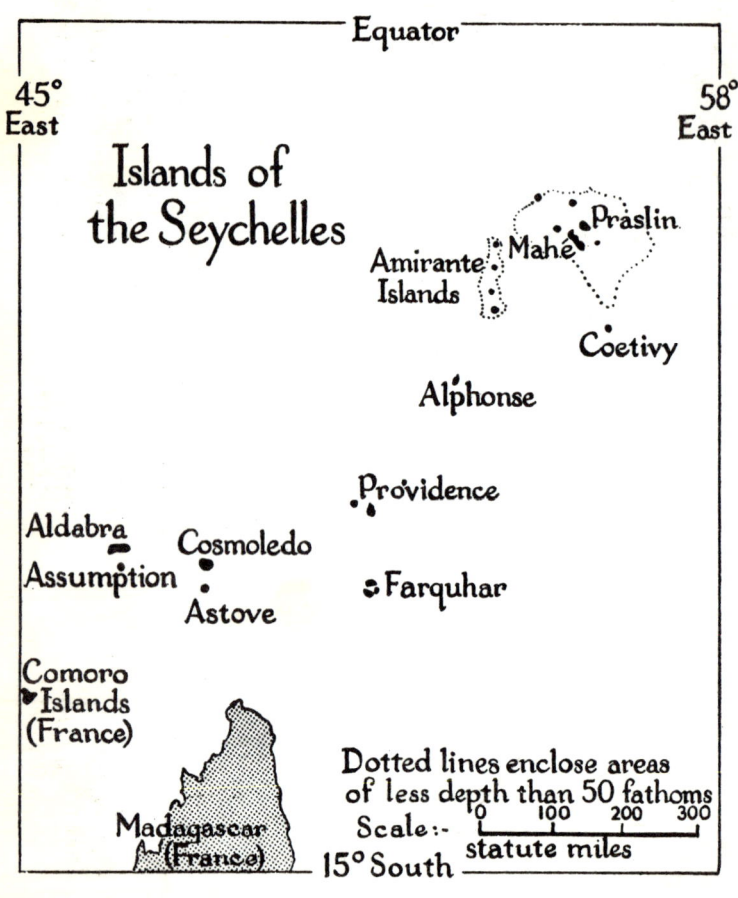

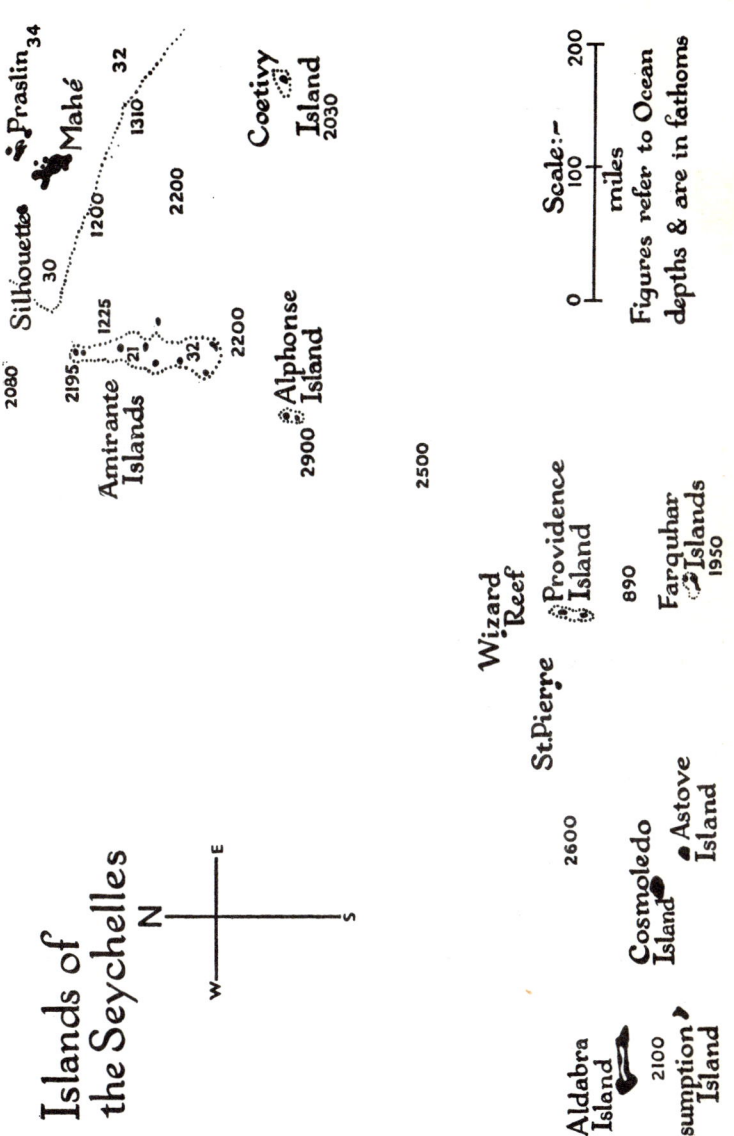

Introduction

It was Christmas Eve.

The distant hum became more definite, audible now above the gusts of wind that sang through the rigging and which gave warning of another vicious squall. Ducking out from under the shelter of what was grandly termed 'the wheelhouse', I looked up into the dark sky, which was made more threatening by the gathering dusk.

As I watched, the aircraft slid from the black interior of one massive cloud and crossed over a valley of clear air. In doing so it was illuminated by a stray sunbeam, so that it glinted silvery and fishlike for a moment, before being swallowed up in the murk. Then it was gone. The first aircraft I had seen or heard for a year, though I knew well enough what flight it was – the weekly Air France schedule from Madagascar to Europe.

For several minutes I stayed on deck, staring across the dark sea towards the low and jagged coral island off which we lay. But my mind was following that aeroplane, whose engine noise had even now died away, swallowed up in the rush of wind. A few spats of rain roused me from my dreaming and I went back to the tiny shelter from which the familiar sound had drawn me.

Within, sitting on the wet floorboards, writing up my log by the light of a hurricane lantern, I thought of that other navigator up there and his probable log entry for that moment: '1815. Over Aldabra Island. Eight thousand five hundred feet. Airspeed one hundred and eighty. Course Three Three Seven. Rain. Moderate turbulence. Estimate Djibuti . . .'

So I sat, my thoughts still accompanying the airliner's flight, conjuring up the passengers and the crew, visualizing the hostesses preparing the evening meal up there.

What would it be?

Something special, no doubt, seeing it was Christmas Eve. Perhaps:

MENU

Petite Crème de Foie d'Oie
Cromesqui façon Cardinal
Pintade en Daube Froide
Fromage
Bûche de Sapin

Vins *Café*
Pouilly-Fuissé
Saint-Emilion
Champagne
  Liqueurs

I knew very well the meal I should soon be having:

A Handful of Cold Rice
Boiled Salt-fish
A Mugful of Rusty Water

I looked around at my companions. There were eight of us in that small cabin over the engine. Two were jet-black negroes, three were coffee-coloured, two near-white and myself. Four other Creoles were tucked away in the tiny chain-locker up in the bows. After six weeks on the *L. Fred*, we were dirty, bearded, ragged and thin. Our skins were burnt and blistered by incessant exposure to sun and salt-water. We had no place to sleep other than these floorboards and nothing to keep us warm, this cold night, other than the animal heat of our bodies.

Yet we counted ourselves successful. Successful because there lay in the hold two hundred full, fat sacks. Successful because these sacks contained eight tons of mother-of-pearl shell; the culmination, for me, of eighteen months' planning and scheming and representing, for them, more wages than they usually earned in a year.

All things considered then, I was glad to be sitting on that battered sailing schooner, anchored in the lee of a tiny island of which few people had even heard, in the middle of the Indian Ocean. And I did not envy, after all, those passengers on Air France Flight Six Two Four, in spite of the undoubted luxury of their reclining chairs and the excellence of the meal they were about to eat.

No, they could go on their airway, with all its modern comforts, and leave me happy and remote at Latitude 9° 27′ South, Longitude 46° 13′ East.

ONE

Mahé

It all started in Zanzibar.

Apart from the usual Government officials, the only Europeans one saw there were those few schooner owners whose trading up and down the East African coast brought them to that island. Hard working, these men had no fixed hours, nor itineraries. Perhaps it was this that first attracted me, contrasting vividly, as it did, with the strict schedules of my own career. Their conversation and anecdotes concerning this strange coast, about which so little is known even today, made me restless and very conscious of the fact that my life lacked real interest, purpose, effort or even satisfaction.

After twelve years of flying the glamour had worn remarkably thin – it had deteriorated into just another humdrum nine-to-six salaried job, although up to that time I had not realized how dull it was.

Eventually, I reached the point where I had to have a change, or else I would burst. Moreover, if a break were to be made, it must be radical and immediate – else I should never do it, and then the years themselves would come to repeat the pattern of each day's work, and that was a depressing thought.

The question was, what could I do? Though I envied the freedom of these schooner owners, I had neither sufficient capital, nor experience with ships to think of doing likewise.

A chance encounter led me out of this cul-de-sac. One of these men, Eric Hunt, who is now dead, had found the famous Coelacanth fish, the second specimen in the world and the first to be secured intact. He had followed up his discovery by catching several subsequent specimens and, although a layman in the science of ichthyology, probably had more empirical knowledge of these creatures than any other person in the world. His graceful ship, the *Hiariako*, always contained a host of strange creatures:

shy and rare Lemurs from Madagascar, monkeys and bush-babies from East Africa, dogs, owls and cats – all living together, if not in harmony at least in neutrality.

It was through Eric Hunt that I met Harvey Brain, another schooner captain from the Seychelles, who occasionally made the thousand-mile journey to the African coast to take part in the clove-freighting, or else on charter to private fishing parties. It was from Harvey Brain's ship that a group of Italian underwater sportsman had seen and photographed a Coelacanth in the Comoro Islands the year before.

This photograph of the Coelacanth, still the only one in existence of a living specimen, had its authenticity hotly contested by certain French scientists, who varied their denunciations from maintaining that it was a case of wrong identification to boldly asserting that it was a premeditated fake perpetrated for publicity purposes! In spite of all this, many scientists and the people on the spot at the time it was taken, including Harvey, were of the firm opinion that it was not a fake, indeed could not have been from the very nature of its spontaneity, and that it *was* a Coelacanth. The French scientists' main objection was that it upset all their previous published assertions that the creature belonged to the abyssal depths, for the Italian party saw and photographed it only about thirty feet down. This insistence on depth was still further shattered later, when additional specimens were caught on hand-lines in shallow water.

Intrigued by Hunt's account of his finding of the Coelacanth and by Harvey's history of the disputed photograph, I saw that here might lie the answer to my problem. For the past few years much of my spare time had been given over to the new sport of 'aqualung' diving and underwater photography. Why not, then, another underwater expedition to the Comores, to try and settle this argument?

Harvey was most enthusiastic over the idea, and together we thrashed out the preliminary charter arrangements. Several friends in England were equally keen, and both the film company and the manufacturers of specialized diving equipment whom I contacted offered us free assistance in the form of technical equipment and advice. The whole scheme grew with snowball rapidity. Zoos, scientific institutions and even circuses approached us with a view to buying live, dead or even portions of any Coelacanth we might obtain. In fact, everything was going along remarkably well when the whole project dissolved into thin air on the withdrawal of our main financial backer.

Regretfully, the expedition was shelved, and I continued with my life of routine, sure that now my big chance had come and gone, while Harvey Brain went back to the Seychelles.

I was all the more surprised, therefore, to receive a letter from him a few months later. This time it was he who proposed the basic idea. It appeared that a type of shell known as Green Snail was being found in the waters surrounding the Seychelles. The market value of these was of the order of three hundred pounds or more per ton, and although they were not too plentiful there, he had heard that a great many were to be found in Chagos Archipelago, an island group a further thousand miles to the east.

The snag, however, was that the shells seemed to be beyond the depths accessible to the few 'skin-divers' on the islands. Moreever, they lay beyond the reefs themselves, on the edge of the great deeps, where no one had ever swum or dived before – mainly on account of the many sharks patrolling there. Anyway, what did I think of the idea of going 'shelling' with him? Firstly a trip within the Seychelles to gain experience, followed by a major expedition on to Chagos?

The more I thought about it, the more I liked the suggestion. I already possessed most of the equipment necessary and thought that I might well be able to make sufficient capital out of the venture, if the price of shells remains stable, to finance my next move in what would be a new life. True, I knew nothing about Green Snail, but for that matter I had little detailed knowledge of anything outside the world of aviation. If I was going to jump on to something new, it might as well be something completely new and, moreover, something about which no one knew very much, as seemed to be the case with these shells.

Even the encyclopedia which I consulted, apart from stating that this 'is the common name for a marine gastropod, *Turbo Mammoratus*, whose shell is utilized in the manufacture of mother-of-pearl commodities', seemed remarkably reticent. The further I looked, the less I knew. It transpired that no one knew very much at all about this animal. The Pearl Oyster shell, yes. There were references and textbooks on all its facets, commercial and scientific. Mussels, welks, conch, cowries and clams; these were there too, their life histories, diet and methods of reproduction, all carefully compiled. But of *Turbo Mammoratus* not a word, except a bare description obviously copied in most cases from the same source of information as that of the encyclopedia.

It was refreshing in these days of expert opinions and technical efficiency to find something simple about which no one seemed to know anything precise. In a sphere with so little competition or foreknowledge it seemed that the most ignorant, in this case myself, stood as much chance as the enlightened – if there were any! At least on the technical side I was as advanced as most people, since to my knowledge modern aqualung techniques had never yet been tried in commercial shell-diving.

And so it was arranged. I was to go over to the Seychelles, taking all the diving gear necessary, not only for myself but sufficient if required to train a team of Creole divers. Harvey would supply the schooner, and we would share the expenses and profits, if any.

On the strength of this, I resigned my job.

There is little doubt that the approaches to Mahé, the principal island of the Seychelles, constitute some of the most glorious land- and sea-scapes possible. So far as I know, it is one of the very few natural beauties of the world that lives up to its reputation. Another that does so is the famous 'Persian Dawn' of the travel brochures. In fact, if one is lucky enough to reach Mahé at daybreak, as I was, the similarity between the two is very striking.

Against a flat, blue-shadowed horizon a stark and jagged fringe of mountains rises up, the edges clear cut and fantastically etched against the flood of pale green and orange light that builds up above the eastern horizon. It has the unreality of a cardboard cut-out and the dramatic texture of a stage backcloth. But there is this important difference between sunrise amid the Persian mountains and that on approaching Mahé. In Persia the revealing daylight proves those mountains to be – in actuality, as they first appeared – massive ramparts of bare rock thrown up abruptly from the earth's crust in wrinkled folds across the plain. In Mahé the sun is kinder, showing those stark precipices to be indeed

MAHÉ

mountainous but wooded slopes, with the dense green of tropic vegetation rapidly building up out of the shadowed valleys.

Only one thing is missing to complete the beauty of the scene; the hordes of sea-birds that one would normally expect to find in such a locality and which were present fifty or more years ago. Since then the islanders have killed off by the hundreds of thousands the terns, boobies, frigate birds and gulls that used to nest on the island and which the old histories record. Now, if one sees twenty such birds together around a ship it is something to be remarked upon.

I was so impressed by all this that even Harvey's news on meeting me at the quay did not then seem so important, nor anything much to worry about. It appeared that his schooner, the *Marsouin*, had broken down and he had cabled me to bring over certain engine parts from East Africa. He had sent this cable on the day of my departure, not knowing that I had managed to get a berth when I did, so that his message had missed me. Now, with no one to bring these over, and no other ship due for six weeks, we were stuck. Everything else was ready and we should have set out on our first shelling trip within a few days of my arrival, but for this.

There was nothing to do about it but sit and wait as patiently as we could. In the meantime, the season of the north-west monsoon, which last from October to the beginning of May and which constitutes the period of calms in the Seychelles, and is therefore ideal shelling weather, was fast drawing to a close. I arrived in Mahé in early February and the vital spare parts finally arrived in April, nearly two months later.

During this interval I was busy trying once more to find out what I could of the Green Snail shells in the vicinity and also in getting together a diving team. The first task presented no difficulties. I could find out exactly nothing beyond what we already knew and also that certain Creole fishermen were collecting them around Praslin, second largest island in the Seychelles and only nineteen miles from Mahé.

The second task also presented few difficulties. Within a week of arriving it was known throughout the island that I was willing to employ suitable skin-divers. ('Skin-diver' means a diver equipped either with mask and swim fins, or with mask, swim fins and aqualung; that is to say, having no mechanical connections with the surface, such as are used in a diving suit with its air and safety lines.)

The Seychelles are greatly overpopulated in proportion to the employment they offer. In 1956 the population was around forty-six thousand, compared with an approximate seven thousand in regular employment. Consequently opportunities of steady work for young men are very few and far between and any new opening is immediately sought after. Each day would bring a fresh quota of men to me, all of whom announced that they were superlative swimmers and divers. I was quite ready to believe all this. The bathing facilities here were glorious and with work very difficult to obtain, it seemed only natural that they should have spent a lot of time swimming and lazing around the beaches. They had no money and the sea was free to all. I considered each one as a true potential Polynesian in the water.

Having picked out a dozen of the most suitable, it only remained to try them out. With the first four I took the *Marsouin*'s dinghy and anchored it just outside the harbour, alongside a coral reef in about thirty feet of water. Since none of the divers had as yet used mask or flippers, I though it wisest to let them swim and dive without, before getting on with the real tests. Seeing them all sitting glumly there, not making a move, I picked on the nearest one and told him to get into the water, to dive down and try to touch the bottom. Without saying a word, he got to his feet and, holding his nose tightly between thumb and forefinger, took a flying leap over the side, to disappear with a mighty splash, feet first. I was so surprised at this manoeuvre, that it was not until the bubbles had cleared and I could see him kicking spasmodically some three feet under the surface that I realized he had no more idea of diving than of flying.

His head emerging, he made a wild grab at the boat, missed it and would have sunk again, had I not caught him by the hair and hauled him unceremoniously back. When he was finally in the dinghy he confessed he knew nothing about diving and could not swim, at least not 'when out of his depth'! The rest, it transpired, were just as bad, two flatly refusing to enter such deep water.

And so it was with all who came to me for the job. I felt sorry for them that they must be prepared to take such an unpleasant step as having to demonstrate their inability to swim, swallowing a lot of sea water in the process, on the chance of being selected. What I could not understand was how they ever thought they could get away with it.

Luckily, before my arrival Harvey had managed to find one young boy who could not only swim and dive, but could also use mask and fins. Though at first I was reluctant to make use of him on account of his age, for he was only fourteen, there was no other choice. Physically he was slim and wiry, but of a comparable muscular development to a European youth of seventeen. As I soon found out, he was like an eel in the water and mentally sufficiently alert to have picked up a working knowledge of English, which was unusual, for though the Seychelles are a British Colony, English is barely used.

The *lingua franca* is a primitive Creole patois, which bears little or no resemblance to French. The vocabulary is extremely poor, verbs do not decline and persons are limited to 'you', 'me' and 'him'. It has neither grammar nor syntax, and constitutes the colony's greatest single handicap, shutting off its inhabitants from general contact with the outside world. It is of no value commercially and prevents many from emigrating to other countries where they might otherwise be employed. There is, moreover, a definite prejudice against English, and although it is taught in schools, family and local influences bear down upon the young people to forget and discard this essential skill. If it were indeed French that was spoken, there would be no grounds for criticism, but this Creole tongue has no historical or cultural background, no possibilities of development, no literature and no value as a language at all. Yet it is as hotly defended by the inhabitants as if it were a sacred trust.

By now February had gone, March was drawing to a close, and still no spare parts. It became more and more apparent that our plan for a major expedition to Chagos would have to be abandoned, for with the onset of the south-east monsoon, diving on the outside of the exposed reefs there would be impossible. In order to salvage something out of the mess, we decided that on the arrival of the spares we should at least go over to the island of Praslin and get hold of the fishermen who were picking shells there at the time. We should see their methods and then, either by working with them or employing them, try to improve on their results. It was the only thing we could do in the circumstances. In the meantime we had made contact with a mother-of-pearl shell dealer in East Africa who was prepared to buy shells at two hundred and forty-five pounds sterling per ton.

After all this talk of Green Snail shell, what do they look like? Their general appearance is much the same as a Garden Snail, but greatly enlarged and with a less pointed apex. A big one, with the flesh removed, would weigh two pounds or over and have a diameter of nine inches, with a shell thickness at its lip of a quarter of an inch. The colour varies. When young and fresh the exterior is a pleasant mid-green (hence the name), though occasionally a reddish-yellow type is found. Running in a spiral around its whorls is a dark stripe, usually only apparent when seen in a good light. But an older shell would present a completely different appearance. Encrusted with coral, which grows upon it with ease, the shell would take on the same colour as its surroundings and its outline, too, would be obscured by the growth. The lime of the coral attacks the outer layer of the shell and if chipped away the polished green 'skin' will be found to have disappeared, so that it now has a dull and uninteresting mottled, chalky surface.

But it is in the interior of the shell that its value and beauty lie. Turn it over, having first removed the snail itself, and an iridescent spiral tunnel of mother-of-pearl is revealed. Whereas the nacre of the true Pearl Oyster has a slightly bluish tinge, that of the Green Snail retains the faint greenish tint of its original surface. This nacre extends throughout the convolutions of the shell and is, in fact, the actual shell itself, the deceptive outer layer being only a thin veneer. This nacre may be as much as a quarter of an inch thick, or as little as a tenth, depending upon the size of the shell as whole.

The animal that lives within is, again, a larger edition of the Garden Snail, complete with foot-mouth and sensitive horns or feelers. Its skin, however, is a rich dark green, black lipped at the edges and with the underside of its foot a drab yellow. In one obvious way only does it differ from the Garden Snail. Attached to its foot is a circular trap door of heavy calcium, behind which it can barricade itself within its home, secure against attack. This operculum, as it is called, is a rose-tinted disc, white on its exterior and convex side whilst the flat inner side, where the muscle joins, is dark sepia. These 'doors' will

MAHÉ

vary according to the shell, from two inches to five inches across and up to a quarter of a pound in weight. They seem to have no commercial value other than as ornamental paperweights, for which they are ideally suited.

Of the habits of the Green Snail, we as yet know nothing, though local verbal information was not lacking:

'They come up from the deep with each new moon . . .' said one.

'They go down into deep water each new moon . . .' said another.

'You catch them in fish-traps, using crab-meat as bait . . .'

'You'll never pull them off the rocks, they stick worse than clam-shells. You must use a crowbar on them . . .'

'Don't eat the meat, it's highly poisonous!'

'The meat makes wonderful curry . . .'

'Be careful not to touch the creature itself, you'll come up in a rash. You must only pick it up by the shell . . .'

'Green Snail? Oh, yes. The good ones are over two hundred feet down. You'll never reach them . . .'

'Where there are Green Snail, there are sharks – don't say I didn't warn you!'

'How do you think you'll ever get any Creole to dive beyond the reefs? You'll only do it once, yourself! One thing, you won't have any funeral expenses to pay . . .'

'Look, why don't you just go back to East Africa, and forget about it . . .'

And so it went on.

The sum total of all this was that nobody knew anything at all, though many thought they did, and we were no wit the wiser when all the talking was done.

Eventually, the parts arrived and within two days we were ready to put to sea. As well as a three-man crew, we took the young diver, Albert Durand, so that I might go on with his training.

No sooner had we cast off and got out in the middle of the harbour than a fuel pipe fractured. All the frustrations and disappointments of the previous two months' waiting seemed about to be re-enacted all over again and at that point I was perfectly prepared to go back to East Africa, and might have done so had there been a ship available! As it was, the damage proved to be reparable locally, and by dusk we were able to continue.

Indeed, since Praslin was only a few hours' run we were able to find our anchorage there in time to settle down to a quiet night's sleep.

Next morning we were on deck as soon as it was light. The village of Anse Boudin, off which we lay, consisted of a dozen palm-thatched cottages placed some twenty yards back from a narrow beach. These were so screened by an intervening row of young palms and takamaka trees that it was impossible to catch even a glimpse of the settlement from the schooner. All that served to show that the village was, indeed, there, were some tendrils of grey smoke that coiled up in the clear air from behind the foilage. A hawksbill turtle swam up to have a closer look at us, but quickly paddled off when I jumped in after it. It was the first time I had seen one underwater, and I was surprised to realize how agile it was. Using its two front legs in a powerful breast-stroke, it shot through the water in a series of rapid lunges with which my swim-fins could not compete.

After breakfast, we had another visitor, a nearby coconut plantation manager, who paddled out to us in his pirogue. A pirogue is a narrow, doubled-ended canoe peculiar to the Seychelles, whose black silhouette is as characteristic of those islands as the outrigger-canoe is of the Pacific.

'I hope you enjoy your swim,' he said, as soon as he climbed on board. 'Personally, I never bathe here, nor does anyone from the village. You see those rocks,' and he pointed to some half-awash granite boulders that lay between us and the shore, 'every week we put down a dead dog there with a steel hook sewn in its stomach and a chain fastening it to a ring-bolt on the largest rock. Last Sunday night we got a twenty-two-foot Blue Shark, and the week before one we estimated at eighteen feet. We could only estimate because from just behind his head all was missing. Taken off at one bite! So you see why we don't bathe. But what can I do for you?'

Over some mugs of coffee we explained our need to enlist the aid of any local fishermen who knew where the *Burgaux* (as the Green Snail is called in Creole) were to be found. Our new acquaintance told us that there would be no difficulty about that. The pirogue fleet from the village would be coming in with the morning's catch at about ten. We should meet them before they got to the beach and dispersed to their homes and should ask for Jean Batiste. He would be the man for us.

We thanked him for this useful information and Harvey and I took advantage of his returning to shore to go with him and have a closer look at Anse Boudin. When we got back to the beach it was in time to see our cook and bo'sun rowing desperately ashore in the dinghy, obviously trying to cut off half a dozen black pirogues which were sweeping in across the bay at a pace that left them standing. The fishermen in these canoes were paying not the slightest attention to our crew's frantic gestures and imploring cries. This, I found later, was a characteristic Creole reaction. To wave or attempt to communicate with them from a distance would be looked upon with great suspicion and would usually result in their making off in the opposite direction as quickly as possible. This time, however, they were caught, for Harvey and I were there to greet them when they landed!

In reply to our query, 'Jean Batiste?' a middle-aged man stepped forward. He had a strong Mexican-Indian cast of countenance, sombre features, unrelieved by a big black moustache, and a flat straw hat with an exceptionally wide brim.

Jean Batiste did not say anything while we explained our mission. Then he turned to the others, shot a few short sentences at them in rapid Creole and, without waiting for their replies, turned back to us. How many pirogues did we want? Were we able to tow? Would we give them diving-masks? Could they sleep on board? Would we supply rice, salt-fish, tea and tobacco?

Eventually, it was all arranged. Jean Batiste would supply three pirogues, three men to each, who would lead us to where the Green Snail were to be found. We should be at liberty to watch them at work, providing we did not interfere. In return, we would tow them from place to place, provide basic rations and buy their shells on the spot, thus saving them the journey to Mahé, where the shells were normally sold. They would be ready to start at sunrise the next day.

The business concluded, each party went its separate way, the fishermen to their homes and we to continue with our walk.

TWO

Praslin

Praslin, perhaps even more than Mahé, is a very lovely island, particularly when viewed from the sea.

That morning, sailing along close under its granite headlands and steeply wooded slopes we saw it at its best. The sky was cloudless and the sea flat calm, with only an occasional heave of its surface to show that we were not on some vast inland lake. Under the guidance of Jean Batiste, who stood in the bows peering out at the passing coastline from under the shade of his huge sombrero, we crept in to within twenty yards of the land, diverting momentarily now and then, in obedience to his signals, in order to avoid some sunken pinnacle of rock that lay across our path. Even so near in, we usually had sixty to eighty feet of water under our keel, the island structure plunging to comparatively deep water without any fringing reef or sandy slope.

A few terns flickered around us, and over and amongst the foliage of the upper slopes the white crescent shapes of others cut swift arcs. It was strange to see these sea birds, whose normal environment is bare rock or sandy island beaches, dashing in and out amongst the trees in this fashion. Occasionally, the whole sea would quiver and ripple over a large area as a shoal of mackerel broke the surface, their mouths agape, scooping up and sieving the plankton life that floated there. Behind us the line of black pirogues danced along in our wake, the whole string guided by a solitary sombre black figure, who sat on his haunches in the stern of the rearmost, steering by means of a paddle held obliquely over the side.

After continuing thus for about an hour, Jean Batiste waved us towards a granite promontory, whose smooth slopes ran down at an angle of fifty degrees straight into the sea without a break. Against this buttress the water surged and fell in great sighs, yet without forming either waves or surf.

PRASLIN

For safety's sake Harvey took the *Marsouin* out a hundred yards or so, before heaving to. Scarcely had we stopped than the fishermen came out from the shade of the tarpaulins and sails under which they had been sleeping, grabbed their new face-masks, pulled their pirogues alongside, jumped into them and paddled away towards the cliffs. Taking one of the crew as oarsman, Albert and I tumbled into the dinghy and followed. Arriving within five feet of the rock-face each pirogue crew set about its business. Two would balance and fend off the narrow craft with deft paddle strokes, while the third member squatted in the centre, his head over the side. From the boat it presented a strange sight. Against the light grey wall of rock the slim canoes were strikingly etched. In the bows and stern of each stood a black shadowed oarsman, while in the centre was visible only the white cotton-clad buttocks of the third member, pointing alarmingly skywards! As soon as we arrived on the scene Albert and I jumped into the water and each swam up to a different pirogue. Clinging on to the stern with one hand, we were able to see exactly what was going on.

Below the surface the granite continued to fall away at the same angle for some twenty feet, after which its smooth outline was broken up in a jumble of huge boulders and fragments which continued on down at a much shallower slope for another thirty feet, before levelling off into a barren and featureless submarine plain. One thing that struck me at once was the complete lack of live, growing coral. The scene lacked, owing to this, the colours and interest which I had expected. In the diffuse light the granite took on a leprous green shade. Amongst the jumble of boulders lower down many fish swayed and swung with each successive heave of the sea, but none of these were of the glorious scintillating colours found in coral fishes. Brown sand and muddy greens were the predominant shades, with here and there a glint of silver scales.

Suddenly a thumping of feet on the floor-boards of the canoe above my head indicated that something was about to happen. Then a black figure shot down in a cloud of bubbles and, frog-like, groped its way obliquely underwater, not towards the bottom, but along the granite slope. This, I now noticed, was not perfectly smooth but marred by cracks and shallow fissures which ran diagonally downwards across its surface. It was along one such crack that the man was clawing his way. About twelve feet down he stopped and fumblingly ran one hand on a little further along and within the flaw. Then with a sharp wrench and much to my astonishment he pulled out of its hiding place a large Green Snail shell. Pressing the soles of his bare feet against the rock he kicked off towards the surface, the shell outstretched before him. There he handed it in and scrambled back into the pirogue. The whole operation had not taken more than fifteen seconds and it was only afterwards that I realized that he had not used his mask, but had taken it off prior to diving, which is why he fumbled so blindly for the shell, his open eyes incapable of focusing underwater.

I put my head over the side of the pirogue and with the assistance of Albert asked him why he had left his mask behind; the mask was to enable him to see under the water; that was the whole idea of it.

His answer was odd. Apparently he did not *want* to see. But why had he used the mask in the first place? Oh, that was in order to spot the shell before diving in. Once he had seen it from the canoe, he noted the spot and then went down and hunted till he got hold of it. But why didn't he use the mask under water? It would help him. At last we got the answer. He didn't *want* to see beneath the water, in case he *did* see. In case he *did* see something unpleasant. *Un grand bébête noir et malin.*

In other words, a bogey! A bogey or a shark. It was for the last reason that he remained in the canoe and peered awkwardly over the edge, instead of staying in the water like us, clinging on to the pirogue while it towed him along. He was afraid of a large shark stealing up behind him.

At this I felt a certain qualm of uneasiness. That there were very large sharks in the area was unquestionable, particularly after the evidence of our friend at Anse Boudin. However, from what I had experienced in other areas, I was fairly sure that such specimens passed the daylight hours in the great deeps, only venturing with the dusk into the comparative shallows to scavenge and search for prey. Since both Praslin and Mahé stood on a great raised submarine plateau, nowhere deeper than forty fathoms, and since the nearest edge of this plateau was twenty miles from us, I felt reasonably secure. Still, the thought of an eighteen-foot shark cut in half by a single bit within two miles of where we swam, and that within the last few days, was not too comforting. Albert looked a bit glum at the fisherman's explanation and for a moment I thought he was going to get into the pirogue as well, but he did not.

As it afterwards turned out, my theory proved in practice to be correct, and we never came across any really big sharks by day whilst around Mahé and Praslin, though the same did not apply to the other islands of the Seychelles. Anyway, for the next few weeks I kept a very sharp look out and made sure that Albert did not stray off on his own by mischance. But it was apparent that no argument I could offer would alter these fishermen's ideas, and as I was there basically as an observer I told them to carry on as they were accustomed.

And so our little flotilla progressed.

At first, Albert and myself could never pick out the shells where they lay tucked away in crevices or on shadowy rock ledges, but after about an hour closely following each successive headlong plunge we began to get the hang of it and by the end of the morning were picking up as many as were the fishermen. In fact, by lunchtime we had evolved a better system. If we saw a shell in shallow water, that is, down to about fifteen feet, we pointed it out to our pirogue-divers who then dived for it themselves. If, on the other hand, we or they saw any shells beyond that depth, then either Albert or I would collect it, for we soon saw that fifteen feet was the maximum obtainable by the fishermen and that they were consequently missing many as they went along.

This Harvey had already heard when he first wrote to me, but the scale of depths had become rather distorted. By their own account these Creole divers were capable of diving to forty feet, whereas in practice their limit proved to be a mere third of this figure. It was this that led us to believe that aqualungs would be essential for the harvesting of the shells, since we believed the majority to lie in waters beyond forty feet. In actual fact, the majority of Green Snail shells around Mahé were in depths greater than fifteen but never beyond the forty-foot mark. This surface layer all lay within the working range of a trained diver equipped only with mask and swim fins, and on that trip we never had occasion to utilize all the specialized equipment I had brought specially for that purpose.

In the afternoon Albert was sent off with the fishermen to continue diving, whilst Harvey and I thrashed out our plans in the light of what we had learnt. When they returned with some eighty shells we put before them our new scheme, to which they agreed. We would continue to pay and feed them on board ship and would now return to Anse Boudin so that they might collect any personal belongings needed for a ten-day tour around the coasts of Mahé and Praslin. Albert we would pay separately. The shells would be weighed at the end of each day and each pirogue credited with its respective 'catch'. They themselves would be responsible for the cleaning of the shells prior to weighing.

We got back to the anchorage at dusk and the fishermen paddled away homewards. We went with them for a walk before turning in. Surprisingly enough, there were very few mosquitoes or sand flies which one might expect in such a densely wooded area. So still and calm a night was it that the coconut oil lamps lighting the entrance doors and tiny verandahs of the huts burnt unshielded, with a steady yellow flame in the clear air. But by eight o'clock these tiny beacons were all extinguished and the darkness and silence were complete.

At six the next morning all our new employees returned, each carrying a bundle which contained a clean white shirt, khaki shorts and a tooth brush. We set off at once, having our breakfast as we cruised along, past the many islets and half-covered rocks that are characteristic of this coast line.

For the next week, each day followed the pattern of the previous and all were the same as the first. Following an early breakfast, after we had left our night's anchorage in some small cove, we would reach our first working area before eight, after which Albert and I would go off with the pirogues and begin the day's work. At eleven we would quit the water, return to the *Marsouin* and whilst the fishermen handed up the shells and started cleaning them, we would go off 'spear-fishing' for the day's food. This was never a difficult task and was a welcome break.

After the drab submarine surroundings of the areas in which we found the Green Snail, it was refreshing to get back to the colour and life of the coral outcrops; to have clouds of multi-coloured fish drift around one; to watch the soft, glowing shades of the giant anemones merge and change with each surge of the current that caused their pliant tentacles to move like fields of wheat under the wind. It was a relief to relax and enjoy the sea once more; to think of nothing more serious than whether to have lobster for supper or a tropical bouillabaisse – if the latter, then Albert and I would eventually emerge with a whole string of brilliantly-hued fish, Rainbow Wrasse, Parrot Fish, Red Snapper, Imperial Butterfly Fish, Cardinals and many others. Whatever our choice, one hour was ample time for our hunting.

After a very light lunch, back we would go again, leaving the water finally at about four. Then tea, more shell cleaning, and lastly the weighing and reckoning of the day's haul. In this fashion we would cover some eight miles of selected coast area each day and we learnt more in that first week than we had dreamed possible.

We learnt not to rely too much on the fishermen's selection of suitable places. Often these places were suited to them but too shallow, and better results could be got further out in deeper water, or where the shore-line shelved more steeply. We learned, too, to keep a careful watch on the weighing and cleaning of the shells. About a quarter of those obtained were 'rejects' due to the ravages of various boring parasites. These barnacle-type creatures would attack the outside of the shells and tunnel through the nacre, discolouring and weakening it as they went along, until eventually all that remained was a raddled skeleton. Such specimens were thrown overboard and since we usually carried out the preliminary sorting after anchoring for the night, the sea-bottom beneath the keel rapidly became cluttered with such throwouts. This did not escape the quick eyes of the Creoles, who immediately thought out a scheme to utilize it to their benefit and our disadvantage. Their method was simple and direct. We would examine each shell, place it in a sack, weigh the sack when full and then tip out the contents in a heap into the hold. After a while we noticed that our heap was not growing noticeably larger and then found out that when our backs were turned and we were busy sorting and weighing, one fisherman would swiftly and silently enter the hold through the front hatch and toss up as many shells as he could to a companion who would quietly drop them overboard. Later, a third member, hidden under the bows, would dive down and pick up these good shells, placing them in a pirogue prior to passing them up openly to the *Marsouin*'s deck, as though he were still engaged in unloading his catch!

Thus a shell might be weighed and credited to their account several times over. Even if we heard the 'plop' as the shell went over, we would assume that it was just another reject, and glancing over the side and seeing the litter of empty shells on the sandy floor below, no one could tell whether they were all bad ones or not.

It was no use remonstrating with them or flying into tantrums. Very ostentatiously we locked up the front hatch and afterwards saw that all the pirogues were unloaded and empty before sorting and weighing the shells. The sly grins which these precautions provoked indicated that they understood, and if they succeeded in finding a new loophole in our arrangements by which to benefit, we never found it.

As to the habits of the Green Snail, we were able to discover that they liked algae-covered rocks, but not loose sand or seaweed. They thrived in places directly in the path of current eddies and did not do so well in sheltered waters. Most significant of all, and this I later substantiated wherever I found Green Snail, there seemed to be some sort of 'food link' between them and a small coral fish *Zanclus Cornatus*, commonly known as 'Moorish Idol'. Wherever one found Green Snail one would also find Moorish Idols in the immediate vicinity, though the reverse was not true.

These quaint little fish with their vivid stripes of black and yellow have a grotesque mask-face, which gives them the appearance of a Japanese puppet doll. Their stiff jerky movements enhance the illusion, whilst the small 'whip' that streams from their dorsal fin is like the bladder with which a jester in bygone days belaboured the empty air. So remarkably constant was this combination of snail and fish that in the future I came to look upon Zanclus with great affection, almost as a talisman, and the tempo of a fruitless day's search was immediately enlivened if, even at its close, I saw one of these small fish. There is something irresistibly comic about their busy struttings and they have even less fear of humans than most coral fishes, pottering about coral heads, twisting in and out with abrupt pirouettes and taking no notice at all of any intruder. What is the exact link between this little creature and the Green Snail I still do no know, but suspect that they share a common food item, in all probability a lichenous alga. At all events, this one point was to prove of great importance throughout subsequent shelling trips.

Another point of interest was that I never saw any Green Snail on the move, though I watched individual ones for as long as two hours at a time. However, since their positions relative to one another alter from day to day, they can walk about but probably do so only at night, although this I have never managed to verify. At that time we presumed them to lead static lives, resting on one shelf or rock throughout their life-span. Later, we were to see just how wrong we were.

Apparently sea temperature did not affect them as much as some other types of shells. The same submarine temperature might extend for another thirty feet down, yet at a certain level in any one place the Green Snail would stop abruptly. At the time I put it down to the food supply fading out at that depth, but I was wrong about that, too. Most of our Creoles had met with clinical thermometers in the dispensaries or on the occasional visits of the local Health Officer and the sight of me diving down and inserting similar instruments under and around various selected Green Snail never failed to cause them fits of laughter and they could only explain it as just another case of *'zou-zou les blancs'* (Europeans' play), not to be taken seriously.

Other more practical things we learned. How to cut through the muscle hinge of the operculum by sliding a thin knife blade in around its edge, then, with a quick turn of the wrist, to scoop out the whole animal in one piece, leaving the shell completely clean and free of all remnants that might decay and putrefy within its convolutions. Harvey discovered, by trial and error, the best way of towing the string of piroges behind his schooner. Being so slim and having flat bottoms they tended to careen erratically from side to side in our wake in a series of mad rushes. At one instant they would be jerking heavily at the end of the tow-rope, and the next travelling parallel with the *Marsouin*, spume and foam hissing under their bows and along their black flanks. This made an exhilarating picture, but unfortunately usually ended in one or more capsizing and being pulled under. After we had lost a whole pirogue load of shells, plus paddles and thwarts in this fashion, we were more careful and experimented till we found the correct method.

Although so frail and temperamental, the pirogues were ideally suited for the job. In heavy weather they could be pulled on board in a trice and then stacked one within the other, like soup plates, so that they took up very little deck space. In launching they were simply shot over the side by hand, landing with a tremendous splash, but then 'skidding' on the surface without any water entering. Being pointed at either end there is no 'bow' or 'stern' and these canoes travel in whatever direction one chooses to paddle. For my part it took several days to learn to get into or stand up in one without upsetting it, for their balance is as critical as a light sculling craft. It proved to be the same as riding a bicycle: once learnt, never forgotten.

So, day by day, we searched more of the coast. When we had finished Praslin, which is only about eight miles long, we went to the still smaller islands around it and after those were finished, put out to sea to look at the various half submerged granite rocks that are common in the area. With these we did not do so well, finding very few shells. Here the fishermen flatly refused to enter the water, for though they thought we should find Green Snail, they were even more sure that we should find les grands bébêtes! Nevertheless, they were only too keen to paddle me over to the actual rocks, while the *Marsouin* lay off a little distance to avoid the heave and swirl of the disturbed water.

As I slid over the side, at the first of these places, I too was a little uneasy. The Creoles had spent their lives around these islands, they should know what was safe and reasonable from what was not. Once I put my head underwater, I forgot all about these fears, the sight was so enthralling. Sheer, smooth bastions of granite rose like castle walls out of the blue depths. Almost vertical, above surface they would have presented unclimbable rock faces. As it was, with the aqualung which I was wearing, they presented no difficulty – it was a simple matter to launch myself into space and glide down along this precipice. Even at the surface I could faintly see the sea bed at one hundred and eighty feet, so clear was the water. This extreme transparency heightened the illusion of flight and gave a feeling of vertigo. It was the 'flying' sensation of dreams and an experience that stands out among thousands of other dives. For the first few minutes I was so enraptured by the surroundings that all idea of shell-hunting was forgotten. Then, remembering my purpose there, I hurriedly looked around, saw that the area was totally unsuitable, surfaced and yelled to Albert that there were no shells, but to come and have a look. Then I went back.

I soon discovered that I was not the only living thing swimming among those giant pinnacles of grey rock. Rounding a corner I came face to face with a large Red Snapper, weighing perhaps fifty pounds. We both jumped with surprise and then proceeded to examine each other with caution, like two strange dogs on a lonely street. Each satisfied as to the harmless intention of the other, we went on our respective ways. I discovered more and more of these big fish which peered out from dark fissures or hung motionless in the shadows of rock outcrops.

At fifty feet I could make out the bottom quite distinctly, an uninteresting undulating plain of sand and coral fragments. By turning on my back, I could see the bean shape of the pirogue, like a water-beetle, moving along the surface, this surface which was for me a leaden mirror, the ceiling of this new world. Behind it, 'walking' like a fly on that ceiling was Albert looking down at me. I waved and continued. To pass along between the pillars and rock corridors required no effort. Invisible hands clutched and pulled me through each gap, twirled me gently round once or twice and then, like the wind playing with a leaf, allowed me to go on. Soft gurgling and snorting sounds came from every side, as the sea too wound its way in and out. Merely to hang, suspended in a shaft of light, and watch the shadows of surface ripples play across a granite slab was enough.

Eventually, I started on an upward slant towards the pirogue. Half-way there, I saw what seemed to be a small shark way below me, climbing in lazy spirals. It was only when near the surface and with this new arrival growing steadily closer that I realized he was not small at all. Far from it, it was merely that the clarity of the water had enabled me to see him when he must have been right on the bottom. Since the shark would catch me up anyway, I thought it best to stay and meet him. Albert was already out of the water, which was a good thing. Turning, I swam back down towards him. He was a handsome beast. Dark grey above, white below, with each fin white-tipped. Perhaps ten feet long. Not huge by any means, but big enough to be nasty should he wish. Perhaps this was what the fishermen had feared, but if it was, they grossly overrated the danger, for after completing several cursory circuits around me, he pointed his nose downwards and dropped away back into the blue depths.

There were many more shoals and rock outcrops such as these which we examined. At none of these were there Green Snail shells, due, I think, to the steep angle of ascent and smooth surface of the stone which would prevent the shells from either crawling up it when adult or adhering to it when in the 'free swimming' stage. For the Green Snail propagates its kind by means of spat, which develop into animalcules, almost invisible to the eye and which are capable of limited propulsion, but rely mainly on ocean currents to carry them along. Arriving, by pure chance, in contact with a suitable stone or coral surface they adhere and then commence to change into their shell form and thus begin a normal cycle of growth, reproduction and death. All this we found out later. For how long the free-swimming stage lasts or for how far the animalcule can be carried still remains a complete mystery to me.

After several more days of this unproductive exploration we realized that the Creole fishermen had exhausted their store of local knowledge as to the shells and were picking areas entirely at random, hoping that there might be something there. After all, they were being fed, which was a pleasant change for them and a unique opportunity to get free transport to anywhere they wished. Naturally, they made the most of it.

Albert, too, was having a wonderful holiday. He had managed to catch by hand under the water a baby Hawksbill turtle, and this quaint little fellow now accompanied him everywhere in the water that he went. He had attached a very light transparent nylon line from the turtle's carapace to his belt. On being set free the first time, the little creature rowed off as fast as it could, all four flippers kicking furiously, only to be brought to an abrupt halt when it ran out of line. This invisible restraint it could not fathom, but after a few fruitless attempts accepted it as being a part of life and would not stray further from Albert than its leash allowed. It learned this in about a quarter of the time a puppy takes to tolerate a lead, which was remarkable. The pair of them presented an odd sight when out looking for shells. Albert swimming along the surface and, about ten feet below him and slightly in advance, having no visible connection, a baby turtle the size of a large soup-plate, also happily kicking along. When the boy dived the Hawksbill would wait until he was at the same level, then cock its head sideways at him as if to say 'Hang on, I'm coming too', crane its neck as far out of its shell as possible and, bending his tiny head downwards, follow him on down. If Albert, on reaching the rock or whatever it was he had dived for, stayed there for more than a second or two, the turtle would swim in small circles just over his head, like a queer bird.

However, this state of affairs could not go on for ever and reluctantly I told him to let his pet go. We chose a nice spot that was sheltered, free of any sharks that might eat it up and with a nice sandy bottom covered with large patches of 'turtle grass', that flat broad-leafed seaweed on which these creatures feed. It was only then we struck a difficulty. The baby turtle didn't want to go! On being liberated it took up the normal position ten feet in advance of Albert and there it stuck. They swam like that for about half an hour, then Albert got back into the pirogue. This really upset the turtle who paddled desperately alongside, head out of the water, waiting to be picked up. Every now and then it would claw at the side of the canoe with its front flippers as if to draw our attention to its presence. It took the whole of an afternoon to teach the little reptile that Albert was no longer a part of its life. This we finally managed by getting it to feed and then stealing quietly away. The first few times we did not get very far before being found out, and then there was a frantic rush to catch us up. Gradually, however, it allowed Albert to get further and further and eventually we were able to creep away altogether without it paying any attention. And there we left it.

By the time we had scoured the islets and coast of Praslin the role of the fishermen had changed to that of mere boatmen and diving attendants, for by now Albert and I had become thoroughly accustomed to the work and found the clumsy efforts of their divers more of a hindrance than a help. Ninety to one hundred and twenty good shells per day was about the average amount we gathered which, though not great, resulted in our leaving with three-quarters of a ton of clean shells to our credit down in the hold.

We came back from Praslin bringing our pirogue fleet with us. They were eager to try their luck around Mahé and though their divers were no longer necessary, their pirogue had proved indispensable, as it was impossible to manoeuvre a dinghy as close to the rocks and cliffs as the work demanded.

At Mahé the underwater situation proved to be much the same. Isolated groups of Green Snail along the granite rock areas; poor shelling, but nevertheless worthwhile. It was here that I first made aquaintance with the Seychelles Giant Rock Cod, sometimes known as the Giant Grouper or Jew Fish. This monster is held in great respect and all sort of grim stories are told about its man-eating capabilities. The sheer size of these great fish is quite alarming. Eight or nine feet in length, with a girth as big, or bigger than a beer barrel, they have dark, warty and tattered skin, bulbous protruding eyes and a thick-lipped sneering mouth. It is this mouth that gives it such a sinister appearance, for when required the lower jaw gapes wide to reveal a cavernous maw, lined with row upon row of small backward-sloping teeth. And this mouth is capable of being opened to the same circumference as its body!

Within the entrance to the cave chosen as its lair, it hangs motionless most of the day, barely visible in the shadows. When any unwary fish passes close by, that great gullet is opened wide and, by a powerful suction action, a large volume of water plus the luckless fish is 'breathed' in. The water comes out again through the gill arches, but not so the fish. Occasionally the Giant Cod will leave its home to make a tour of the neighbourhood or else surge upwards to engulf, from below, some other prey swimming near the surface.

It is on such occasions that its man-eating habits are supposed to manifest themselves. In this fashion many young children are supposed to have been taken while having a swim. No shriek, no swirl of bloody water as would occur in a normal attack by a shark. Just a slight upheaval, an arm momentarily upraised and then, perhaps, the shadow of a huge rotund beast slipping quietly away. It does present a sinister picture, but not a true one. In all probability in ninety-nine cases the victim has drowned, probably through a sudden attack of cramp, since children here often bathe immediately after a large meal, which is asking for trouble. The hundredth case could well be the work of a stray and large shark. A Tiger Shark of fifteen feet, for instance, is quite capable of swallowing a small human whole, and would normally do so rather than bite the poor wretch in half.

PRASLIN

On the north-west coat of Mahé there are some of the biggest and sheerest cliffs in the whole of the Seychelles Archipelago. Beneath the surface of the sea these precipices are split and serried into gloomy chasms and fissures and it is within these that the huge Rock Cod lurk. Not knowing this, I had dived down under an overhang of rock and was busy groping around to see if any Green Snail had tucked themselves away in that recess. My eyes, gradually growing accustomed to the dark, picked out something lighter in colour than the surrounding blackness. Something that moved gently back and forth about a yard from my face. Stretching out my hand towards it I touched something hard and faintly slimy, which gave slightly under the pressure of my fingers. Feeling back along its contours, this firmness gave way to something round and polished. At the same instant a miniature tidal wave hit me with such force as to push me violently out of the cave and to tear the mask off my face. Once on the surface I realized that I must have had my hand on the forehead of a large fish which had remained motionless until my inquisitive fingers found its eye. The 'tidal wave' had been the backwash from the tail as it surged away, perhaps even a glancing blow from its tail.

Borrowing Albert's mask, I went down again to recover my own and to find out what it was that lay within the cave. By approaching at an angle and moving round cautiously I was able to silhouette the fish against a light-splashed wall of the cleft. The long sloping forehead and protruding lips proved it to be indeed a Giant Rock Cod and the 'lighter patch' I had first seen moving gently up and down in front of my eyes was a yellow-tipped pectoral fin gently fanning to keep the monster suspended, otherwise motionless, between sandy floor and rock ceiling. This time he did not let me get so near but backed away slowly, eventually turning and disappearing down a side corridor.

After this unexpected encounter, I felt much happier. If ever a Giant Cod had a chance to engulf someone it was then, since my head must have been practically within its yard-wide mouth. Later I got Albert to go and have a close look at another area. He was so elated at the 'debunking' of these monsters that he was all for swimming down there and then putting a hook, fastened to the end of some rope, right into its mouth by hand and dragging the fish out bodily. I vetoed the suggestion, partly because I was coming to regard these brutes in a new light and partly because I didn't want a pirogue smashed up, which the six to eight hundred pound fish was quite capable of doing.

Within a stretch of four miles there were more than twenty of these monsters. Each had its own cave castle, at the entrance to which it stood guard. Some specimens were dark green with mud-green patches; others nearly black; others, like the first, touched here and there with yellow. Probably all belonged to the same family, but in common with all large marine creatures, such as whales and whale sharks, each differed from the other in minor details of colouring and proportions.

By the time we had swept the major part of the coast of Mahé, Albert and I had improved our technique to a large degree. Not that we were collecting many more shells per day, but we were able to do so without expending half the energy of our earlier efforts. Now, when we spotted a shell, instead of diving down at once towards it, we would float above it on the surface and carefully examine its immediate surroundings. Usually, a minute thus spent would bring to light one or more additional snail tucked away in a crevice or pot-hole, with its outline blurred by coraline deposits or obscured by shadows. Having decided that we had marked all those that lay below, we would position ourselves in such a manner as to be upcurrent and with the shells lying in a rough line away from us. Only then would we swim down, pick up the first in passing, be carried on by the movement of the water to the second, which would be collected in the same manner, then, with the two shells tucked under one arm or in the crook of the elbow, swim on to any others that might remain. In this fashion we might gather in one dive what would previously have taken us three.

For it is not the swimming or the actual picking up of the shells that is tiring; it is the plunge down to twenty or thirty feet. A dive to this depth, in itself, is nothing at all. But one hundred and twenty such dives to that depth in the course of a day is very exhausting, and by cutting this number by half or more, though we swam just as far, made a tremendous difference.

Eleven days after our departure we arrived back in Port Victoria. The near-ton of Green Snail, cleaned, weighed and now sacked, we sold to a dealer on the spot for £200. After paying the fishermen, the crew and Albert, and accounting for stores and fuel, it left Harvey and me a little over £115 profit. Although we had more or less cleared out the shell of Mahé and Praslin this was very encouraging as it gave an idea of future operating costs and had already given us the necessary experience. It also provided a reserve fund out of which the next long voyage could be partially financed. We were very pleased with all this and set about our preparations the same day.

For the next three days we hardly saw any of the crew nor any of the fishermen, as they were all busily engaged in getting as drunk as possible. When the crew did appear it was in time to do the actual loading of drums of fuel oil, water kegs and sacks of food that had been ordered and had arrived in their absence. The fishermen came to find out whether they might come with us as well, and it was finally arranged that we would take six of them, together with two of the best pirogues. Living space being limited for a six-week trip we could take no more.

A few days before leaving we gave the crew some money and a sample Green Snail apiece and told them to find any labourer or fisherman who had worked on the outer Seychelles islands, buy him a drink or give him a small tip, show him the shell and ask if he had ever come across anything similar on the island on which he had worked. In this fashion we would get far more pertinent information than if Harvey or I asked directly. This was the sort of commission the crew loved. Something that gave an excuse for a drink, paid for it as well, and which hinted at intrigue.

Whilst they were away doing this we went to see the various owners of the islands around which we intended to work. There is something about the possession of an island that makes people jealous and suspicious of any visitor, however harmless his intent. Though their legal right covers only the land as far as the high-water mark, many owners have come to regard the reefs and littoral waters as theirs too, and some mentally extend their domain to cover all the high seas as far as the horizon encircling their possession! We were prepared for this and in each case explained the exact purpose of our visit, gave our word that we would not go ashore or in other ways trespass and that we were willing to take out or bring back any cargo or mail that we could manage, free of charge: all this to establish 'goodwill', so that if we did run into difficulties at any island we should not feel that we were imposing by asking for assistance. Knowing that no one else was doing any shelling in the Archipelago, we hypocritically offered to work in with the owner in each case if he were 'engaged in this work already'.

On the whole this round of visits was well worthwhile. In only one case did we meet with open hostility, and this from a person who seemed to claim a Divine Right to most of the Indian Ocean and certainly all that lay within several hundred miles of his islands. For the rest, they varied from tacit acceptance of our proposed visits to downright encouragement and aid in the form of letters of introduction to island administrators, promises of water and vegetables and helpful advice as to the best anchorages.

Our crew, too, had done well. They had obtained definite information that our shells were to be found at two of the islands on our list. In both cases, this came from fishermen who had worked there and had collected the molluscs to eat the flesh, afterwards throwing the valuable shell away. I had already heard rumours of this, as one island owner had mentioned it, but only on hearsay. Since in each case the same island was mentioned, this now seemed fairly conclusive and was very reassuring, as up to that moment the whole trip had been based on pure speculation. Whilst we knew that there were Green Snail around Mahé and Praslin, we had no evidence of colonies at any of the other islands of the Seychelles. Moreover, since those we had found had lived on granite and there were no other granite islands, we had no real basis for concluding that we should find any elsewhere.

These isolated granite-cored islands amongst the rest of the group need explaining. The Seychelles cover almost five hundred thousand square miles of ocean and can be divided into three distinct areas. In the north lies a large submarine plateau from which thrust up the granite outcrops forming Mahé and Praslin and their associated islets and rocks. These granite islands are interesting, since there are no others like them anywhere in the world. All other islands thus placed far from continents or large land masses are of coral or similar detritus composition. These unique granite peaks seem to have been linked in the remote past with Madagascar, whose rocky backbone is of similar form. In all probability a vast continent once joined India with southern Africa. Now all that remains are the tips of this land mass, represented by present day Madagascar and these few Seychelles islands, stepping stones across the ocean towards the Indian subcontinent. Some geologists and historians refer to this sunken continent as Lemuria, while to others it is the fabulous Atlantis.

Separated from Mahé by a deep channel and about one hundred and fifty miles to the west-south-west are the Amirante Islands, the second natural division of the Seychelles. They lie in a line north to south over a distance of one hundred miles along the length of another plateau. These islands are mainly mere elevated sandbanks, fringed by coral reefs. Sea-birds nesting there throughout thousands of years have provided a top covering of guano, in consequence of which the larger islands have been brought under cultivation and the birds driven away. The third and last division of the Seychelles is made up of various scattered islands, lying mainly to the south, whose construction is of coral rock. These rise up individually from depths of over two thousand fathoms, more than two miles, to attain their height of twenty or thirty feet above the level of the surrounding sea!

None of these three divisions has much in common and as they are everywhere separated by abyssal depths the chances of one colony of Green Snail spreading to the others is not very great, if even possible. So this definite news of other shell colonies in the outer islands was of primary importance to us and it was in a very optimistic mood that we finally set off on the second trip.

But we still did not know what awaited us beyond the reefs!

THREE

Alphonse

We had decided to make our way direct to Farquhar 650 miles to the south, the furthermost of the islands of the Seychelles. In this fashion we should work back towards Mahé, so that when the south-east monsoon broke, as break it must within the next month, we should have it behind us, instead of pushing against its relentless wind. However, this did not stop us from calling in at Alphonse Island, since it lay directly on our route.

The first sight of that island was one which I shall never forget. Right up to its encircling reef the brilliant blue of the deep ocean continued. There it was slashed with white as the breakers curved up and crashed down again in a turmoil of foam. A majestic booming could be heard above the noise of our engine, the roar of everlasting war waged by the sea against the coral ramparts. But beyond that savage borderline lay a lake of translucent green water, the quiet lagoon, dappled with cloud shadows. On this surface Alphonse Island seemed to float, like a vessel in a sheltered anchorage. Casuarina trees, their dark green delicate plumes contrasting with the paler waters on whose surface they were mirrored, bordered the narrow white-sand beach along its entire length. Behind these could be seen the tops of tall coconut trees, whose stiff fronds formed a jagged fringe to the island's silhouette.

Out across the lagoon came two sea-going pirogues, six times the size of our little canoes, each manned by ten oarsmen whose long strokes sent their narrow craft racing through the water. On a little raised platform in the stern of each stood a coxswain, steering by means of a long paddle. They came on, aimed directly at the line of raging surf that marked the reef. As they reached it they backed on their oars a few moments, then at a gesture from the figure in the stern sent the pirogues leaping forwards again into the white swirling waters. Carried on by their rapid

ALPHONSE

oar-strokes and by the backwash of the wave for which they had momentarily waited, each pirogue shot through the danger zone into the comparative calm of the open sea beyond. Then, at a slower pace they rowed up to us where we lay, hove-to, a hundred yards from the reef.

The first to come on board was the island's manager and it was he who had acted as coxswain in the leading pirogue. A slim young man, whose obvious pleasure at the sight of an unexpected ship did not quite overcome his naturally serious manner. We had some mail to deliver and also a few supplies, so he suggested that we anchor for the night within the calm of the lagoon opposite the settlement. We were glad to accept this offer as it would give us the opportunity of having a bath as well as seeing over his island.

Leaving one pirogue to make its way back again across the reef and towing the other behind us, we continued on southwards, parallel to the reef, towards where he assured us lay the safe channel into the lagoon. Speaking of this way in, he referred to it as 'La Passe des Morts' which was not too encouraging. After we had gone about a mile and were opposite a portion of the reef upon which the sea fell with exceptional violence, the young man startled us both by calmly announcing, 'All right. Here we are. Turn in now.' Harvey asked if he were sure of this, a question which was dismissed as though idiotic, and I looked closely at the white line of surf to see if there was any break in it that might indicate a deep-water channel, but there was none. Very reluctantly we edged in closer, and I dashed down to the engine room to tell the mechanic to be double quick about it if Harvey rang down 'Astern'.

It was not until we were thirty yards from the breakers that the pass became apparent, and it was then that I understood why it was called 'Dead Men's Channel'. There was a break in the reef, true, but not a clear break. Rather, the reef formed two pointed horns, one overlapping the other. The way lay straight past the tip of one horn, directly at the next; but once past the first line of breakers an abrupt turn had to be made and the channel continued parallel to and between the two lines of the reef that lay twenty yards off on either side of the boat. Down this narrow channel the water slid, deceptively calm and oily smooth, but it needed full speed for us to make any headway against the powerful current that ran out of the lagoon into the ocean.

For a hundred yards we continued thus, then the reef on our right hand fell away and we were able to edge the *Marsouin* round until she was on her original course, pointed straight for the island itself, but this time inside the reef barrier. Once away from the channel, the current slackened off rapidly, and we were able to make our leisurely way across the mile-wide stretch of lagoon that here separated the island from the reef.

Eyes twinkling behind his spectacles, the young administrator admitted that it was a bit frightening the first time. Even the captain of the schooner which called there regularly every three months and which had done so for years, never attempted it on his own, but waited outside the reef for a pilot. It was not so much that the channel was complicated: left turn, a hundred yards, right turn and there you were, safe inside. The trick was to know exactly *when* to turn in, since the 'horns' could not be seen until one was almost on them.

In a way, Alphonse is one of the 'show' islands of the Seychelles. It is everything one imagines such a tropical island to be and more. Nearly circular and about two miles in diameter, it represents an almost self-supporting and highly productive kingdom in miniature. In common with all the Seychelles, the staple product is copra. I must admit that until I arrived in these islands I had no idea what this was, except that it was a product from which coconut oil was produced. Now, I learnt that the coconut kernel itself, split open and dried on racks in the sun, constitutes copra. Consequently the main work on Alphonse was in growing, collecting and preparing coconuts. But besides this there were a hundred other minor activities. Fish were caught in the lagoon in traps, or by hand-line from the big pirogues that went off on long fishing expeditions away from the island. These catches were then dried and salted for export. Chickens were bred for consumption in Mahé. Pigs, roaming loose over the island, provided meat. Beehives there were in neat white rows behind the administrator's house, their honey destined for Mahé, but the raw beeswax for India. In one corner of the island guano was dug from rocky pits, not for export, but for use in the extensive market gardens that occupied the sheltered centre of the estate.

ALPHONSE

Then there was the village, two straight neat lines (like bigger beehives) of whitewashed cottages in which the labourers lived. A mill, driven by a donkey, whose companions carried the loads of nuts in from the plantation. A shop, dispensary, church and jail, all run by the manager. Alongside the landing beach, half in the water, was a turtle pond for housing those poor reptiles until the schooner arrived and carried them away, on their backs and kicking feebly, destined for the butcher's slab.

Up from the beach, just under the shade of the casuarina trees which served as a wind break and which continued right around the island, was the pirogue shed. With its shade and because of the cool breeze that always blew under its wall-less thatched roof, it was a favourite place for men to gossip after work whilst the women prepared the food in the cottages. It was peaceful here, with the black shapes of the giant pirogues, like sleeping dragons, against which to prop one's back whilst looking out across the lagoon to the distant reef. The projecting thatched eaves served as a visor against the glare and the noise of the wind sighing through the casuarinas was infinitely soothing. Away in the distance, masking the horizon, a band of haze capped the reef: spume and spray flung high and vaporized by the endless surf. And as a background to all this the faint and unforgettable 'booming' of those faraway breakers.

It was while sitting thus in the pirogue shed that I came across an interesting fragment of local history. Glancing up towards the rafters, I saw balanced there a most extraordinary-looking boat. It was coffin-shaped, flat-bottomed, slab-sided and about eight feet in length. Thinking it might have been built by a child perhaps, for paddling around the lagoon, I would have dismissed it had not the administrator noticed my studying it.

'You see that,' he said. 'That was the boat the American came in.' 'What American?' I asked, and he proceeded to tell me the following tale.

In 1951 an American engineer, by name Rowe, was passing his time by sailing alone around the world. Not a very wealthy man, he had nevertheless sufficient capital to have himself built a well-fitted yacht; and in this he made his way slowly across the Pacific, past Australasia, calling wherever he wished and for as long as his interest in the locality held. After Australia, he ploughed on past Indonesia, then Ceylon and finally the Maldive

Archipelago. Continuing on westwards he was then wrecked on one of the many uninhabited Chagos Islands, that group amongst which Harvey and I had originally intended to go shell-diving.

His yacht was completely destroyed, but certain of the provisions were washed ashore, along with himself. On this tiny island he lived for two months, feeding mainly on sea birds and their eggs. During this time he built himself a boat. None of the timbers of his original craft had come ashore, nor had he any nails or cordages. Consequently his 'coffin-craft' had to be made of box-wood, 'sewn' together with twisted grass fibres and plugged with wooden dowels. The whole he caulked with a mess of sea bird excrement and pulped feathers. A three-foot length of bamboo served as mast and a piece of ragged canvas as a sail. Rowe had just enough room to lie down in this coffin. There was a foot space at either end in which he stowed tins of fresh water.

The wind blew but fitfully at that time of the year and the current ran towards Africa, over two thousand miles away. Knowing all this, but preferring the idea of positive action to a Crusoe-ish life on sea bird eggs for maybe the next twenty years, the American, a man already in his forties, paddled out one calm day away from his island and from safety.

For six weeks he drifted, not knowing where, for all his charts and navigational instruments had been lost in the wreck. Quite often large sharks came up alongside him, rubbing their rough skins against the thin planks, scratching themselves to get rid of sea lice and other vermin, as cows might use a post in a meadow. When this happened he would lie flat on the bottom of his frail punt, as the brutes threatened to overturn him. At other times the plugs would dissolve away and he would have to stuff more feathers into the cracks and holes through which the sea poured.

Eventually one morning he heard the roar of breakers, and by standing upright could just make out a line of surf and beyond it the shape of an island. For hours his 'coffin' wallowed there, now drawing nearer, now drifting away with each change of the current or tide. Rowe's weak paddling had no effect. In the afternoon the wind increased with the rising tide, gathered him up and swept him in onto the reef. By some miracle he came through the surf intact and the waves took him straight in over jagged coral to the quiet lagoon. Here a gentle current took hold of him and quietly carried him straight up to the beach, where he stepped out. Mr Rowe had arrived at Alphonse Island after a voyage of nearly two months and having covered a straight line distance of over twelve hundred miles.

But he was a modest man and no magazine or sailing journal ever printed his story. After a week's stay at Alphonse, he got a passage on board a schooner to Mahé, from whence he returned to the United States. The manager, Gendron, still gets Christmas cards from him, but the memory of his epic voyage is fast fading and few people in the Seychelles now remember it. But his 'coffin-craft' is still there in the rafters of the great pirogue shed at Alphonse. Gendron has treated it with anti-termite solution and is doing his best to preserve the cockle-shell. He had it brought down and taken outside so that I might photograph it. In the sunlight alongside the massive pirogues it looked unbelievably fragile, a pigmy amongst giants. But a pigmy that had undergone a sea journey which made the expeditions of those great fishing pirogues puny in comparison.

Early next morning I set off in search for Green Snail within the lagoon. By midday it was obvious that there were none and I thankfully gave up the task. Thankfully, because the lagoon was dotted with deep pockets. Most of these lay out of the path of the direct tidal stream and so contained semi-stagnant water. Their edges were lined with dead and rotting coral and below fifteen feet, in the pocket itself, everything was opaque and slimy, with visibility reduced to an arm's length. In each of these submarine pits I had been 'bounced' by large and singularly repulsive Giant Cod. Their sudden appearance at such proximity was hard on the nerves and the whole environs had such a sinister and unpleasant aspect that I was secretly glad I found no shell life at all, other than a few small mud oysters.

Following lunch we decided to continue on to Farquhar, after first examining the outside of Alphonse reef. Gendron came with us as pilot to guide us through 'La Passe des Morts' and as he waved goodbye from the stern of his pirogue I could not but wonder at his life. There he was, a hard-working and intelligent young man, in sole charge of an island whose gross profit was of the order of £25,000 per year, responsible for some eighty persons, with power of magistrate, doctor, priest and employer, his own accountant, storekeeper and boat builder. There he lived with his wife and two young children out of touch with the world, except for a schooner that called every three months and for short spells of leave every three years. For this he received the princely salary of £7 10s. per month, plus a semi-furnished house. In a few years' time his children would have to go to Mahé to school and his wife must accompany them. How would he manage then? No wonder so many of the younger educated Seychellois are emigrating whenever possible. Soon there will be none of his calibre left, but by then it will be too late to think of a palliative.

Once outside the reef we turned southwards and followed it around for a short way. Then Harvey hove to and I set off in a pirogue to see if there were any Green Snail. I had left Albert behind on purpose, much to his relief. Alphonse, in common with all these outer islands of the Seychelles, plunges straight into water of abyssal depths, and as I have explained, whilst the shoal waters of the great bank on which Mahé and Praslin are placed had given us a certain amount of protection from large sharks, here there were none. No one had ever bathed outside these reefs before and Gendron had told us that quite a few Tiger Sharks patrolled there. His verandah was decorated with the jaws of one of these. Agape, it could pass over the head and shoulders of two people standing back to back, without touching either of them.

Previous meetings with large sharks in other seas had dispelled some of the instinctive dread of these beasts that is, in reality, the diver's chief foe. However, whilst I was fairly certain that I could safely get myself out of any trouble should it arise, I did not want the responsibility of having young Albert on my hands at such a time. Not for a start, at any rate.

I slid over the side, well out from the breakers, in about fifty feet of water. Here was a different world from that which lay within the lagoon. The sea was crystal clear and cold. Colder by far than the sun-warmed shallows of Mahé. The immensity of the scene was frightening and I felt very insecure and small. I swam in towards the reef quickly, to start the search in shallow water. There, confidence soon returned, though each time I looked out and away from the reef face, towards where it slanted down and disappeared into the abyss, I felt a spasm of nervousness. It was the first time I had ever dived alongside such tremendous depths. I had expected the two-thousand-fathom drop to fade away into deep gloom, perhaps even inky blackness, but strangely enough, the reverse seemed to be the case. Looking downwards over the coral precipice it was as though way below, far out of sight, there lay some secret source of intense illumination that bathed the sea with faint light. This blueness radiated, not from the sunlit air above, but upwards out of the depths. As this light 'poured' up it became mixed with the sunlight and grew paler, so that the surface layer was hardly tinted at all with this miraculous colour.

Seen from the *Marsouin* the line of breakers had seemed most impressive, but near to they resolved into comparatively small and harmless waves. The 'blooming' of the reef was not so much caused by the waves crashing down upon it, as I had expected, but by the surging backrush of water flowing in their wake. Near in, the reef was worn smooth and flat by the action of the tides and presented a slightly sloping surface right up to its inner lagoon edge. The lagoon water, spilling out over this rim, ran down this slope and undercut the incoming swell, causing it to heap up and then fall in a turmoil of foam back upon itself. It was this stretch of swirling water that give rise to most of the noise of the reef. At its inner edge the depth varied from five feet at high water to zero at low tide when the reef lay brown and bare, exposed to the coral-killing sunlight. This rim whereon the breakers fell was about two hundred yards across and the depth of water at the outer edge was perhaps only six feet greater than that at the shallowest point. Seawards, it fell away at a steeper angle, no longer flat and smooth, but a delightful coral garden brilliant with colour and alive with movement. This continued for another hundred yards, by which time the coral lay some sixty feet or more below the surface. Finally came the edge of the great cliff, the step-off into the abyss, but this I did not examine too closely at the time, as it frightened me.

Swimming along, eyes straining to pick up some submarine feature in common with the Green Snail terrain of Mahé, all unconsciously I drifted into shallower water. It was some time before I noticed how rapidly the bottom was sliding by beneath me. By then it was too late.

Caught in the swiftly flowing current that was now making itself felt with the rising tide, I was carried along, willy-nilly, at an oblique angle, up over the reef and deposited with a gentle 'plop' into the lagoon beyond. Lesson number one – the current across such a reef at the change of tide is far too strong for any skin diver.

Just as a saucer will hold water beyond its apparent capacity until the critical last drop is added, whereupon the liquid pours out over the lip all around, so it is with these circular reefs. The sea 'heaps up' until finally it has to find its own level and pours out (or in, depending upon whether it be high or low water) in a sudden rush simultaneously along the entire front of the reef.

To get back by swimming across the wide coral lip was impossible, but by wading in the shallower parts and clawing my way along the bottom when that was no longer practical, I was able to regain the outside of the reef where the pirogue lay waiting. As soon as I was a very few yards away from the shallow reef top the current petered out and I was free to continue, but each time I drew in towards it I would feel its pull upon me and, wiser now, swam back to deeper water and to safety.

On I went, working parallel to the great reef, but without seeing so much as a trace of a Green Snail. To tell the truth, I was not even sure what I was looking for, for I could see that if there were shells there they must be living under totally different conditions and probably at different depths from those I had seen around Mahé. Here there was no granite, no boulders, no green algae, so that these snails would in all probability present a completely different appearance. I could see that my eye, trained to spot the shells under one set of circumstances, would find it difficult to 'unlearn' all that it had just acquired. Also, I was still too preoccupied with my own insignificance in this great sea and the extreme proximity of that awful gulf, out of which might come a huge monster at any instant, or so I imagined!

Consequently, with half my mind alive to this possibility and only half trying to concentrate on a completely new set of surroundings and conditions, this first survey was very incomplete and unsatisfactory. I consoled myself by remembering that Gendron, who had a keen faculty for observation and who had been on the island since he was a boy, had stated categorically that he had never yet seen a Green Snail, not even a dead one, on any part of the coast or reef of Alphonse.

Anyway, it was getting a little late now. The sun was hidden behind a bank of clouds and the coldness of the water was no longer something to be ignored. With the overcast sky the colour of the underwater scene faded too, until only the blueness remained, which emphasized the loneliness and the lostness of that place. Shivering, I climbed back into the pirogue and we returned to the *Marsouin*. There, as a result of what I had seen, we decided to continue on our way rather than waste more time on what appeared to be an unpromising area.

The four-hundred-mile journey down to Farquhar was uneventful. Both wind and current set us back so that for four days we saw nothing but empty horizons. The ocean itself seemed deserted and the feathered lure we hopefully towed astern remained untouched. Once, for a short half-hour, two small beaked whales came and played alongside. In the transparent water it could be seen how they used the movement of the swell itself to help them on their way. Just below the surface, they would cut obliquely up a long hill-slope of water. Then, with a flick of their tails to lift them over the top, coast down the other side, gaining speed, until they reached the trough, then losing it again as they mounted the next oncoming wave. They played with the sea, using it as they wished, in the same way as gulls use the air and turn its most violent gusts into a force to propel them wheresoever they wish to go.

What is it about a distant island that exerts such a powerful and mesmeristic attraction upon the eye of the beholder? We first saw Farquhar as a frieze of palm trees that seemed to rise on their own from the blue sea, and it was some hours before the low-lying island itself appeared over the horizon. Yet in that intervening time, whatever else we were doing on deck, our gaze continually strayed back to that faint and far-off fringe upon which our hopes were centred.

While we were still several miles away the scent of the island reached out towards us. At first there were indefinable nasal sensations which set the nostrils quivering with each faint puff of air that came off the land. After a week at sea our nostrils were burned and cauterized by the strong clean wind of the ocean. Now, like long-cramped limbs in which the blood has renewed its flow, they tingled with the promise of new life. Later, when we were nearer, the humid perfume of the island became as heady as strong wine. It was a female smell, heavy and overpowering. Its ingredients were rich vegetation, moist warm earth, soft carpetings of casuarina needles, a touch of jasmine or frangipani, and a trace of peppery and acrid guano. All these combined to form a strangely exciting feminine presence, contrasting sharply with the rough male scent of the sea, to which we had grown accustomed.

Off the reef on the north-west side of the island we saw the beacon that marked the anchorage and for which we had been advised to look out. Moored alongside it lay a large pirogue obviously awaiting us. In all these remote islands the arrival of a ship is quite an event, and any labourer seeing a vessel, no matter how distant, raises the cry 'Sail-O' (which dates back 150 years) and this is shouted from one individual to another until the news eventually reaches the village. The usual sequel to this is that the entire population, apart from those engaged in essential work, flocks down to the beach to help and watch those fortunate few who have been selected by the administrator to accompany him to escort the newcomer in.

So it was with us.

Once on board the manager, Monsieur d'Unienville, having read the letter of introduction which Farquhar's owner had given us before leaving Mahé, invited us to stay on shore in his house for as long as we wished. He added, moreover, that M. Moulinie in his letter had said that he was to give us any assistance we might need during our stay which, to say the least, was very kind of him.

Once again, we were guided in through a narrow pass in the reef's perimeter, but this time it was not such a hair-raising channel as that at Alphonse, though the current was even stronger. Once again, we dropped anchor just off a white sand beach in water so calm that we might have been on any small lake. Once again, we walked up past a shady pirogue shed, along an avenue of trees, to an old-fashioned wooden house set in a little clearing.

The similarity between the two islands, Farquhar and Alphonse, was everywhere apparent, but that did not detract in any way from our enjoyment of the scene. Later, we were to find much the same environment at many islands in the outer Seychelles.

That evening, after dinner, listening dozily to the quiet conversation of our host, the calm tempo of this island life was vividly brought home to me. There were six of us, d'Unienville, his son, the two deputy managers and ourselves. The room in which we sat was high-ceilinged, cool and furnished somewhat austerely, in a sparse but not uncomfortable Victorian style. On the table and sideboard two oil-lamps gave out a warm yellow light which cast into relief the shadows of the lizards clinging to the bare walls with their splayed feet. Outside the evening breeze rustled through the coconut fronds and occasionally swept in a misguided beetle, who, lumbering heavily, would complete a few puzzled circuits and then buzz heavily out into the night again.

Against this setting the quiet voices rose and fell. There were long periods of silence, but the silence of contentment, not of awkwardness or boredom. Sentences did not clash nor overlap with one another. One spoke if one had something to say, not for the sake of breaking the silence in that room, whose very quietness was friendly and companionable. No one minded if one dozed a little or paid more attention to the lizards than to the speaker.

On a small table in one corner stood a radio, and although I had already been told that it was in working order, it was obvious from the fine layer of dust that covered its controls that it had not been used for several weeks, perhaps months. I understood perfectly why that was so. The wireless, with its never-ending stream of time signals and programme announcements, is a constant reminder of civilization's 'now':

'. . . at the first stroke it will be *exactly* 6 p.m. Greenwich Mean Time.' 'It is *now* seventeen minutes past two, on Sunday, the twenty-third of March.'

'Our programme for *tomorrow*, Friday the 15th of September . . .'

All these incessant reminders have no meaning for island such as these. Here, 'exactly' becomes 'two or three *months* before the schooner is due'. 'Now' is 'the *season* of the south-east monsoon'.

There was work to be done, surely, but it was continuous work throughout the year, a general programme of advancement, not a meticulously parcelled-up package of separate time-units. In such a place a radio had little purpose, other than as a warning system during the cyclone period.

Monday, Tuesday, Wednesday, did not exist.

'Come-day-go-day-God-send-Sunday' was enough . . .

And along with it went peace.

The next morning, since the weather was a little rough for operating outside the reef, we decided to take the *Marsouin* as far south within the lagoon as possible and to try and penetrate the reef from the inside by pirogue, when we could get no further. M. d'Unienville gave us one of his coxswains as a guide, since the lagoon was dotted with innumerable coral heads and culs-de-sac which made the eight mile journey hazardous for a vessel the size of the *Marsouin*.

The land portion of Farquhar atoll is composed of a narrow strip, running from the north edge, where the settlement is placed, along the eastern reef face. There, it peters out and only the reef continues to mark the perimeter, until right around on the north-west side where there are a further three tiny islets. The various islets comprise only eight and a half miles out of the thirty-mile circumference.

Our pilot took us down the eastern side of the lagoon, until we were opposite the southernmost end of the main island chain. Beyond this point it was not safe to go, since the lagoon became shallow and the currents over the reef unpredictable. Taking the biggest pirogue, Jean Batiste, Albert and three others, I set off immediately in an effort to gain a tiny raised sandbank that lay a further two miles to the south, just inside the reef. By examining the sand on its seaward edge for minute fragments of dead shells which might have been cast up by the waves I hoped to determine whether or not any mother-of-pearl shells lay on the far side of that eastern reef. The tide was low, and so we planned to walk on the reef itself, comparatively dry-shod. Accordingly, we struck off at a tangent to gain the reef as soon as possible and then work our way along it towards the sandbank, Ile Goelette (*Goelette* is the local name for the Sooty or Wideawake Tern).

Once there, however, we found that the 'reef flat' was so serried by little tideways and so pitted with rock pools that our progress was extremely slow and it was also very hard on our feet. Leaving one man with the pirogue, with instructions to pole it around the reef until he reached the sandbank, the rest of us set off to wade directly across the lagoon which, with its level, sandy floor was far more comfortable, although the water was up to our chests.

Soon, the five of us were spread out over a comparatively wide area, each person choosing his own particular route. Coming to a shallower stretch, where the water only came up to my hips and thinking it likely to continue so, I signalled to the others to join me. As soon as they had done so, we continued, but had scarcely gone a hundred yards when once again the fishermen began to stray off on their own. Suddenly one of them gave a high-pitched yell, at which the rest of us turned round. At first I could see no reason for his evident consternation, but by following the direction in which his hand pointed I saw, some twenty yards away from him, the unmistakable dark silhouette of a very large shark, stealthily drawing nearer still.

The others were standing petrified and all looked at me for some sort of guidance. Thinking any action was better than none I beckoned them to converge on me and then clapped my hands, palm downwards, on the water, to divert the brute's attention. Luckily, at this the ominous shadow stopped its advance and those nearest it were able to retreat until we were all in a tight little cluster. Then the shark started to move in again, and no amount of hand-clapping deterred it, until presently it reached a point some ten yards away, at which distance its true bulk became apparent. It was, I should say, fourteen feet or more in length. In the waist-high water its dorsal fin-tip just broke the surface, whilst its pectorals ploughed up furrows of sand which stretched behind it like vapour trails from some weird aircraft.

If any group of people were in a mess, it was us! Completely unarmed, with not even a stone to lay our hands on. Our masks and swim-fins lay in the pirogue, half a mile away. We were up to our waists in water and the loose sand on which we stood made each move a clumsy lunge.

After a minute or so, that which I had feared, happened. The shark, discarding all pretence of concealment, began to move in a steady circle around us, its dorsal fin now well clear of the water and its belly no longer hugging the bottom. As it moved, so did our little group, turning with it, constantly facing it. I glanced sideways at Jean Batiste. Nothing could be read in his face, no emotion whatsoever, but beads of sweat trickled down his cheeks and clung to the stubble on his chin. Beyond him, Albert's thin face seemed unnaturally pinched and he was very pale. I had no time to check on the others.

The great beast increased the pace of its circlings and then diminished them again. I had expected it to come in at our legs once it had worked itself up to a frenzy, but it had not. Presently it stopped altogether and lay dormant, now only six yards from us, a little more than its own length away; blunt, broad head pointing directly at us.

There was nothing to be gained by waiting there. Besides, the tide had turned and already we could feel the pull of the current around our feet. With a jerk of the head and at the same time stepping slowly forward one pace, I indicated to the others what we must do. To their credit, they stepped out too, though I heard Jean Batiste, on my left, suck in his breath between his teeth as he did so. Very slowly, but uniformly we advanced. By the time we were four yards from the brute our pace had slowed to a crawl, but we at least went through the motions of moving our reluctant feet. By now, I did not know how this could end, and was too scared to think about it. Someone on my right stumbled and his foot kicked up a whorl of sand. That was the turning point. I saw a shiver flex the tail of the monster and then, with a tremendous surge it shot forward, rolling on its side as it came. I experienced an instant of pure blind panic and then the fisherman on the extreme left collapsed in a welter of foam. Seconds later he was on his feet again, but the whole scene was so jumbled that I was still sure he had been taken and caught myself shouting idiotically in English 'But your legs! He took you by your legs.'

It was not until we had all looked each other up and down in amazement that we realized that what we had taken for an attack was retreat. In doing so, the shark had not sufficient space to clear us and so had bowled Georges over, with one side-sweep of its lashing tail as it swung around. The tension broken, we behaved like schoolboys, slapping each other on the back boasting that we *really* knew all the time it would run!

Then Albert pointed and we saw the sinister dark cigar-shape quietly watching us from about thirty yards' distance. That had an immediate sobering effect, but we now felt morally superior and were able to retreat in good order to the safety of a dead coral, upon which we climbed and then felt reasonably secure with the water only ankle-deep. From that vantage point we waved, hooted and shouted until the pirogue saw us and came to fetch us off. The shark, meanwhile, cruised about nearby, but never came nearer than twenty yards, and once we were in the pirogue it sheered off altogether and we saw it no more.

On the way across to the sandbank the rest chattered away, recounting the experience with many lies and much laughter. But I was seriously worried. This shark had shown deliberate aggressiveness. It was large, and its blunt head, dark skin and absence of fin-tip markings made me pretty certain that it was a Tiger Shark, of which I had heard a lot about but never yet met. Moreover, it was inside the lagoon. How many others, then, patrolled the outside of the reef, where we intended to work? That was the question.

Ile Goelette was a disappointment. The tide-lines yielded an enormous amount of shell fragments, of all descriptions except those of the particular shell for which we were looking. There were multi-coloured cones, volutes, olives, cowries, harp and hare shells – from minute slivers to perfect beach-washed specimens. But not one trace of any mother-of-pearl-bearing shell other than a few trochus, of a type not suitable for commercial acceptance. The seaward edge, where it abutted the reef, proved impossible to examine underwater, since the rising tide brought swirling eddies and vicious cross-currents. Anyway, the surf on the reef itself was far too heavy to penetrate and it was obvious that our idea of getting through that way would have to be given up for several days until the water grew calmer.

Not meeting with the rest of the fishermen, I was wondering where they might have got to when a tremendous clamour arose from over the low brow of the sandbank. Seconds later, an enormous number of sea-birds rose up from behind its shelter, screaming with rage and fear. Like a whirling dust cloud they formed a huge inverted cone of dark wings, twisting and turning, concentrating their fury and despair upon something that remained hidden from me by the intervening hillock. I scrambled up the slope, knowing full well what I should find, and hoping that I could reach the scene before too much damage had been done. Sure enough, there they were, my missing group of fishermen, and already they had half a dozen or so limp, feathered bundles dangling from their hands. Before I got to them several more birds were literally 'plucked from the air', as they clamoured and beat around the men's heads.

Like many native peoples the Seychelle Creole is supremely

indifferent to animal suffering and it is his own ceaseless butchery that has resulted in many of the islands being denuded of all wild life, save for those forms which are completely inedible. To the end of our acquaintanceship these fishermen could never fathom my continued intervention in what was to them 'fair game', and this strained our friendship to near-breaking point on many occasions. Had we been on a restricted or monotonous diet it would have been a different matter, but they would grab or club any bird simply for the sake of it, leaving the pathetic corpses to litter the ground.

Goelette Island seemed to be incorrectly named, for there were few if any Sooty Terns to be seen, the whole sandbank being covered with little brown Noddies (*Macoa* in Creole). These would remain squatting on the ground, which was here covered with tenacious creeper-grass, until we were almost on them; then, with a plaintive 'peep', take to the air. Once aloft, our presence which they had hitherto virtually ignored seemed to offer a new and intriguing perch and they would do their best to alight on our heads and shoulders as we walked. It was at such moments that the fishermen would grab them and wring their necks. One thing I noticed at once. Any man who carried a dead or flapping bird became the immediate target for a thousand feathered protests, and his progress was marked by a swirling mob of Noddies. Once the men had put the bodies down and moved on a few yards the birds promptly forgot whatever it was that had excited them and even the ruffled bodies lying on the ground grew scant attention. A man by himself was not cause for alarm, although he might strike at other birds as he went. Their own dead were similarly ignored. But woe betide any man who picked up a bird, whether alive or dead. Instantly he became a target for every Noddy within sight, their plaintive 'peeps' turning to harsh and strident alarm-notes and their soft flutterings becoming desperate and reckless lunges.

By the time we had walked across the sandbank to where we had left the pirogue, I had managed to make all the fishermen release those birds that they held and which were still alive, and discard the bodies of those they had already killed. Luckily, the Noddies had not as yet started to lay or else my men would have done a hundred times as much damage.

The next day the weather was, if anything, worse, and we gave

ALPHONSE

up all idea of doing any serious work. Harvey took advantage of the strong breeze to go back to the settlement in the sailing dinghy and collect some bread which the manager had promised to bake for us. For the first hour or so after his departure I busied myself about the ship, then, growing bored, decided to paddle over to the long islet behind which we were anchored, and look around.

South Island, as it is named, presented a completely different aspect from Ile Goelette. Low bushes lined the beaches, behind which coco-palms and casuarinas grew in jumbled profusion. The whole island, however, had the appearance of having been under heavy shell-fire at some time during the past few years. Many palm trunks were snapped off or uprooted. Casuarinas were twisted into weird shapes and the ground beneath them littered with torn-off branches. Those trees that remained standing were all leaning at an acute angle as though they had been pushed over by a giant.

Then I remembered M. Moulinie telling us how Farquhar had been hit by a severe cyclone in 1951 and of the damage it had caused. On the main island, owing to a vigorous programme of cutting away and replanting, most of its traces were now covered up, but here, on this remoter islet, the full force of the holocaust could still be measured, vividly recorded in these scenes of destruction. I myself believe that the actual centre of the hurricane passed directly across South Island, for I found a hundred-yard-wide belt in which not a tree was left standing. On either side of this flattened strip the debris lay piled high, all pointing obliquely inwards towards the razed pathway that stretched right across the island. Even here, however, young casuarinas were already beginning to mask the desolation with their soft and luxuriant plumes. Self-seeding, some of these trees had already reached a height of twenty or thirty feet in the short time that had elapsed since the cyclone struck.

Following this 'Roman road' of the storm's path, I pushed on towards the eastern edge of the island, wishing to examine the reef and coastline on that side. As I went, the acrid and peppery smell of fresh guano became stronger, and now I could hear a mounting cacophany of strident squawks rising above the sound of the distant surf and the noise of the wind through the treetops. Coming to the top of a short rise I looked down into a little valley. This had obviously escaped the full force of the storm and the destruction was considerably less noticeable. No palms grew there, but a multitude of casuarinas; great mature trees, upright and stately and in many cases dying of old age. Amongst their branches was the most extraordinary colony of birds I had ever seen!

Many times before, particularly when far from land, I had watched for hours the deliberate flight of the great Boobies, those sea birds very much akin to and closely resembling the Gannet of northern Europe's remote coasts. I had automatically assumed that Boobies, like the Gannets, chose nesting sites on rocky headlands or steeply sloping ground, from which they might take off and land with ease. But here was a large colony nesting in trees!

Even as I watched, several adult birds came sweeping in from over the opposite hillside, executed a steep turn into wind over my head and planed down into the valley to alight (with a splintering of many small branches and the loss of several feathers), each on its selected bough. Each such arrival was commented on by all the other birds in that particular tree with a rising chorus of harsh cries, as if to say 'Look out. *Look out.* LOOK OUT. Cling on. Here he comes. Sqwaaaaark . . . !' The clamour would reach a climax as each newcomer settled with a tremendous flapping of pinions. The whole branch would often bend and sway with the impact, for these birds were as big as a small goose and had a wingspan of five or six feet.

For half an hour I stayed there, looking down entranced at the scene. Sometimes a Booby might make four or more attempts before his landing was successful, particularly if his nest were awkwardly placed. These nests were parsimoniously made, being for the most part mere 'rafts' of dead casuarina twigs, lined with a layer of casuarina needles and usually situated at the crotch of some minor branch. Occasionally, however, they rested on one branch only, hanging down in a limp fashion on either side. All in all, they were not very inspired examples of home-building, but they seemed to suffice, since most of them housed one or more chicks. So far as I could see, these Boobies must lay not more than two eggs and those spaced at an interval of six weeks or more, since in no case could I see two fluffy chicks in one nest. Usually there seemed to be one small and very fluffy chick on the nest itself, and alongside him, clutching the branch and not in the nest at all, an elder brother or sister, already discarding his down and sprouting half-formed feathers. Since the nests were often side by side, I was not altogether sure that the two chicks belonged to the same family; if not, then perhaps only a single egg was laid and hatched by each family.

Presently, I walked down into the valley in order to take some photographs. This was not without hazard, since as I passed below each nest the parent or chick above me would disgorge a partially digested fish upon my head. On examination these all proved to be flying-fish and at no time did I come across any other article of diet. The ground below the trees was bare, all vegetation having been burned away by the excessively rich and phosphorus-containing excrement of the birds, which gave off a pungent smell, but was not altogether unpleasant to the nostrils. Many of the trees which I had thought to be dying of old age were, in fact, poisoned by these strong droppings, their bark peeling off where it had been splashed.

Seen from immediately below, the arrival of the parents was even more spectacular. Screened by the intervening branches, one had only the mounting crescendo of the other birds' cries to warn one of the approach. At the peak of this there would be a rushing of wings followed instantly by a shower of twigs and feathers as the newcomer floundered through the branches, which would bow under his weight, a few more squawks as the chick was presented with a flying-fish, and then peace for a minute or so until the next arrival or departure.

Finding one nest lower than the rest, I was able to climb up alongside it and photograph the mother and chick at very close range. This parent obstinately refused to leave the nest no matter how near I approached. She watched my antics calmly until I trespassed too near, whereupon she bobbed her head up and down in mock-threats, occasionally opening her long beak to give vent to a drawn-out and goose-like hiss. The chicks on their own, like enormous powder puffs with protruding black beaks and over-large pink webbed feet, had no fear and allowed themselves to be picked up and handled without any fuss at all.

All the Boobies I could see seemed to belong to one species, the Redfooted Booby (*Sual Piscatrix*. Creole: *Fou-Bête*) and no other sea-bird shared their valley, though I did see a solitary and shy Warbler, which I could not identify.

Leaving the valley I went on to gain the far side of the island. Here the reef 'flat' seemed to extend much further out into the sea than I had imagined possible, for there were heavy breakers indicating shallow water, stretching out as far as a mile or more from the shore. Once again I searched the tide-lines and the bottom of rock-pools for traces of Green Snail shells but without success. This was not entirely unexpected, since both M. Moulinie and M. d'Unienville had said that they had never heard of any being found there, but that they *were* to be found off the three islets on the north-west side of the atoll, diametrically opposite to where I was. This was also one of the places mentioned to our crew by the labourers they had questioned in Mahé, and we were placing great hopes on this information which had come from two different sources.

It was past midday and as I was hungry and thirsty I returned to my pirogue. Before setting off, however, I had a bathe to rid myself of the slimy flying-fish residue and other tokens of affection bestowed on me by the inhabitants of Booby Valley. At tea-time Harvey returned bringing, besides the bread, the welcome news that d'Unienville thought the weather would moderate sufficiently during the night for us to go out through the Pass again and to work the reef off the Three Islands. That night, before going to bed, I checked all the diving gear and the aqualungs, in case we might need them. By nine, the rest were all asleep, but I lay awake for some time wondering what lay in store for us, outside, on the other side of that reef.

FOUR

Farquar

Eight o'clock the next morning found us outside the lagoon. Since the only other break in the reef's perimeter was far too intricate and possibly also too shallow for us, we had motored right back, up past the settlement, and then out through the channel by which we had first entered. We should have gained the open sea much earlier, for we had up-anchored at first light, but for the tremendous current that poured in through the Pass with the rising tide. As it was, that half-mile stretch took us fifty minutes, with the engine at maximum revolutions, and for minutes on end we seemed to make no appreciable progress against the inexorable flow of water.

On the outside of the reef conditions were good. The wind had dropped completely and though there remained a long swell – the aftermath of the previous day's 'blow' – the reef face looked workable, particularly on this sheltered western side of the atoll. The first attempt was to be at the Three Islands, those three tiny hummocks of coral-rock capped with sandy soil and boasting a few casuarinas. On these, small turtle-fishing camps had been erected in the years past and it was the labourers who assisted in this work who had first told us that they gathered Green Snail there at low tide, on the reef itself, in waist-deep water.

Once abreast of these islets we launched the two pirogues, by the simple expedient of throwing them over the side, while the *Marsouin* lay off a short distance. Catching the crest of an incoming wave the pirogues sped in, surf-riding in a thunder of foam, to be deposited high and dry on the little sand beach we had chosen for our landing place. While the fishermen pulled them up out of reach of the rising tide, Albert and I waded out to explore the now submerged low-water area.

We paddled up and down over the reef 'flat', all around the islet, and in depths ranging from three to fifteen feet – but without seeing any trace of Green Snail, or of any other shells for that matter. If there had been shells there once, certainly none remained! Disappointed, for we had pinned much hope on this information, we swam back to the islet, where Jean Batiste was busy roasting some crabs that the others had managed to catch in the tide-pools. After these had been eaten, there remained no excuse to keep me from what I had to do. There lay the reef edge, way beyond the breakers and that was where I had to look next.

With Jean Batiste and Fouquet as crew, I took one pirogue back out through the surf to the deeper water beyond; there, telling him to be sure to keep up with me, I dropped over the side.

I had expected the usual glorious spectacle: live coral, of many different varieties, and amongst its branches swarms of brilliant fishes, some as big as parrots and others smaller than humming birds – the bird-like inhabitants of this submarine forest. The water was clear. The coral was there also. But where was the colour and movement? What had happened? Instead of the coral bed – that fairly smooth and uniform slope on which grew the usual coral bushes and bigger 'nigger-heads' – everything was topsy-turvy. Huge hunks of coral rock lay scattered about and all round them coral débris. Fragments of every type littered the sea-bed, right up to the final drop-off into the abyss, which lay some fifty yards out. There were piles of Antler coral, like heaps of dead branches; pieces of Organpipe coral, intermingled with stumps of Millepora and crushed by great boulders of Nullipore. It was as barren of life as a lunar landscape and as depressing. I swam along, forgetting the pirogue, Tiger Sharks and everything else. What could have caused this?

The further I went, the more apparent became the true magnitude of the damage. For a while I thought that there had been an underwater earthquake, but the actual atoll foundations were untouched, only the surface layer had been disturbed in this violent fashion. It was as though an immense explosion had torn up the reef face along its entire length – the place looked like a battlefield. The destruction was as bad as that caused by the cyclone in its passage across South Island.

That must be the answer! It *was* the cyclone that had caused this. Just as the howling wind accompanying the storm had

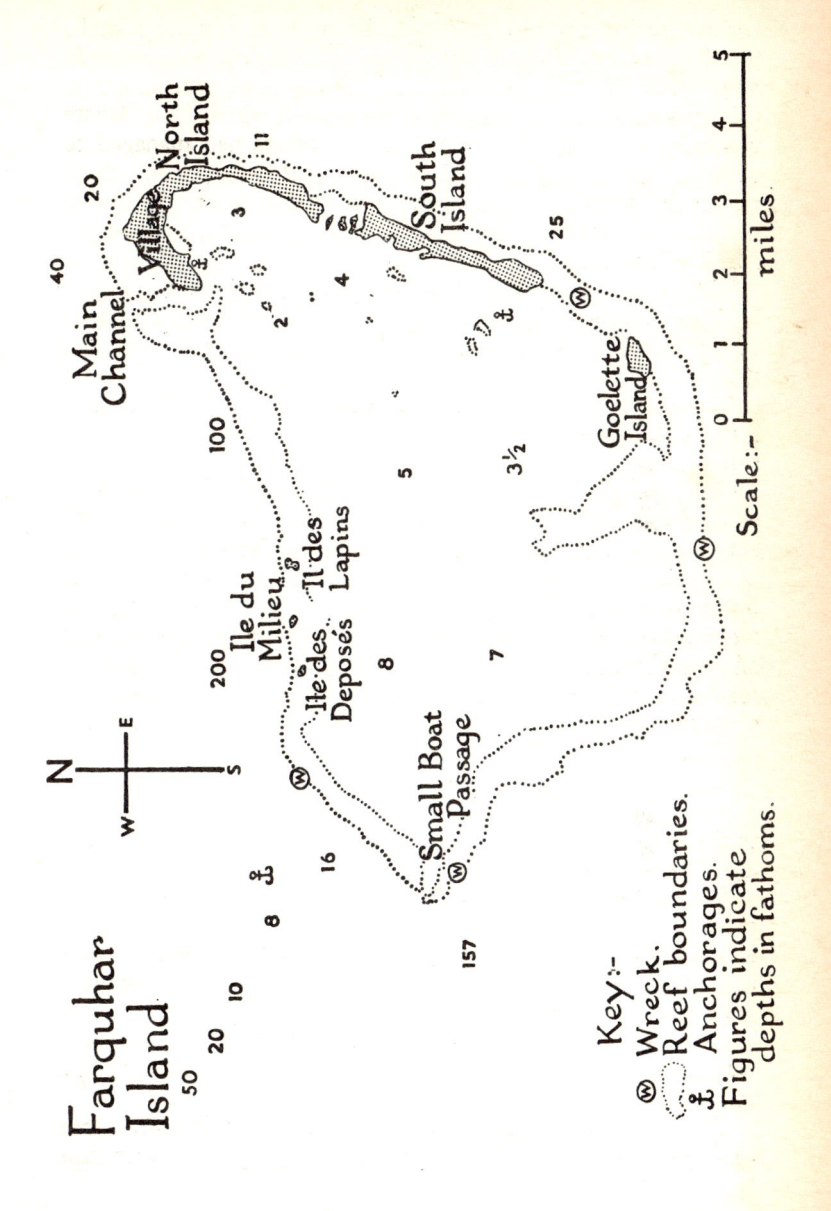

FARQUHAR

torn up trees, so had the lashing waves flattened the submarine vegetation, beaten down the coral bushes, torn up the limestone pavement until everything was destroyed. The fish – which had probably fled to the safety of the depths – returning found their homes destroyed, their food supply dead, the area inhospitable and indeed uninhabitable. They had either stayed and died, or gone elsewhere. Now there was nothing left.

Or was there? Even as I thought about it, two small Rock Cods, possibly the first of the slowly returning colonists, swam up from out of the shadow of a boulder of Nullipore and came right up to me. I dived down to look into the cranny that served them as a home. It was dark down there, and I pushed my hand under the ledge to hold myself in position until my eyes grew accustomed to the gloom. But there was nothing there apart from those two half-curious, half-frightened fishes that now skulked within. I shifted my grip, preparatory to pushing off up to the surface again. As I did so, my hand brushed something – something rounded and vaguely familiar.

My breath could not hold out many more seconds, but I had to make sure. Already clear of the boulder, I half turned, and pulled myself right under the shallow ledge. There it was, wedged in a corner, jammed under the weight of the rock. I could curl my fingers around it but it would not move. By now I was really uncomfortable; I had stayed down far longer than I had intended, but I had to get it out. I could have gone up, got my breath and come down again in a leisurely way – that would have been the proper course. But no, I had to take this thing with me, there and then. I slid one leg under the shelf and pressed with the flat of my foot against the inner wall. The object moved, then jammed again. I pushed with all my might; there was a crunching sensation and I had it, or at least part of it.

I wrenched free of the ledge and let my body rise limply to the surface. There, I was too spent to do more than beckon. Jean Batiste pulled me out of the water and I flopped into the bottom of the pirogue, sprawling full-length. But I still had my Green Snail in my hand. It was old, it was long-dead, and my last wrench had broken it in two, for it was very rotten. As a shell it was valueless, but it proved that these shells *had* lived there up to the time of the cyclone. This one and maybe many more, had been trapped underneath rolling fragments of coral. The others, what had happened to them? Probably starvation had taken some, and perhaps the rest had made their slow way down into the depths to reappear again on some other undamaged reef. Whatever the answer was, I would never know, but this I did know. We should not find any living Green Snail on this section of the reef.

And so it turned out to be. The reef remained desolate and void. So much so that I sent back for Albert to come and join me, for I was sure no sharks scoured this lifeless coast. By one o'clock we gave it up, having only seen three more Rock Cods and one very small and lonely Butterfly fish, whose vivid colouring seemed strangely out of place in those stark surroundings.

While we were drinking mugs of hot, sweet tea on board the *Marsouin* Harvey sailed on down the reef, until we came to our next area. Albert and the others were still fairly optimistic, for did not my find indicate that there were Green Snail on the reef? I could not be persuaded, however, though I did not discourage them, for I had now a very good idea of the immense forces at work in a cyclone, of the large area involved and of the time necessary to repair its damage.

The place we had chosen for this next foray was a stretch of the reef on which lay an old wreck. It was an 11,000-ton steamer, the s.s *Aymestry*, which had been caught off guard in another severe cyclone in 1897, and had been driven ashore by the huge waves, until eventually she lay beam-on, right up on the reef flat itself. Since then, the pounding of each successive monsoon had gradually broken her up, but even now there remained the keel, boilers, propellers and some of the bridge structure, grim evidence of the tragedy. D'Unienville had told us that the wreck was visible at all stages of the tide and, sure enough, though we arrived at high water, there it was, the gaunt tower-like framework of its bridge rearing twenty feet above the waves, like some Wellsian fortification above the line of breakers.

Using this as a mark, Albert and I began our patrol along the edge of the reef, working steadily southwards, in the same direction as we had so far sailed. Sure that this coast also would yield nothing, neither shells, live coral, fish nor sharks, I nevertheless put the young lad on the shallow inside position, in about fifteen feet of water, while I kept to a parallel track within sight of him at about thirty feet. The pirogue, for we had only one this time, was in the middle, so that we might both easily reach it in an emergency.

On we went, and the same scene of desolation unfolded beneath us. After about an hour, however, there was a slight improvement, in that clumps of living seaweed began to appear. Soon, these clumps became whole pastures and the usual weed-inhabiting fish, brown, drab and dull, matching their surroundings, could be seen nosing amongst the fleshy leaves. Here, the underwater visibility rapidly decreased, as it always does in such places, owing to the suspended sediment of rotting vegetable particles. The earlier reef scenes had been devoid of life, but at least they lacked the sinister gloominess of this portion of the atoll.

Occasionally we came across bare and deep canyons, whose narrow fissures ran up on to the reef flat, and sometimes right through into the lagoon itself. In these places we were often 'jumped' by twenty- or thirty-pound *Babonnes* (*Plectropona Maculatus*). I soon saw that these were the adults of those few I had seen that morning, and which I had incorrectly identified as ordinary Rock Cod. In none of the grottoes did we see any small specimens, which perhaps meant that the young ones, after hatching, escaped to remote areas and thus avoided being eaten by their elders. We had no spear guns with us, which was sad, as these big fish make excellent eating. So on we went.

By half past four we were both very tired, and had still not seen even a trace of Green Snail. The *Marsouin* had gradually closed in, so that now she was only a hundred and fifty yards out from where we swam. It would be quite an effort to haul ourselves into the pirogues, and no sooner in than we should have to clamber up on to the *Marsouin*'s deck. So I decided that Albert and I might as well swim directly to the *Marsouin*, keeping close to Jean Batiste for safety's sake. This we started to do, but had not gone more than fifteen yards when Albert pointed downwards. Peering up at us from under the shelter of a massive overhang was a real Rock Cod, barrel-bodied, goggle-eyed and weighing well over one hundred pounds. It was the first one we had seen at Farquhar and both of us felt as though we were meeting an old friend.

I dived down, with Albert close behind, and was able to get within a foot or so of the old fellow before he backed slowly away into the recesses of his sanctuary, leaving us to arc upwards to the surface. I had only a few scant feet to go before my head burst through into the air, and already my eyes were upturned towards the leaden ceiling, when a torpedo shape hurtled past within a yard of my chest. I was so startled, I let out all my breath in a long whoosh of bubbles and only just managed to tilt my head back and draw in another quick breath before I sank down again. I knew what it was all right. A shark! The question was, where was it now? I hadn't far to look. Right below me, perhaps ten feet down, it shot by again, this time travelling in the opposite direction.

I swung round to find Albert. He was on the surface, perhaps ten yards away, looking anxiously down at me. I swam up towards him, for it was essential we stayed together. As I did so, I saw the shark beyond him, at the same level as myself, closing in again. I could see it was about eight or nine feet long, pale grey with short head and with very big and fleshy pectoral fins. Afterwards I found out that this particular type was known locally as '*Requin Grandes Ailes*' and in South Africa as 'Soupfin Shark'. Just then, however, I was not worried about the name. I was only thankful that it wasn't a Tiger.

Not daring to lose sight of it for an instant, I delayed my surfacing and swam on straight towards the brute. It kept on coming and I knew my only hope to avoid, at the very best, a collision was to dive on down underneath it. So we passed. Albert was on the surface, frantically trying to keep his legs up and out of the way, then the shark, and just beneath it myself. I came up just alongside Albert, gasping for breath. We had no time to talk and talking meant lifting our heads out of the water and losing sight of our grim friend. Nor had I time to wave to the pirogue which I saw had gone paddling on, blissfully unaware of what was happening behind it.

No sooner had I put my head under again, than the shark cruised straight past nearly on the surface. As it was going in the same direction as previously I thought it must have executed a quick turn, when Albert pointed feverishly downwards. There, hugging the bottom, were two more! The same type. The same size. Active and dangerously agile brutes. They moved in short, vicious dashes, and I knew what that meant. They were hungry.

When a shark is gorged, or at any rate not hunting, it moves lazily, sliding along, coasting through the water without apparent effort. When it turns, it does so in a smooth graceful arc, rolling slightly. But sharks on the prowl have decisive, quick movements, 'nervous' as one authority describes them. When they come across prey, then their movements become rapier-fast, quicksilver flashes of immense power, dazzling in their ability to hurl their immense bulk in any direction and at any moment.

They can accelerate to terrifying underwater speeds in the space of a second or two, and equally rapidly come to an abrupt stop. In this way, by sheer speed and fantastic manoeuvrability they can outswim and outwit smaller and seemingly more agile fishes. A hunting shark is probably the most efficient killing mechanism ever devised, and one of the most frightening.

There and then I found that out for myself. I grabbed hold of Albert by the shoulders, and swung him around in the water, so that we were back to back. He got the idea, or at least he did not budge from there. Like that we had some hope, as sharks do not usually attempt a frontal attack if they can avoid it. The two on the bottom curved up a little and then broke away, one passing either side of us, about ten feet off. A second later, another cut across my line of vision travelling downwards in a shallow curve. Almost at the same instant a shark streaked past in front of my mask, perhaps two feet away. It was so close, I never saw anything except an eye, a blur of gill slots, and a grey-white wall of flesh. It was just a momentary impression. After that, things go so muddled I really have no idea what went on. Looking back on it, I reckoned there were probably between six and nine in the pack altogether, but they closed in so rapidly and zig-zagged so abruptly, we never really knew how many there were. It was for our legs we were both most worried and we both found ourselves instinctively drawing up our knees to our chins each time we had a glimpse of a head coming our way.

Idiotically, we both lashed out with our feet and fists whenever a shape passed us, but we were always too late, and never made contact, though twice I felt the firm skin of a shark's flank pass across my legs, and once my elbow dug something smooth and fleshy.

Ironically enough, it was the very aggressive nature of their attacks that saved us. Jean Batiste, not dreaming anything had happened, glanced casually around for us and was horrified to see, immediately beside us in the water and all breaking the surface at the same instant, two large dorsal fins and one complete tail, all belonging to different sharks. Luckily for us he never hesitated but jumped right round and sent the pirogue slicing through the water with strong, quick paddle strokes. Pirogues being pointed at each end can be propelled in either direction and this was an occasion when manoeuvrability paid.

A second before he got to us, he must have dropped his paddle, stooped down and made a wild grab at each of us as the pirogue passed. With Albert he succeeded, and with one heave hauled the boy right out of the water into the bottom of the craft. With me he missed.

The first I knew about his arrival was a heavy blow on my shoulder from the bow of the pirogue. By the time I had glanced up and realized what it was, the canoe had almost passed, and in normal conditions I should never have been able to catch it. As it was, I simply picked myself out of the water and flung myself at its beaked stern, grabbed it and was out of the water flat on my face on top of Albert before I had even thought about it. It was lucky that I came in over the stern, for had I attempted the same amidships my weight would have capsized us and that would have been that.

In the pirogue, I lay where I was for a few moments, not thinking, not caring, oblivious to everything, until Albert beneath me was sick, either from excitement, fear, relief, or maybe just my weight!

When we got to the *Marsouin*, my legs felt like rubber and I needed Jean Batiste's assistance to clamber on board. I did not feel like talking about the incident, and merely told Harvey that we had found no shells, that the area was unsuitable and that we had seen a few sharks. He was too disappointed with the day's results to bother me about sharks.

Looking back on it, I realize how lucky we were. I know you should not get in a panic when you come across one of these beasts, and normally it is fairly easy to avoid doing so, *provided that there is only one of them*, no matter how aggressive or large it may be. To kick out, to splash violently, to act instinctively – as we had done – only serves to attract more sharks that may be in the vicinity and to stimulate those already there to press home their attacks. I knew all this, and yet had disregarded it. My only answer to myself is that when one is confronted with a group of hunting sharks the very nature and complexity of their sudden rushes and swift manoeuvrings prevents one from keeping a rational picture of the proceedings; one can no longer keep mental track of the 'battle', and feels so entirely out-classed and inferior as to be unable to act or even think in a logical and reasoning way. The awful thing is that I am sure that, faced with the same situation again, I should once more fall a victim to blind panic, in exactly the same manner as that first time off the reef on the south-west side of Farquhar atoll.

It was already far too late for us to return to the lagoon anchorage, so Harvey decided to pull out a couple of miles and try to find decent holding-ground on a long sandspit that ran from this corner of the reef, out into the deep. We had no difficulty in locating this sandbank, since the colour of the water over it was pale turquoise green compared with the deep blue of the rest of the sea. By six o'clock we were securely anchored and after a light supper went to bed, depressed with the apparent outcome of our six-hundred-mile journey, which seemed to be taking on the nature of a wild-goose chase.

I was swimming along over an immense reef plateau. The coral that lay beneath me was thickly carpeted with Green Snail shells, each and every one a perfect specimen. Adjusting the aqualung mouthpiece to a more comfortable fit, I was just preparing to dive down when someone shouted '*Requins! Guette ça requins! Requins bébêtes!*' I looked around but the sea remained void. Should I go down, or had I better get out? Even as I thought about it, the cries became more pronounced, others taking up the chorus. '*Requins! Requins! Requins Grandes Ailes!*' The shouts were louder, more distinct, drawing nearer. Louder and louder still! And then I woke up. The reef, the sea, the Green Snail were gone, but those cries were still there, echoing down the hatchway from somewhere above my head.

By the time I got on deck, everyone else was there too, peering over the rail into the clear, green water. It was immediately apparent at what they were looking. Twisting and turning lazily just beneath our keel were dozens of medium-sized sharks, identical with those we had met with yesterday. I looked along at Albert. He caught my eye, and nodded glumly. We were both thinking the same thing. What chance had we of getting up any shells on this part of the reef – even supposing there were any – with all these brutes around.

The cook brought up a heavy shark line, to which he attached a six-inch steel hook baited with a piece of turtle meat. For security he tied the free end to a bollard and having done so, hurled the hook as far out as he could, exclaiming as he did so, '*Mange ça!*'

The meat hit the water with a splash, and in a second all those sharks that had been idly wallowing beneath us turned and sped straight to where the bait was now slowly sinking. The first group shot straight by it, and then curved round to sweep back in again, but they were too late. Another, slightly slower off the mark, had already taken it. The shark cruised right up the bait, paused imperceptibly and went on again. I had neither seen the jaws open nor close, yet now the heavy line was stretched back from its mouth like a taut bow-string.

The cook managed to get his fingers out from under the line where it crossed the bulwarks, which was just as well, for now it was biting the wood itself. Thirty yards out I could see the vague outline of the shark's tail stubbornly beating the water in a grim attempt to tear itself away from this unknown force that held it in check. First it pulled directly away from the ship, then when that failed, it went down and rolled along the sandy bottom right beneath us, stirring up clouds of sediment in its wake. But by now the Praslin fishermen had emerged from their daze and had seized the finger-thick line. That was the end as far as the shark was concerned. Remorselessly it was hauled up, kicking and squirming, until it lay alongside. There it had a brief respite while a rope sling was made ready for securing its tail. As Jean Batiste slipped this noose up over it, one of the other sharks, more daring than the rest, slid alongside and took a neat shovel-sized and spoon-shaped bite out of the flank. But, before we lost more of it we were able to get our catch on board.

All this time the rest of the crew had been preparing other lines, and by now a dozen lay neatly coiled, baited and ready on the deck. Harvey had allocated each man a place along the length of the ship and the fun began. In just under an hour we caught twenty-two of those *Grandes Ailes*. The smallest was about seven and a half feet in length and the longest ten and half. Many were bitten and mauled by the others before we got them on deck, and it was not uncommon for a shark to burst right out of the water in a desperate effort to gain a last mouthful before its prey and erstwhile brother disappeared for ever.

While this was going on I got up on the cabin-roof where I was well out of the way, for I could see that anything I might do to try and help in this work could only result in hindering the 'professional' thoroughness of the Creoles. This was work for which they were born, and I soon saw that beneath the apparent chaos of lines, hooks, snapping jaws and flailing tails, there lay a high degree of efficiency and a minimum of wasted effort.

At last the sharks stopped biting. They were still there, all around the ship, seemingly as many as before, but now they were no longer interested. The fever of hunger had passed as quickly as it had come and nothing we could offer would tempt them. Apparently, that was quite a usual occurrence and the fishermen did not waste much time in coiling down their lines and setting about the unpleasant work of carving up their catch for salting down in the hold. While they were doing this I talked over the situation with Harvey. Having seen the number of sharks that were all around, and after our experience of the day before, of which I now told him in greater detail, he insisted that it would be extremely foolish to continue looking for Green Snail along this portion of the reef. I agreed with him, particularly after examining some of the bites that had been taken out of the sharks that now littered the deck. Into some of these cavities, the result of a single snap, Albert and I jokingly put our heads and there was room for a third head alongside ours.

We decided to carry on southwards trying the area well away on the south and south-east of the atoll. By the afternoon we had rounded the south-west corner but it was at once apparent that it would be impossible to work there. Already the long swell that foretold the coming of the south-east monsoon was in evidence, battering the reef and hurling tons of water high into the air with each successive roller. Not even the feather-light pirogues could manoeuvre in there and I foresaw that the heavy back-wash from off the reef would reduce underwater visibility to a few feet. There was no possibility of these conditions abating for another seven months, until the end of this season. There was nothing we could do about it. We were too late, or the monsoon too early. We turned round and dispiritedly sailed back, across the sandbank where we had spent the previous night, past the wreck of the s.s. *Aymestry* whose interior I would now never explore, past the Three Islands and in through the channel to drop our anchor opposite the settlement as the sun was setting.

D'Unienville, sensing our disappointment, did his best to cheer us up. After an excellent dinner he started to tell us many interesting anecdotes about Farquhar and soon I, at any rate, had forgotten most of the past few days' disasters. 'You called at Ile des Deposés, the southernmost of the Three Islands?' he asked, after I had mentioned our roast crabs. 'Do you know how it got its name? I'll tell you. You must first know that Madagascar, which lies only one hundred and sixty miles away, was partially occupied by the Portuguese during the sixteenth century, but finally they abandoned their settlement there. During the seventeenth century the island came under the rule of the French East India Company. During the eighteenth century their ownership was disputed by a large and formidable influx of pirates and corsairs who had been driven from other parts of the Indian Ocean by the great naval powers. From 1774 onwards the island came more and more under the influence of France, though it was not until 1840 that the inhabitants of the northern provinces formally requested the French authorities to take them under her protection to escape the cruelties and excesses of their own native rulers.

'In actual fact the whole island did not become a French possession until 1895, when France sent an expeditionary force there to settle matters once and for all. But that takes place after our little islet got its name. When it happened exactly, I don't rightly know, but probably around 1860, when the French were having a little political trouble with one of the minor native kings of the ceded northern portion of Madagascar. This gentleman quietly hopped off south into native-administered territory each time a small force was sent to bring him in. Eventually, however, he was caught. Some say by a woman, but no one really knows. Once the French had him, the question was, what to do with him. Mauritius was too near, he might well escape. So was Réunion. So they sent him off to France, along with his personal treasures, bodyguard and harem.

'Well, the ship he was on was wrecked. Wrecked right here on the western reef, and all were drowned save for one boatload containing *the deposed chief and some of his party*. They came through the surf intact and fetched up at "Ile des Déposés" as you have guessed. There they stayed for three or four months until a ship picked them up. Or rather picked him up. For the only one left was the chief, and he was stark staring mad. I think the authorities finally got him to France, where he lived for many years but never recovered his sanity.

'But the story does not end there.

'Some years later, a visitor to Ile des Déposés came across five graves in the little hollow that constitutes the centre of the island. Four were arranged in a square, and the fifth lay in the middle. Each grave had a casuarina seedling growing at one end, but there were no headstones or other evidence of a Christian burial. In those days people were not so nosey as they are nowadays, and so the graves were left strictly alone. Moreover, amongst the labourers working on the atoll there arose the story that the islet was haunted – some even went as far as to say by a great fat black man with a curved sword in his sash. But others said by the evil ghosts of pirates, so I shouldn't take much notice of that! Eventually, the legend included a tale of buried treasure, as do all such tales of the Seychelles. And eventually, again, his story got to the ears of a very great friend of mine. This was many years ago now, but I cannot tell you his name, for he is still very much alive.

'This man – he was young then – came to Farquhar on some pretext or other, and after a few weeks' stay made an excuse to go over to Ile des Déposés, ostensibly to look for turtles. He took with him a blanket, some biscuits, a bottle or two of cognac in case the nights were cold, several shovels and a crowbar. I saw him again when he came back, two days later.

'That evening he took me aside and told me what he had found.

'He had started digging at one of the corner graves, since legend had it that the four outer mounds hid the treasure, whilst the central one only contained a body. He dug half the night, for the roots of the casuarina, now grown tall and stately, hindered his shovel work. Then he found something. A few shreds of mouldering cloth, a brass button and the skeletal remains of a body. But what a body! Even in death my friend swore that from the skull to the heel it measured over six and a half feet.

The rib-cage was enormous, more like that of an ape than a human. There was no coffin, no weapons and no jewellery.

'At this stage my friend sat down to rest and drank most of one of the bottles of cognac. After he had done that he set about the grave in the centre, for, as he reasoned, if legend had it that the four corner ones contained the treasure and the centre the cadaver and he had found a corpse in one of the corner ones, might not the centre one then contain the treasure?

'Anyway, he dug again, and this time it took him even longer to find anything. When he did so, the mystery merely deepened. He unearthed the remains of what must have been a very small child, perhaps two years or less, wrapped in a garment that might have been a shawl. Within the shawl lay a little silver crucifix on a thin chain. Now my friend was a young man, and not over-pious, but after this he dug no more. He put back the remains and covered them up as best he could, but by now he was very tired.

'In the morning he came back, and since then no one has dug any more. Only he saw these things, if he did see them. No one can explain their meaning or their history. They are just one of those odd unconnected incidents in which these islands abound.'

After this little story we went to bed.

When the others had gone to sleep, I lay awake, wondering. For although d'Unienville did not know it, I had walked right across the centre of the hundred-yard strip of elevated sandbank that went by the name of Ile des Déposés. I had found the depression in the middle of the islet, and in it there did grow five casuarina trees. Moreover, at the foot of each one there did lie a mound that looked remarkably like a grave, though at the time that thought did not cross my mind and I had dismissed them as old guano pits or turtle laying mounds. And it was true that the centre one was not of such smooth and regular contour as the others, as though someone had dug into it at some time in the past. I seemed to remember also that one of the others was similarly disturbed, but perhaps that was imagination. Two skeletons, that of a child and a huge man – what lay under the other three hummocks? More human remains? The vaunted treasure? Perhaps nothing at all! At that point I too went to sleep.

After breakfast I tried to get d'Unienville on to the subject of

Ile des Déposés again, but he would not be drawn. I asked him point-blank if he had made it up, and whether the mounds were old guano pits or turtle egg hatcheries, but all he would say was 'Perhaps', in a noncommittal way. Whatever the truth, it was a good story and served its purpose in diverting our minds momentarily from the depressing thought of our failure at Farquhar.

After further discussion we all agreed that it would be pointless to delay our departure in the vague hope that the monsoon might abait temporarily. All we could do was to strike north, homewards, in an effort to out-run this wind and the resultant swell that put paid to our exploring the exposed outer reefs.

By midday we were once more outside the atoll, but this time heading away from the island. Our decks were loaded with baskets of fresh vegetables, crates of chickens, and somewhere forrard two pigs squealed their displeasure at being uprooted from their island home. However, that evening one of them squealed his last and subsequently figured prominently on the menu.

Our next objective was Providence Reef, sixty miles to the north. To avoid arriving there during the hours of darkness, once through the pass at Farquhar we stopped the engine and carried on under sail alone. Noon on the next day saw us there.

At the north edge of this reef is Providence Island, on which lies the settlement, and at the extreme south end, the only other above-water portion, some sandbanks known as Cerf Islands. The twenty-mile stretch between those two island groups is all reef, visible as a long dark brown thread that seems to float upon the surface of the sea, like a gigantic tendril of seaweed. It was at Cerf Islands that we first began, since, although there was still a fresh wind from the south-east, we saw that we should be able to work in comparative calm in the shelter they provided.

This time we took every available person in the two pirogues. One party was to be landed on the foreshore, making their way along the coast, scouring the reef in waist-deep water; the rest of us were to swim parallel to them further out. Periodically, I was to branch out at right angles from the reef to examine a vertical section as far as the drop off into the abyss. In this way we should cover the widest possible area.

Once again we were doomed to disappointment. No sooner had I entered the water than I knew it would be no good. Yet here was another place at which we had been assured that in previous years Green Snail had been found.

It was cold. Far colder than anything I had ever found in any other tropic sea. The water was clear with the chill intensity of a fresh-water mountain stream. Coral was there, yes. Glorious coral, not broken or smashed by mountainous seas as it had been at Farquhar, not pounded into débris. The delicate fingers, the turrets, the bushy growths were all intact. But where was the colour, the soft violet hues, the vivid yellows, the pinks, purples and clarets of these incrustations? All was drab brown, blanched and dead. All this huge reef that, a few years previously, had been an enormous living entity, was now a corpse, killed by this sudden influx of icy water. Not a fish to be seen anywhere. An empty void. The reef itself, with its buttresses and ramparts, a haunted land, dotted with empty coral castles and desolate pathways among which Albert and I appeared as two strangers, trespassers in that spell-bound place.

The surface level was cold enough, but when I dived and reached a depth of fifteen feet the shock of its icy impact on my skin caused me to release all my breath, and I could stay there no longer than a few seconds. Even so, in that short space of time, I saw that already the wearing down process of the sea had commenced. Coral tips that should have been wafer-thin and delicate were blunted and at the base of each growth lay a little heap of coral mortar swirling like dust in each swing of the tide. Another few years and all these intricate coral structures would be reduced to mere blobs of masonry. Another twenty and the whole reef would be a sandbank, unless the icy current were diverted elsewhere.

For two days we made our way northwards along this lifeless reef. In the many hours I spent in the water, only once did I see any living creature and that was when a huge Manta Ray went past. This giant, with a span of fifteen feet or more, came lumbering up to me, plainly inquisitive as to what other creature had strayed into this lonely place. For a while we kept each other company, and each time, when even the slowest beat of her great wings outpaced me, she would wheel and swoop back to take up her position alongside again. I could see that her arm-length and flexible 'horns', which curled up from the tips in the same fashion as Christmas party 'blowers', were yielding but poor results in their work of supplying wafts of plankton-loaded water to her cavernous mouth. The sea here was crystal clear and devoid of any of the usual forms of zoo-plankton or diatoms, other than those types which are completely microscopic and transparent.

I had met these giant rays previously in other seas, and their friendly curiosity never failed to amuse me. This most docile of animals, whose inherent gentleness contrasts strangely with its enormous bulk, has undeservedly gained a world-wide reputation for evil. 'Sea Devil', 'Devil Ray', 'Devil Fish' are but some of its local names, and many are the legends concerning its supposed maliciousness. Nearly everywhere this harmless ray is looked upon as being vicious and dangerous, a monster to be feared beyond all others – yet nothing could be further from the truth. It is true that it will occasionally scratch itself against an anchor rope to rid itself of parasites and has been known to get tangled up in so doing and has ridden hastily off, towing the unfortunate fishing boat with it! Perhaps it is from such rare incidents as this that it gains its unfounded reputation.

At the end of the second day it was obvious that the whole reef was barren and it would be useless to continue. Twice now had we been defeated by natural cataclysms. The cyclone of Farquhar had wiped out one colony of Green Snails, and now an extraordinary cold current had brought disaster to this area.

Many months later, a friend in the East African Fisheries Research Organization was able to unearth the possible cause of this. For many years it had been known that ice-cold water of the antarctic region, on meeting with the warmer and less dense seas of temperate latitudes, sank down under the latter, but continued to flow outwards from the Pole towards the Equator. This cold mass of water maintains its original characteristics throughout its journey northwards along the deeper levels of the Indian Ocean. In 1948 a Swedish oceanographic survey ship located an unexpected 'up-welling' of this icy water in latitude 10° south, longitude 80° east. This was confirmed subsequently by the British Research Ship *Discovery IV* in 1953. This particular area of up-welling lay in the same latitude as Providence but one thousand miles to the east. It seems likely that the cold current which we experienced was another uncharted and probably only recently formed Antarctic up-welling. This was not wholly unexpected since an increase in the total amount of Antarctic surface water (and therefore outpouring) had already been observed. Such an increase must either result in a greater area of original up-welling or in new localities with similar characteristics.

All this we did not know at the time, however, and for a long time I did not dare mention this freak occurrence to anyone. Whoever heard of ice-cold water practically on the Equator!

The third day produced a flat calm. The south-east monsoon had temporarily withdrawn and the sea lay oily calm beneath a sea-blue sky. These shades of colour were so exactly similar as to make it impossible to distinguish between sea and sky. There was no horizon, no sea, no sky. Just a great bowl in which the *Marsouin* floated. When one of the crew paddled off in a pirogue on some errand or other, it appeared as though the crescent-shaped canoe left the sea and mounted up into the sky. The whole scene lacked perspective, and had that blue translucence found only in Chinese water-colours. Such a day was ideal for examining the far side of the reef, that eastern edge on which the heavy seas had previously prevented us from working.

From where we lay, it was about five miles directly across the dead reef and the intervening lagoon to the far side. Once over the reef we had expected the usual deep water, across which we might easily paddle, but this was not the case. The lagoon here just about dried out at low tide, and for most of the way we had to carry the pirogue, the water being less than six inches deep. Occasionally, we came across deep pits of stagnant murky water, stinking of dead seaweed and rotten coral. Twice, on our approach, the surface of these murky pools was violently agitated by some large creature that sought refuge in its depths. Probably these were large Rock Cods. Amongst the twisted and matted stems of the fleshy weed that covered the ankle-deep water we found numerous oysters. These, although less than five inches across, would have been well worth gathering, for the mother-of-pearl interior was of good quality and of reasonable thickness, but they were all raddled with parasitic borers that rendered them valueless. There were other shells as well: cones, cowries and helmet shells, for here the water was sun-warmed and presented an amazing contrast with the coldness of our anchorage.

Towards the eastern edge of the reef we came across our first identifiable fish-life, hordes of grey reef-eels, morays, that squirmed away from our feet as we passed. Occasionally, one of these ten-inch specimens would go for us, throwing itself across the reef surface at our ankles. Then we would skip and hop out of the way, and bombard the little brute with mud or coral fragments till he retreated. Jean Batiste, scorning such unmanly antics, stood his ground and got bitten for his pains, a neat slash of razor-thinness that bled profusely but healed cleanly.

The far side of the reef was another disappointment. I had expected the classic pattern of lagoon, reef 'flat', reef edge and seaward slope on which would lie the shells, if there were any. But this eastern edge of Providence reef seemed to follow no general law. There was no reef 'flat', or rather it was all 'flat' with no determinate edge. Instead, pools and pits broke out directly into the sea. There was little or no coral, but pavements of Nullipore on which seaweed and other fleshy algae had attached themselves. The water was murky and fish were few. Strangely enough, it was not cold at all, but retained a normal temperature for several hundred yards out, which was as far as I ventured. No shells, no coral, few fish. Just as we rowed back and were disembarking on the reef, the water swirled and boiled a few yards off. I caught a glimpse of a white belly and a large tail. Anxious to see what it was, I cautiously eased myself into the sea again and swam quietly out.

Ahead of me, on the bottom, in about twenty feet of water, I saw a large object thrashing around in a cloud of sand and weed particles. Circling up-current, I gradually made out what it was. A large bull-headed shark was pulling and nosing at something which was frantically trying to burrow its way in to safety beneath an overhanging ledge. As I watched, dark tendrils of blood blotted out the scene as effectively as a smokescreen. That was enough. I turned and very quietly slid back to dry land, keeping a good watch behind me. Scarcely had I arrived and had started to tell the others what it was, than someone yelled a warning and leapt into the pirogue which was standing, as we were, up out of the water on the reef.

No one waited to see what it was. We all scrambled aboard in a mad jumble of arms and legs. Then we turned. In from the sea, right on the surface, came a shark, swimming desperately towards us. Straight on it came, running up high and dry on the reef alongside the pirogue. It wriggled on in, flat on its belly, beneath our astonished eyes, until it came to an abrupt halt in a shallow pool that was not more than eight inches deep. An awful grunting sound from behind us caused us to swing round again. There was the most horrifying thing I have ever seen, trying to follow in the wake of the other. Lying on the reef, half out of the water, was a Tiger Shark of about fifteen feet in length. Its great bulk, no longer supported by the water, spread out obscenely over the coral as it tried to hunch itself forward after its quarry. Its drawbridge mouth gaped wide, and from its maw came awful pig-like grunts. Its gill-slots were half exposed, and a mixture of water and air gurgled and wheezed within. Each time it pushed forward its pointed snout shot up and the rows of kukhri-shaped teeth sprang erect, presenting us with a hideous and terrifying spectacle. When it did so, its dead eyes came up above the level of the pirogue's side, some ten feet or less from where I crouched.

But luckily it could make no progress. It was too deep-bodied and big to get any further. After about a minute of these ghastly lungings, it bent its ugly forepart round, and with several sweeps of its tail succeeded in dragging itself off the reef into deeper water, where it disappeared with an ominous swirl, to reappear again after a few seconds practically on the surface a few yards further out, at which distance it proceeded to patrol up and down along this section of the reef in full view of us all.

Satisfied that we were secure from it for a while we turned our attention to the other shark that had lain motionless all the while, gill-slots feebly pulsating. It was an *Endormi* (*Nebrius concolor*), a harmless type of shark that feeds on shellfish and whose small and soft lipped mouth hides nothing more dangerous than a set of 'crushers' with which it grinds its food. The *Endormi* is the biggest fool in the animal kingdom. Lazy, sluggish and defenceless, it will grow to ten feet or more. It feeds mainly by night and passes the day tucked away fast asleep (it is one of the few fishes that do sleep) in some convenient cave. Often though, on account of its bulk, it is difficult to find a retreat that will accommodate it in its entirety. When this happens the Endormi contents itself with merely tucking its head away in some crevice and sleeping just the same, sure that since its head is out of sight the rest must be too! On countless occasions I have seen the absurd spectacle of a huge tail and trunk protruding right out into the open from under the shelter of some diminutive ledge, beneath which the *Endormi*'s head is wedged. If you dive down, and pull hard on its tail, all the fool does is to stir lazily and try to push still further in. In many places fishermen, seeing the gentle waving of the tail amongst the corals, will lower a noose down over it and haul the fellow out, struggling sleepily against this unfair treatment. I regret to say also that it is this large but timid and harmless shark that many spear-fishermen shoot, boasting afterwards of their intrepid shark-spearing abilities.

But, this particular *Endormi* did not suffer that fate, for as we approached, it died. Turning it over, we soon saw the reason. Its genitals and half its stomach were missing, 'spooned' cleanly away by two gigantic bites. Further back, the caudal fin was all but severed from its body, presumably in the first attack when the Tiger Shark had dragged its victim out bodily from whatever place it had chosen to sleep.

The tide had now turned, and already trickles of sea-water were draining into the little pool in which the corpse of the *Endormi* lay. Another half an hour and the water would be sufficiently deep for that grim and persistent watcher beyond the reef to make its way in and finish off what it had already begun. When that happened I did not want to be around. Not that we would be in danger in the pirogue, but it would be a grim and messy business. Besides, there were no shells and it was pointless to delay our return. We had traversed the lagoon, had examined this eastern edge, and now could go back to report another failure.

The following day we sailed on up to the settlement, paid a brief visit to the manager there, and returned to the *Marsouin* with some fresh vegetables and a supply of milk-coconuts to drink.

The manager confirmed that the fishermen used to find Green Snail on the 'south banks' as he called Cerf Island, but had not done so for several years past. He did not know anything about the cold current, which was not surprising since all the island's fishing was done off the eastern side of the reef where the temperature seemed normal. Though the settlement lay on the western side and the reef off it was directly in the cold stream no one ever bathed there on account of the sharks, so no one had noticed it.

By now both our time and possible shell localities were running out. There remained one more possibility. Twenty-five miles north of Providence lay a submerged reef, called the Wizard. Ships that had accidentally come across it in the past had reported huge shoals of fish and great coral formations visible in the shadowy depths. One small fishing vessel had taken over four tons of fish there in one day, four years previously. Where there were fish of that quantity, there must be living coral. Where there was living coral, there must be shells. Where there were shells, there might be Green Snail. It was worth a visit anyway.

We set off before it was light, in order to arrive there by lunchtime. In the past many ships had searched for the Wizard, but few had found it, since between Providence and it the ocean currents are often violent and unpredictable, and drove the searchers far off the course. By keeping careful check on our back-bearings from Providence and by taking repeated sun sights we hoped to find the elusive reef without too much difficulty, and sure enough at ten o'clock the masthead lookout reported a possible shoal about a mile ahead. As we drew nearer we were able to see the ocean 'hump up' as the flat ground swell passed over the sunken reef. Before closing in, we crept around the periphery of the shoal in an effort to gauge its extent. It seemed to be about three miles long and perhaps a mile in width, and although we saw no fish, the whole area was rimmed with extensive coral growths, visible as dark blobs against the lighter colour of the sand or rock that formed the sea-bed.

After that, we buoyed the reef so that we might locate it and re-orientate ourselves on it easily the next day, should we drift off during the night. By the time all this was done, it was four o'clock and the underwater visibility would have been too poor to allow much exploration. So we contented ourselves with finding a reasonable anchorage, trying our luck at fishing off the western edge of the shoal water. Apart from a few very small sharks we caught nothing, and I for one was glad that the bigger specimens seemed conspicuous by their absence. Tomorrow looked like being a hectic day for Albert and me, so we turned in early.

First thing in the morning we threw out a few more shark lines, while we had breakfast, but they too remained empty. Considerably reassured, Albert and I set off in a pirogue to commence diving in the middle and to spiral our way outwards round the reef. No sooner were we in the water than, once again,

BEYOND THE REEFS

I saw that we were too late. The surface temperature was about normal, but the coral was all dead and the reef deserted. Here, the cold water stream lay about eighteen or twenty feet down, and the dividing line was very marked. One could feel one's body making the transition, and one shrank from entering the cold layer as a bather in cold climates might shrink from the water's edge having tested its temperature with his toes.

We swam on, zig-zagging in every direction in the hope of finding a corner of the reef that had been spared. But it was no good, the icy water had done its work too thoroughly. I think the only fish we saw in our two-hour search was one miserable specimen amongst the weed that had already started to cover the dead coral with its drab cloak. Dejectedly we returned to the *Marsouin*. As a last resort we trailed out a line over the stern, to which I clung while Harvey steamed slowly around and across the area. But it was no good. A few small sharks came up and had a quick look at me, did not like what they saw and disappeared into the depths.

That evening Harvey and I took stock of our predicament. Outfitting and provisioning for this trip had swallowed all our profit from the earlier expedition around Praslin, and we were now in the 'red'. Moreover, although we had taken on the fishermen on a 'results only' basis, we could not let them return to their homes after a month or more without anything to show for their labour. There was only one thing left to do. Go on back up to the Amirantes and there try to catch turtle. It was late in the season for them too, but we might just be lucky. *Might*. A turtle would fetch seven pounds ten shillings in Mahé, and twenty or so would do much to save the situation. We could also try to do some shark fishing on the way.

Anyway, we knew what lay beyond the reefs now; sharks, no shells and ice-cold water!

We reached the Amirantes in record time, blown thither by the renewed monsoon that came hard after our departure from Wizard reef. For five days after our arrival there we were forced to hang out for shelter behind several of the various islets that make up the group, until once again the seasonal wind abated temporarily. Even after the 'blow' subsided there remained a long swell that would not allow us to approach within easy distance of any beach. At each sandbank and cay we visited we drew a blank. The turtle had already fled, back down into the Mozambique channel from which they would not stir until the calms of the north-west monsoon drew them northwards to their breeding grounds once again.

One of these islets in particular I remember. Etoile Cay – for that was its name – presented much the same aspect when viewed from the sea as many of the others we had visited. A long, low bar of sand, perhaps a third of a mile in length, whose summit was crowned with a thin green strip of tough creeper-grass, the only growing matter there. As usual, the heavily breaking surf on the weather side prevented us from approaching nearer than half a mile, and even on the lee it was not safe to venture nearer than four hundred yards on account of the strong tide-race that swirled around past the island's twin promontories.

Taking one pirogue, with Jean Batiste as crew and Albert to accompany me, I managed to get within two hundred yards of the shore before the turbulent water threatened to capsize us. There Albert and I slid over the side and swam ashore, keeping close together and watching out for any sharks. There was no reef, nor coral, and we came in over tussocks of eel-grass to a shelving beach of loose sand. Above the tide-lines there was ample evidence of turtles; their tracks, like lorry tyre treads, gouged deep into the soft sand. But they were all old, and we could see that no turtle had made its egg-laying pilgrimage here for several weeks or even longer. Once again we were too late. However, since we were now there, we thought we might as well look over the islet.

The central portion consisted of a plateau, raised some twenty feet above the level of the sea, and on which grew a matted layer of coarse verdure. No sooner had we put our heads up over the rim of this plateau than a cacophony of hoarse cries went up, and in an instant the whole sky was blotted out by tens of thousands of dark wings. In a few seconds these had sorted themselves out into three varieties. The first off the ground, but now those circling lowest above it, were the Wideawake Terns. Next off, and occupying the middle airspace up to some three hundred feet or so, were the Noddies. The last to become airborne and those birds which occupied the higher reaches were the Boobies, their gooselike silhouettes extending far up to a thousand feet or more, glistening brilliant black-and-white in the afternoon sunshine.

We walked on in towards the centre of the plateau. Already many of these birds had begun to lay, and the ground was carpeted with eggs and chicks. Soft wings fluttered nervously around my head, but the strident alarm notes soon lessened to petulent cheeps as the birds grew accustomed to our strange shapes. I soon realized that they had no basic fear of us, but were only alarmed at our sudden and unexpected appearance over the edge of the nesting area. In all probability they had never set eyes on a human form and so had not learnt to fear man as have so many other creatures. I sat down on the springy grass, motioning Albert to do likewise. Within thirty seconds of my doing so one Wideawake had settled on my head, plainly intrigued at finding a new and unoccupied perch in this overcrowded island. I stretched out my arms and tried to imitate a scarecrow. Soon I was entirely covered with birds, and many, unable to find a landing ground on my person, alighted on the ground nearby from where they regarded me with curiosity. Two mottled chicks scurried up in short, sharp dashes and sheltered from the gentle wind beneath the cover afforded by my thighs. A baby Booby, looking like an animated powderpuff, regarded me solemnly until, disturbing the rest of my new-found colony, I placed a hand, palm uppermost, upon the ground. This it regarded thoughtfully for a few moments and then waddled purposely forward, halted and after further deliberations clambered on to it, to settle in its centre with a shaking out of downy plumage. From this vantage point it surveyed the rest of the assembly with a lordly air, as if to say, 'You must realize, you chaps, that only the very best Boobies rate this treatment!'

After a while I put the chick down on the ground again and lay on my back, looking up into the blue sky. Normally to do this one would have to shield the eyes against the blinding glare, but here this was not necessary. The thousand upon thousand of birds that circled overhead acted as a screen and only rarely could I glimpse the blue sky through momentary chinks between successive layers of white wings. The call-notes of these sea-birds were half smothered in the roar of the surf and the overall effect was very soothing.

FARQUHAR

Before we swam back through the waves to the pirogue that waited there outside for us, we walked right around the sandbank. On the far beach – the one facing the wind – we found row upon row of empty crayfish carapaces, cast up there by the tide. From the quantity that were there, hundreds of these crustaceans must have been living among the rocks a little way out, but the sea was too rough for us to try and we came back empty-handed.

My last view of the islet from the stern of the *Marsouin* was of a thin yellow hump that seemed to float suspended on the turquoise sea. Above it hung a solitary fleecy white cloud, and between the two the air was mottled with hazy specks, like gnats over a pond, the birds of Etoile, still circling that remote place . . .

Right through the Amirantes we sailed, spending each night tucked away behind the shelter afforded by island, sand cay or reef. But we found no turtle, and very few shark. We were wasting our time and merely running up more expenses, so reluctantly we set course for Mahé. The first time we had been absent for ten days and had returned with a ton of shells. This time we took six weeks and came back with nothing. Perhaps if the spares had arrived earlier we should have made our trip to Chagos and then things might have been different.

Perhaps . . .

FIVE

On My Own

After our ignominious return there were only two courses of action left open to me. One was to give up the whole idea of shell-diving and to take up something else, and the other was to carry on but along different lines.

Eventually I decided to go on with it. One reason for this was that I realized how sketchy and impractical our approach to the problem had been; another was that I still felt sure there must be Green Snail shells in quantity somewhere within the Seychelles group, if only I could track them down. The final factor involved was innate personal stubbornness.

Certainly I had plenty of time during the south-east monsoon period to think out a new approach to shell-diving and to try out various ideas and improvements. The first and obvious mistake which had to be rectified was that of proportions. I had been quite unprepared for the relatively enormous areas of reef it had proved necessary to search and the joint attempts of Albert and myself had proved totally inadequate for the work involved. There was only one answer to this: more skin-divers. And since these were not readily available (as I had found out earlier), they must be trained.

The second consideration was speed. With the limited fair weather period at our disposal it would be essential to take full advantage of each diving day, and this meant the ability to travel both under and above water at a far greater rate. The third consideration was equipment for handling the shells when, and if, we found them. But this would come later, when practice had shown us those requirements most suited to the work involved.

Rather than have the tedious work of weeding out non-swimmers and 'barely-swimmers', I decided to start from absolute zero and train young lads who quite definitely could *not* swim, but who were basically fit. In this fashion, though there would

ON MY OWN

be a lot of rejects during the course of the months, at least those who emerged would be competent right from scratch and, more important still, be trained as I wanted them and accustomed to my own particular faults and idiosyncracies. In this fashion I should know what they would be likely to do in an emergency. I did not want other ideas, nor whims; I had quite enough trouble dealing with my own. All I wanted was duplication. Other legs, arms and eyes, which would act as extensions to my own, multiplying my own efforts ten-fold.

In the Seychelles, although there is no 'colour bar' – nor could there be on account of the complexity of the population – there is a very definite and intuitively defined 'social bar' arranged according to skin tone. In general, the darker the skin the more destined the owner for a life of labour, while the white-collar positions are filled by those whose complexion matches it. This is often regrettable, since in many instances the results of overmixed marriages and a tendency to interbreeding amongst certain sections of the population give rise to children of fairer skin but inferior physical and mental qualities to those of pure negroid strain. Yet the octoroon is assumed superior to the quadroon, the quadroon to the picaroon and so on. This situation gives rise to an interesting local nomenclature. A prosperous or well-to-do person, whatever his colour, is known as a '*Grand Blanc*' (intimating that success is the prerogative of the white-skinned), whereas a labouring man, even though he is white, is referred to familiarly as '*Mon Noir*' and thinks of himself as such.

Faced with this extreme colour and class consciousness, I made sure that my first recruits were as black as possible. In that way, when at a later date I took on lighter-skinned divers, there would be no possibility of their bullying the '*noirs*' (not physically but by social approach), since they would be inferior 'new boys' compared with the original more negroid divers. Moreover, any white young man who turned down the job due to these conditions presumably did not need it, and I needed people who would work hard, not for fun or pleasure, but because they had to. If the undertaking materialized there would be exertion to the limit of endurance and I did not want anyone faint-hearted on account of colour or social standing. The highest wages and greatest responsibility would go to those who earned it by prowess, not by pigmentation!

BEYOND THE REEFS

Starting off with four likely *'noirs'*, I took them over to live with me on an island in Port Victoria bay, facing Mahé. Here in the shelter afforded against the monsoon we were able to work in peace. After a week three out of four were returned to the main island as not showing sufficient promise and another three taken on.

After a month I had two apprentices who were coming along very well and who were now fully competent with mask and swim-fins and who could dive to twenty-five feet. At this stage I loaned them spear guns and sent them off fishing whilst I went on training the next batch. All the fish they caught was theirs to eat, sell or send to their families as they wished. Since they had been accustomed to one bloater-sized fish with their rice per day in the past this was sufficient encouragement to keep them in the water all day long, unconsciously hardening and training their muscles for the work that lay ahead.

Once again with the newcomers I began the schedules of dog-paddle, developing into crawl-kick with swim-fins; then mask and breathing tube, then surface diving – all the time in progressively deeper water and for longer hours. Another six weeks and another four divers were ready. And so it went on until life became a succession of basic instructions, made the more difficult by the paucity of the Creole tongue. By the end of three months I had a final selection of seven first-class skin-divers plus a reserve of ten, and had brought back Albert into the team as well. Five times as many had been dropped as being too slow mentally or physically, too tired, or too unwilling.

Then came the major step.

It was imperative that these skin-divers became fully competent aqualung divers. The main difficulty here was a technical one. Briefly, there are two basic types of aqualung. There is the popular and better-known compressed air system, which is comparatively simple to use, safe, and requires relatively little experience. Then there is the far more complicated, difficult (and in inexperienced hands definitely unsafe) oxygen re-breathing apparatus. With the compressed air lung one can descend to relatively great depths but endurance is limited, the equipment bulky and, more important, one needs the continual services of a complicated air compressing station to recharge the air cylinders that are carried on the diver's back. With the oxygen system one is limited to moderate depths but has a far greater endurance. The equipment is light and compact and the recharging made easy since the amount of oxygen used is only a fraction of the compressed air required in the other type and can therefore be supplied by compact storage cylinders carried on board.

Until that time only professional divers, such as naval frogmen, had been trained in the use of the oxygen system and then only after an intensive course of theoretical instruction, covering such items as diving physiology, general science and hydraulics. Oxygen apparatus was considered too difficult to master for normal civilian purposes, yet here was I committed to training a group of young men in its use of whom ninety per cent were illiterate. The Army principle, 'One can teach anybody anything by numbers', seemed the only possible solution. For how can one explain gas tensions within the blood stream, or Boyle's Law, to a person who cannot sign his name?

By the end of a fortnight Albert and the other foremost seven could take the aqualungs to pieces and reassemble them blindfold. They walked with the equipment on, ran races with it on, rested with it on and had become so accustomed to it as to have altered their whole natural respiratory actions and now no more considered breathing through their noses or at a normal rate of fifteen inhalations per minute than they would have of entering the water without swim-fins.

Then came the actual submarine training. This I had to undertake individually, for each diver now required my full attention. Taking them in turn, I descended down a shot-line, placing my hands on their shoulders and keeping my face mask right in front of theirs, so that I was able to watch their every facial movement. There was a special reason for doing this. Although they had all been told to signal on the slightest ear or sinus pains which the unaccustomed depths would be likely to produce, I knew that many of them would rather have caused themselves severe internal injury than admit to pain which they thought might result in their being thrown out of the team. Signals they might not give, but there is no person living who can repress the instinctive grimaces that such pains produce and it was for these tell-tale signs that I watched.

Soon their initial awkwardness had been overcome and all the divers were quite at home in the equipment at moderate depths.

From there we went on to faults and emergency drill. It was no good telling them what oxygen lack or carbon dioxide poisoning was like, they must experience it. That way they would remember.

So down they went to a mere fifteen feet, stayed there until their oxygen supply was completely exhausted and then kept on down till they fainted. Then they were rapidly hauled up, the salt-water they had swallowed pumped out of their lungs, and left to vomit in peace. The next day down they would go again, the aqualung charged with an exhausted or empty canister of the carbon dioxide absorbent. After a minute or so they would begin to pant and their respiratory rate would increase along with the build-up of carbon dioxide within the lung, until they went into mild convulsions and collapsed, whereupon they were brought to the surface, 'pumped out' and, feeling very groggy, given the rest of the day off.

It was cruel and dangerous, but it had to be done. I had to make sure that these lads, though they could never understand the causes of the maladies that struck them thus, were always alert for the faintest symptom of their approach. As a sequel to this, I taught them to trust no one but themselves as to the serviceability of their equipment, frequently issuing out one aqualung among the lot as allegedly serviceable but in reality lacking oxygen or absorbent or inoperative in some vital respect. And woe betide that particular diver who trusted my word and entered the sea without checking his gear, only to ascend ignominiously again on discovering the fault.

To improve underwater efficiency I invented games aimed at teaching them to be able to swim at one level without reference to depth gauge, or out of sight of both surface and sea-bed, in what is known as the 'blue zone'. Here there is no horizon by which to orientate oneself, no directional indications whatsoever. 'Up' is where the bubbles go, and with our closed circuit aqualungs there were no exhaust bubbles! To establish the true vertical it was necessary to let slip a tiny globule of precious gas from out of the corner of one's mouth and then trace its upward flight. To ascertain direction and to keep on course over a featureless sea-bed I taught them to note the angle the sun made with the horizon as seen on the surface, then, when at cruising depth, to keep the polarized rays of light that filtered down from above at the same inclination. They were shown how jerky movements or splashing fin-beats attract predatory fish and that an infallible way to precipitate attack by passing sharks was to jump directly from a boat into the sea, rather than to lower oneself overboard, so as to create as little disturbance as possible.

After three months of this work I had a fully trained aqualung team of eight Creole divers and a reserve second line of some seventeen who could be brought into use if we had any casualties or withdrawals. In actual fact, throughout the months that followed there was never any necessity to call upon this reserve, though at a much later date they served to provide Harvey Brain with a separate and independent group of divers.

These foremost eight provided a typical cross-section of Seychellois, having nothing in common with one another except their language, their poverty and their newly acquired diving skill. At the head of them and the original one of all to be chosen was Ti Royale. His real name was 'La Moitié Joseph' (Half Joseph) but someone, perhaps his mother, had called him 'Little Prince' (Moitié Royale) as a babe-in-arms, and 'Ti-Royale' it remained. He was jet-black and eighteen years old. He had a nose that spread out all over his face, very full but well shaped lips, and was built like a bantam-weight boxer. Always cheerful and with an alert mind and strong will, he proved to be one of the most remarkable and nicest persons it has been my fortune ever to meet. In the water he was superb and within two months of learning to swim was more at home below the surface than I could ever hope to be. In his work he showed dogged determination and tremendous stamina and already could spend eight hours in the water without showing signs of fatigue.

Then there was Donald, slim, bird-like, and brown-eyed. Crinkly black hair contrasting with the straight nose and nut-brown skin that marked his predominantly Indian origins. He was quick and as agile as a fish, capable of keeping up high swimming speeds for moderate periods – but it was his bird-like eye that was his chief asset. Nothing on the sea-bed ever escaped him, and when underwater conditions were such that to me the reef beneath us might be almost totally obscured by drifting clouds of sediment or plankton, Donald would dive down unerringly and pick up that for which we were looking and which was lost to the rest of us. Above water I found him quiet and even sullen, lacking in humour and difficult to approach, but he was good as a diver and that was what was wanted.

Next came Teddy Hoareau, a 'white' Seychellois, indistinguishable from any European boy. At that time his lanky frame had not filled out, but his big bones gave evidence that he was going to become a hulking young man. He was strong too, but basically lazy and it was difficult to make him exert his full strength. Under training he developed a very good and smooth style of swimming which he could maintain for hours upon end. He was as easy-going as a young St Bernard puppy and like that animal only lived to eat, lie in the sun and, very occasionally, indulge in a little gentle exercise.

Conrad possessed none of these qualities. He was squat and ungainly and with just sufficient dusky 'bloom' on his skin to give him the perpetual appearance of a coal miner. Though he was as young as the others he had an old face and his hands were gnarled. He had a long, thin crooked nose and two screwed-up eyes that peered out at the world from under an unruly thatch of hair. His actions in the water were as ungainly as his movements on land and his style was awkward in the extreme, earning him the nickname of 'The Tortoise'. But he had a wonderful pair of lungs within that scraggy chest and on his second attempt at skin-diving his frog-like body threshed its way downwards to fifty feet, while I watched dumbfounded from the surface.

His character matched his shape, being full of strange quirks and unexpected humour. He was a grotesque clown and as such served an additional useful purpose in providing a continual butt for the jokes of the others. He was a bit of a coward, too, but had the sense to make fun of and exaggerate his own failing, so that it became something to laugh about rather than scorn. At this stage they were all secretly afraid anyway, for they had begun to realize that diving in these sheltered bays of Mahé was very different from our eventual hunting-grounds on the outside of the great reefs in the remoter islands.

But now it was time to think of the best way of employing these and the rest of the divers in order to cover the greatest search area with the minimum amount of wasted effort. Experiments proved that dinghies powered by outboard motors and each containing a pair of divers gave the best results, but produced another problem in turn. Now it became necessary to recruit divers' attendants to man the dinghies and to look after the others.

The first of them to be enrolled was Andrea, the bo'sun of the *Marsouin*, whom I knew to be efficient and reliable from our previous voyages and who already had an inkling of what was required in this shell-diving. Andrea brought with him a friend, Joseph Labiche, and in doing so gave me a new and valuable lead.

This Joseph was a quiet, stocky little man in his early forties, neat in his person and bearing all the unmistakable signs of the professional seaman. Talking casually to him about the work I asked if he knew anything about Green Snail, since it was quite possible that he had never even seen one. To my surprise he replied that he was quite familiar with them, having helped to collect many tons in the past. Thinking this must have been somewhere in the Pacific or Australian seas which I knew he had sailed, I was very surprised when he added that he supposed we should be working that same place.

Seeing that I looked blank he repeated his statement, this time naming the island to which he referred. It was Cosmoledo – an atoll some two hundred miles west of Farquhar and one which we might well have visited in the *Marsouin* had not the early arrival of the monsoon prevented us. But why did no one else in the Seychelles know of the shells there if there were so many? To this, Joseph gave a simple and logical explanation. Five years previously he had been bo'sun of a trading schooner on the East African coast. During this time her owner and master, hearing of these shells from some source or other, took his ship direct from Mombasa to Cosmoledo and after filling up with Green Snail sailed back again, without having called in at any other island in the Seychelles. Questioned further, Joseph said that they had only been able to collect the shells at very low water, whilst wading waist-deep on the reef, and although they had taken some fourteen tons from the atoll, they had only touched the fringe of the colony, for they saw many more lying in the deeper and to them unapproachable water on the outer reef slope.

This was news indeed and at the first opportunity I went across to Mahé to check up on certain details. My first stop was at the Meteorological Office where I checked all the outer island weather records for reports of cyclones within the past five years. There had been no such report from Cosmoledo, which meant that the atoll reef there should be still intact and not devastated as at Farquhar. Next I examined the ocean currents charts at the Post Office, anxiously looking to see if there was any possibility of the cold Antarctic water which I had found welling up near Providence being carried across to Cosmoledo. All the charts showed that any such water would be swept far to the north and therefore could not affect that atoll.

That was the second vital point in our favour. No cyclonic destruction. No icy current. What else there might be I could not know, but the last expedition had taught me not to rely too much on reports of shell that were several years old, no matter how definite they might appear.

However, with this information on Cosmoledo at least we had a starting point for the new voyage and now the time had arrived to look for a schooner suitable for the work. After much searching I came across what appeared to be a reasonable ship; a local vessel, built for inter-island trading but differing in several important features from the usual run of these craft. In the first place she was well built. In the second she was well rigged and in the third she had a reliable engine. She was thirty-eight feet in length, twelve-foot beam and four-foot draught. Though originally christened the *Louis Alfred*, a wharf-side accident had removed most of the wooden name-plate fastened to the stern, and all that was left was '. . . . lfred'. So as the '*L. Fred*' she was now known!

Her owner was equally unusual. For one thing Ravile Esperance did not drink. That, in itself, was enough to set him apart from the majority of his fellow Creoles. The son of a plantation owner, he had shown unusual enterprise in electing to go into the schooner business rather than spend his life hanging around Mahé until his father's death placed him in charge of the estate – which is what most Seychellois would have done. Having made a success of his passenger and freight hauling he reinvested the profit in a larger ship, the *L. Fred*, and the profit from this in turn had gone into a new diesel engine, which he was busy fitting that very monsoon.

In appearance Ravile was a big man, well built and with a tendency to run to fat in spite of his youth. He had semi-negroid features but his dark skin had a certain smoothness about it that

ON MY OWN

might have indicated a Chinese strain. Most other Seychellois boat owners established on a paying but routine run would not have been interested in risking their vessels on what might well have been a wild-goose chase and which, in any case, would involve extensive ocean cruising running into thousands of miles. Ravile, however, with his progressive outlook was quick to realize that such an undertaking, if successful, might well give him a unique 'ground-floor' opening in a new business, and soon we were agreed upon the general basis for a charter arrangement, to begin that coming November.

Having settled this basic requirement I went back to continue with the training of the divers. Before long it became obvious that the maximum number I could control under or above the water were three dinghy units, comprising six divers (myself included) and three attendants. With this knowledge I was able to pair off the best divers into definite teams along with their respective boatmen, and with each team one diver was made senior to the other in order to avoid any argument between them.

The first team consisted of Albert and Conrad, with Albert as senior and Andrea as attendant. The second team was Ti-Royale and Donald with a newcomer, Sadi Morgan, to look after them. This Sadi was lean, nervous and excitable – with a proud hawk-like face and a smouldering temper. But he was a first-class seaman and under the stimulus of reward in proportion to labour showed himself capable of excellent results.

Finally there was myself and Teddy, with Joseph our boatman. Teddy I had to have with me, he was far too lazy to leave with anyone else. Albert had to be separated from Ti-Royale, for the two were jealous of each other and if coupled together would have fought rather than worked. Donald, in turn, had to be away from Conrad, for here colour consciousness came into it and he would have sulked had he been placed under someone whiter than himself, automatically assuming that the other had been put in command because of his colour.

All this took time to work out and it was September before the final difficulties were settled. By now our underwater practices had shown up what equipment we lacked and this we made up on the spot and altered and sometimes discarded again, as necessary. Amongst other requirements we had to find something to hold shells in when submerged and after experimenting with wicker baskets, weighted hessian sacks and other such, we decided on rope bag-nets, shaped like oversized string shopping baskets but having a two-foot-wide iron hoop at their mouths through which the shells could easily pass and which served to keep the bags from floating when empty. These were connected to the surface by means of buoyed lines so that the attendants in the dinghy might haul them up when full of shells – when and if we found any.

Among the ideas we discarded was that which became known as the 'Live-bait-Bar'. In order to increase our speed in underwater reconnaissances I introduced a trapeze bar, fitted with stabilizing fins, on to which one clung and was towed along behind the motor-powered dinghies. In this fashion one could scan the sea-floor without having the exertion of swimming and at a far greater speed.

This was all very well but for one factor. I soon found out that a towed but otherwise inert human body was an object of great interest to every predatory fish, and even the small, timid sharks of four or five feet that we met with round Mahé came up fast behind one, following far too readily and too close at one's heels for comfort. I could very well picture what might happen if a diver was towed on this trapeze along an open reef patrolled by fourteen-foot Tiger Sharks! No. It was a good idea and it worked well – but the risk was too great. Reluctantly, therefore, I discontinued the 'Live-bait-Bar' – much to the relief of the others.

By October the amount of gear that had been assembled to equip the diving team had reached such proportions that another problem had arisen. The *L. Fred* was now scheduled to carry twelve people (in place of her normal complement of four), three dinghies, ten huge oxygen cylinders, three outboard motors, three tons of provisions, two ton of miscellaneous diving gear, twelve barrels of fuel oil, ten of water, half a ton of salt, plus the normal ship's stores. All this the schooner could just manage, but the whole arrangement ignored one vital factor. It left no room for any shells!

No matter how I tried it proved impossible to prune down our requirements any further. That left only one alternative – we would have to have another ship! I could not back out at this stage but was committed to seeing the expedition through, though I dared not think of what would happen if the voyage was a failure and we found no shells.

But it could not fail. The shells were out there beyond the reefs somewhere and I knew it. The diving team was fully trained, our equipment tried and proved. We must succeed!

My own convictions must have seemed genuine enough for within a few weeks we had the second vessel. Bentley-Buckle was a tea-planter from Ceylon. Although he was supposed to have retired, during the few years he had been in Mahé he had managed to collect a hotel, half a dozen islands in the Amirantes group, a large schooner and sundry other undertakings. Now he was committed to the shelling business as well.

It was arranged that his ship, the *Argo*, would accompany the *L. Fred* down to Cosmoledo carrying part of the stores. There she would wait a few days and then return to Mahé bringing back any shells we might have gathered, my report on the area, and a list of our further requirements. One month later Bentley-Buckle would send her down again to meet us at a rendezvous among the islands.

The last two weeks passed in a whirl of last-minute alterations made all the more hurried by the dying away of the monsoon wind and the commencement of the calm season.

It was time we were off.

The stores and equipment were loaded a dozen times before the *L. Fred* was passed as fit for the long voyage by Ravile who had brought along two of his original crew to help him with this work and to provide a skeleton crew to run the ship while the diving teams were away in their dinghies. First there was Ton Pierre, a tall emaciated gipsy of a man, whose weatherbeaten skin was creased in a thousand wrinkles. Then there was Wyn, Ravile's younger cousin. Ton Pierre was a worker, Wyn was a loafer. The old man was quick-witted; the young one was dim. Ton Pierre was a character, Wyn was a lout whom I disliked on sight. But Ravile was adamant – Wyn must come. He was a cousin and that was that. This was the first and last time Ravile went against me. He knew Wyn's faults better than I, but they were of the same blood and against that fact my arguments were useless.

The two ships finally set out from Victoria early one evening. A flat calm sea and the unwinking stars gave evidence of further

BEYOND THE REEFS

good weather to come and I remarked upon this to Captain Calais, the dumpy middle-aged Seychellois whom Bentley-Buckle employed as master. From where we sat on the peculiar flying bridge that spanned the poop of the *Argo* we had an uninterrupted view out over the stern towards where the lights of Mahé receded in the distance. Our conversation continued along similar lines until Calais got to his feet in order to point out a particular star about whose navigational significance he was talking.

'Look,' he said, 'there it is. Right over there. Just over the fo'mast of the *L. Fred*.' But I never did get to see his star, at least not that night, for as he said that he took a step backwards and disappeared from sight as neatly and completely as the Demon King in a pantomime!

I stood dumbfounded for a few seconds before realizing what had happened. The little captain had stepped right off the bridge and was now somewhere out behind us in the darkness, bobbing about in our wake. Then I remembered something else. To make matters worse, he could not swim.

No one besides myself had noticed his disappearance, for we had been the only occupants of the bridge deck, so the helmsman was singularly surprised when he heard me shouting to put the ship about and on turning round saw me diving over the side with Calais nowhere to be seen at all.

On surfacing, all I could think of doing was to swim back along the phosphorescent wake and hope to find him. My chief concern at this stage was not so much his safety as the fact that if I could not find him we should have to put back to port and waste weeks in useless formalities. Callous, possibly, but true!

The sea was like a mill-pond and once away from the disturbed swirl of the propeller wash I put my head down so that my eyes were only just clear of the surface and scanned the soft night horizon for any dark hump that might be a floating body, but without success. Arriving about where I thought he should be and still seeing nothing but empty horizons, I took a deep breath and for want of a better idea, dived down into the velvety sea.

At about ten feet I opened my eyes and after a quick glance up at the leaden-glowing surface to check my direction, continued swimming downwards. Suddenly, a few yards away at a lower level than myself, I saw a vague and blurred square of whiteness, which continued to sink as I watched. I kicked towards it and was within a yard before I realized what it was, the white cotton singlet of the *Argo*'s captain and, more important, he was inside it! Beneath the dark sea his dusky body was invisible, as were his khaki shorts. Only that one patch of whiteness in the night, and I had struck it. Another yard away and he would have been lost to me in the blackness.

I got one hand in the waistband of his shorts, another under his groin and lugged him upwards. Luckily he was quite limp and almost at equilibrium with the surrounding water, which made things relatively easy. Even so, by the time we gained the air I was in a bad way and only had the time to snatch a short breath before sinking again, for now I had shifted my position and was supporting the little captain from below. To make matters worse he now began to revive a little and started thrashing around.

I came up for another breath and in the brief instant my eyes were above water I saw two black shapes humping their way towards us. Two of my divers were on their way. By the time they arrived I was all in and left Calais to the support of their fresh arms while I lay on my back and got some air into my lungs. Suddenly, into the night air from right beside me there rose a shriek of fearful human agony!

'*Aieeeeeeeee! Y morde moi!*' (It bites me.)

It was Conrad and it flashed through my mind that only one thing in the sea could produce a reaction like that, the bite of a barracuda! I had visions of a pack of these voracious night hunters closing in on Conrad, who already sounded as though he might have lost half an arm. I knew it could not have been a shark, for then there would have been no scream, just a swirl in the dark water and silence.

'*Qui morde ou? Ou-li?*' (What bites you? Where is it?)

'*Içi même! Capitaine morde moi!*' (Right here! The captain's biting me!)

At this point I nearly sank again with laughter bordering on hysteria. Conrad had grabbed Calais's head with one hand and the strong teeth of the semi-conscious captain had sunk into it. But our troubles were soon over, for the *Argo* had turned back and was now alongside us. Aided by those on board, Albert and I put a sling around Calais and heaved him out of the water, after which we helped Conrad up.

BEYOND THE REEFS

On deck I stretched Calais out flat and pumped the water out of him, then took him below, gave him some brandy and rolled him up in his bunk with a blanket and hot-water bottle. After that it was Conrad's turn for attention. On examination it turned out that Calais's teeth had closed on his middle finger just below the knuckle joint and then had stripped the flesh clean off the bone, right back to the finger nail, so that two long strips of mangled meat hung limply in the air and the sinews and bone gleamed palely in the lamp-light. On seeing it I understood that agonized scream and forgave him the fright he had given me.

After I had sewn it up and given him a shot of penicillin as a safety measure, I left the *Argo* in the capable hands of the mate and, along with my divers, went back on board the *L. Fred*, for by now we were well away from Mahé and it was time we got on course.

Later that night, alone at the helm of the little schooner, I wondered what lay ahead of us. It had not been an auspicious start, but I had been fantastically lucky in finding Calais like that. If only that same luck would enable us to find those shells that were reputed to lie along the reefs of Cosmoledo, seven hundred miles in front of us, way over the horizon.

SIX

Cosmoledo

The *L. Fred* was a typical inter-island trading schooner, designed for short twenty-mile runs, whose pleasant exterior completely belied the extreme discomfort of her interior accommodation.

The fo'c'sle provided just enough space for five to sleep there in extremely cramped positions. In the hold the drums of fuel and fresh water, the diving gear, dinghies and outboard motors, the stacks of firewood and provisions, the sacks of salt and fishing tackle took up every inch of space. Even so, we managed to squeeze three in there, by making them all curl up in one small dinghy! The attractive cabin structure aft proved to be, on inspection, merely a hatchway down into the engine room, which provided shelter for the helmsman against the wind and the rain. Alongside the engine itself Ravile had managed to fit five shallow coffins arranged in tiers, and it was here that the remainder of us were supposed to sleep. After one look I decided to lie on deck, come what may, for an unsilenced diesel engine within eighteen inches of my head did not seem exactly conducive to sound slumbers! As it was, after two days at sea I had yet another reason for being glad of this decision. Where Ravile had obtained the planking for these engine-room bunks I do not know, but before long they began to exude a steady stream of bugs, which oozed from every crack and joint with the coming of each night and which continued to plague us throughout the entire voyage. The more squeamish occupants of these bunks followed my example and tried the open deck, but the rain showers which fell each night soon drove them back to their pest-ridden but dry sleeping quarters.

Seven hundred miles of empty ocean is a big stretch under any conditions. In a small sailing schooner, overburdened with four tons of equipment and carrying twelve people, it seemed even more formidable – particularly since our destination was a small atoll, so low as to be invisible from a distance of eight miles and totally deficient in beacons, buoys, lighthouses or other landmarks, and around which powerful and uncharted currents were known to sweep. Moreover, it was my first trans-ocean voyage in command of any vessel, and I was extremely conscious of the fact that these men knew nothing whatsoever about navigation and had placed themselves entirely in my hands. Under the circumstances I felt justified in diverting slightly from our direct route in order to call at Alphonse Island, which landfall, if successfully attained, would give the crew a little proof of my capabilities and give myself a check on the performance of the compass, my estimation of the oceanic drift and the accuracy of my sights.

Emboldened by the fact that our arrival at this island went off according to plan, and bolstered up by the very careful note I had made of the concealed pass in the reef on our previous visit in the *Marsouin*, I decided to enter the lagoon without waiting for the pilotage of Alphonse's manager, Gendron, whose pirogue was already on its way out from the settlement. Sending Joseph to perch up on the bowsprit to watch out for any coral heads in case we left the main channel, I put Ti-Royale in charge of the engine and took over the wheel myself. As we turned in towards the reef with its solid line of breakers I looked around at the rest of the crew. The exuberance they had displayed on first sighting Alphonse had now changed to marked anxiety as they realized what I was going to attempt, for 'La Passe des Morts' has an almost legendary fame throughout the Seychelles. But it had to be this way. If they were to obey without question in the weeks ahead, they must have complete confidence in me. As it was, they were well aware I knew comparatively little about sailing and the mere fact that we had arrived at Alphonse, perhaps by chance, would soon be forgotten. But going through the channel at Alphonse without a pilot they *would* remember; and if I could not do it I certainly had no business taking them down to Cosmoledo.

As the breakers drew close under the bow the crew were all far too concerned with the proximity of the reef to bother about me, which was perhaps as well, for I was sweating to a greater degree than called for by the actual temperature. Once within the pass the thunder of the surf all around us effectively drowned

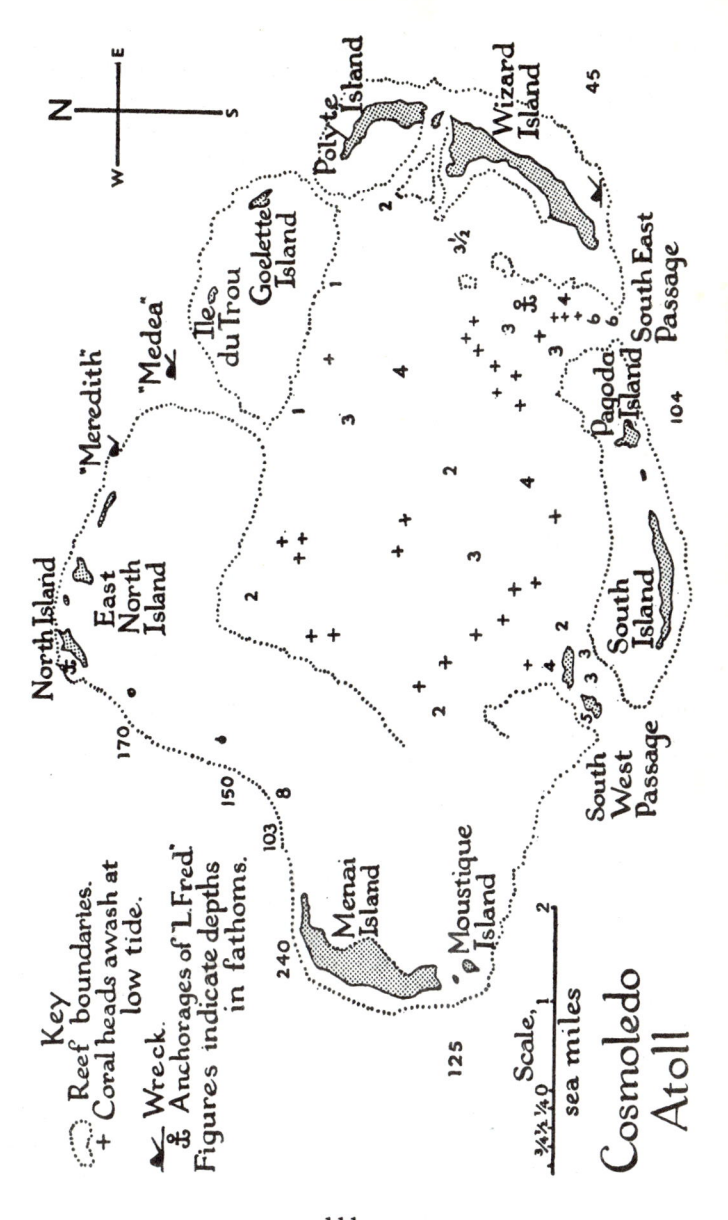

COSMOLEDO

all other sounds including the voices of those of the crew who had begun to mutter amongst themselves. Even when we were within the lagoon the crew did not chatter as usual, but crowded aft to stare out over our wake at the receding danger. Not until we halted momentarily to allow Gendron to come on board was the spell broken.

They were a different bunch of men! Before, outside the reef, they had been just an odd collection of young boys, local fishermen and mature seamen. Now they were a crew, they had shared an experience together, and the sharing of it had knitted them into a team. It applied equally to me, for now I was part of this thing, this team, as well.

After we had exchanged greetings, Gendron smiled in his shy fashion and said that he had guessed I must be on this schooner. He knew no Seychellois would try the pass without a pilot, and there was no normal reason why a vessel of this size should make the long journey to Alphonse. He had heard that our expedition of the previous spring had been a failure and also that I was going to have another attempt at shelling this season, therefore this strange little schooner that came straight through 'La Passe des Morts' must be mine.

We left the next day and this time Gendron did pilot us through 'Dead Men's Channel'. Our deck was piled high with baskets of vegetables and fruit, crates of chickens, and running loose amongst all this the inevitable pair of squealing piglets.

The long journey on down to Cosmoledo went quickly enough. Besides the inevitable helm-watches (for I considered that only six of us – Ravile, Ton Pierre, Joseph, Andrea, Sadi and myself – were reliable enough to steer a decent compass course), there was the navigation to attend to. Each dawn and dusk the little row of crosses on the chart that marked our position drew steadily nearer our destination. During the daylight hours each patch of shade gave shelter to a sleeping figure, though at night the same deck was deserted. Sometimes, waking in the night and gazing up through the cordage at the stars that seemed to wheel and dip with each soft heave of the ship, it was as though I was way out there myself, beyond the earth, out of space, beyond the bounds of time, alone in the bowl of the universe.

At some time during each successive night there would come a sharp shower of cold rain, followed by a chill wind that left one shivering and icy. Soon I became an expert at rolling up my bedding with the onset of the first few spots and tucking it beneath a hatch cover while the rain lasted. Being wet oneself was nothing, as long as there remained a dry, warm bed into which to crawl as soon as the squall passed. While it lasted I would shelter as best I could and in this fashion found a friend, a surviving piglet. One we had slaughtered the second day, but this other we resolved to keep as live 'emergency rations', meat on the hoof. This survivor also spent the night on the open deck, and was not long in discovering that the warmth of two is better than that of one. As soon as the rain began the little sow would tear around the deck, skidding and sliding on the wet planking, squealing peevishly until I was located. Then, with a few sudden companionable grunts she would wriggle in wherever I was, kicking and pushing until sure she had gained the utmost advantage of shelter and warmth. As she was a clean and fat little animal I did not object very much, and after a few nights grew to appreciate her point of view. She was quite right – two were better than one under such conditions.

Even more than the cold rain, the piglet loathed the heat of the noon sun. Since every patch of shade was always occupied, and no amount of squealing or shoving would oust the crew from their positions, she was eventually forced to find other shelter, and it was in doing so that she got her name. Desperate in her search for somewhere cool to lie, she finally precipitated herself backwards, squealing in fear, down into the dark interior of the fo'c'sle. There she rummaged around until she came to the low bunk in which Conrad was dozing and promptly snuggled in beside him. Feeling this fat, warm little body next to him the young lad sighed, turned over and tenderly embraced the young pig, exclaiming throatily as he did so, 'Aaaaah, Alice . . .' We never discovered who Alice was, but the next night, seeing me huddled in with the piglet to avoid the rain, one of the crew woke up Conrad to tell him he had better look out – his girl-friend Alice was sharing the Captain's bed. From that day onwards it was apparent that no one would eat Alice, no matter what the emergency – for now she was one of the crew!

The sixth night after leaving Alphonse should have brought us to Cosmoledo, but on the afternoon preceding that the far horizon was obliterated by driving squalls and distant thunderstorms. Not wishing to go blundering on to the island's reef in the dark I altered course to take us on a long 'dog-leg' to the north. From midnight onwards I took the helm myself. By then the storms had all cleared, leaving the night air fresh and cool with excellent visibility and, as the sea was dead calm, I ordered the sails to be furled and dispensed with the look-out. Then, at half-throttle I turned the *L. Fred* back south again, towards where I calculated Cosmoledo to lie.

The stillness would soon have lulled me to sleep on any other night, but now I was eager to see how our landfall would work out. Three o'clock came, and still no slight hump on the thin horizon to mark the island. At four I cut the motor and listened for any sound of breakers, but all was deathly quiet save for the creaking of the ship's timbers. At 4.45 a.m. came the first sign. A rush of heavy wings, and two black silhouettes pulled up over the bows and scudded over the mast: boobies on their early morning outward flight from their nesting grounds. They had come from dead ahead. The island must be there somewhere, there was no other land within a hundred miles.

In the next five minutes several more pairs came over, all from the same direction. Cosmoledo must be at hand, out there somewhere in the dark. I lashed the helm, left the engine on 'Slow Ahead', and went up to the bows. There I was joined by Ravile's mongrel terrier. But still I could see no sign of our destination. At five minutes past five the dog whined and then growled a little in his throat. He stretched forward, his nose twitching, his head lifted to scent the air. He whined again.

Then I got it! The unmistakable soft fragrance of the land. A mixture of warm earth and vegetation, humus and guano. We were there! I could not see the land, but we were there.

Many birds were by now cleaving the dark sky above our heads and I could hear the distant calls of those still on the ground. But still I could hear no surf, nor see any sign of the atoll. To make sure I sounded. Fifteen fathoms. We must be very close, since Cosmoledo was steep-to. I shut down the engine and returning forrard let slip the small second anchor and forty-five fathoms of coir rope. The *L. Fred* swung to and settled down comfortably. All this time the dog and I were the only two awake on the ship, and we stayed there in the bows to keep an anchor watch and wait for the dawn.

COSMOLEDO

It was ten minutes to six before it was light enough for me to make out exactly where we lay. Then, and only then, I saw that we had approached the atoll at an oblique angle and had crept in to within two hundred yards of the reef itself. But so calm a night had it been that the sea swirled over the coral rampart without forming waves or any surf. We had missed the main islets that broke up the reef's periphery and so had approached this north-east side without having any raised land in our path to block our horizon and give us warning of how near we were to the reef itself. Now I could understand how ships could pass within eight miles of the ten-mile-wide atoll in broad daylight and never even see it. We ourselves, on a clear night, had been within a quarter of a mile and had had no visual indication of its presence. I wondered how many ships had been lost here on Cosmoledo owing to this. There were two old wrecks on this side that I knew of, and maybe many others in days past, of which no trace now remained.

By seven o'clock everyone was on deck and the novelty of watching the crew's surprised expressions as they saw the atoll alongside had long since palled. But before moving further up the coast to where we were due to start our search I had to make sure of something.

Putting on mask and flippers I dropped over the side and swam up to the bows where the anchor rope slanted downwards into the depths. There, taking in as deep a breath as possible, I jack-knifed under and pulled myself on down, hand over hand, eyes closed, into the cool sea. At about twenty feet I cleared my ears, and again at thirty. On, on, down. At last I stopped, unable to go further, eyes still shut. After travelling a quarter of the way across the Indian Ocean I was frightened of what I might see, the cyclone-racked and Antarctic-water-washed reefs of Farquhar and Providence still photo-clear in my mind. But I must open them for my breath was fast running out.

It was all right! It was all right! Below me, perhaps a further thirty feet on lay the coral, a mass of soft colours, amongst which swam multitudes of brilliant fishes. It was all right! They were all there, even as I had often imagined them – Imperial Butterfly, Emperor, Croisant, Soldier and Parrot Fish. Even a couple of Zanclus, my talisman, scooting along, twisting and turning among those stiff coral branches. It was all right!

I clambered back on board already certain that here at Cosmoledo we should find our Green Snail shells. Joseph had said that on his first visit with Captain —— they had collected a good quantity on the reef opposite the wreck of the *Meredith*, a steam vessel that had driven straight up on to the atoll in 1926. To my mind the presence of the Green Snail there meant only one thing. That these shells had travelled up into the shallows from some specific spot that lay nearby, in the deeper water, for I knew now that Green Snail did seek the reef shallows under certain circumstances. If what our coxswain had said was correct it only meant a systematic underwater search to track down the original colony, and that was what I proposed to do.

On this portion of the atoll there were no islets to serve as useful reference points, but luckily the rusted iron bow-work of the *Meredith* itself still showed above water two hundred yards out from the reef. Needless to say, the word had got round the rest of the crew that the *Meredith* was our starting point, and I had the greatest difficulty in preventing all the diving teams from making straight for the reef, and starting to collect Green Snail at once. If we had done that, having removed our 'chain' of evidence (i.e. the shells that we might find there), nothing would remain to help us track down the parent colony.

Once opposite the wreck we hove to and started to unload the three dinghies. As soon as the first was in the water it was sent off, with Joseph in charge, with instructions to land on the reef and try to see if they could find any shells there at all. If they did, however, they were not to disturb them but merely to signify their discovery by waving an oar in the air.

While his boat was doing this the rest of us got on with unloading the other two and making ready the gear. Before we had finished Ravile called my attention to where Joseph was making frantic signals high up on the reef. They had found some! Now the hunt was on. I sent in the other two boats to join the first. On arriving at the reef one team was to work along towards the south-east and the other in the opposite direction. Both of them were to continue until the portion of the reef they were working produced no more Green Snail, upon which they were to retrace their steps until they began to appear again. No shells were to be picked up. No one was to go further out than five feet depth. I knew that they would obey this latter instruction, for all of them were secretly very scared, mainly on account of the stories Albert had related of his adventures off the reefs of Farquhar.

Once they had located the limits of the shell-ground to their own satisfaction they were to stay there and plant an upright oar on the reef to act as a marker. In the meantime Joseph was to come back and tell us what exactly he had found. Away they went and it was not long before the first boat returned, bearing a triumphant Joseph whose usually solemn face was puckered with exultant laughter.

He had in his hands a specimen shell, thereby displaying more sense than I, who had told him to leave them alone. Now I could see why the Snails of Cosmoledo were so sought after. A perfect shell, weighing not more than a pound, whose glossy exterior was neither marred by coral, nor pitted by borers, and whose underside glistened with a pearly dewiness such as I had never seen in any other shell before. As to his news, Joseph said that there were far fewer Green Snail in evidence now than on his previous visit, but that nevertheless there remained a worthwhile quantity. To him it looked as though the island labourers had been busy collecting these shells recently, as he had found several operculums loosely thrown down on the reef and showing knife scratches upon their edges. Before the day was out we were to have proof that this was indeed the case.

After about an hour one party on the reef raised an oar, and shortly afterwards the other boat followed suit. Quick bearings taken on these two marks and transferred to the chart now gave us a fairly accurate idea of the length of front over which the shells lay.

Now began the real work of tracking down the colony, if such a thing existed, as I believed it must. First we picked up the two groups on the reef, and then motored back up to the approximate centre of the area they had defined and which we had to search. Here we anchored, and leaving the skeleton crew, comprised of Ravile, Ton Pierre and Wyn, on board, the rest of us split up into our respective teams and motored off inshore again in our dinghies. My idea was simple. The three boats would start searching the sea-bed in parallel swathes along the reef, commencing in shallow water and gradually working out, strip by strip, into the deep. If anything lay there we must discover it, sooner or

BEYOND THE REEFS

later. Donald and Ti-Royale would take the inside run, then Conrad and Albert, and lastly Teddy with myself, on the outside edge as a 'watch-dog'. Each dinghy would accompany its respective pair of divers. For the moment we would do without aqualungs – that would come later, after we found the shells and then only if they were in deep water. But even then, perhaps we might never find the true colony. Perhaps it might lie below the hundred-foot level, way past our limit. What then? It was all still very much of a gamble.

Before going in Donald asked me a bit sheepishly if we should take our heavy diving knives with us. I knew what he had in mind – sharks! And I knew equally well that should we get into any situation even remotely like that of Farquhar a knife or any other similar weapon would be absolutely useless and one would be more likely to gash oneself or slash one's neighbour than inflict any damage on the real enemy.

I told him that I was not going to take mine, but that anyone who wished to was welcome to do so. Reassured, he did not bother about it, nor did anyone else, I was glad to see. As always, the waiting to start was the worst part. Once in the water all doubts and fears vanished. Here was work for which we were trained in mind and body. It fell back into its standard pattern. The clarity of the water, the colour, the host of glorious corals and the myriads of scintillating fishes all helped to make the reef an attractive, inviting place that November morning. By the time we had traced our first swathe along a half-mile stretch of the atoll all was going well, each diver no longer glancing nervously about him but concentrating his attention on the sea-floor that unfolded like a moving carpet beneath him, but meanwhile keeping his correct distance from his neighbour. Now I could see that all our training would pay dividends, and what a difference from the haphazard attempts of Albert and myself that spring!

Our first beat down the reef was with Donald on the extreme inside in about five feet of water, and myself in about twenty. On the return trip that young lad overlapped my first track in about twenty-two, whilst on the extreme outside I was in about thirty. The reef at Cosmoledo formed a shallower slope than that of most of the other atolls of similar structure, and everywhere the hard coral rock base, the 'platin' as it is called, provided a good foundation for other more specialized and living corals, amongst which the coral-fish swam and had their homes.

Occasionally, one or other of us would see a Green Snail lying tucked away behind some coral 'bush', or else wedged in some shallow crevice upon the sea-bed, but these were merely noted and passed by. We were not going to waste our time on such isolated specimens. Not now, at any rate.

Up and down along the reef we went. Once a school of horse-mackerel swept in to see what was going on, and their sudden and unexpected appearance reminded me of my sole purpose – that of look-out and guardian to the others. All I hoped was that no large predators would arrive with so little warning, for this school of sixty-pound fish lanced in and out of the depths, completed several circuits around me and had departed into the blueness once again before I had time to realize what was going on!

By the time we had commenced the fourth 'beat' I had begun to give up hope of any success, for by now the general depth of water was perhaps forty-five feet, and still no signs of any marked increase in the shells. Coming to the end of our patrol line I decided to continue on for a little before turning, for above water I could see the rusty hulk of the *Meredith* in line with us and only a hundred yards ahead. Since we were now so near we might as well make this our turning point, and I signalled to the others to continue.

As we approached the wreck the reef shelved upwards towards a narrow coral spur on which the ship had foundered. So clear was the water that the vague outline of the vessel, with its curving ribs and overhanging stern, became apparent at fifty yards, though the castellated shape was blotted out now and then by clouds of bubbles which followed in the wake of each turgid wave that surged up on to the inshore reef.

As we got near I could see that great quantities of fish swung lazily around the wreck. Sergeant-majors by the thousand, and hosts of Surgeon fish, whilst lower down within the iron framework slid dozens of *Gaterin* and clumsy Yellow Lipper. I was so intent upon identifying all the species there that it was not until I was right over the stern that I saw something else as well. The entire wreck was covered with Green Snail. Here was our colony! Every single plate provided a grazing ground for one or more of these gastropods. Behind the shelter of each rib clustered a little group. They occupied the riven boilers and housed themselves among the craggy piles of anchor chain. Where the bubbles were thickest and the sea surged at its strongest, there were the most to be found. Young ones, old ones, even the decayed husks of the dead shells lay there. Here was our shell city, in the place I had least expected it.

I had no need to tell the others to begin work. They had gone mad at the sight of all this. I saw Albert scrabbling along the iron platework, four shells tucked under and along his left arm and another cluster in his right. Weighed down like this he could no longer rise, and seeking to gain the surface was pushing off desperately with his feet in his vain efforts. But it was no good, and reluctantly he had to jettison half his gains before he had sufficient buoyancy. Those that he dropped twirled downwards and settled on the bottom, operculum uppermost, their pearly interiors glistening against the drab metal hull.

This action of his brought into being one of our first operational rules. Each little diving group was working for itself. The shells that they collected were credited to them alone. It was thus unfair, if one person discovered a hoard, for another to take part before the first divers had been able to harvest it. So I laid down there and then the following maxim. Any shell which a diver might see but be unable to raise on one dive was still his, as long as he was able to turn it upside down, revealing the operculum, on his first dive. He might thus bring up four shells, but if he was able to overturn a further six those also remained his property. The necessity of this rule became apparent within a matter of minutes. The divers' attendant, called by one of his charges to take on some shells, would leave the other to flounder helplessly on the surface weighed down with an armful, whilst below him dozens more awaited his attention. With this new method, a diver could go on 'stock-piling' shells on the sea-bed until the dinghy was able to attend to him.

Within half an hour great conical piles of Green Snail lay ranged along the length of the wreck, and the dinghies made their slow way back to the *L. Fred*, loaded to the gunwales with their cargoes of shells, on top of which sat their respective boatmen. While they were away I called a halt, for the excitement and pace of this work was killing. One would dive down, scoop up as many shells as possible, claw one's way along the metalwork to the nearest personal heap, drop them there and then regain the surface to snatch a quick breath and repeat the process. Though the depth was not excessive and did not warrant the use of aqualungs, each twenty-five-foot dive was no mean effort, particularly since we had had no practice for the last two weeks.

To rest we crawled out of the water up the barnacle-encrusted bows that rose some five feet above the level of the sea. Here we perched and chattered with excitement, like a flock of starlings on a chimney, until our boats came back. While we waited there I tried to puzzle out the reasons for this colony of Green Snail within the wreck. As I saw it the *Meredith* had produced artificially three major factors. Firstly, a series of comparatively level surfaces, the ship's plates, upon which algae could grow and where these shells might graze and move around without being baulked by coral obstructions. Secondly, an adequate constant supply of aerated water, caused by the sea swirling around and over the deck. This also would provide currents and eddies which would disseminate food particles and 'spat' and yet retain both these items within a limited area bounded by the walls of the wreck itself. And thirdly, sufficient dark spaces and shadowy retreats wherein the Snail might browse, for I had noticed that the majority shunned the directly illuminated and sunlit portions of the wreckage. But before I had time to think any more on this, Joseph was back and Teddy and I dropped into the water again to continue where we had left off.

As soon as the *Meredith* had been partially cleared, I swam off on a tour of inspection. One side of the vessel, that nearest the reef, was largely broken down, and beyond it the bottom sloped gently upwards towards the atoll. For the most part this slope was covered with the usual coraline structures, but to one side lay a shallow and flattish gulley devoid of any such growth. Along this pathway at varying intervals were dotted further Green Snail, some solitary, others in small clusters of two and three. More important still, they were all facing the same way, and although none were moving, it was immediately apparent that they were coming *from* the wreck and heading *towards* the reef 'flat'. Again, they were all of the same size, moderately young shells, 'teenagers' as it were. This avenue eventually petered out, forming side alleys and minor roadways that spread out lengthways along the reef. Following these it soon became clear that the rest of the shells on the reef were all along this level or slightly further in. In other words, these Green Snail that had come in along the main pathway from the comparatively deep level of the wreck, once having struck the reef periphery, ranged along it in either direction but without going back into deeper water again. This 'frontal' line or 'level' proved to be very important in later searches, though I did not know it at the time.

But I had gone far enough and hastened back to the *Meredith* to see how the others were getting on. I arrived in time to see Donald emerging from the black depths of a boiler and scaring the life out of a six-foot Black-tipped Shark that happened to look in to see what all the fuss was about. An hour earlier and Donald would have been the one to turn and run, but now he had work to do and the shark was merely an intruder that was not worth bothering about. A few minutes later I saw Ti-Royale similarly ignore a large Moray that oozed its worm-like shape out of a crevice into which he had stuck his head searching for hidden shells. There was no need to worry. My divers were at work and all their misgivings seemed to have been effectively dispelled.

By the middle of the morning the three dinghies were once more barely afloat under the load of shells that had been taken from within the wreck. Whilst we had been diving and thus taking no notice of what went on above water, the *Argo* had turned up and now lay at anchor alongside the *L. Fred*, her glistening white hull contrasting vividly with the scruffy appearance of the smaller vessel. I wanted to see Captain Calais about transhipping out shells directly on to the *Argo* and since all the divers had worn themselves out prematurely in the mad scramble around the *Meredith*, I called a halt and back we went to the *L. Fred*. Although the boats were too full to embark the divers, not wishing to repeat the episode of Farquhar when Albert and I ran into the shark-pack, each pair of swimmers was instructed to cling on to the stern of the dinghy and was thus towed back to the schooner. We saw no sharks, but it was not worth risking an unfortunate encounter at this early stage.

Captain Calais spotted me from afar and on drawing nearer I could see that his chubby face was wreathed in smiles. He had reason to be pleased, for with each ton of shells he took back with him to Mahé he would receive a substantial bonus. On board the *L. Fred* all was apparent chaos. Along one side of the deck were ranged three enormous piles of shells, the carefully guarded and zealously separated 'catches' of the three diving teams. On two of these piles Ravile and Ton Pierre had already begun work – sliding their knife blades around the operculums, prising them open, removing the meat from within with a deft twist of the fingers, and finally making two new heaps of cleaned but unwashed shells. The meat and operculums they tossed over their heads on to the other side of the deck to wait for attention later. I had expected and had told Wyn, the so-called mechanic, to join in, but that was far too much hard work for his liking and he contented himself with sitting in the bows under the shade of a furled sail, idly strumming Albert's guitar to pass the time.

During the entire voyage this useless young man did nothing but loll around, eat as much food as he could scrounge, toy with this guitar and only open his mouth to tell dirty stories. Coercion, threats, abuse or wheedling availed me nothing at all. Strangely enough the others accepted it, and did not grumble at the obvious fact that we were all working extra to make up for this 'passenger'. Indeed, had I done what I felt like doing on many occasions and given him a good hiding, the rest would have risen against me. Often when I scolded him severely, as I did at first, the mounting tension on board was very noticeable and instinctively the crew slid back into the automatic reaction of 'All-Creoles-together-against-the-foreigner'. (Usually known colloquially as *'Baiser les Anglais'*!) It was no good, so in the end I gave it up.

Leaving the divers to their hot tea and the rest to the work of shell-cleaning I went over to the *Argo* to talk with Calais. Here, after a discussion which involved the other two unofficial captains, Coletto the coxswain, and 'Le Gros Soula' (Big Drunk), the fat cook, we decided to sail up around the north-west corner of Cosmoledo to a more suitable anchorage before transhipping the shells.

This first conference on board the *Argo* was quite an eye-opener to me. I had heard that Calais, Coletto and Soula had been shipmates throughout their lives. The three of them were all over fifty and Calais, on getting the job of master of the *Argo*, had spared no pains to install his two henchmen alongside him. The Captain, a kindly man and growing perhaps a little lazy through over-indulgence, though the master in theory was never captain in practice. No, the triumvirate ruled supreme. Calais the easy-going arbitrator, Coletto the meteoric and dynamic and Soula the masterful terror of the crew.

That very morning I had occasion to witness just how masterful. Albert, ever inquisitive, had followed me over to the *Argo*. He nosed around the engine-room, peered in the hold and, ever hungry, was not long in finding the galley. Here, he prised up saucepan lids and tried the contents, helped himself to some of the coffee that was always available for the three rulers of the *Argo*, and eventually wandered up into the bows where he sat munching a ship's biscuit on which he had spread a thick layer of condensed milk. There he was discovered by Soula who, on retiring to his kitchen from the conference, had instantly seen that someone had trespassed into this holy-of-holies in his absence. The first thing Albert knew was that an enormous podgy hand grabbed him by the neck and raised him effortlessly into the air, while at the same instant his buttocks caught the full impact of a deftly wielded cast-iron frying-pan. After a few seconds, during which Soula managed to land several more blows, Albert wriggled free and fled, still clutching his half-eaten biscuit.

Soula, surprisingly agile for all his bulk, raced after him, brandishing the frying-pan in one hand, and, I was horrified to see, a meat-axe in the other. There followed two complete circuits of the deck and then, realizing there was no other escape, Albert shot up into the rigging, paused for an instant to cram the rest of the biscuit in his mouth, grinned derisively at his fat purser, dived neatly into the sea and swam back to the *L. Fred*. Soula contented himself with hurling abuse and firewood at the retreating figure and then, somewhat mollified, squeezed his enormous bulk back into the narrow confines of the galley. After that, none of my lot ever dared come on board the *Argo* without first asking permission from 'Le Gros Soula'.

All that afternoon we toiled away at the cleaning, sorting and bagging of the shells. Eventually this was all finished and the resultant twenty-two sacks were ferried over by dinghy to be stowed in the capacious hold of the *Argo*. It had been a wonderful start to the work. A ton or more of first quality Green Snail, more than we had got in a month of diving on the previous expedition!

Just as we had finished a pirogue rowed up to us where we lay tucked away in the shelter of that islet off the north-west tip of the atoll. The occupants had been out fishing to feed the rest of the labour force living at the settlement on the main island on the south-west side, and which we had not yet visited. They would not come aboard, for they had been warned by the manager not to have anything to do with us. The reason for this was that we were regarded somewhat in the nature of pirates or poachers. It appeared that the lessee of the island had also discovered that Cosmoledo housed Green Snail and had ordered his labourers to comb every inch of the encircling reef at low water. Since, however, the reef lay outside his lawful tenure and since he had made no effort to seek out the shells by organizing skin-divers to work on the outside of the reef, this did not worry me unduly, as I did not feel we were in any way trespassing. Moreover, I knew that no Seychellois would ever dive in these waters unless he were first shown by personal example that such a thing was safe and feasible, and this I knew the lessee could never do.

After our friendly reception at all the other islands it was strange to arrive at a place definitely hostile to us and I realized that it would be foolish to think of obtaining any help – even for such a vital necessity as water – from these people. It was not their fault, they had their orders and I was glad that we had fitted out the *L. Fred* so as to be as self-sufficient as possible, for now there was no other alternative. The fishermen were obviously afraid that even their harmless visit might be wrongly interpreted ashore and were only too anxious to paddle off again once their initial curiosity had been satisfied, for they had been told to report any strange boats and especially to look out for 'La Barbe' (myself).

That night we dined on Green Snail curry. These snails had a flavour very akin to that of lobster but the consistency of the meat was too rubbery for my liking and I could see that such a diet would be too rich and indigestible to keep up for long. Even after that first meal many of us were kept awake most of the night and I subsequently banned Green Snail from the menu of all the divers. One person on board, however, thrived on this meat and that was Alice, the piglet. After a few days she would touch nothing else and would root around the heaps of unopened shells in a fury till someone opened a few and fed her with the molluscs. On an exclusive diet of Green Snail she grew at a tremendous rate, and her skin became glossy and tight-stretched over her fat little frame.

The next day the *Argo* left to continue her voyage, and I arranged with Captain Calais that our next rendezvous would be in six weeks' time. As the white-hulled schooner pulled out I felt a momentary pang of uneasiness. Now we were absolutely on our own, with no one to help us but ourselves. The others, too, were depressed and I hastily started on the daily schedule of work that was to become automatic in the weeks that followed. Firstly, all the three diving teams were assembled on deck with their respective crates of equipment. These were then unpacked and re-packed after I had inspected them to ensure that nothing was missing. Each crate contained:

2 pairs swim fins
2 masks
2 schnorkel breathing tubes
1 spare mask glass
2 spare mask straps
2 thick belts
2 heavy knives
1 shell net and sixty feet of line
1 aqualung fully charged and with seals intact
1 weight belt
1 depth gauge
1 box of aqualung washers, spanners, etc.
1 nose clip
6 miniature buoys and weighted lines
2 whistles
1 pair heavy gloves

and lastly a canvas cover to protect all this from the sun.

This complete, I would pass on to Andrea, Sadi and Joseph to check that they had each dinghy loaded with:

a pair of oars
a baler

COSMOLEDO

an anchor and anchor rope
a pair of rowlocks
a painter for towing
a supply of ready-mixed outboard fuel in sealed cans
a working outboard motor with spanners and spares
a flag for signalling
a turtle spear with two spare heads and sufficient line.

When this was done I would check each diver's feet and hands for coral cuts, scratches or bruises and ask if anyone had any earache or sinus trouble, or if anyone did not feel like diving that day. I never made a diver enter the water other than of his own accord. While this was going on Ravile would be checking the fresh water and provision supply and would give the engine a trial run. Finally, we would up-anchor and cruise to where I had decided to begin work.

That first day after the *Argo*'s departure produced an unexpected hitch. I knew that a few more sackloads of shells still remained in the *Meredith*, but that we should be wasting time if all three diving teams concentrated there. My idea was to leave one team on the spot to finish off while the other two continued on down the coast. But they would not have it so. No one was willing either to continue or to clear up the *Meredith* on their own. The truth of the matter was that they were not yet confident enough to dive without me alongside them, so reluctantly I decided to leave the *Meredith* till a later day.

Opposite where we lay the island had its hard coral rock base covered with soil, bushes and even a few slender casuarinas trees, but once we had pulled up around its northern tip this gave way to a low rock promontory that presently merged with the perimeter of the atoll, a circlet of sepia brown reef that surrounded the ten-mile-wide lagoon. It was only at a distance, however, that the reef assumed this drab colour. Close to, a hundred shades of purple, claret, violet and pink were discernible even through the light-filtering medium of the sea. But it was only when one entered the sea that the true nature of these subtleties was revealed.

Those early beginnings of our organized shell-search were interesting as they brought out the character of each young diver. People are automatons to a large extent and instinctively the boys took up the same positions in the work as I had detailed the previous day, but while their places were identical their individual behaviour was not, and as they worked and became experienced so their habits crystallized. On the extreme inside, Donald searched the shallowest water. Quick and wiry he would forge far ahead of Ti-Royale who, adjacent to him, would cover every inch of the terrain with dogged and untiring persistence, never pausing, never looking up as the others did to see how the rest were getting on, concentrating on his own beat and nothing else. Next came Conrad, an ungainly frog in the water, as grotesque as his young-old face, with a tendency to clown and act the goat, and rather frightened about it all, splashing and laughing to cover his nervousness.

Then Albert, a born gutter-urchin, quick and sharp, determined to excel if not by fair means then by chicanery. In order to make sure his strip alone was not bare of shells he would zig-zag erratically, swimming all out to poach on either of his neighbours' preserves. It was Albert who always kept an eye above the surface, and the instant he saw a pair of upturned fins, a sure sign that another diver had found a shell, he would leave his area and speed across to join the discoverer, but if he himself found the shells he would slide gently under the surface, making as little splash and commotion as possible! He was very selfish and covetous, but very good, and worked his thin wiry body to its utmost limits. By the time we had finished he was a brittle stick of a youth, all bone, sinew and hard knobbly muscles, with skin burnt black by the sun and his head crowned with a halo of golden sun-bleached curls.

In deeper water still was Teddy, lazy, strong as a bull and cheerful. By now he could swim magnificently and with his great depth of chest could remain under for minutes on end if he so wished, but he seldom did, for he was too lazy. Teddy was simply 'born tired'. That was why I had him with me in order to chase him the whole time. He was very good-natured about all this and took my scoldings and bullyings in good part, but if my attention was diverted for an instant he would be floating on his back in the sunlight, or else clinging on to the dinghy for a free tow while Joseph poked ineffectually at him with an oar to frustrate his barnacle intentions. Lastly there was myself, a third of my attention devoted to watching the deep for anything that might come out of it, another third concentrated on keeping tabs on all the others, seeing that none strayed or lagged, that the line remained even, with no gaps and that each dinghy stayed close to its respective pair of divers, the remaining third portion perfunctorily and intermittently occupied in scanning the bottom for such signs as slope level, reef contours, presence of Zanclus or sympathetic corals and algae – and lastly for the shells themselves.

The boatmen, too, had their characters etched in their work. The hard, proud and ambitious Sadi exhorting Donald to slow down and Ti-Royale to speed up, ever scornful of their efforts, laughing if they were successful, dour if they were not, zealously attentive. Andrea, watch-dog to Conrad and Albert, easy-going, chatting all the time, shouting pleasantries to the others or discussing old times, old places, old ships with his friend Jojo (Joseph) – or cursing Albert's zig-zaggings in an easy, uncomplaining fashion, even though it caused him to row twice as far as the others. Finally, Joseph, attentive and serious, mindful of my words, keeping right with us the whole time and anxiously following when I penetrated beyond the abyss to see if anything lay there; continually chiding Teddy for his laziness in a quiet voice.

In this fashion the nine of us went on down the reef. Before long a curious eight-foot Black-Tipped Shark put in an appearance and to test the others' reactions and their obedience I stuck my head out of the water and yelled *'Requins! Requins!'* Startled heads popped up from all over the place, looked at one another and then at me and then, remembering, swam quickly towards me. The boats too closed in, Andrea and Sadi rowing frantically, while Joseph, already right by me, shouted them on.

The shark was still there by the time they all arrived. Last was Donald, and he and Conrad shouldered their way up close behind me, visibly frightened, trying to hide themselves in the centre of the group. Albert, knowing from the brute's behaviour that there was nothing to be worried about and wanting to steal the limelight, pulled out his knife and dived down towards it. At this the shark lazily turned away and glided on effortlessly downwards, keeping some yards ahead of him. His breath exhausted, Albert surfaced, the bright knife-blade glistening in his hand. Something else had seen that shining object as well. A large barracuda suddenly materialized and followed stealthily up after him. Barracudas, like jackdaws, love bright and glittering things, and the only occasion on which I have known someone to be 'attacked' by one (in spite of the many tales as to their ferocity) was due to the individual wearing a steel wrist-watch which caused the fish to lacerate the man's arm severely in a lightning snap at the glittering object.

With Albert on the surface, I explained to them all how silly it was to threaten any fish with such a shiny thing, since it only served to attract their unwelcome attentions still further. To demonstrate I took the knife from Albert and dived down in the vague direction of the barracuda, which was still slowly circling us. Getting within fifteen feet of it, I halted and worked my wrist to make the light play and ripple along the steel blade. Intrigued, the barracuda moved forward. Another tremor of the knife and on it came to within about five feet of my outstretched arm. That was near enough and I was just about to hide the weapon away out of sight of its bulgy staring eyes when a flash of something large and silvery streaked past over my shoulder and hit my wrist with stunning force. At the same instant there was a metallic ringing sound, and the knife was torn from my hand to spin slowly downwards into the green depths.

Before I had time to recover, this new attacker had shot by, curved up over my head and swept down again to survey me with a puzzled air. But it was only a large sixty-pound Horse Mackerel whose sinister shape had so surprised me and whose rows of small pointed teeth had merely blunted themselves on the knife blade. The newcomer surveyed the torn skin along the inside of my wrist with contempt as though to say 'Well, my friend, if you will hold a shiny tempting fish in your hand what *do* you expect? By the way, where did the little chap get to anyway? I was sure I had him.'

I sent Albert on down to get his knife which lay amongst the coral forty feet below us. It was good practice for him and it was his showing off that had started the whole business. But it was a very good object lesson, almost too good, and the others were suitably impressed. And I had a sprained wrist which served me as a painful memento for several weeks!

As we worked our way along the reef it soon became obvious that here all the shells lay along a certain line due to the Green Snail, on leaving the *Meredith*, having 'fanned out' sideways along the reef after reaching a given shallower level. This I had already noted in my brief survey of the previous day, but I insisted on Teddy and I keeping out in the deeper water, although we appeared to be missing all the chances of success and only had a bare half-dozen shells to show for our pains when the other boats had already sixty or more shells apiece. But I knew something the others did not. I knew that further on (how much further, I was not sure) there lay an additional wreck, not marked on the chart or mentioned in the Pilot Manual. This was of another guano-carrying ship, the *Medea*, and although smaller than the *Meredith* I had hopes that it, too, would house another colony. Sure enough, before we had swum more than three miles from the *Meredith*, Teddy came across the first signs, several encrusted plates and a bollard, lying on the bottom in some thirty feet of water. In the cavity beneath one of the plates sat a family of three Green Snail.

Calling up the others I explained the position and we began to comb the area to track down the main hulk. We were disappointed, however, for this we never found and it became obvious that successive monsoons had broken up the wreck completely, although we did fairly well from the débris that remained. Ti-Royale found a heap of anchor chain in a great rusted pile, on which the molluscs clustered like garden snails on a midden heap. Albert hit on a boiler, from whose dark interior he pulled out more than fifty snails. Each of us made his own little discovery and set about exploiting it. Teddy and I made a discovery of another sort.

Coming upon a slab of rusted ironwork I was surprised to see a huge Rock Cod sally forth from its shadows and head directly for us. That these oafish fish were curious I knew full well, but was totally unprepared for this particular Grouper's subsequent actions. Teddy had just dived to retrieve a solitary shell that lay under a coral bush. The Grouper, seeing this strange being hanging there, holding on to the coral with one hand, legs beating slowly to keep itself in position head downwards on the seabed, swam right up, circled the unsuspecting diver and then deliberately, and from a range of about three yards, took a short run and butted him hard in the middle of his back.

That it was hard, I could see by the string of bubbles that soared upwards from his schnorkel tube, as Teddy, the breath knocked out of him, was hurled over backwards by the attack. Puzzled and completely oblivious of what had happened he struggled towards the surface while the Grouper hid himself in a nearby gulley. When he had got his breath I pointed out the ungainly fish to him and then dived down to see if the Grouper would do the same to me. It did, and I was very sorry I ever thought of tempting it. Hardly had I reached the bottom and even before my back was turned, 'wham', I was flying violently head over heels, losing all my breath, as had Teddy. When I got to the surface Teddy had almost sunk through laughing, but the humour of the situation was lost on me!

By playing a game of tag with that crusty old gentleman we soon discovered that, firstly, he would only butt when you were not looking and would courteously withdraw when approached directly; secondly, the intensity of his rushes varied inversely with the distance from his home under the wreckage – the nearer we were the more furious the attack, but these attacks petered out altogether at fifty yards from his dwelling. Lastly, if we pressed on right into his home, violating his domain and the laws of property, he would give up in disgust and sulk or retire, completely outraged at this behaviour which obviously broke all the rules of the game.

I have seen the same comedy of 'spheres of influence' dominating the lives of countless other reef fish; and a fish's courage increases in proportion to its nearness to 'home', whilst an intruder's diminishes the further it is away from its own. Hence the apparently idiotic but quite normal sight of a tiny fish specimen in hot pursuit of a fellow ten times its size. But never before had I seen a fish actually assault a skin-diver. Eventually there comes a stage when the diminishing courage of one matches the mounting courage of the other and a border-line is established between their two territories.

By two o'clock that afternoon we had had enough. We were not in practice and the six hours we had spent in the water proved very tiring. Yet, we had no cause to grumble, for the day's yield proved to be well in excess of half a ton. On the way back to our anchorage behind the islet, these shells were cleaned, sorted and stacked below. The shell meat joined that of the previous day in a great salt barrel where it would remain till sold in the local market on our return to Mahé.

COSMOLEDO

Before we had our evening meal we had to catch it, so I took the divers out spear-fishing. We were too tired to fool around and shot as many fish as we could in the shortest possible time. Swimming back to the boat I eyed with curiosity the black gulf over which her stern hung, wondering whether there were indeed any large sharks in the area and if so whether they ever came in along the reef. There was only one way to find out, so back on board I strung together a series of buoys made of bamboo logs, from each of which I suspended a short piece of manila rope to which was attached the biggest steel shark hook I could find. These, when baited, were allowed to stream out over the bows, the current carrying them in diagonally towards the reef.

It was in the middle of our meal, just before sunset, when Ravile pointed silently across the darkening sea. Turning, I saw one of the five-foot bamboos furiously bobbing up and down. Even as I watched it disappeared and the two flanking buoys were pulled violently inwards as whatever it was on the end of the line sounded. I looked at the others and they looked at me. We all knew the size of creature that it would take to submerge such a buoy even momentarily, let alone disappear with it for ever. Before the light had finally gone from the sea another buoy silently disappeared into the depths. It was a quiet and thoughtful group that went to bed that night.

Early next morning I set out in a dinghy to examine the lines. Four out of the six buoys were missing, but by the way the remaining two lay I could see that they were still connected though the intervening lines were not visible. I cursed myself for the stupid idea. Not only had I thoroughly frightened everyone, but now I had to go down with an aqualung to retrieve the remaining lines and hooks, for they were all we had and we might need them later on.

The first buoy lay a little distance in from the edge of the abyss, for which I was very grateful. Nevertheless, the water seemed unduly cold as I reluctantly slid over the side. That first one proved to be straightforward. Something had merely eaten the bait and the hook shone bright and clean in the clear water. One saved at any rate. From here on, however, things were not so easy. The connecting-line sloped downwards towards the deeper water, pulled taut at the nearer end by the upward thrust of the first buoy.

Turning on the aqualung I pulled myself hand over hand into the depths. At fifty feet I reached the coral-strewn bottom and saw that the line lay looped around and under various coral boulders. Following it, I came to the wreckage of the buoy, split open like a ripe banana by the pressure of the water. Here one trail ended, for all that remained was a frayed end to which the hook had been attached. I cut the line free, allowing Joseph in the dinghy above to haul it in. The main line still led on to the edge of the abyss, on the brink of which another buoy was trapped by the coral. This had not burst and when released it shot upwards to the surface, dragging me with it till I cut loose. Back on the edge, at sixty-five feet I found the hook and this one was definitely not empty. Hanging from it, suspended over the precipice and waving in some unseen current was a nightmare head. When I first saw it I nearly died of fright for it was a giant shark's, the eyes glassy and the great jaw foolishly agape. I stared at it petrified for a few seconds and then, realizing it must be dead, edged my way forward. Once I was at the brink and able to peer over I saw why. From just behind its pectoral fin all was missing, taken off at one bite. Little fishes nibbled at the ribbons of pale flesh that hung from the ragged eyes. One thing I knew. I could never allow the others to see this monstrosity or not one of them would ever enter the water again knowing that such things could happen so near to the reef.

I swam on down over the edge keeping my eyes away from the depths that gaped below. Hanging on to the line with one hand and sitting astride that grim snout I cut with my knife deep into the palette that lay behind the rows of glistening teeth, in an effort to free the hook that was firmly embedded there. It was fully five minutes before this was done and so intent was I in the job that I had let go my hold of the rope and was using both hands to press down on the knife handle. Consequently, when the hook tore loose the whole head began to tumble gently down the side of the submarine cliff into the abyss, carrying me with it. Luckily my buoyancy was such that I had no difficulty in getting free from the death's head and I shot up again as fast as I could to regain the overhanging coral lip.

There, having freed the adjacent portion of line, I tugged twice on the free end as a signal to Joseph to pull it in and hurried on to finish the job. The next buoy was afloat and pulling myself up the sagging line I could see from far off that this hook was still intact, the bait having been taken in the same fashion as the first. Pulling myself down again on the far side of this buoy to where the line disappeared amongst the corals I was unreasonably startled when a small immature shark of about four feet slipped close past me and curving downwards vanished over the cliff edge with a flick of its tail.

It was apparent that I was in a pretty nervous state and hanging there in the blueness I felt very isolated and small. Down amongst the corals it was better. The proximity of those familiar structures bolstered my diminishing confidence. The line led me on, a thread in the weird labyrinth, and disappeared finally into the dark interior of a cleft between two fused coral masses. Alongside lay the fifth buoy, stove in and smashed. Pulling on the line I felt it give slightly and then it moved inexorably back into the cavern taking me with it. There could only be one thing on the end, I knew, and I was not frightened of that. A foolish Giant Grouper had taken the bait and now lay within its house wondering what on earth this was all about. I pulled myself in hand over hand. It was inky black inside and even my hands on the line close to my face were invisible.

After a few yards I came to the metal swivel to which the chain of the hook was linked. That was far enough, and I gently sawed through the line at that point. It was all I would do and I hoped that the harmless giant would survive with the hook deep in its gullet. Actually its biggest threat would be from the four-foot length of chain now hanging from its mouth, which might easily entangle in some rock and hold the Grouper prisoner till it died of starvation. As the line was severed the chain fell away to chink against the floor of the cave. At this there was a slight commotion as the unseen fish, now freed, withdrew still further into the recess.

Once more on the outside, casting around to pick up the train of the sixth and last line, I soon found a neatly severed end and that was all. Secretly I was thankful that it was so, as I had had enough of the submarine Minotaur-chase and wanted no more unpleasant surprises such as the trunkless shark. I now had recovered three shark hooks out of the six and most of the line as well. I rose to the surface, happy in the silver cloud of bubbles that accompanied my ascent, resolving never again to set any more night lines and scare everyone alike, myself more than anyone!

That day we continued on around the northern side of the atoll, finding no more colonies but nevertheless collecting about a quarter of a ton along the reef itself. By now we had fallen into our routine and the whole day passed without a hitch. A few small sharks and some big barracuda materialized and I was glad to see that now everyone, after giving these intruders a rapid scrutiny to gauge their intentions, paid no other regard and went on with their work. Muscles, cramped after the long voyage, were now loosening up and the speed with which we all worked and the ease with which we dived to twenty, thirty, or even forty feet was very encouraging.

By the evening, having seen nothing startling during the day, the incident of the previous night's buoys was largely forgotten and after our meal I was asked if we might have the wireless on. I had brought this battery-operated set not only to listen in to time signals and meteorological broadcasts for the navigation but also for the express purpose of keeping everyone amused. No sooner was it switched on and everyone clustered around than the inevitable squabble arose as to what programme should be heard.

We decided that each night's recital would be the choice of one person taken in turn, the whole arranged on a rota system. The results of this experiment proved very interesting and showed how racial characteristics were reflected in musical taste. Individually, their choices worked out in this fashion: Ravile, a typical dark Creole, loved the programmes from Madagascar – rather honky-tonk dance music with a distinct native beat. Ton Pierre, older and lighter-skinned, chose the dance music programme relayed to the colonists of Madagascar or Mauritius – jazzy little pieces with a piano-accordian accompaniment or old-fashioned little French tunes such as one might hear in Quebec. Under the spell of these he would go into ecstasies, jigging around the deck in an unconscious parody of the folk dances of fifty years back. At these antics several of the younger divers nearly fell overboard with laughter. Personally I thought Ton Pierre had more musical sense than most of the others. The point in all these selections was that no one knew what station or country's music they were listening to, they merely twiddled the dial till they found something that struck a pleasant personal chord. Wyn, Albert and Conrad only responded to Hill-billy tunes, all exactly the same and usually intoned by some adenoidal popular vocalist of the day. These programmes might be heard from Nairobi, Radio Ceylon, Luxembourg, or even the BBC. The three young men would try to ape these performers on the guitar they now shared, until at last I had to put a stop to it in pure self-defence – their twangings and flat notes becoming a hideous monotony which might be heard at all hours of the day or night!

Teddy, probably the 'whitest' of the lot, took a liking to Viennese waltzes and for him I spent hours trying to find Radio Austria, which proved rather difficult to tune in. Prior to this he had never heard any, but responded to their sway at once, closing his eyes and tapping out the one-two-three, one-two-three on the deck with his knife with evident enjoyment. Joseph and Andrea did not respond to any music whatsoever. The only comment I ever got from them was when we came across an Arabic concert, when they looked up in disgust and announced in unison that the musicians must all be 'dead-drunk' (*sou-net*) to produce such a noise.

Sadi, whose swarthy colouring and black straight hair I had always assumed to indicate an Indian strain took straight away to the hot tangos and rumbas that emanated from Portuguese East African radio stations; preferring finger-snapping, fire-crackling varieties to the langourous and heavy slumberous rhythms. The more I watched him the more certain I was that his origins might well have been Spanish rather than Dravidian. His sudden temper and choleric nature contrasted strangely with bursts of gaiety and, for a Creole, almost scintillating wit. The way in which he held himself aloof and proud from the rest, considering himself a better being than they, all combined to give me a new insight into his temperament. All other music he contemptuously dismissed as 'foolishness'.

Ti-Royale, true to his almost pure African descent, loved all rhythms and would listen entranced for hours to the excellent programmes of modern African music that came from Dar-es-Salaam and Nairobi. Though he had never heard it before, he also had an inborn sympathy for the Kiswahili language and really did not mind if a commentary in this tongue replaced the music during intervals. I would watch him, long after the others had gone to bed, his head cocked to the loud-speaker, his lips silently forming and following sentences of which he did not know the meaning.

Donald had no particular choice and would listen to any with equal interest but no particular enthusiasm. Every programme except one that was, and in that he was joined by all the rest. Each evening, after the others had had their one-hour radio period, I would try to pick up something of my own choice and, if I was lucky, before long the mathematical cadences of Mozart or the sonorous chords of Bach would sound out into the still tropic night.

At first the others would listen astonished and then quietly but determinedly the circle around the wireless would break up, figures stealing away, soft-footed, to the other end of the ship, away from this strange music, that, I truly believe, was hurtful to their ears since no other programme brought about this graphic reaction. As for myself I would listen enchanted. For that quiet anchorage was an ideal setting, with each note dropping gem-like into the velvety darkness and no outside influence or distraction to break the spell the music cast.

Without those evenings life on the *L. Fred* would have been very hard indeed.

SEVEN

Turtle Hunt

By the end of the week we had scoured the whole of the northern coast and had over a ton of shells to show for our labours. Sunday was a rest day, to allow us all to recover from excessive exposure to sun and salt-water and to give our cut hands and scratched feet a few hours in which to heal. I let them practise with the aqualungs, but only for half an hour as I thought it better if they stayed out of the water altogether. Mostly we lay around the deck and slept and ate. Some went fishing in the dinghies, whilst others played cards or dominoes.

That first Sunday I went off alone, ostensibly to explore the lagoon, but my real intention was not that at all. Having watched all week the Boobies and the Frigate birds that had their nests on the islet in front of our anchorage, I wanted to see them at close quarters. If the others knew I was going ashore they would naturally want to come as well, but this I could not allow, as they would be bound to filch eggs, knock down sea-birds, break off branches for firewood and otherwise behave in a slightly vandalous fashion and this must not occur, particularly since the lessee had warned us against trespassing.

Once in the lagoon I turned up inside the islet out of sight of the *L. Fred* and soon found a little bay in which to beach the boat. Ashore the old pungent island smell that I liked so much assailed me and the feel of the warm earth under my bare feet was infinitely reassuring.

This islet was different from many I had been on previously in that there had been at one time an obvious attempt to cultivate Sea Island cotton and now these tangled and withered bushes, each bearing its flecks of cotton wool, covered much of the central portion. At the far end, along the rocky spur that ran out into the sea to join the reef, lay a belt of screw pine and some pemphis. Among their roots large scarlet and black land-crabs strutted importantly, and in the matted branches the Boobies and Frigates had their nests. I had read that the Frigate Bird is a relative of the Pelican, but to me it always looks far more like a type of oceanic kite. It has the same puff-chested appearance, the same scimitar wings, cranked sharply backwards at the elbow joint and the same kite-family forked tail, which opens and shuts scissor-fashion in flight.

The Frigate leads a glorious life, and is aptly named. All it does is to lie await aloft, until it spies a gorged Booby homeward bound. Then down it sweeps and chases, bullies and chastizes the poor Booby until the latter, in disgust, obligingly disgorges its flying-fish lunch on which the Frigate then pounces. And the Booby never learns one simple fact by which it could escape this fate! The Frigate always hangs high above the reef-line and never fails to intercept the Booby it has marked down, because the full-fed Booby always flies in *low*, right down on the water, in an effort to sneak under the vigilant airborne footpad. A Booby that is not gorged flies in at any level and is never molested, nor even looked at. If only the laden Booby would do the same, instead of acting suspiciously and arousing immediate interest, it would get away with it.

Yet the full-fed Booby must fly low, obeying his natural instincts, and the Frigate catches him every time and so the comedy goes on. It is only due to the fact that the Booby far outnumbers the Frigates that the baby Boobies ever get fed at all for, as it is, sooner or later the Frigates are full of Booby flying-fish and let the parents fly in to their nests in peace.

On this northern islet of Cosmoledo all the Frigates, Boobies and Terns showed the same lack of fear towards humans as I had already witnessed in other remote islands of the Seychelles. The Frigate chicks in particular were very interesting. At birth they were as snow-white and as powder-puff-like as the Boobies and only distinguishable by the vicious little hook on the end of their beaks and by their feet which lacked the webbing of the Boobies. At a later stage the long sprouting forked tail became obvious and the dark flight feathers lent further distinction. Some of these chicks were perched in the most precarious places and it was difficult to see how the eggs from which they came had ever balanced on the bare and slippery branch on which they crouched.

TURTLE HUNT

On the inside edge of the islet, the one facing the quiet lagoon, other birds had their homes. There, snowy egrets stalked about, their heads hunched down on their shoulders, looking like little old men marching up and down with hands clasped behind their backs, engaged in serious contemplation. On the rocks at the water's edge Oyster Catchers stood in small groups, their black-and-white livery out of place in the general colour-scheme of greens, browns and blues. Far out in the lagoon shallows stood tall creatures whose upright figures I first took to be those of men, but which turned out to be Goliath herons, hunting for crabs and small reef eels. All the time around my head twittered the ever-restless forms of the Terns, glossy white save for their little black caps and beaks. Bees were there on this island too, and their heavy 'bumbling' seemed strange against the noise of the distant surf. Before returning I plucked some green fronds from a casuarina tree, the young live tips of which I added to the curry that evening as an added source of vitamin C, much to the amazement of the others who would have carefully picked them all out again and thrown them away had I not been watchful.

According to Joseph we had not even begun on the Green Snail of Cosmoledo as yet, for the most prolific reef areas by far were those that lay on the south-west side of the atoll near the main island of the group, and it was there we sailed at the beginning of our new working week. I was sure that not many would remain for us in the shallows, since these were easily accessible to the labourers, who had merely to walk across a wide stretch of reef-flat from the settlement. However, I knew that the shell colonies which fed the reef here and which must lie nearby, would be untouched somewhere in the deeper water and it was on our eventual discovery of these hidden colonies that I relied.

Full of confidence of the outcome of our standard pattern of organized underwater research, I was absolutely unprepared for the sight that met my eyes on entering the water there. As soon as I looked round the sea-bed I knew that something once again was radically wrong. In place of the clear water and organized reef pattern of the atoll's northern reef, here lay gloom and murk and desolation. Once again, as at Farquhar, huge coral masses had been uprooted from the bottom and all around lay the piled débris of dead coral. In places great canyons had been formed, their fissures choked with clouds of drifting sand, the wearing-down process of the sea upon dead coral rock. Here and there drab growths of fleshy seaweed, such as I had grown to loathe, struggled for survival in the wilderness of decay.

Once again, a valuable shell-bearing portion of the reef had been destroyed by some vast destructive force. The damage seemed identical with that of Farquhar, yet I had found no record of a cyclone having hit Cosmoledo in the past decade. Whatever it was, it was no use expecting to find any shells along this side of the atoll and I signalled to the rest of the divers to remain in their dinghies. To make sure of this bareness, however, I stayed in, tracking the whole reef face, zig-zagging to cover different depths. In mid-morning I sent all the dinghies back to the ship except my own. By midday I was tired and when I finally quitted the water at three it was with the dubious satisfaction of knowing that no Green Snails were to be found at any place on that nine-mile stretch of the reef in any depth whatsoever. Back on board I did my best to cheer up the others, but it was a pretty dismal crew that went to bed that night.

The next day produced similar results and by the evening I knew that some diversion must be found to combat the dismal 'cafard' that had set in as a result of two consecutive days of failure. The Seychelles Creole does not have much stamina in times of defeat and will soon sink into a useless apathy if allowed to. This was particularly noticeable amongst the young divers and I was thankful that all the diving attendants were older and more mature men who did not respond quite so readily to a temporary setback.

There was one thing that would get them out of this, I knew. A turtle hunt! And the meat would be a welcome change in diet. The average Seychellois fisherman goes completely crazy as soon as he sees a turtle. Just as many foreigners cannot understand a certain class of Englishman's grim pursuit of the fox, so to an outsider the Creole's enthusiasm for turtle-hunting seems similarly mysterious. True, one can eat a turtle, which is more than can be said of a fox, but even if this were not so I am sure that all my crew would have been just as fervent.

Accordingly that evening I took the *L. Fred* in through the narrow pass that lay on the south-east side of the atoll and which

TURTLE HUNT

led into the confines of the lagoon. Here, on waters glassy calm, we anchored for the night and the work of preparing for the hunt began.

The psychology of turtle hunting is very interesting and arises from certain inflexible instincts which the reptile possesses. During the months following the south-east monsoon hordes of Green Turtles stream northwards from the Mozambique channel, bound for the lonely islands of the Seychelles and the remote coasts of Northern Kenya and Somaliland. The Green Turtle is used in all turtle food dishes and is consequently sometimes known as the Edible Turtle. The Hawksbill Turtle is a much smaller beast and is only of value because of its shell from which 'tortoiseshell' is made. There is nowadays little or no demand for this product and consequently the Hawksbill enjoys a far less perilous life than of old.

The cumbersome turtle cannot climb rocks or steep slopes and thus its laying ground must be flat sandy islands, or coral atolls along which sandy-beached islets are interspersed, and it is off such places that the courtships and matings take place. Most of the Seychelles islands other than those composed of granite are ideally suited to the turtle's requirements.

On arriving off the chosen island, the male turtle cruises around the reef, feeding on turtle-grass seaweed to make up for the semi-starvation of his pilgrimage. At frequent intervals he surfaces, craning his head out of the water periscope-fashion, and having a good look round. If he sees another head similarly engaged he paddles off to interview the newcomer, and should it be another male a cumbersome fight may ensue, or else each Romeo will disappointedly look elsewhere. When at last the long-sought-for females arrive there is a great to-do. There is nothing bashful about a turtle. A brief introduction and then the happy pair will interlock their flippers and waltz sedately round on the surface while mating takes place. Owing to there being many more males than females, a mating couple will often be surrounded by a ring of six or ten envious males awaiting their chance to carry on the courtship where their lucky rival leaves off.

The actual catching of the turtle is limited to four sets of circumstances, the harpooning of the male turtle when on the prowl in search of other turtles or coming to the surface with his head raised high; the harpooning of male and female or both during the act of mating; the harpooning of the turtle when feeding on the bottom or resting on the sea-bed; and finally, by overturning the female on land after she has laid her eggs and is on the way back to the sea – this is known as 'turning' (hence to 'turn turtle').

The harpoon used by the Creole is a highly specialized weapon based on a great deal of practical experience. It has a slim wooden shaft about six feet in length, to which is coupled a 'push-fit' and detachable metal head of curious shape:

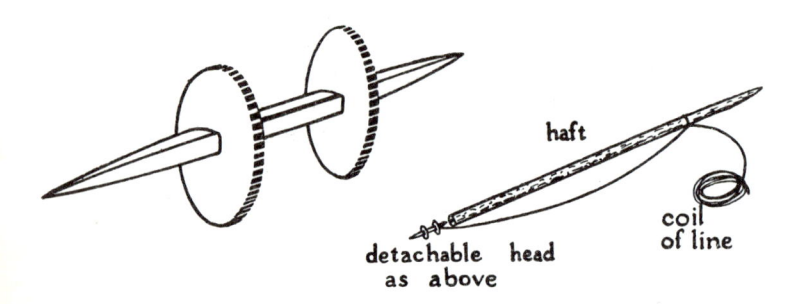

haft

detachable head as above

coil of line

The idea is this. A swimming turtle has the back plates of its shell relaxed and loose. The harpoon, on striking the carapace of the turtle, sinks in and the first ring breaks through the shell, allowing the point to penetrate a little way into the muscle. Feeling this the turtle instantly locks his plates together as a definite reflex action – but too late. This merely prevents the second ring from passing through the shell and the harpoon head is now securely locked within the turtle, one metal ring on either side of the carapace. Away goes the turtle, pulling downwards with all its might, and towing in its wake the canoe of the harpooner, to which it is now attached by means of the line linked to the metal head. At this stage, the loose wooden haft pulls out and floats to the surface to be recovered later. The reason for this is that were the harpoon in one solid piece the turtle could use the haft as a lever against the coral on the sea-bed to tear out the head from its shell. As long as the turtle pulls away, its carapace muscles are locked tight, anchoring the head

TURTLE HUNT

of the harpoon firmly within. When the turtle surfaces, however, the hunter must be quick to slacken off all tension on the line for at the moment of inhalation those muscles relax and the barb will otherwise pull out.

Eventually the tired-out turtle is brought alongside and hauled bodily into the canoe, where it lies wheezing on its back, harmless and immobile. Much has been written about the cruelty of keeping turtles in this position, but in actual fact it is the only humane method – if kept they must be – for when lying the right way up on a hard surface the weight of the carapace is such that the lungs are crushed down and the beast suffers great difficulty in breathing and may eventually even die of suffocation. Turtles cry as well, great glistening tears that ooze remorsefully out of their luminous dark eyes and which they sniff up their nostrils, causing them to snuffle in a most pathetic manner. This again is not so sad as it may sound, for the turtles' eyes are designed to see under water and these 'tears' place a layer of liquid over the eyeball which enables them to focus correctly when out of the water. A turtle, even on such a happy and natural occasion as when shambling up a beach to lay its eggs, weeps profusely and sighs in a most distressing fashion.

But to return to our preparation for the hunt. No one bothered to listen to the wireless that night. Harpoons were assembled, and the hafts shaved and whittled down to conform to the various harpooners' exact idea of balance and proportions. Lines were made up to the required length and carefully coiled down ready in each dinghy. Rations in the form of kegs of water and hard biscuits were similarly placed and there were long arguments as to who would go in each dinghy and which of them would have the key position as harpooner.

At first light tea was already brewing and the dinghies ready with their outboard motors. There would only be room for nine, so I gave up my place to Ravile, and Teddy, out of pure laziness, gave his to old Ton Pierre. As the sun came over the blue-rimmed horizon the three little engines broke the lovely silence of the still lagoon with their infernal cracklings and the whole party buzzed off, leaving Teddy to sleep, Wyn idly to pluck the strings of the guitar which now badly needed retuning, and myself to overhaul the engine of the *L. Fred* and to think out our next move.

It was dusk before the distant gnats' hum of the outboards announced their return and by the time they had drawn alongside it was quite dark. Cosmoledo, in the past, used to yield over seven thousand turtles a season, but slaughtered in these numbers the poor brutes have been largely annihilated and are now comparatively rare. For this reason I had forbidden the hunting party to take any from within the lagoon, on the land or even on the reef. Consequently the three they had succeeded in catching that day represented a highly satisfactory total.

To get the 300-odd-pound giants on board entailed the use of a block and tackle. On deck, grotesquely straddled on their backs, I examined them. One proved to be a female and since the other two would be sufficient to provide us with meat for a week at least, and also because females were so much rarer, I ordered her to be set free. Unceremoniously dumped over the side with a mighty splash, she stoically swam down to the sandy bottom for a well-earned rest, and we could see her dark silhouette spread out on the sand floor that gleamed palely in the moonlight. In the morning she was still there, but after feeding on a patch of turtle grass nearby she swam off and we saw her no more. Her back plates would soon grow together over the small hole left by the harpoon and the half-inch-deep cut in her flesh where the point had penetrated would heal in a few days.

That night we fed well. Turtle meat I had eaten previously had come from animals kept long in captivity and in, as I now realized, very poor physical condition. But this! It was tender, succulent and full-bodied, yet completely lacking the slightly reptilian tang I had come to associate with turtle. The best cuts came from under the centre of the carapace, the 'plastron', as it is known in Creole. I had not realized how monotonous a diet of fish could become and the savoury aroma that came from the cook pot during the preparation was almost too much for our jaded palates and eager nostrils, and we stood around – a ragged throng – sniffing hungrily.

Before we went to bed we started preparing the calipee. Previously I had wondered how turtle soup was made and had presumed that the necessary turtle meat was salted and dried before being exported to Europe. Now I discovered that the meat played no part in this but that the main ingredient were segments of the carapace, cut and prepared in a special way and termed

TURTLE HUNT

'calipee' of 'calipash', depending upon whether it came from the underside or the upper portion of the shell.

After the turtle offal had been removed the two halves of both shells were hacked with an axe into strips, the size and shape of which were determined by the natural divisions of the carapace. The under-shell of the turtle proved to be much more flexible and also thinner than the heavy upper armour and differed, too, in its colouring – being a pale mustard yellow. All of this under-shell was cut up and then put into a large boiler, which the crew had prepared out of an old fuel drum. From the upper carapace only the curling edges and side plates were taken, the rest of the saucer-shaped shell-casing being jettisoned. These pieces were added to the cauldron and the whole left to boil for several hours, after which the water was drained off and the strips, now much reduced in size, were tipped out on the deck. When these had cooled off I picked one up to examine it. Under the boiling the shell had altered, becoming rubbery and glutinous, and the small, flat, bony plate that lay within was now easily extracted. This left a chunk of yellowy, green-black substance resembling nothing so much as a curly fragment of motor-car tyre.

During the next few days all these strips were laid out on deck until judged to be sufficiently sun-dried, by which time they had taken on the same consistency and near indestructibility of tractor tyres! This, then, was the famous calipee and calipash from which the 'Soup of Kings' was made. From a large turtle, perhaps only two and a half pounds' weight of this material might be obtained, which is one of the reasons why it commands such a high price.

This interlude of the turtle hunt had completely changed the outlook of the crew. Overnight they had become keen and eager again, all traces of despondency had vanished and it was a cheerful group that set off shelling in the dinghies the following morning. Once outside the lagoon we turned and continued on around the south-eastern corner of the atoll, which we had not as yet searched. Almost at once we found Green Snail, at first singly and then becoming more numerous. It was Conrad who stumbled on the colony this time and nearly passed right over it without realizing the fact.

On this portion of the reef in comparatively shallow water, perhaps only twenty feet down, the limestone 'plating' on which the coral grew had been torn and 'stretched' laterally (perhaps by submarine volcanic action) leaving deep fissures with heavily and constantly undercut stratas of rock which gave a 'puff-pastry' appearance to the sea-bed. It was within these crevices and under each successive lateral overhang that the shells swarmed. Once again, they had taken on the same algae growth as here covered the 'plating' and this made them difficult to pick out. But they were there all right, hundreds of them!

Since these pockets lay along an extended portion of the reef the divers were spread out over several hundred yards, each taking on a section which we demarcated with little coloured buoys, whose vivid reds, oranges and yellows showed to their best advantage in the clear blue water. These we had made out of sealed and empty cannisters of cigarettes, to the bases of which we attached miniature reels from which a weighted nylon line ran out to moor the little markers to the bottom.

Here, too, we made the first use of the shell-nets, for it was impossible for the boatman to cover the activity of both of his charges simultaneously. The ring-nets were dropped open on to the sea-bed near the shells and the diver did not then bring his catch to the surface each time, but rather piled the snails into the bag before returning to the surface. In this way each man would have a netful containing twenty or thirty shells all ready for his attendant to hoist up from the bottom into the dinghy as soon as he had returned from serving the other diver. This proved very successful and it did away altogether with the not unhumorous sight of a diver frantically treading water but so loaded with an armful of shells that only the top of his head was above the surface and he was thus unable to call the attention of his boatman to his plight.

As it was, Andrea, Sadi and Joseph were always hard put to keep up with the constant demands of their charges and soon grew to be amazingly accurate in placing the dinghies alongside the surfacing diver. This was no easy matter, for if they misjudged the position either the divers would break the surface yards away and waste considerable time and energy in swimming across to them and, moreover, risk losing sight of other shells they had just marked down on the bottom; or else, if the boat were exactly over the spot, the diver would come up with a bang right underneath it. When this happened all the shells would drop down again, the diver would have a very sore head and the

TURTLE HUNT

attendant a further cursing. On the whole it was easier to be a diver than a boatman!

By mid-morning we had cleared up this small colony and went back to the *L. Fred* which had followed us out from the lagoon and now lay a little way off. Our haul again proved to be a little more than three quarters of a ton of good shell, which was most encouraging and the others were all very pleased and excited. But I was not so sure. True, we now had collected two and three-quarter tons of good shells but we had just above covered the entire periphery of Cosmoledo atoll and these results, although satisfactory, were considerably poorer than I had hoped for.

However, I now knew almost exactly where to look for colonies of these snails, since the latest find confirmed my previous assumptions. All colonies were contained within an area which had definite physical boundaries beyond which the shells found difficulty in passing. Such places might be made artificially, as within the wrecks we had discovered; or naturally, as in the fissured reef we had just worked. These places must have adequate currents to disseminate food and spat and must contain balanced proportions of light and shade. Furthermore, such coral growths as might occur there must not be of too luxuriant a nature, otherwise the shells could not travel about in search of food. I knew all this, but now it seemed as though this knowledge might have come too late, for once we had completed the exploration of Cosmoledo's reef, where then?

All our information was based on this one atoll which had not given the total yield of shells we had anticipated, owing to the unsuspected and still unexplained area of underwater destruction at the very place we had expected the best results. I could see that very shortly I would have to make another decision, and I knew that it must be correct first time – otherwise the crew would not continue searching endless and unknown reefs in a vague hope that we *might* be lucky, but would want to return to Mahé to spend the money they had justly earned. While we had tea and a few cubes of lean roast turtle, I studied the maps and current charts in an effort to correlate my findings with other localities. In this I was constantly disturbed by Alice who, full-gorged on her beloved shell meat, sought the shade offered by my body, pushing, grunting and squealing until at last I was forced to put my books away and scratch her back.

BEYOND THE REEFS

By one o'clock we were back in the water and were beating on northwards along the eastern edge of the atoll. Shells here proved very few and far between, the coral gradually giving way to sand and turtle grass, and it was hereabouts that the three turtles had been taken the previous day. Along this side of Cosmoledo lay some of its most extensive islets, two of them, Polyte and Wizard, being over three miles long. Arriving empty-handed at the quarter-mile-wide pass that separated these two I thought that we might as well have a look at the edges of the reef flanking this channel. No sooner had we entered the pass, however, than we met with an exceedingly strong current coming from the lagoon with the now falling tide.

It was pointless our all battling against this, so I left the others to return to the ship, with the exception of Ti-Royale whom I judged to be the strongest and the most dogged swimmer of them all. We two struggled on into the gradually shallowing and narrowing funnel. In various little crannies and backwaters along the coral slopes we saw numbers of Green Snail but the current was too strong for us to dive and we contented ourselves with noting the most promising areas, resolving to come back again at slack water the next day. Eventually we had worked our way about half a mile in and now Polyte and Wizard islands lay directly on either side of us. Ahead, we could see the raised 'sill' beyond which the channel must grow wider and deeper again as it led into the lagoon, and we knew that once past this bottleneck the going would be considerably easier.

Suddenly, from dead ahead, up over the sill came a turtle – going all out, flippers thrashing madly. Neither we nor it had time to alter course and carried on by its own velocity and considerably aided by the powerful current, the turtle shot between us and disappeared from sight in a flash. Before we could recover from our astonishment an enormous grey bulk loomed up in its wake. I had an instant's vision of a head as broad across as a fair-sized table and three huge fins – one vertical and two slanting outwards and downwards on either side of the vast body. I tried to pull to one side but I was far too slow. I felt a tremendous buffet across my knees, a swirl of water and something hit my head like a thunderclap, shattering the glass of my face mask.

By the time that I had groped my way to the surface the shark

TURTLE HUNT

had vanished on down the channel. According to Ti-Royale, who had pulled a little to one side following the turtle's passing and had thus avoided a similar collision, the shark – which he judged to be about fourteen feet in length – had swept by paying not the least attention nor diverging in the slightest from its path. Ti-Royale saw my shins hit the brute just below its mouth, which was luckily shut, and it was the leading edge of one of its pectoral fins that had slammed against my knees. As for the blow on my head, this he was unable to account for, since the shark's body had been between us, hiding the rest of me from sight, but he guessed that it was probably caused by a side-flip from its tail. At this stage, however, I was not very interested in his explanations for my head was buzzing like a hive of bees and I was busy picking fragments of glass out of my beard!

After this incident, by mutual and silent consent, we turned back downstream and Ti-Royale led me (since underwater I was now blind) out of the channel and back to Joseph. Once there, we lost no time in getting into the dinghy, thinking that if the turtle had got away, a hungry shark of that size might possibly return to investigate those two queer fish which it had passed in the defile. As it was, it was two rather subdued and very frightened 'fish' that returned to the *L. Fred*.

With Polyte and Wizard islands our tour of Cosmoledo was complete and obviously it would be pointless to remain at that atoll much longer. True, we might pick up a few more shells if we went over the ground once more, but the effort would not be worthwhile and the divers would soon become restless with such poor rewards. By now they were just on their mettle and it would be a good time to try elsewhere. But it had to be the right spot, good shelling grounds first time, otherwise the whole crew would be clamouring to return to Mahé.

The next morning, while they were all engaged in restowing the gear and arranging our load to trim the ship correctly for sea, I set out in a dinghy to have a last look at the pass we had tried to force the previous day to make sure that the far side of it, which we had not yet examined, did not house any worthwhile colonies. To do this I motored up and down the channel pausing now and then to examine the reef below the surface by means of a glass-bottomed box. There was nothing there and after an hour or so I turned back, convinced that Cosmoledo concealed no colonies of Green Snail shell which we had not already discovered and plundered.

It was pleasant cruising down that narrow channel back towards the *L. Fred* which lay at anchor in the lagoon beyond. In order that I might study the reef more closely and yet be in a position to avoid any coral-heads I stood right up in the bows, steering by means of a turtle spear lashed to the tiller of the outboard. Idly watching the reef unfold beneath the dinghy, I was thrown completely off my balance when without any warning whatsoever there was a tremendous jolt and the dinghy momentarily stopped dead. Picking myself up off the floorboards I turned round to see the outboard motor canted right up on its hinged mounting, propeller in air, coughing and spluttering. My first thought was that I had struck a hidden coral-head, but that was absurd for I was in relatively deep water and would have seen any such mass from my position in the bows. Puzzled, I went back to see to the motor. It seemed all right and, having disengaged the clutch, I lowered the propeller into the water again, let in the clutch and opened up the throttle.

Hardly had I done so and the boat was barely moving forward again, when there was a swirl in the water just astern and a second later a tail, a great glistening back and an enormous dorsal fin broke the surface. I gazed at this apparition in astonishment and then my hair stood on end. From out of the water rose the most devilish-looking head I had ever seen! It was a good yard across, flattened, wedge-shape and horny-looking, with fixed and staring eyes as big as golf balls faired into its extremities. This whole reared up to display a down-curving mouth that seemed to be full of three-inch spikes.

With a sickening 'chopping' sound the head sank back again as these jaws were snapped shut. The motor jumped right up from its mounting and fell forward, pushing me down once more on the floorboards. This time it had stopped and no wonder. The Hammerhead, for that was what it was, had gone and I never saw it again. Judging from the number of teeth it left splintered around the propeller boss and shaft it must have had even more of a shock than I.

Back on board, having rowed the rest of the way, my story did not arouse much comment. Apparently it was not unusual in the Seychelles for Hammerheads to strike at the propellers of small craft, presumably being attracted by the bright, whirling discs as other fish are to metal trolling spoons. What with our encounter of the previous day and now this incident, I judged it was high time we left Cosmoledo and as soon as the dinghies were loaded, we raised anchor, sailed out of the lagoon and set course to the west.

EIGHT

Aldabra

Our destination was Aldabra Island.

Looking through the Pilot Manual I had come across a reference to a large wreck which was supposed to lie on the southeastern side of this island and which was reported as being moderately intact and partially visible at low tide up to a few years ago. Moreover, the current charts showed a constant and powerful oceanic drift flowing permanently from Cosmoledo towards Aldabra.

I had no idea for how long the freely swimming Green Snail spat could live or be carried, but I thought that the colonies of Cosmoledo might conceivably have engendered similar groups on this other island that lay a mere seventy miles away. And what more likely place for a new colony than within a large wreck? But for all my theories and deductions I knew very well that it was only a guess. There were too many unknown factors, too many gaps in the evidence, and when all was said and done no one could really predict what lay beneath the sea there.

Aldabra, unlike Cosmoledo whose atoll-ring only partly succeeds in breaking the surface, is a very substantial affair, some twenty-three miles in length. Although technically an atoll it has the external appearance of an island, for the land rim is well-nigh perfect with only a few narrow channels through which the sea may enter the land-locked lagoon. The whole terrain at some time in the past has been raised above the level of the surrounding ocean, so that its rocky foundations form fifteen-foot-high cliffs which encircle its coastline. To speak of Aldabra being 'raised' is probably incorrect since all indications are that the sea itself has receded fifteen feet, probably during one of the glacial periods, leaving Aldabra high and dry.

Owing to the extremely rocky and barren terrain only one very small portion has ever been cultivated and that on the north-west side, diametrically opposite from where we proposed to work. If any shells were there I knew that they would be untouched, for the island was virtually impenetrable even from the lagoon, where thick mangrove swamps formed a barrier to anyone seeking entry to the land rim from that side. No paths existed and the only way to reach any of the tiny sand bays along its coastline was to sail right round from the settlement.

Aldabra! The name had a magical ring, perhaps on account of the obvious similarity to 'Abracadabra'! The Pilot Manual had it that the word is a corruption of the Arabic *Alhadra* (the Green) and was supposedly bestowed on it by some long-forgotten constellation of stars and was so called on account of its navigational significance. No one really knows. Aldabra has always been Aldabra and its discoverer remains unknown.

As we drew closer and the long line of stark cliffs grew more distinct, 'the Green' seemed the last possible name for this jagged coast. We passed to the south of Cape Hodoul, a sinister rock promontory on the eastern tip, named after a notorious local buccaneer. Here, the current drift which I had thought might have propagated the shells divided, one limb passing on either side of the cape, and this division was made apparent by the many rips and overfalls which violently disturbed the surface of the sea.

Great shoals of tunny clove the waters, wallowing after the gonito which strove frantically to escape, leaping desperately into the air to do so. Flying fish, too, skimmed the surface but there was no safety in flight for many of them, since the sky above was mottled with clouds of Boobies, while over the dark cliffs hung squadrons of watchful Frigates, awaiting to pounce on the Boobies in turn! I made a mental note as we passed that a locality so obviously rich in food might well house Green Snail and would be worth trying at a later date.

According to the chart the wreck of the *Glen Lyon* lay on the reef itself, some eight miles further along the southern coast and it was this spot we now sought. Arriving there we saw no sign of a 'conspicuous wreck' at all, until the quick eyes of Andrea picked out two objects that looked like large coral boulders cast up on the reef flat. He was quite right, they were not boulders but portions of a rusty boiler – the wreck – but definitely not conspicuous. By now it was nearly dusk, so, having marked the

BEYOND THE REEFS

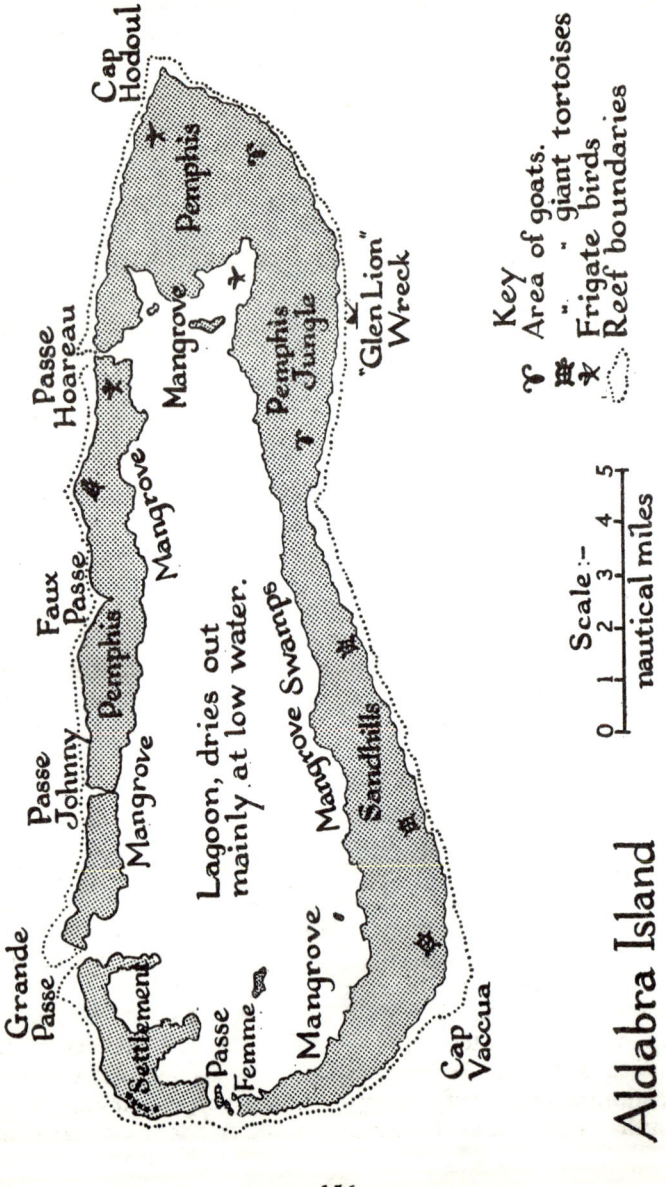

spot, we continued on a little way to take up our moorings in a small bay that offered some slight protection against the uncomfortable swell caused by the current.

The next morning, back again alongside the *Glen Lyon*, it was only on entering the water that the true size of the wreck was made apparent to us. The twisted débris and shattered fragments of the eleven-thousand-ton hulk were scattered over a wide area. Here the sea itself had a strange metallic bitter taste, 'brassy' and unpleasant, caused no doubt by minute particles of rusted iron and verdigris. This derelict, unlike the *Meredith* whose red rust framework had shown up bright and vivid in the clear water, was totally covered by slime and the whole presented a leprous and blotched appearance. On account of this verdigris the water was opaque and the sunken ship only partially visible, the major portion hidden from the diver by a cloying fog whose smoky tendrils coiled about the twisted wreckage in ghostly fashion. But we took no heed of the sinister scene for here were Green Snail again, even as I had hoped, ranged in lines along each metal cornice and clustered within every dark opening.

Within a matter of minutes the mad scramble was on, each pair of divers selecting an area of wreckage and clawing their way down through the grey mist, groping around and, on returning to the surface, unceremoniously dumping their armsful of snail on to the floorboards of their attendant dinghies. As the divers thrashed around, so the fog grew thicker, clouds of grey sediment covering everything until all of them looked prematurely aged, their faces ashen and their hair plastered to their skulls in piebald patches.

Soon the dinghies were loaded and I sent word back with them to bring us cotton singlets and heavy gloves, for already we were covered in scratches and cuts from blundering blindly into the jagged ironwork and the barnacle-encrusted superstructure. Thus protected and the initial fervour having died away, we made better progress. We knew now that here there were enough shells for all of us and that there was no desperate hurry.

By mid-afternoon we had taken out over a ton of shells and were worn out. Battered and bruised we crawled back on to the *L. Fred*, spent and listless, but very happy. A haul of this size constituted earnings of over eight pounds sterling per man. Two months' wages when compared with the standard low payment

BEYOND THE REEFS

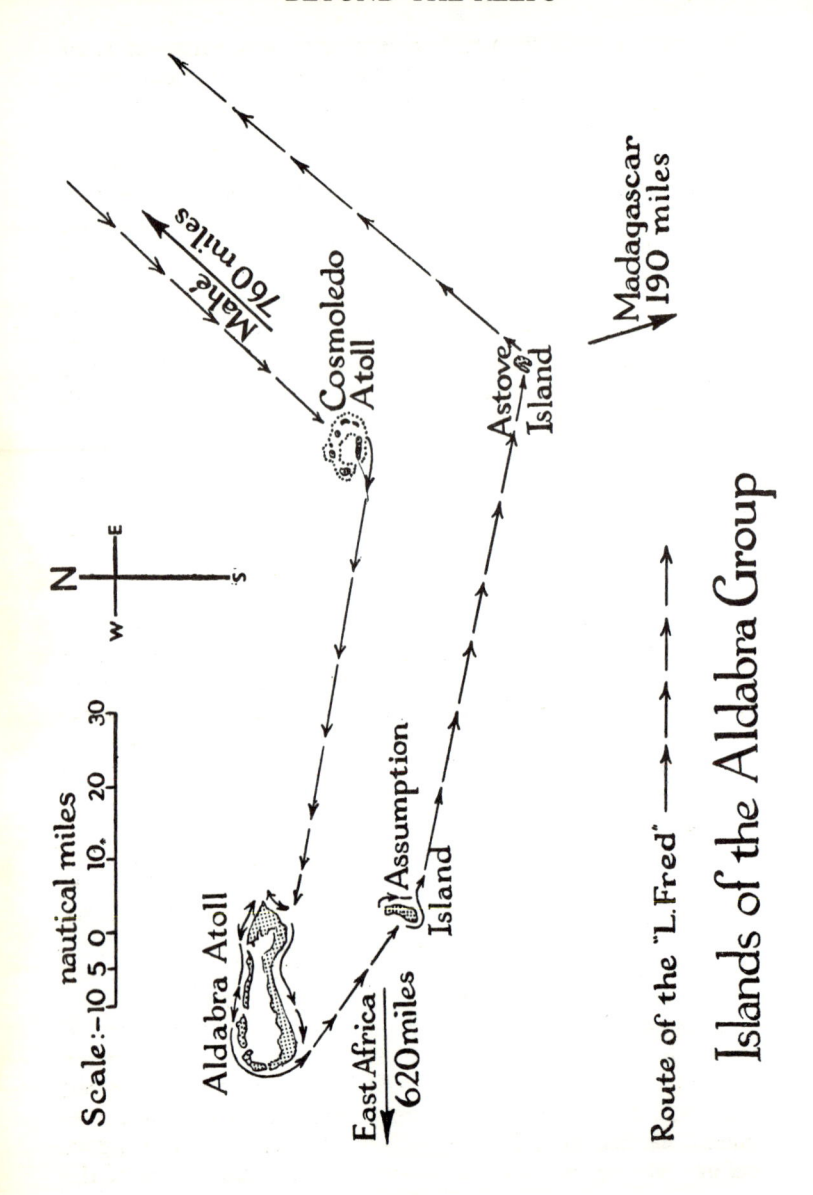

Islands of the Aldabra Group

Route of the "L. Fred" → → → →

these people might normally expect if they were employed at all. Even the discovery that a third of these shells were rejects, owing to the prevalence of borers and also to the high percentage of old ones amongst them, did not discourage us unduly.

Strangely enough, all the shell meat had a 'brassy' smell as well and rather than risk contaminating the meat we had already salted I ordered the lot to be thrown overboard, not even allowing Alice a share, much to her fury. I knew that fish caught in the vicinity of such verdigris-covered wrecks are often highly poisonous, the livers in particular being very deadly, and I was taking no chances with the *Glen Lyon*. Some of us who had swallowed a certain amount of the murky water while diving, myself included, vomited that evening, which made me still more suspicious of the wreck. For that reason I was very careful to wash and dress thoroughly all the cuts we had suffered, fearing some sort of septic condition might set in if they were left unattended.

It took us three days to clear out the wreck, by which time we had put on board over four tons of shells of which just over two were finally passed as satisfactory. The sea-bed beneath our anchorage became a temporary charnel house of glistening operculums, discarded shells and quantities of shell meat. This last brought in hundreds of fish, Red Snapper, Horse Mackerel, small sharks and in particular Rays, whose disc-shaped bodies browsed over the sand floor, rooting like pigs for fragments of the molluscs. But so efficient were these scavengers that by the time we moved on no particle of flesh remained and the area was as clear and clean as it had ever been.

Before leaving the *Glen Lyon* I 'sowed' the wreck with selected live shells to ensure that a new Green Snail colony would grow up on the spot. This I had already done in selected areas off Cosmoledo as a possible investment for the future operations in the years ahead, for I thought that this shell-diving might well become established as a regular and paying concern.

Once again the question was where to look next and I decided to search in the vicinity of Cape Hodoul, since it was relatively close by. The strong tide rips which we had previously noticed prevented the *L. Fred* from approaching the area and consequently we had to undertake a four-mile journey in the dinghies before reaching it. As soon as we stopped I knew that if the shells were there we would have a tremendous battle to get them, for the vicious current swept close under the cliffs and there was no shelter from it.

As usual I went in first to see what conditions were like and in doing so received the surprise of my life. Clinging on to the stern of the dinghy to prevent myself from being carried away I looked down at the sea-bed. Sure enough there were shells there, resting and feeding on flat algae-covered terraces that lay thirty feet below. But there was something else as well. The whole place was swarming with sharks!

Right under my legs, twisting and turning gracefully, seemingly oblivious of the current a dozen or more of the brutes circled complacently. At a glance I could pick out four separate species: *Nez-nez Pointe* (Pointed-Nosed), *Peau Claire* (Greater White-Tipped), *Requin de Sable* (Brown, Sand or Grey Nurse Shark), *Grandes Ailes* (Soupfin Shark). All were of good size, the smallest must have been six foot and the biggest perhaps ten or eleven. So far none of them had paid me the compliment of even noticing my presence and after having satisfied myself that they were all keeping well down near the bottom, I took stock of the surrounding terrain.

It was first-class shell territory and to prove it the shells were right there. The sea-bed here was smoothed out, presumably by the action of the currents which may have also formed the terraces which rose in shallow steps towards the cliff base some fifty yards away. Few, if any, corals were noticeable, but red and green algae provided a patchwork covering to the rock and produced grazing grounds for the Green Snail which were scattered all over these pastures like goats upon a hillside.

And still the milling sharks took not the slightest notice of me, continuing their girations without pause. By their movements I judged that not one of them was hungry. There was no 'nervousness' about them, no tell-tale quick tail lashings and sudden jerky movements. If it had been only one or two of the creatures I should not have minded, but here they were everywhere, coming and going, being joined by others, sculling off elsewhere. There must have been hundreds in the area.

Well, it was up to me. There lay the shells; the question was, could I get them?

Letting go the boat I tried a brief and shallow dive to about ten feet keeping a wary eye on all the sharks within range. No reaction. Surfacing, I found that I had forgotten all about the current and the dinghy now lay a good fifteen yards away. For a moment I panicked. Supposing the brutes came at me now, I could never reach safety. But a quick glance around restored my confidence. They were still ignoring me. I paddled back to the dinghy taking care not to splash. This took a minute or so on account of the fast-flowing water and before I tried another dive I swam on a little ahead so that this time I should not fall so far astern.

Down again, this time to twenty feet, but at that level seeing no hostile movements I continued on to the bottom. Then a quick look round. The nearest *Nez-nez Pointe* was about twenty feet off, cruising along, minding its own business. Furtively I snatched up a shell that happened to be near and, feeling exactly like a pick-pocket who has worked his trade amongst an assembly of burly policemen, scuttled up again. There I found I had again drifted astern, but managed to reach the dinghy after a brief but hard swim. Handing in my shell to Joseph I noticed that he and all the others were watching me curiously, oblivious of what lay beneath and wondering why I had not given the word to begin.

But I had to make sure first. Three more times I went down and still no response from the big carnivores, though on the second attempt I had made a *Grandes Ailes* (not to mention myself) jump and beat a hasty retreat when I turned around suddenly to find it lazily fanning past just behind my head.

It seemed safe enough, so I called Andrea over and signalled Albert in, telling him to keep close to me. He slid over the side, put his head under and, in a single movement, apparently without touching the sides of the dinghy, leapt back into it again! I beckoned again. He shook his head. I dived down and brought up another shell and beckoned once more. Gingerly he lowered himself into the sea with a look of abject martyrdom. There we stayed on the surface while I pointed out the lack of interest the sharks were displaying and their lazy movements. Then we dived on down together. Once on the bottom instinctively he went to work and seized two shells before the current pulled us away. Then, his eyes signalling appealingly heavenwards, we came up and regained the boat.

Next thing I saw was Ti-Royale lancing down towards the

terraced rock floor. Seen from above it seemed strangely unreal as his lithe ebony body was momentarily blotted out by two large *Requins de Sable* that crossed above him. Then he was on his way up again, body relaxed and seemingly quite as much at ease as the sharks that prowled around him.

I told the others to remain in the dinghies. Two divers were all I could manage under these conditions. Moreover the current would soon tire them out and the others could then work in shifts.

Looking back on it the whole incident has a dreamlike quality about it. Never had I seen so many medium-sized sharks gathered so near the shoreline. If anything, their numbers increased as time went by. Once I thought I counted thirty, all in sight at the same time, but it was difficult to reach an accurate total although they were only moving in lazy circles and figures-of-eight for the most part. It was the colour contrasts that were so remarkable. The skin tones of the sharks varied from the pale dove-grey of the *Grandes Ailes* to the shiny black upper surfaces of the *Requins de Sable* and against these grim silhouettes criss-crossed the pastel sepia, bronze and café-au-lait skins of my divers.

Instinctively we had all adopted the lazy movements and slow rhythms of these big predators so that shark and diver, on coming face to face, would turn gently away from each other with slow, unhurried grace, curving and spiralling past one another in smooth arcs of motion like a weird ballet sequence. Perhaps it was this factor that gave the scene its dreamlike quality. But dreamlike or no we were getting the shells! Eventually, we had to give up. Not only was the current forcing us to over-exert ourselves but the tension of working amid beasts that might at any instant burst into savage and deadly action was considerable. By mid-morning we were finished and felt as though we had been in the water for a week.

On our way back to the *L. Fred*, the episode now safely over, the young men went through a violent reaction that took in each case one of two forms. Either they felt unutterably tired and just dropped off to sleep sprawled on top of the heap of shells they had collected, or else they became almost feverishly talkative, giggling and laughing inanely at the slightest thing. Anyway, they had earned a holiday for the rest of the day. Once on board and our adventures accounted to the incredulous crew, we sailed back to the anchorage, where we had a feast of turtle and rice, sweet potatoes, tinned fruit and condensed milk, cheese and hard biscuits and as much hot, sweet coffee as we could wish for. After this we all slept, leaving the cleaning and sorting of more than a quarter of a ton of hard-won shells until the evening.

On the following day we went back to Cape Hodoul. The sharks were still there, still as nonchalant as before, but nevertheless after two hours' diving we had to give up. It was not only the sharks that beat us but the current, for now we were working right alongside the promontory and the closer we got to it, the more violent became the swirling water. Eventually, penetrating too close, we were caught up in a particularly vicious eddy that took hold of the three boats and those of us clinging on to them, whirled us around and took us willy-nilly past Hodoul's jagged rock-spur and several hundred yards out before dying away.

As we were first sucked into this tide-race I pushed Donald and Teddy, who were with me at the time, back into their dinghies, but I stayed on to have a quick look at the sea-bed as we went swirling across it. In the path of the main current the limestone terraces had been flattened completely, no algae were to be seen and only a few patches of ragged weed clung grimly to such scant shelter as was afforded by the almost levelled sea-bed. No sharks nor other fish swam there, presumably having more sense than to bother with such a wilderness. Only once did I see a Green Snail and that was bowling head-over-heels, tumbling down the slope, dragged from its precarious hold by the surging water.

For some unknown reason the far side of the cape, once away from the current, presented an entirely different type of terrain. Deep sand pits alternated with craggy rock columns, the whole obviously unsuited to our snails and in fact we did not find any along that coast at all. Once again we were back on the schooner by mid-morning and although there still lay a large quantity of shells as yet untouched in the neighbourhood of Hodoul Point I could see that they would remain there, for we could not safely bring up any more, lying as they did in deeper water still and with even stronger currents passing over them.

Once again the problem arose as to where to look next and this time there were no more clues. All we could try was a systematic search along the entire coastline and the only way to ensure that the crew held their interest in the work was by allowing them as many diversions as possible, chief amongst which would be the inevitable turtle-hunts, for here at Aldabra there were many more turtles than in Cosmoledo, owing to these distant coasts being so many more miles away from the labourers' settlement.

To conserve our efforts against the time when we might need them, only one diver on each boat now entered the water, so that our searchline was reduced to three swimmers, the 'spares' resting in the dinghies, keeping a lookout for turtle and awaiting their turn to take over the work. On the *L. Fred*, Ravile, Wyn and Ton Pierre now motored off down the coast each morning to await our arrival at some prearranged spot and do some line fishing in the meantime. In this fashion we were able to cover some four miles of new coast each day.

Working thus westwards along the fringing reef on the south side of the island we found relatively few shells, but nevertheless at the end of the day each dinghy team had usually managed to collect one full sack. It was hard, monotonous work and the skin of our backs soon became scaly and cracked with the constant and alternating exposure to the sea and sun. By now all the divers had lost considerable weight and we were rapidly approaching the peak of condition.

Each day we would sight dozens of turtles and usually one or other of the boats would be successful in harpooning one, frequently venturing right into the surf during the chase, oblivious of the possibility of staying in the boat and losing all the equipment! At such times I would stand aghast as the whole team was at times entirely hidden from sight in the middle of foaming breakers and crashing surf, but more by luck than skill they always came out unscathed, often bearing their prize with them.

Every day also, we divers met more and more turtles underwater, for by now the breeding season was well advanced and fresh arrivals were constantly increasing the numbers that spent the daylight hours roaming the reefs in search of a mate. On seeing us the amorous and perhaps short-sighted creatures would hastily swim right up, hoping to find a new spouse, but in this they were disappointed and would content themselves with circling us wistfully at a few yards' range.

If one let one's arms hang downwards and outwards limply in

the water, kicking one's legs in a parody of a turtle's movements, the lusty males would rush up with obvious intent, completely ignoring one's evident lack of turtle attributes, and press home their suit to the point where one was forced to flee to the sanctuary of the dinghy. Conrad, in particular, having a peculiarly graceless and froglike movement in the water, was always being chased and on one occasion we were all reduced to hysterics by his being 'blockaded' in his boat by an enormous bull, who must have been very short-sighted since he continually tried to embrace the youth each time he entered the water! In deference to this gallantry we did not harpoon the old bachelor but left him to find a more suitable mate. The episode considerably shook Conrad who, for a long time after, could be made to swim for his life without a backward glance by someone shouting, 'Conrad! Conrad! *Tortue derrière ou!*'

One thing that was very noticeable was the number of turtles of either sex who were missing flippers, usually one of the hind ones. These, from the scars remaining, had obviously been bitten off by sharks and many of them were freshly wounded. Once, I even saw a female who had lost both rear flippers and one of her front ones as well, but she got along remarkably fast, scooping at the water with her remaining flipper and craning neck far to one side out of her shell to offset the uneven thrust. Of all meat, sharks prefer turtle and a hook bated with the flesh or offal of this reptile will succeed when all else has failed and the brutes ignore all other lures.

Towards the end of each day the turtles would hide themselves away under ledges of coral or shelves of rock, within cave or crevice, in an effort to find safety from the night-prowling Tigers, Hammerheads and other such marauders. Only at full moon would the turtles continue with their love-making throughout the night and then only within the comparative safety of shallow water. Even this did not always provide the necessary security as we ourselves saw.

One evening Ravile and Ton Pierre, bored and wanting a change, borrowed my electric lantern and set off in a dinghy to scour the sea-bed to see if they could find any turtles at rest in the shallow water that lay between the fringing reef and the shore. Paddling silently along, the beam of the torch sweeping the sand-floor beneath the bows, they heard a violent commotion in the water not very far off. A turtle was thrashing wildly about, somewhere out there in the darkness. Perhaps a mating pair! Discarding all idea of stealth they rowed hard towards the noise, which was now close by the shore.

Running the boat up on to the sand, Ravile carrying the torch and Ton Pierre the harpoon, they ran along the beach towards the floundering. In the beam of the light they saw a turtle, half in and half out of the water, struggling desperately to free itself from something that had hold of it, something whose back was awash and whose large dorsal fin rose three or more feet into the air! Not knowing quite what to do, they stopped and at the same instant the turtle tore free and scrambled madly up the sandy ramp that led up the beach. It was almost clear when the Tiger Shark surged up after it, jaws champing futilely behind its fast-escaping prey. Such was the fury of the brute that by lashing the shallows into foam with its powerful tail it succeeded in driving its heavy bulk right out of the water, up on to the ridge of sand, where the weight of its body was supported by the two pectoral fins splayed out like stunted arms on either side of its gross torso.

In doing so it undermined the soft sand, causing the turtle to slide backwards down the slope right into the horrible armed mouth. The shark lunged again and this time its teeth did not close on the empty air but on that mangled hind flipper, this time higher up. As the ugly monster squirmed obscenely in the sand in an effort to wriggle back into the water Ravile and Ton Pierre closed in. Ravile dropped his torch on the sand so that its beam shone downwards along the sloping ground directly at the turtle and into the cold gleaming eyes of the Tiger Shark beyond. He then grabbed the turtle by its two front flippers in an effort to pull the poor creature free. At the same time Ton Pierre reversed his harpoon and beat the Tiger on its upturned snout. Nothing coming of this, he proceeded to jab the butt into the beast's eye which continued to stare at him coldly and without any expression whatsoever until he had reduced it to a sightless white cavity. Only then did the shark let go and then only to turn and snap ineffectively at the harpoon haft. Finally, with a terrific muscular contraction, the brute succeeded in swinging round and half slid, half wallowed back into the sea, covering the two fishermen with sand and drenching them with water under the furious lashings of its tail. There was a swirl, a few wavelets lapped the edge of the sandbank and then it was gone into the night.

Ravile loaded the turtle into the dinghy and brought it back to the schooner where we butchered it to put it out of its misery. It was a female and within the abdominal cavity we found strings of unripe eggs. These were all of yolk, were round, about the size of chestnuts and connected one with another by means of a transparent skin of placenta-like structure. Washed in sea-water to remove this membrane they were dumped in a saucepan and boiled. Dipped in salt and eaten hot they tasted sulphury and, unlike a bird's egg, contained a large amount of fat. We found them both rich and extremely indigestible!

Aldabra, amongst other things, is one of the only two places in the world where the Giant Tortoise is found. The other locality is the Galapagos group, off the western coast of South America. These Giant Tortoises present something of an evolutionary problem. They are relics of a long-past age, about the only living 'prehistoric' animal left. They breed very slowly and live for many hundreds of years. Yet the age of Aldabra itself has been geologically determined as not more than three thousand five hundred years. If so, how do all these tortoises come to be on the island, for there are literally hundreds of thousands of them roaming the barren wasteland and desolate sandhills of this southern part of the atoll. By all accounts they must have been there for millions of years, but by geological evidence they cannot have been. Where then do they come from?

It is hardly likely that they were *brought* deliberately to Aldabra, since the only other place they inhabit, Galapagos, is separated from it by two continents. Another possibility is that these creatures once inhabited the supposedly sunken continent of Lemuria, which may have joined southern India with Madagascar. The catastrophe that removed the land mass (and which is thought to have elevated the Arabian peninsula) may have destroyed all its living creatures save these Giant Tortoises which, secure in their armour plate, survived the eruptions, storms and other elemental furies, floated on the ensuing flood waters and remained as oceanic flotsam until some of them were carried in by waves and currents to the beaches of Aldabra. That theory, again, is rather improbable, but I wanted to test one particular aspect of it and to do this I first had to capture a Giant Tortoise.

BEYOND THE REEFS

I had not far to look. Clambering up over the eroded rock cliff that surrounds the island I came to an area of low sand-dunes whose desolate slopes were partially covered by a species of Marram grass. The ground here was carpeted with what I took, in my ignorance, to be donkey droppings, and it was not until I came across a group of Giant Tortoises peacefully grazing away in a hollow, that I realized that it was they who were responsible for those mounds of dung. That these tortoises would be big I had known, but I was totally unprepared to see just how big. In the herd I first saw there was an old grandfather of more than five feet in length, the arch of whose back would reach near table-height. I crept up to them very carefully expecting that like other tortoises they would withdraw into their shells. But not a bit of it! One or two looked up and regarded me steadily and tolerantly. Walking right among the group produced no result at all. I might as well have not been there. They saw me, looked through me, ignored me. I began to doubt my own existence and felt rather like a small boy wandering unannounced into a conclave of bishops.

A few were asleep and here again their behaviour was odd. A normal tortoise draws in both head and feet, 'shuts its door' so to speak, and then sleeps. Not these giants. They sprawled out, all four legs straddled and yard-long necks extended along the ground. They were as relaxed and unabashed as ancient tramps lying drunk under haystacks.

I sat down on one and it simply marched off in high dudgeon carrying me along with it. Rapping on the shell produced no response other than a turning of the long reptilian neck and a cold unblinking stare. Annoyed, I shouted at it. No reaction whatsoever. I grabbed hold of a sinewy hind leg but was forced to let go as my tortoise stamped off. Only by jumping up and down as hard as possible on top of its back could I make it withdraw into its shell and then only for a second or two, after which it came out again and strode off in a huff.

The truth of these untortoise-like actions is that the Aldabra tortoises have nothing to fear; no enemies exist for them. If they leave their heads out while they sleep, nothing is going to attack them. Their shell, which used to be a fortress into which they could retreat when danger threatened, has now become a useless appendage which they are forced to carry around with them.

ALDABRA

I still had to kidnap one temporarily to try my experiment and this was not so easy as I had imagined. Even a small one, the size of a suitcase, was extremely heavy and the only way in which I could carry it was by lifting the creature up on my head and balancing it there upside down, holding the edges of the shell with my two hands. Thus burdened I set off back to the beach but had not gone more than a few steps when I was confronted with a calm, imperious face staring into mine!

My hostage, by craning its neck as far out as possible and then by leaning backwards (that is, downwards in its present position) and turning its head through a half-circle, was able to bring itself face to face with its captor. Under the circumstances I would not have been surprised to have had my nose snapped at, but my tortoise was far too subtle for that. Having regarded me steadfastly for a minute or so the face was withdrawn and I continued in blissful ignorance of what was about to take place.

Then I became aware that something warm was trickling down my back and drenching the backs of my legs! I gingerly lowered the little horror to the ground, whereupon it marched away smugly towards a nearby patch of grass. The damage was done now anyway, so ignoring the possibility of further such occurrence I picked up the tortoise again and this time tucked it under my arm, a position less vulnerable to its retaliations than my head.

Once on the beach I waded out waist-deep in the lagoon and then gently put my charge into the sea. With all its weight I was confident that the tortoise would sink like a stone and thus ruin the theory that these animals had floated up from a now-submerged continent and had drifted in safety around the Indian Ocean before reaching Aldabra. But lo and behold, it floated. In fact, it barely drew any water at all, only the soft under-carapace resting lightly upon the surface, leaving the head and neck completely clear. Even the legs were hardly immersed and only the tips of each bent foreleg served to act like rudimentary oars as it tried vainly to walk away.

Not satisfied with this, I tried to hold the little creature under for a moment to see if it would continue breathing and thus choke, as might happen in rough weather. This was easier said than done, but eventually by sitting on the top side of the shell I forced the tortoise below the surface. I waited for a few seconds, watching for any signs of discomfort, bubbles or kicking movements. Nothing happened and feeling cheated I let it bob up again, whereupon it floated calmly about breathing perfectly normally.

Down I pushed it again and this time found a little coral overhang under which I thrust it. With it thus locked in position I was free to duck under myself and have a look at the long-suffering reptile. Blearily through the watery medium I could see it resting there motionless, its small eyes unwinking. A tiny bead at each nostril showed that the water had not entered those orifices and, moreover, that the creature was holding its breath. During the next five minutes I made several similar observations and then, thinking the point well enough proven, took the tortoise back to the beach. One thing was certain, these Giant Tortoises would take a great deal of drowning, a point in favour of the theory of continental inundation.

One last thing remained. I plucked some green seaweed off the bottom and proffered it. The little tortoise examined it coldly, then gravely took and ate it all. In a similar manner, then, might it be possible for these tortoises to feed on drifting seaweed if afloat for a very long time.

Before going back to the spot from which I had taken it I gave the tortoise a thorough bath to clean out the sand and encrusted dust from within the creases and folds of its whimple. Afterwards I brushed out the salt crystals with a switch of grass in case they might cause irritation. On the return journey there were no unpleasant incidents and I left my reptilian guinea-pig where I had found it, but now stoically lapping up a bird's egg which I had found and broken by the simple expedient of cracking it on its horny nose.

The other tortoises were all in the exact positions in which I had left them earlier. The biggest one still had half a blade of grass protruding from its mouth. At what point in the past it had ceased eating I did not know, nor when in the future it might continue. I had an eerie feeling that this sunlit clearing was somewhere out of time. That here the sun would never sink and that if I stayed there for what seemed like one short hour I should return, like Rip van Winkle, to find the *L. Fred* long since rotted to dust and my crew already dead and forgotten.

A heavy silence permeated the air and not even the weird lost cries of strange birds away in the thickets of pemphis seemed real. A white Ibis stalked among the sleeping giants, its grotesque struttings brought into sharp relief by their immobility. No breeze stirred the grasses here. A vivid green lizard crouched motionless on a flat stone by my feet; its hard agate eyes, extended tongue of jet and metallic sheen of skin made it not a thing of flesh and blood, but a lifeless exotic bauble, a fit inhabitant of this lost world into which I had inadvertently stumbled and in which I had no place. Shivering a little, in spite of the sun, I got to my feet and left that haunted clearing, unconsciously tiptoeing in order that my unwanted presence might not be noticed.

It was my habit each morning to get up before daylight and watch the sunrise. There was a reason for this. I knew that during the night many large sharks came close to the beaches in search of turtles and I wanted to ascertain the exact hour of their return across the reef out to the depths. Every day as soon as there was sufficient light I would spend an hour or more watching the sea-bed from a vantage point on the bowsprit. Eight fathoms down, the beginning of each day came far later than it did on the surface, and not until the sun was well above the horizon would any fishy activity begin in the coral jungle that lay below our keel. But the night prowlers returned to the safety and darkness of the abyss before this. As soon as the pale lead light of the pre-dawn lay upon the sea you might see their shadowy silhouettes pass, slinking like giant alley-cats, furtively and silent, back over the reef, to curve down in a last smooth arc and disappear from sight.

If several species of shark frequented that portion of the reef off which we lay, they usually sought the deeper waters in the same order. First would pass the *Nez-nez Pointe*, slim pencil shapes, then the blunt and pig-like *Requins de Sable* and heavy Tiger Sharks; finally, long after the others, came the Hammerheads, wagging horny heads with each roll of their sluggish bodies. The *Nez-nez Pointe* cruised past travelling fast, just below the surface, their eyes showing up orange in the dark sea. The Tigers lumbered along hugging the bottom, preferring to cross the smoother reef portions than wind in and out of the coral heads, while the obscene Hammerheads wallowed in the mid-depths, travelling at a slower speed than the others. In every case the last big shark had left the reef within the first hour after sunrise. But just to make sure I waited for another whole hour before we started the day's diving.

Similarly each evening we left the water in good time for the four o'clock deadline and I had reason to be glad that we did so. One afternoon, Sadi's dinghy sprang a leak, with the result that his divers, plus their shells, were loaded in the back of ours. The five of us, our shells and a turtle that Joseph had caught proved too much for our boat and before long we were bailing furiously. Seeing it would be impossible to make the *L. Fred*, which was waiting for us two miles further on, Teddy and I left them and swam ashore, to walk along the beach until level with the schooner where we waited for a dinghy to pick us up. Soon it was past five o'clock and growing impatient I decided not to delay any longer but to swim the half mile back to the *L. Fred*. Teddy, the ever lazy, would not come, preferring to lie comfortably in the shade until rescued. As it transpired, he was wise.

Leaving him I set off on my own. By now the sea was already growing murky and opaque with the approaching dusk. All colour had gone save a drab autumn green. Most of the coral fish had already retreated into crevices and holes and the reef seemed strangely empty. In the shallows a solitary Hawksbill turtle took to instant and panicky flight on seeing me. The shadow of a Booby bird crossing overhead made me start nervously. There was a tension of fear about the place. This reef that had been alight with colour and quick with friendly movement a few hours ago was now 'on edge', withdrawn and deserted, waiting for the night, silent and afraid even as a great primeval forest might await the onset of darkness.

Something white flickered in the gloom ahead. It was the under-surface of a small shark, perhaps three or four foot long, curving up to meet me. It passed close over my shoulder, swung round and cut in again. Normally a baby of this size would have taken to flight, but now with the dusk it was no longer the timorous infant of the daylight hours. It stayed with me for several minutes, only disappearing when a slightly bigger specimen suddenly materialized. This one also came straight at me, zipping close by my flank at the last second. In a flash it was back and continued to 'buzz' me in this fashion until finally I chased it off by diving directly at it and trying to tweak its tail as it swung away.

ALDABRA

By now I was past the shallow reef lip and the coral that lay below was no longer visible, lost in the obscurity of the undersea nightfall. In the intervening two hundred and fifty yards between the reef and the *L. Fred*, I was bounced by three more sharks. Not one of these was more than six feet in length and all were of the common White-tipped variety that were usually so timid in the daytime. But this was not the daytime and already their hunting instincts were roused. A man swimming on the surface would be taken for a queer type of turtle and I could see they thought me just that by the nature of their approach. In each case they appeared from dead ahead and came straight on in. A turtle on meeting them would have swung round, banking steeply to get away with all four flippers thrust out for quick acceleration. A similar quick turn on the part of the shark and it would be in the best possible position for attack – slightly behind, below and to one side, with the nearest portion of the turtle an outstretched hind limb – no doubt the reason so many turtles lacked one or both rear flippers.

Luckily, I was not a turtle and did not play the game according to the rules at all; but like any turtle I certainly heaved a sigh of relief when I felt the *L. Fred*'s solid deck beneath my feet! Those had been comparatively baby sharks. In another half-hour their bigger relatives would arrive to scour the reef for the night's food and that would be a different matter. From then on I was doubly careful that no one entered the water before eight in the morning and that we all quitted it by four in the afternoon. We were after shells, not accidents.

NINE

Goats and Groupers

Mid-December came in squally and vicious. For one whole week we dodged from anchorage to anchorage in our efforts to avoid being driven onto the reef by the constantly changing wind. It was a miserable period. During the daylight hours we crouched under what protection the primitive wheelhouse of the *L. Fred* afforded. Everything stank of mould, of sodden dirty clothing, diesel oil and musty provisions. The two packs of cards finally gave up the unequal struggle, dissolving into a glutinous mass of streaky paste-board. The radio shorted out. At night it was worse, for the wind would invariably shift with each fresh squall and in the darkness and the lashing rain, unable to see whether we were dragging inshore, we would up anchor and beat out to sea, there to cruise up and down till dawn.

Under the influence of the weather the turtles that had swarmed off the beaches disappeared and we were forced back onto our basic diet of salt-fish. I personally developed into a creaking bundle of rheumatic aches and pains and each morning secretly envied the indiarubber suppleness of the young divers, who would prance and racket about the deck whatever the weather, while I lay shivering and stiff, longing for the warmth of the sun. Under such conditions our morale soon dropped to zero and by the sixth day I knew that some diversion must be found. The turtles had all gone, the sea was too rough and the ship too small. What remained?

Looking out at the rocky coast of Aldabra I was surprised to see the whole skyline along the top of the jagged coral cliffs alive with movement. For a while I could not make out what was causing this until a momentary lifting of the rain allowed me to see that the whole cliff edge was a solid mass of great shaggy goats, whose promenadings on the skyline gave the strange illusion that the rock-face itself was on the move. No turtles – all right then, a goat hunt!

The goats of Aldabra, like the Giant Tortoises, present something of a mystery. No one knows who brought them there, or for what reason. At any rate they now constitute one of the plagues of the place. Fortunately, they are all more or less permanently marooned along the south-east segment of the atoll. This area was always barren, its razor-edged rock surface (the '*Champinion*' of the Creole) supporting little but a few screw-pine and a tangled mass of pemphis jungle. Somehow these goats, now completely wild, manage to survive there. Not only survive but have multiplied to such an extent as to overrun the area. Normally they live within the thickets of pemphis, unapproachable and safe, but with the arrival of the wet weather they had sought the open foreshore and rock gulleys away from the dense clouds of mosquitoes that had now hatched out and which made their thorny pastures unbearable.

I was fairly sure that these animals would be both too tough and too rank to eat, but thought that the novelty of a goat hunt might appeal to the crew. Even so, I was totally unprepared for their reaction to my suggestion. With whoops of joy they set to like madmen and within a half-hour had produced the most alarming set of weapons for the chase. Spears, clubs, nets, axes, and even spear-guns were pressed into service. There were slings and lariats and a thing like a bolas. There was even a crossbow! I let all these pass, only insisting that any unfortunate goats be captured alive and examined before being killed for the pot. Then we went ashore.

Arriving underneath the overhanging cliffs we crept along until we were beneath where a group of the animals stood. The smell from the goats was the strongest, rankest, goatiest smell I had ever come across in my life. Even Ti-Royale wrinkled up his nose in disgust and gave out an expressive '*Piee-uuw*'. We climbed stealthily and as we heaved ourselves over the top were met by the most unnerving sight I had seen for a long time. Towering above us, his forefeet right on the cliff edge, was the biggest billy-goat it is possible to imagine. He was almost as big as a donkey, but lean with a lifetime of hard living and carrying an immense coat of shaggy black hair. One horn was missing and the other, gnarled, twisted and menacing, was pointed unmistakably at us in an attitude that clearly meant danger to intruders. We retreated.

So it was every time we sought to get up from the beach. Each time we would be forced back at horn's point by some hoary patriarch who did not care two hoots whether we were the lords of creation or not. Eventually Donald found an unguarded gulley and we managed to gain the terraced cliff-top. Once there the goats were rather taken aback and retreated as we drew near, even the leaders of the troops contenting themselves with vague aggressive gestures in our direction. By now, all thoughts of lassoing or carrying off any of the animals had left us. They were far too big, far bigger than we had even imagined. Aldabra seemed to have that effect on things; tortoises, lizards, turtles, and now goats.

For more than an hour we tried to separate one of the kids from the flock and eventually Donald was successful in grabbing hold of it; but he did not retain his prize for long. At the youngster's first surprised bleat the mother shot forward, closely followed by the nearest patriarch. One look at the angry pair and Donald took the easy way out, dropped the kid and leapt for his life over the cliff into the shallow water below. The rest of us did not have much time to laugh, for having disposed of one tormentor the ram then charged the rest, scattering us like chaff. Ti-Royale stood his ground till the last instant and got knocked over for his pains. So far as I was concerned that was the end of the hunt and clambering back into the dinghies we returned to the *L. Fred*. It was not until half an hour later than I noticed Ti-Royale was not with us. In answer to my questions the others said they 'thought' he had gone off on his own to catch a goat single-handed, his dignity demanding revenge for his tumble.

It was not till nearly four in the afternoon that we saw a weird figure jogging back towards us along these same cliffs, hunchbacked and top-heavy, with long thin legs supporting a monstrous hump from which sprouted great horns. It was as though the Minotaur had come to life. Aldabra now looked like the backcloth to a Teutonic legend

> '. . . with monsters on the skyline, on the rim of it.
> Dwarves with antlers, Falstaffs of the shadows,
> Giants with donkeys' heads . . .'

GOATS AND GROUPERS

But it was only Ti-Royale bent double under the weight of an enormous goat which he carried on his back. Its front legs were hanging down each side of his chest and the bearded chin rested impassively on his own woolly skull. When we met him on the beach he threw down his burden with a laugh at our feet. It was the same goat that had bowled him over that morning. Now it lay on the sand at the Creole boy's feet and his honour was satisfied!

His honour might well have been, but our sensibilities were singularly offended, for between captor and captive there was now no difference, one stank as badly as the other. Poor Ti-Royale! For the next two hours we threw buckets of sea-water over him, we scoured him with sand, we swabbed him with Dettol, but it made little difference. That night he had to sleep in one of the dinghies, rain or no rain, for no one would have him aboard. We released the goat. Only real starvation would have driven one to eat that mound of living carrion.

The following day we saw the end of the bad weather and we were able to start work again. Since leaving Cape Hodoul, although we had on no one day drawn a complete blank, our total haul of shells had been depressing, averaging not more than one hundred pounds per working day. Soon, if we went on like this, we should not only become mentally weary with these slow results but should also pass our physical peak and become stale. But there was nothing else we could do but plod on round the reef. One thing only encouraged me. I was sure that the scattered shells we found along this stretch did not originate from the wreck of the *Glen Lyon* and the indications were that they had 'fanned out' along the reef from some deep-lying colony that we had yet to find.

Accordingly, I concentrated more and more on the deeper levels, leaving the others to search the inner lanes and in this way I missed all chance of picking up the few scattered snail that lay in the shallows. Gradually the total catch of our team fell behind the others'. Teddy, I knew, objected to this, thinking it stupid to waste our time in searching areas of deep and shell-less reef, but was too lazy to voice a determined opinion. Joseph understood what I was up to and continually urged Teddy on, seeing to it that he remained steadfastly in position with me near the edge of the abyss.

BEYOND THE REEFS

The other two teams had asked if they must continue to bring the cumbersome aqualungs with them each time. I told them that it was up to them, but that I would continue to take along ours on every occasion. Albert and Conrad had immediately begun to leave theirs behind as being too heavy, and Ti-Royale and Donald varied as to how the mood took them.

It was two days after our goat hunt that my precautions proved sound. This portion of the reef was no different from that which we had previously traversed, with the outer lip of the 'flat' lying in about fifteen feet of water, from whence it sloped down to the edge of the abyss which lay in about seventy feet of water and two hundred yards further out to sea. On this slope of fairly level and solid 'platin' grew the variegated corals, the tips of each bush alight with the soft colourings of the extended and living polyps. Blues and yellows predominated, contrasting with the clarets and russets of the algae growths. Running down the slope at invertals were shallow troughs, two feet or more across and half as deep. These had been formed by backward-running current streams and eddies off the reef-flat itself.

That morning, I soon knew that the number of shells the other divers were discovering was increasing as we went along. This was carried to me in the form of the sound-waves of their dives transmitted through the water and by the increasing instructions shouted from one to the other. Acting on a hunch, I swam out still further to the edge of the great depths. All along this edge and extending for about thirty feet inwards was a thick belt of large Stag-horn corals. These formed a massive and impenetrable 'hedge' some eight feet high which served as a natural boundary between the outer reef slope and the abyss. I had not come across a similar formation before and dived down as far as I could to see what fishes might live within these tangled branches.

But once down to thirty feet I forgot all about fishes. Along the inside of the hedge, clustered close under its overhanging branches and tucked away in the shade, was a parent colony of Green Snail! They lay thick as autumn mushrooms, palely beautiful, their green and iridescent shells unmarked by coral growths or marred by algae. From where I was I could see the thick brown hedge of antler coral continuing without a single break along the abyssal edge for as far as my eyes could penetrate the blue ocean water. Coming up alongside the dinghy I clambered in, too excited to speak. Joseph was watching me intently, knowing full well that something had happened. I pointed to the box housing the aqualung and nodded. While I was putting on and checking the equipment he got the anchor ready and at a signal from me let it go, to halt the dinghy right on the sixty-foot edge of the submarine plateau. Teddy swam up, eager to find out what was going on. I gave him the shell-net without a word, put the aqualung mouthpiece between my lips, switched on and glided down into the cool depths.

I knew he would be regarding me with amazement, for from where he floated on the surface all the shells were hidden from sight, obscured by the shadows and by the branches of the overhanging Stag-horn coral. There on the bottom, in the liquid silence, I lay and looked along the thick lines of shells that stretched away into the distance. For the first time I had found a 'natural' colony of Green Snail. All the others that had come before had been 'unnatural', in that they had been confined within wrecks or prevented from spreading out by geological and other freaks. But here was the secret; here lay the answer. Here was the reward for all the long hours I had spent in working and scheming. This, in one moment, paid for last spring's failure and the disappointments that had lain between.

Dragging the collecting net with me I swam under the protecting canopy of coral branches and started work. Within two minutes I had a net full, more than twenty shells, and had not moved more than five or six yards. I would have given much to see the look on Teddy's face as he hung up there on the surface fifty feet above me, seeing me come out of the shadows with that bulging net. I saw the image of the dinghy tilt and broaden as Joseph took up the slack on the line and began hauling it in. I was so elated that I rose up with the net, lightly touching it now and then, wishing to savour its bulging rotundity to the full. When I finally dropped back again it was to look up and watch the net rising in a series of jerks, diminishing like a child's balloon caught up and carried aloft by the wind. Even when it was almost at the surface I could still make out the pearly opalescence that shone through the rope strands where several shells had opened their operculums again, giving me a brief glimpse of their shining and nacreous interiors.

For the next two hours I worked my way along the shadowy

hedge. Picking up, sorting, discarding, leaving a few here and there to keep the colony alive in the future. The only sounds that broke the silence were the apparently distant tinkling of the empty net's return to my side, its iron rim ringing against the coral as it dropped. That, and the slow harsh sound of my breathing, echoed and magnified by the flexible lung-bag on my chest. After about an hour I saw that two more duck-shapes had joined the original silhouette on the surface. Soon I heard a 'whoosh', and looking up saw the shiny black body of Ti-Royale arcing down. Swimming right up to me he grabbed a shell I offered him and a grunting noise, which I knew was laughter, came from within his mask, which was flattened against his face by the pressure at that depth. Then he rose again, to disappear in a cloud of silvery bubbles from my world. That would teach them to leave their aqualungs behind! Several times Ti-Royale swam down, but I could see the effort was tiring him and I indicated that he was not to try any more.

Finally, knowing by the reduced hissing in the by-pass valve that my oxygen supply was nearly exhausted, I allowed myself to drift upwards from the dark line of Stag-horn coral that still stretched out ahead of me as far as I could see.

It was only when I surfaced that I realized the full extent of the haul. In one dinghy sat the other five divers and the three older men. The other two boats were piled so full of shells that they formed great conical heaps rising above the gunwales. As a consequence, all three dinghies were so low in the water as to be unable to move without danger of sinking. Someone had planted an upright oar with a shirt attached on top of one of the heaps and in answer to this prearranged signal for assistance the *L. Fred* was even then puffing up along the reef towards us.

As the others pulled me over the side and took the gear off my spent body I did not notice the metal-polish taste in my mouth (the result of two hours spent at fifty feet), nor the dull ache that the mask had left imprinted across my forehead, not yet the cut fingers and grazed knees, the dizziness and partial deafness. No, all I was conscious of was those two beautiful boatloads of shells that wallowed on the placid sea in front of me. I could have gone on looking at them in silence for a long time had I been left alone.

When the shells had been cleaned and sorted the total came

to more than half a ton. Over a thousand shells in one hundred and twenty minutes! More than we had got in all since leaving Cape Hodoul two weeks ago! Everyone on board realized the significance of this, save possibly Alice, who could not see and did not wish to see any further than the huge mound of shell-meat which littered the deck and about which she snuffled happily.

That night, the first for many weeks, all the divers went about the daily aqualung checks without any prompting. It was just as well they did, for I fell asleep over my supper.

That south and south-western side of Aldabra yielded us five tons of shells in exactly five days. Moreover, for those five days we worked only three hours per day, for I made it a rule that each diver must not spend more than one hour and a half on aqualungs each day. Even so, at the end of each period we were tired enough, for no matter what arguments are put forward to the contrary, the human body is just not designed to take long immersions at great pressure, no matter what diving gear is used, and the fatigue rate at sixty feet is many times that of the surface levels.

In those five days we learnt much and adapted our original technique to suit the actual conditions under water. We found that heavy gloves were not enough, for our knees suffered quite as severely under the wear and tear of close contact with the coral. To rectify this we bound on thick pads of cloth but right to the end these gave trouble, working loose and slipping down to our ankles. We learnt to use the lung-bags as buoyancy bags to enable us to life up the full shell-nets and carry them across the bottom. We learned to rely more and more upon the guidance of the diver on the surface for, though he could not see vertically downwards as well as we, his oblique vision was better, since it was not obstructed at sea-bed level by intervening coral bushes and hedges as was ours. Thus the 'man upstairs' would act as a bird dog, pointing out the next areas to search and calling our attention to any shells we had missed.

It was his duty also to see that the aqualung diver never went deeper than sixty feet and for this a tag of red cloth was attached to the shell-net line at that distance from the net itself. When the surface swimmer felt or saw this mark slip past his fingers he warned the diver by tugging on the line and would not pay out any more, thus preventing the man below from working at greater depths. Those few groups of Green Snail that lay beyond the ten-fathom mark I collected personally if I judged the effort worthwhile.

We saw many sharks, but chiefly small ones. Even those few medium-sized specimens that came to see what was going on paid not the slightest attention to the aqualung divers near the bottom, but reserved their interest for the man on the surface. This all led me to conclude what I had already supposed, namely, that a diver is safe from shark attack in daylight as long as he stays down. The danger lies on or near the surface. Like all rules of safety, this is not infallible, but it does fit the vast majority of cases.

Of the other marine inhabitants only one gave us any trouble. The long and sinister barracuda proved harmless enough. They would materialize out of nowhere, hang around speculatively like touts at a race course and then quietly drift away. They were no danger in spite of their crocodile jaws and evil aspect. The trouble lay with our old friend the Grouper. We soon found out that at set intervals the wall of Stag-horn coral grew out in horns towards the reef. Thus the whole coral slope was divided up into large three-sided hollow chambers by this coral 'fencing'. Each of these chambers was perhaps one or two hundred yards long and the side walls of antler coral extended some fifty yards up the slope towards the shore. Each chamber was the domain of a particular Grouper, who ruled his territory like a benevolent but despotic ogre and who usually had his hide-out somewhere in the thickest part of the coral forest lying at the base of the chambers.

None of these fish was very big, being for the most part between fifty and sixty pounds in weight and about four or five feet in length. All were exactly alike. All were fat, bulbous, frog-eyed, ugly as sin and looked like the illustrations of Tweedledum or Tweedledee in *Alice in Wonderland*. But they were hereditary lords of their respective little kingdoms and lords they intended to remain.

It was on the second day that I first met one. I had left the surface and was sinking down with arms outstretched, when I noticed a Grouper gazing up at me from below, hanging vertically on his tail, pectorals fanning lazily to keep him in position. As I slid obliquely downwards so he moved across the coral floor towards where I intended to alight. Ten feet off the sea-bed and

GOATS AND GROUPERS

with the creature now right below me I halted, remembering the 'butting' I had received from similar Rock Cod at Cosmoledo. After a minute's thoughtful pause the Grouper drew off a little, as though to say, "All right, then. You can come on down now. But *mind you*, I won't tolerate any funny business around here!'

Once on the bottom I forgot all about the fish and started looking for shells. Scarcely had I picked up the first and was about to put it in the net when something touched my shoulder. Peering over my shoulder, its gill case touching my mask, was the long and lugubrious face of the Grouper. My hand, in the act of placing the shell in the net, halted and I did not move, waiting for something to happen. After a few seconds a large globular eye, previously directed forwards, rolled sideways until it was looking into mine. Gingerly I opened my gloved fingers, allowing the shell to sink into the net. The body on my shoulder flexed and for an instant I thought the fish was going right into the net after it, but he settled down again. Slowly I picked up another shell. This time I brought it right back holding it just in front of the Grouper's nose. Then I rotated it slowly, revealing the pearly underside. At this the eye swivelled to peer at me again, as if to say, 'I say, this is absolutely fascinating. But what on earth are you doing?' So I moved the shell right up to the fish's loosely shut lips. He looked at me again and then hesitantly opened his mouth, revealing row upon row of sharp white teeth, all pointing backwards towards the gullet. I pushed the shell in a little. Very deliberately the jaws closed and I heard the faint grating of teeth upon the lip of the mollusc. After a brief pause for rumination the jaws opened again allowing me to take the shell away. Once more that eye regarded me quizzically.

After that it was finished. Wherever I went, the Grouper went. If I scratched under a ledge, he thrust his big ugly head under so that I had to push him aside. Twice he tried to get into the net bag. Once I nearly sat on him. If I peered around one coral corner, he would creep round the other. At first he did not like my touching him, but within half an hour I had to push him out of the way continually. If I scratched his side the fish would roll up his eyes and float motionless, finally rolling over on his side like a dog. When I left off he would stay in ecstasy for a few seconds before rousing himself with a shake and moving off a few yards with an embarrassed air.

The first time I went up to the surface he goggled slack-jawed at me as I went, like an ugly child sadly watching a helicopter disappear out of its ken. On the surface Teddy told me the news. I was not the only one who had troubles. Both Ri-Royale and Albert had had the same experience. Moreover, Albert had made the mistake of feeding his fish a piece of shell-meat prised out with his knife and now the Rock Cod would not take 'no' for an answer, nuzzling each shell that the boy picked up and rummaging around the shell-net like an alley cat in a garbage tin.

By the end of the morning we could do anything with those fish. Anything, except make them meet. Each had its territory to which it stuck no matter how hard we cajoled or threatened. The nearest we ever got to an encounter was with one fish on one side of a coral hedge and another on the other. But then there was no reaction and the two fish carefully looked the other way, each pretending the other did not exist.

Those five days passed with a strange, dreamlike tranquility. I can no longer distinguish in my memory one day from another, nor one incident from the next. The whole period flows together to form one overall impression of blue translucent sea and coral-lined quadrangles; in the foreground groups of pink corals round whose tips swarm hosts of brilliant fishes; along one side the coffee-coloured hedge of Stag-horn in whose shade the pale mushroom shapes of the snails cluster thickly; in the middle distance the opposite coral hedge and above and beyond that, merging into the blue haze, the weaving figures of the next pair of divers.

Occasionally, a silver globule would come clean up over the intervening hedge and be drawn up rapidly towards the water-beetle shape of the dinghy that waited patiently above. Following the rising net might be the aqualung diver himself, balancing it lest the valuable cargo spill and tumble again to the bottom. When this happened the diver looked like a water spider, clutching tight to the precious bubble of air held in place by the network of its silken web. Occasionally, too, behind the diver, yet another shape, a small miniature Zeppelin that never dared to rise right to the surface, for these attendant Rock Cods' curiosity would only draw them a certain distance out of the depths and away from the coral domains.

Each night the hold space in our schooner grew less and eventually someone coined a phrase, '*Aldabra monter, L. Fred*

GOATS AND GROUPERS

descendre!' for as our load increased so the ship settled deeper in the water and the low-lying cliffs of the island seemed to grow correspondingly higher.

By the sixth day, our cargo had grown so alarmingly that we spent the whole morning rearranging the sacks of shells, the drums of fuel and barrels of water in order to adjust the trim of the ship. It was just as well we did, for that afternoon brought a long, heavy swell from the south-east and, foreseeing bad weather, we up-anchored and motored off around the south-western corner of the island to gain the comparative shelter of the other side. Here we lay for four days while the gale blew. From the security of this anchorage we could see a line of heavy breakers extending way out to sea from the promontory, on the other side of which we had so recently dived in lake-calm stillness. Now all that region was a mass of foam, of discoloured water and vicious undertow. But sixty feet down the shells lay safe and snug, cushioned by the depth of water against these surface disturbances.

With the excitement of finding these natural colonies all our other activities had stopped. Consequently we now had neither turtle meat nor fresh fish. The tinned meat I was keeping for an emergency, so once more we returned to a salt-fish and rice diet, fortified by vitamin tablets, but these did not make it any more attractive. Once again we were constantly soaked by driving rain squalls and a plague of cockroaches swept the vessel. These horrible insects found sanctuary during the day within the convolutions of the shells sewn up in the gunny-sacks and, short of opening all the sacks again, there was little we could do about it. They ate the rice, clustered around the sugar, and even began to nibble the skin off the toes of some of us at night while we slept.

Christmas Eve came and went, no different from any other day except for a glimpse of an aircraft that appeared momentarily through a rift in the clouds at dusk. It was the first I had seen for almost a year and its familiar shape brought back a heavy feeling of nostalgia. Christmas Day, however, broke fine and clear and the *L. Fred* blossomed like a weird Christmas tree, the rigging, booms and masts covered with strange decorations; mattresses, blankets, sacks of provisions, and motley collections of tattered clothing, all drying in the welcome sunshine. A foolhardy turtle surfaced near us and that was Christmas lunch taken care of. I dug out the two dozen bottles of beer I had hidden away and decided we could spare a bottle of brandy from the medicine chest as well.

After lunch we all stretched ourselves out under makeshift deck awnings and went to sleep. Before very long I was disturbed by a strange and persistent sound. Puzzled, I went to find out what it was. In a corner of the hold, his head covered with a sack, crouched Ravile, sobbing bitterly. At his side sat old Ton Pierre, making soothing and clucking noises while he patted the other man's shoulder. Mystified, I asked Ravile what was wrong. The sacking was raised and a tearful and smirched face peered out at me.

Now Ravile was a man of thirty-four or five, a big, powerful fellow with an air of responsibility and of maturity. Yet the face I saw and the voice I heard was of a small schoolboy and into his cry went all the anguish of a child's heart. '*Aieeeeee, aieeeee!*' he bawled, 'I want to go hoooome.' And so saying he replaced the sack and sank back against the bulkhead, his shoulders heaving inconsolably. Ton Pierre explained what was the trouble. Ravile, though a fisherman born and bred, had never spent more than ten days away from his family in all his life. After lunch he and Ton Pierre had started talking about their families on Praslin Island and what they would be doing seeing it was Christmas, and who would visit whom and what about the dancing and the feasting, the drinking and the new clothes, the upshot being that Ravile had been smitten with an acute attack of home-sickness, made the more violent since he had never experienced such a thing before.

Luckily, none of the others was similarly affected. The men were mainly too old and had all spent years away from their families, while the boys were too young and excited with the adventure to care about anything else. True, Conrad looked a bit miserable but soon perked up when I gave him a packet of cigarettes, as I had now allowed any of the divers to smoke since leaving Mahé.

Boxing Day found us back working on the southern side of the island amongst the familiar Stag-horn coral and the ever-attentive Groupers. But that was the last day. Not that we had collected all the shells, but simply that the *L. Fred* would hold

GOATS AND GROUPERS

no more and now sat the water like a lead-filled duck, barely afloat.

Our rendezvous with Captain Calais and the *Argo* was only a few days off and we were all badly in need of a rest. This last effort had tired us out more than we had realized and the damp and discomfort of the previous week had not helped. Now every evening all the divers had fresh coral cuts to dress and our earlier abrasions were continually breaking open and festering. These coral sores are an occupational malady of the shell-diver and the only real cure is to stay out of the water until every pustule had disappeared.

On the day scheduled for our meeting there was no sign of the *Argo*. However, I knew the difficulties involved in keeping exactly to a prearranged timetable, particularly over such a long ocean crossing and was not over-worried. On the fourth day, however, I could no longer ignore the possibility that the *Argo* had broken down somewhere, and I began to think of alternative plans. Luckily, although the whole crew had been awaiting the arrival of the other ship with great eagerness, their overall tiredness was so great that they did not fret over the continued delay, but passed the time between meals by dozing fitfully wherever they could find some shade. This left me free from interruptions and able to concentrate upon the problem of what to do if the *Argo* did not turn up.

Thanks to the rain our water supply presented no difficulties, but we were running short of provisions. Under other circumstances I would have set course back to Mahé, but if I did that and the *Argo* arrived afterwards Captain Calais might well spend a month or two searching for us throughout the islands, thinking we might have got into difficulties and had beached the boat. Even this I would have risked had we not been so heavily laden. As it was, it was impossible to risk such a long passage in this condition. The question was, what could we do with our overload of shells? I could hardly ask the islands' manager to guard them for us until we returned, since the lessee so strongly objected to our activities around Aldabra. Nor could I risk landing them on some deserted beach and making a cache somewhere in the scrub; not that the trespass worried me, but that it was quite likely we might be seen and our horde of shells would then be fair game once we had left. I would not risk losing five tons in that fashion!

Eventually I decided to give the *Argo* a full week and if Calais had not turned up by then, to make preparations for our return by jettisoning as much gear as we could afford and then making a submarine storage depot of our excess sacks of shells. Even this was not safe, for a strong gale in our absence might easily scatter and destroy our horde, either by pounding them on the reef if left in too shallow a place, or by dragging them back into the abyss if too deep.

The seventh and last day dawned and we were just hoisting sail when into our little anchorage sailed the other schooner! From far off I could see the tubby figure of Calais standing on the cabin roof, his favourite look-out point. As the other ship drew near I could see too that he was clothed in his favourite costume: peaked cap, white cotton singlet and white cotton underpants, which gave him the appearance of a chubby baby in rompers.

As the *Argo* let go her anchor close alongside us, all Calais could do was to point speechless at the *L. Fred*'s water-line, for in the slight swell each roll caused our decks to run awash, so low were we in the water. He knew very well what that meant! Oddly enough his first words were not about the shells at all but as to whether we were all all right. When I replied that everyone was fit and there had been no accidents or illnesses, he chuckled. Pressed as to the reason for his enquiry, Calais told me that the mother of one of the divers, feeling worried about her son, had gone to a renowned sorceress in Mahé, who was said to have second-sight, and had asked for news. This oracle, on payment of a large fee, had pronounced that while her son was still alive, three of us were already dead! One had been drowned and two taken by sharks. I myself was one of the victims. Moreover, the prophetess had divulged that a further two of us would die and one other be maimed for life before the *L. Fred* returned. The news of this had already spread throughout the island, to the usual accompaniment of 'I-told-you-so'.

While the two crews were busy preparing the ships for the transfer of our cargo to the more capacious hold of the *Argo*, I checked on the mail the Captain had brought. Chief item in this was that Green Snail shell now stood at £450 per ton. With over a ton already in Mahé, and more than eight stowed below in the *L. Fred*, the expedition looked like being highly successful. And

GOATS AND GROUPERS

there were many more shells as yet untouched. The whole idea of shell-diving in the Seychelles that for so long had assumed a will-o'-the-wisp nature seemed to have changed in an instant into a highly profitable enterprise, making all the disappointments and failures of the past year insignificant.

But the *Argo* had brought something else with her as well. Greed! Up to that moment our harvest, though obvious, had seemed somehow a little remote, a little unreal. Previously, it was as though we, alone on the *L. Fred*, were independent of time and the rest of the world. Consequently, the mounting store of shells did not resolve itself in our minds into its actual monetary value. Now, with the arrival of the bigger schooner and her envious crew, all that was changed. Instead of thinking, 'Today we have reached our eighth ton of Green Snail,' as we used to, we now thought, 'Eight tons, of which my share is a ninth [or a twelfth, or whatever it was]. That makes so many rupees . . .' Or in my own particular case, 'Yes, that makes expenses such-and-such, leaving a net profit of so-and-so . . .'

In a word, we had changed from men who seemed to be doing the thing for the sake of achievement, to men who reckoned the gain for work in hard cash. From that day forward we were different. The old happy-go-lucky atmosphere gradually died out, giving way to a rapacity, a hardness, a greed that was reflected throughout our work. For now we had shell-fever!

TEN

Assumption

With the coming of the *Argo* our material position changed overnight, for from this moment on she was on continuous charter to us and accompanied us everywhere as a mother-ship. This meant we had decent places to sleep, no more bug-ridden clothing, hot food and other people to talk to.

Le Gros Soula, in spite of his apparent cantankerousness, produced marvels for us on his galley stove: turtle done in new and strange ways, fish with good sauces, fresh bread and puddings; for on the strength of the initial load of shells I had ordered as many provisions and extras as I could think up, knowing how we should need them by the time the *Argo* next saw us. As a result of that earlier decision we now lived well.

Captain Calais, in particular, thrived. A great lover of turtle meat he would eat three pounds of steak at a sitting and then confess sadly that he was no longer capable of managing the six he could swallow as a young man. Day by day he grew rounder, redder and more like an advertisement for a well-known baby food. He told me that in his youth he had suffered from the 'turtle sickness', as did many Seychellois who came to work on the outlying islands. When I asked him what that was he said it was difficult to explain, except that when one began to eat turtle meat in quantity one did not care for any other food. Just turtle, the meat, the green fat, the gravy and perhaps a little rice. Nothing else. Morning, noon and night, only turtle. Then eventually, one's hair fell out and one's skin erupted and one became very sick. Many had died from it in the past.

All at once I realized to what he was alluding. Scurvy – the old scourge of the sailing ships when long voyages and no refrigeration made it impossible to preserve fresh fruit or vegetables. Scurvy, essentially a lack of Vitamin C – but here in the Seychelles where there was any amount of that vitamin in the fresh coconuts, the pawpaws and the pumpkin, the people still fell victim to it and blamed it on the harmless turtle!

Although we had more comfort and better food and might have been expected to be more cheerful and exuberant, the reverse was the case. The work went on and each day our total of shells mounted. Each day we had more reason to be elated and yet we were not. Perhaps it was simply because by now words were unnecessary, we knew the work too well, we drove ourselves too hard and so the shouted commands and exclamations that had accompanied our diving previously were now superfluous. But our silence was more deep-rooted than that. There was a hardness about us now, a selfishness that had settled on us with the coming of the *Argo*. The bad characteristics of each person became more evident and the good seemed strangely absent.

Amongst the divers Albert started poaching on his neighbours' preserves and helping himself to the other team's underwater 'stockpiles'. Donald took to hiding any fresh discoveries from the rest, passing over good areas deliberately, then sneaking off back again and working quietly on his own later, when the others were busy elsewhere. Sadi lost his temper frequently, claiming his two charges were not working fast enough. Ravile became morose and Wyn more foolish.

In spite of the improved diet all the divers continued to lose weight. Previously, if a small shark or barracuda appeared on the scene we paid it scant attention. Now we deliberately harried any such intruder, gaining spiteful satisfaction in making it flee. At the least incident frayed tempers would explode into open fury.

One place where we moored every evening for a week was inhabited by a very large Hammerhead shark. Early morning would see this particular giant scull lazily past our schooners, right on the surface, coming away from its nocturnal reef wanderings. Each evening would see it rolling in again, head wobbling obscenely from side to side as it searched for prey. In consequence of these regular appearances I was particularly adamant that no one should bathe from either of our ships when at anchor and that we knocked off diving sharply at three-thirty p.m.

On account of the size of the Hammerhead neither of these rules were difficult to enforce until one evening. We had finished work and were busy transferring some sacks of cleaned and graded shells from the *L. Fred* to the *Argo*. Somehow or other during the proceedings one bag was mishandled and fell into the sea, where it spun gently downwards out of sight into the water that was already growing dark with the approaching dusk. Nerves, now permanently on edge, found temporary respite in invective, each of the several people involved accusing each other of carelessness. It was some minutes before all the shouting died away. Now although a full sack represented about a twentieth part of a ton and therefore a relatively large amount of money, with the number that were already stowed away in the hold I was not particularly worried and would have let the matter rest there. It was nobody's fault. But a few minutes later, hearing some movement and whispering in the fo'c'sle, I found the divers drawing lots to see who should go over the side and try to fasten a line on to the missing sack. All of them were dead scared of the Hammerhead and each was only taking part in the draw thinking it was an eight-to-one chance against his being the unfortunate loser. I broke up this little meeting, telling them all not to be such fools and to forget about the lost shells.

They agreed, but sullenly, and I realized it was quite likely that one or other would later be driven to undertake the venture, even by night if necessary. They were scared, but they were greedy for shells. Unfortunately that left me no alternative but to go and get the wretched sack myself. Previously I had not been particularly worried about Hammerheads. For their size they have a relatively small mouth as compared with other sharks, and are none too manoeuvrable in the water. Though in most other areas they are considered fairly harmless, here in the Seychelles, however, they had a bad reputation and I knew from previous experience that with sharks the behaviour of identical species may differ widely from locality to locality and that the 'safeness' of any particular type can never be guaranteed. I still remembered all too vividly the one that had attacked the propeller of my outboard motor in Cosmoledo lagoon a few weeks back.

All these things I recalled while changing into my still wet gear and by the time I went over the side I had succeeded in scaring myself thoroughly. Once in the water my one idea was to gain some depth as quickly as possible and I scrambled head first down the anchor chain in a mad rush to some thirty feet, where I paused to get breath. Once there I felt secure. If the Hammer-

ASSUMPTION

head did pass now I should be below it and could always seek the safety of the coral sea-bed if necessary. Having decided that, I was freer to enjoy the quiescent approach of submarine twilight on the great reef. Here there was only one colour. Pale grey-blue, like wood smoke amongst trees, it permeated the whole scene and robbed the corals of their daylight shades. The place was still and hushed, without any of the customary bustle of the reef. Nearer the coral I could see a few inquisitive snouts poking out of crevices and from beneath overhangs, but their owners displayed none of their daytime boldness.

It took several minutes to find the missing sack, for instinctively I was looking for an object with an above-water colouring of sandy brown and in so doing almost overlooked the irregular shape clad in the universal blue of the sea's twilight. To make sure I did not lose it again and also because its surface was kinder to my seat that the surrounding corals I used it as a perch from which to wait for nightfall. Soon the beetle shape of the *Argo* above my head lost its clarity and it became just a darker patch in the shadowy heavens. A small turtle flapped past anxiously, like a late crow flying low and fast towards a distant nesting place. Soon I could see no further than six or seven yards and everything within that radius was a deep and luminous madonna blue. I might have sat like that for hours had not a sudden jerk on the lifeline brought me back to reality. Hurriedly I slung a noose around the bag and then pulled on the rope twice, telling those on the surface that they could haul away. Only when the bundle was jerked upwards out of sight did I feel insecure again and swam up quickly after it, mounting in a cloud of loquacious bubbles that burst from lungs upon which the pressure was fast diminishing with each fathom gained.

Only when I was on board the *Argo* again, chill in the evening breeze, did I remember the Hammerhead.

The weeks that followed found us at work along one part or other of the reef. But now that coast had lost its attraction and what had been exciting and glamorous passed by unheeded. No longer was each day memorable save as another pencilled mark on the chart, another two-mile stretch finished.

We must have presented a ludicrous spectacle at that period.

BEYOND THE REEFS

Our original bathing costumes had long since worn out, cut to pieces on sharp corals and rotted by the salt air. Consequently we wore what garments we could find – old khaki shorts, cotton singlets and tattered headgear. One day I caught sight of my reflection in the glassy sea and was compelled to burst out laughing. On my feet were odd ankle socks, to prevent swim-fins from chafing. Around my knees two puttee lengths, as padding against the corals. From there up I was naked except for the crowning item. About my chest was the top half of a once smart black Bikini whose label proclaimed it to have come from the Eden Roc Sports Shop. This, once promenaded and admired on the plage at Cannes, now served to protect my salt-sore skin from the irritating friction of the aqualung! Others were equally oddly clad. Conrad wore only a beret and socks and Albert's sole garment was an old pullover. Donald sported a G-string made out of sail canvas and shark line. The crew were hardly any better off, having surrendered most of their garments to us.

The incidents that now stood out were those that occurred above the surface or which concerned matters other than shell-diving.

Aldabra, which had already proved so interesting, continued to surprise us with many strange phenomena. Off one place along the northern coast we came across a submarine freshwater spring with so powerful a freshet as to make the sea-water drinkable over a wide area.

This is all the more remarkable since the settlement on the island relies entirely upon cachements of rainwater for its supply, and it is largely this perpetual semi-drought that is responsible for the island's barrenness. Yet here was all the fresh water imaginable, yet beyond the reach of those who had possessed Aldabra in the past. As far as I could find out we were the first to discover this underwater spring.

Further along the same northern side of the island we came to the main entrance of the huge lagoon that lies within the raised land rim. This lagoon is everywhere shallow and for the most part dries out at low tide. With the rise and fall of the sea the major portion of the lagoon water must enter or leave through this narrow channel, called Grande Passe. As a result great currents are set up in its vicinity and we had been warned of the possibility of our being sucked into this lagoon efflux should we

ASSUMPTION

try to cross at the channel mouth itself. Consequently the first time we approached it I put out to sea for half a mile. An ugly streak of brown water, caused by the powerful undertow stirring up the sea-bed, indicated exactly where the current-stream lay.

As we drew near this took on a sinister oily appearance, contrasting with the wave-dappled blue waters that elsewhere rimmed the island. The sea within the tide race had a heavy look, with strange humpings-up and slow coiling eddies breaking the surface, and marking it with thick coffee-coloured scum. However, at that distance out from the channel I felt that we would have no difficulty in crossing to the other side and was quite unprepared for what happened. As soon as the *L. Fred* entered the current she shuddered right throughout her hull as though I had run her on to a sandbank. Then, slowly but deliberately, her bows turned inshore. I put on as much rudder as was possible but to no avail. The schooner carried on in a gentle arc till she had completed a semi-circle and her prow broke out into the blue waters again, whereupon at once she steadied and answered naturally to the helm.

Three times I tried to get her across that stretch of water and three times she deliberately refused, as a horse might refuse a fence. Each time we penetrated no more than twenty yards into the quarter-mile stretch of brown and turgid water. Each time we were waltzed inexorably around and pushed right out again the way we had come! It was not till an hour and a half later, during the slack-water period, that we were able to traverse to the reef on the other side of the channel. Here we found a moderate quantity of shells on the steep side-walls of the channel which, under the action of the tremendous current over the years, had been scoured out, forming a deep submarine canyon. Soon, however, we were in difficulties, for in the channel itself there was no slack water and each time we allowed ourselves to drift away from these side walls we would be sucked into the stream and carried many yards further into the pass before we could regain the comparatively calm waters near the edge.

Fish, too, were having the same difficulty. The disturbed water here formed a rich feeding ground and along its edges and lining the banks hung hundreds of hungry fish of all sizes and varieties. Sharks, Snapper, Grouper, Garanx, Barracuda and Wahoo – all eager to snatch up any tit-bit, alive or dead, that might whirl past. But even they were forced to make quick dashes into the maelstrom, gulping their prey and darting back as quickly as they could.

With all this whirling around the diving teams had become mixed up and presently I found myself alongside Ti-Royale, passing our shells to Andrea. Now Aldabra is noted for its unique specimens of Hawksbill Turtle, known as the 'blonde' turtle, owing to its honey-coloured carapace from which the very finest tortoiseshell is obtained. Suddenly a magnificent Blonde Hawksbill appeared, joy-riding on the current into the lagoon, where it presumably intended to feed. In a flash Ti-Royale flung himself into the current after it. Realizing that he must not be left alone I plunged after him, first beckoning to Andrea to follow us in the dinghy. But in our haste, both of us failed to notice that the Hawksbill was already being hunted. In a moment Ti-Royale, I and a large shark were all in hot pursuit of the poor turtle, while Andrea's dinghy danced attendance in our wake.

Ti-Royale managed to seize the unsuspecting reptile's hind flipper which swung it sharply round across the current. The shark and I both shot past and, lacking the turtle's flat saucer-shape, had difficulty in turning back. On the surface, Andrea tried desperately to stop the mad rush of his little boat with short back strokes of his oars. The shark and I swam hard upstream and though we closed the gap that separated us from the others we were both, in actual fact, moving steadily backwards. The shark, puzzled by all these girations and still cautious, was not venturing too near, nor using the major portion of its strength, which was why I was able to keep pace with it. Myself it completely ignored, as merely another predatory out after the same prey.

So Ti-Royale and the turtle whirled around in a flurry of foam, the boy clinging desperately to that hind flipper, the shark and I steadily closing in upon the pair, while Andrea did his best to steady and hold the boat alongside us. And all the time our strange quintet was held fast in the current that every second took us many yards further down the pass into the lagoon.

Eventually Andrea was in a position to help Ti-Royale with the struggling Hawksbill. Leaning over the side of the dinghy he tried to slip a noose over its fore flippers. In this he partially succeeded, but with catastrophic results. He managed to pinion

ASSUMPTION

one flipper, but it proved to be the one on the same side as Ti-Royale's. The turtle's remaining two limbs now thrashed madly, both on the same side, causing it to spin like a top in the water. This pulled Andrea off balance and he fell in on top of the animal which promptly sank under his weight!

In his surprise Ti-Royale let go his hold and the turtle continued on downwards, dragging the unfortunate bos'n with him by the short length of rope on which he had maintained his hold throughout. Now Andrea could not swim, which was perhaps why he clung so desperately to the line. Moreover, he was fast disappearing towards the bottom.

Ti-Royale dived after him and took hold of his ankle, which slowed down the turtle, and as the boy passed beneath me I went on down and by sliding my fingers under the 'lip' of the turtle's shell, below its tail, was able to push down upon the creature's rear end. This had the effect of tilting its head upwards and since a turtle always follows its nose, up we all went! Once on the surface, Andrea let go his hold on the rope and away went the Hawksbill. Meanwhile the shark's departure at some time during the proceedings had passed unnoticed.

Luckily the same current that had been the cause of all the trouble in the first place now brought our dinghy drifting downstream on to us and we were able to push Andrea into it without too much difficulty. After that Ti-Royale and I took the boat back to the ship, as Andrea was in no condition to do any more work that day.

At another point on the northern coast of Aldabra we found several small flocks of flamingoes, whose classic colouring and exotic shape seemed completely out of place in this sea-girt island in the middle of the Indian Ocean. Captain Callais, who unlike most Creoles was both observant and genuinely interested in natural history, told me how he had discovered accidentally, as a boy, how to catch these great birds. One day, seeing a small group of flamingoes in a clearing amongst the pemphis he had walked towards them, approaching from down-wind and doing so slowly and quietly but in full view. As he drew near, the flamingoes moved up the clearing away from him, showing no great fear of this animal that showed so little stealth. Before long they had unwittingly herded themselves into the top corner of the open space, leaving no room for the take-off 'run' their great bulk required in order to clear the tops of the tangled wall of undergrowth. Calais now walked quickly up, whereupon the birds lost their heads and scattered, the wiser ones throwing dignity to the winds and scrambling madly out of his way and the more foolish trying desperately to take off in the insufficient space they had left to themselves. Those that tried this floundered straight into the pemphis branches from where Calais had to rescue them and take them back into the middle of the clearing before releasing them.

He had tried this experiment several times and it had always worked but he had never shown it to any of the labourers there, knowing very well that if he did so within a month not a single flamingo would remain.

While the flamingoes of Aldabra are resident, other birds use the island as a temporary resting place on their migratory routes. Many of those that we saw came from Madagascar and amongst them were ducks, waders and other wild-fowl, while in their wake followed the Saker and more occasionally the Peregrine falcons and Eagle owls. Several times the lonely silhouette of a huge bird, a Wandering Albatross, crossed high over the island. Seemingly oblivious of the wind it would slant down and rise up, turn and tack without so much as a single wing beat, and continue thus till it was out of sight.

Here at Aldabra we saw immense schools of porpoises, numbering several thousand or more. Usually they would appear early in the morning, the splashes they caused looking like distant breakers until they were close enough to distinguish their individual hump-backed shapes as they broke the surface. When these porpoises were following a run of small caranx or bonito they would travel as a line of fantastic cavalry, breaking clean out of the surface in their haste, snorting and puffing. Sometimes, presumably having already eaten their fill, they would hunt for fun, throwing the fish they caught up into the air, catching them again and letting them go, rolling and wallowing in their sport. They took no notice of us and once we were engulfed in such a stream when diving. The sea then became a jumble of sleek fat bodies that appeared, passed us and disappeared again in smooth arcs of movement. Below the surface the noise was extraordinary. Gruntings, squeakings, crashes and bangs reverberated through the water. It took half an hour for the school to pass, by which

ASSUMPTION

time we were dazed by the continual cascade of ebony bodies sliding past us through the clear water.

Our entertainment at that time was provided mainly by Captain Calais and his unique crew rather than through the radio, for the most grotesque incidents were continually occurring on board the *Argo*. One evening, having drawn up alongside in the *L. Fred* at the end of the day's work, I shouted across to Calais asking where he would like to anchor for the night. To this he replied emphatically and without hesitation, 'Over there, just off that spur on the reef there.' At this pronouncement a bellow of raucous laughter came from the galley and a moment later the Gross Soula appeared, exhibiting a freely sweating face and brandishing a frying-pan, his permanent symbol of office.

'You hear that, Coletto,' the cook bellowed at the bos'n who was preparing the anchor winch. 'You hear that! That bloody fool wants us to anchor our boat over there. Sweet mother of God! Did you ever hear the like?'

From my position up in the bows I could just make out Coletto's muttered reply, 'Just like him! In that case he can do it his-bloody-self. You don't catch me letting go forty fathoms of chain only to pick it all up again when the tide swings!'

'That's right,' said Soula, 'and you don't catch me getting up in the middle of the night to heat up some turtle meat for our valiant captain when he cannot sleep because of the rolling. Oh no, not me!'

To all this Calais paid not the slightest attention, merely waiting for the innate rumblings to die away like distant thunder. When all was quiet he turned to his two lieutenants, spread wide his arms in a gesture of appeal, and said, 'Come, children. Now, let us have a little bit of advice from you on this pressing matter.'

'Now the bloody fool asks us!' screamed Soula to Coletto. And then turning to Calais, 'I don't know, Captain Calais, I don't know. I am only an ignorant cook, not like your esteemed self. But if you anchor over there you can bloody well cook your own meals for the rest of the trip. How would you like that!' and he spat deliberately on the deck.

'Enough, enough. Tut, tut. Some advice please, my friends, my old shipmates. *Please.*'

'Well,' said Soula, somewhat mollified and in a quieter voice. 'Now you are actually *asking* us, how about over there?' He pointed in the opposite direction, towards a little sandy bay. 'You remember in '32, Coletto, how we sat tight there in the old *Ziphora* for a whole week? No rolling, no dragging.'

'That's right,' said the squat bo'sun, 'and the fishing's good there too and we'll be sure to get a turtle there tonight with this moon and that should please old fat-guts!'

'That's better, my children,' broke in Calais. 'Now we are getting somewhere.'

Then turning to me he announced calmly and in all seriousness, 'Oh, Mr Travis, *I* have decided to anchor up there, in that little bay, after all!'

But there came an end to it and one morning I realized that there was nothing further to keep us at Aldabra. The shells were not exhausted, but we were. Mentally as much as physically.

Still obsessed with the idea of filling both vessels to their very limits I decided to sweep the other two islands that lay in the vicinity, hoping that the change of locality might act as a tonic to our jaded enthusiasm. So we set course southwards again, but only for half a day's sailing, since Assumption Island lay a bare twenty-five miles away, just over the horizon.

Although so close, Assumption has nothing in common with Aldabra. No atoll this, but a true island. No jagged rock surface here but extensive sand-dunes. The earth is not poor and acrid, but rich with guano. In previous times Assumption earned its various owners large fortunes from these deposits, but nowadays a Government embargo rests upon the remaining stocks as a precaution against the island turned into a barren dust heap, as has happened with other similar islands. Consequently, though there are still labour lines, storage sheds and rain cachements for six hundred people or more on this three-mile long stretch of land, it is run nowadays by a manager and a scant twenty labourers on a 'care and maintenance' basis.

In its heyday the sandy beaches of Assumption had provided wonderful laying grounds for Green Turtle too, and in the past as many as four hundred were 'turned' in one night on their egg-laying pilgrimages. Now the turtles have practically vanished,

ASSUMPTION

fewer than thirty a month being seen off its shores during the season. The Seychelles Government has placed an embargo upon the killing of these reptiles here also, but in all probability this measure has been taken far too late ever to result in a reintroduction of the turtle to Assumption in any numbers.

It was here that Cousteau filmed much of 'The Silent World'; for in his many voyages throughout the Indian and Atlantic Oceans, the Mediterranean and the Red Seas he was unable to find any place having the same clarity of water and such extensive and colourful reef-life as that which he found at Assumption. It represents one of the finest submarine sites in the world, and yet we drew no benefit from it.

For us, Assumption was just another reef along which to search for Green Snail shells. The coral, the fish, colour and shade, we saw not, nor remembered. For us, Assumption was the island where the whole expedition nearly came to grief.

Towards the end of our work there the weather began to deteriorate with massive banks of heavy clouds lining the horizon to the east and fitful gusts of wind that blew from every quarter of the compass. At night lightning flickered incessantly in the distance and the growling of thunder could be heard above the noise of the breakers.

It was obvious that a major disturbance was building up, for now was the cyclone season, and the sensible thing would have been to sail right out of the area while we still had time. But each day our departure was delayed on the pretext of 'Just five more sacks of shells!' and when the five had been collected then the target figure was raised to eight, and then ten – until finally it was too late.

Conditions that last morning were bad but it was still possible to work along the more sheltered portions of Assumption's reef. True, the sky was now wholly covered by low, leaden clouds and a vicious short sea was getting up. Under the circumstances I set off with only two of the dinghies, leaving the third team to help the crews of the two schooners in preparing their ships for sea, in case we might be forced out of our anchorage later.

Once at work on the reef, cut off from surface conditions by the eight fathoms of water above our heads, we soon forgot our early morning misgivings and it was not until I surfaced for the mid-morning break that the full seriousness of our position struck home. By now the clouds had lowered until their ragged undersides almost touched the sea, heightening vividly the impression of their movement. The wind moaned steadily from the southwest, toppling the wave crests and streaking the grey waters with invisible fingers. In the two dinghies Joseph and Andrea had stowed away all the loose gear and had roped their boats together for additional security. The weather was rapidly worsening and it was imperative that we returned to the schooners as quickly as possible.

No sooner had we started the outboards and had got under way than a wave rose up behind our sterns, hung poised for a brief moment and then broke right on top of both the motors. In a second the two dinghies were half full of water and the engines spluttered to a stop, carburettors flooded and ignition systems shorted out. From then on it was a question of hard rowing. In this we were spurred on by the thought of the difficulties that would attend the hoisting of the two dinghies on board the larger vessels should the wind increase still further, but it was not until we were able to break out around the promontory beyond which lay the schooners that our predicament became apparent.

There we met with the full force of the gale and the sea, already heavy for such small boats as ours, now became wellnigh impossible. Under the relentless gusting of the wind, the waves here drove in against the shore in line upon line of huge rollers, whose crests were barred with foam which the shrieking air clawed off the surface, so that flying spume and vicious spats of rain intermingled to reduce the visibility to a scant few yards. As each breaker spent itself against the island it set up a backwash and the resultant wave ran out away from the land. Where each of these met with the next incoming surge the sea heaped up and the two conflicting crests, now interlocked, rose high into the air to add their ruin to the turmoil of the warring sea.

Luckily, we lay to seaward of this area, else we must have foundered. As it was, the driving wind threatened to sweep us into the surf – but it was not this that caused me the greatest concern. It was something far more vital. Neither the *L. Fred* nor the *Argo* were anywhere to be seen. Unable to withstand the storm that threatened to drive them up on to the reef each must

ASSUMPTION

have up anchored and sought the comparative safety of the open sea. The question was now, what could we do?

A landing on the island was impossible, for we would never have been able to live through the breakers that swept the surrounding reef. I was sure that one or other of the ships would be somewhere out there beyond the wall of enveloping rain to seaward and, with any brief lifting of the visibility, would sweep in to retrieve us if it were humanly possible. Our only hope was to try to hang on then in this bay that was now facing the direct force of the gale.

Accordingly I slung over the bows two shell-nets, full of shells, and by paying out line allowed us to stream back before the wind. This rough sea-anchor served to bring us head on to the waves and to a great extent to arrest our inshore drift. In this fashion and by taking short spells at the oars in turn, we were able to keep our position more or less in the centre of the little bay.

We stayed thus for half an hour while the wind tugged furiously at us and each successive wave threatened to swamp us. Then, quite unexpectedly, out through the greyness on our left wallowed the *L. Fred*. It was no use shouting for the tumult of the gale drowned all other noise. Nor would our waving attract attention on a sea so wind-streaked and broken as this – yet we did both, more by way of showing relief than in the hope that it would help the others to locate us. For a brief moment we thought we might be passed by and then, as an intervening wave crest rolled on, we saw that the little schooner had altered course and that her bows were now pointing directly at us.

Within two minutes they were alongside, a tow rope had been passed and the three other divers had scrambled up on to the *L. Fred*, leaving Andrea to hold the dinghies steady by means of a steering oar as we were towed along, and Joseph and me to bail out the water that now slopped in over the sides with each sudden jerk of the tow rope. In this fashion we managed to pull round the eastern side of the island, where we found sufficient shelter to hoist the two dinghies on board. While we were doing this the *Argo* motored up and lay nearby until we had completed our preparations. Then, of one accord, we put out to sea and set course northwards, running with shortened canvas before the storm.

Towards dusk, the weather showing no signs of improving and anxious not to get separated during the hours of darkness, we decided to rig a connecting line between the two ships, so that we might keep station the more easily. As the *Argo* and the *L. Fred* manoeuvred to effect this I became more and more worried. In the huge seas that now ran, each successive wave lifted high first one ship and then the other, so that at one moment we on the *L. Fred* were looking down upon the cabin roof of the *Argo* and the next moment our sky was blocked out by the hull of the larger schooner, which now towered over us so that we were able to see more of the copper sheathing that lay below her water-line than of the white paint above water.

With the wind at near-cyclone force it was impossible to throw a weighted line from one ship to the other until we were right alongside each other. At this point I turned away. There was nothing I could do to help and it made me ill to watch! Ravile on the *L. Fred* and Calais on the *Argo* had been used to sailing schooners all their lives. This was their show, not mine. All I knew was that an error of judgment now might easily result in one or other of the ships being badly damaged and our precious shells endangered.

After long minutes of jockeying for position the line was successfully passed and made secure. Then, as the *Argo* started to forge ahead and the *L. Fred* dropped astern, a near catastrophe took place. Ravile, in order to keep the bows of his ship clear of the *Argo*, had been compelled to exert all his strength on the wheel. All of a sudden there was a snapping noise and he fell sprawling across the deck. One of the wooden hand-studs had snapped off flush with the rim. The wheel, released from his hold, spun haphazardly for a few seconds before Joseph, who was the nearest and the first to assess the danger, hurled himself skidding across the sloping deck, seized it and spun it as hard as he could in the opposite direction.

But he was almost too late! The bowsprit of the *L. Fred* swung inwards, dipped as one wave passed under her bows and then came up under the *Argo*'s port quarter, neatly skewering that vessel's flying bridge. For an instant the two ships lay locked together, then, as the wave passed on under the *Argo* she slid down into the trough previously occupied by the *L. Fred*. There was a groaning of wood tortured beyond its limits and audible

ASSUMPTION

above the noise of the storm. This was followed by several almost simultaneous reports, like giant pistol shots; a portion of the *Argo*'s bridgework splintered into matchwood and our bowsprit broke clear, trailing pieces of cordage and adorned with one of the other ship's lifebuoys which neatly ringed its tip.

All that night and for two days afterwards the two ships rode out the gale, sometimes hove-to under stay-sails, sometimes running before the wind. Cooking was impossible and indeed forgotten, everyone being too concerned with the safety of the ships to worry overmuch about hunger. We slept where and when we could and lost track of the hours.

It was only on the fourth day that a pale and watery dawn showed a world seemingly less inimical to us. By that nightfall we had recovered sufficiently to have got some semblance of order about the two vessels and had started on a long slant to the south-east, destined to take us to Astove Island.

ELEVEN

Astove

At Astove again we met with a type of island differing from the rest of the group. We had been first to Cosmoledo, a true atoll, then to Aldabra, the barren and unique 'raised' atoll. Assumption was a mount of guano built up on the underlying sand and now this island proved to be a volcanic crater. All these four islands lie within an area seventy miles long by twenty-five wide, far from any other land mass, and yet the four have nothing in common.

At Astove we were met by the manager in his pirogue and invited ashore, but first we had to moor the schooners. This was not so easy for, owing to its peculiar geological structure, this island has no anchorage. On the western side, facing the settlement, a narrow coral shelf extends for about a hundred yards outwards from the shore, the water being not more than two feet deep. Then, absolutely abruptly, the reef fringe stops as though cut with a knife and in the space of a yard the bottom drops from two feet to several hundred fathoms.

Later I stood on the extreme edge of this shelf and looked down over it. The cliff was actually overhanging in most places, undercut by the strong currents that run parallel to the shore and which never cease. Ships loading island produce often have to sail up and down outside all the time, which the cargo is carried out to them in pirogues. We were lucky, for when we arrived the wind blew from off-shore, so that the administrator was able to lay a buoyed cable from the settlement across the reef out into the deep, and we lay strung to the end of this, tethered like goats to the island itself.

This sheer submarine precipice continues right along the western side and, although there is a shallow sunken bar extending out from the north-west, the vicious currents and tide rips across it that arise from the deep trench alongside render an anchorage there impossible. On the eastern side of the island the water is too

ASTOVE

shoal and the perpetual breakers that pound its coral shelves prohibit the use of that portion in other than flat calm conditions. Without assistance from the shore it is virtually impossible to land on Astove which is the reason why it has only been inhabited in recent years, although the island itself is rich.

I had read previously that there was an old anchor lying on the reef off the north-west edge, but when questioned about this the manager said that nothing had been seen of it for many years and that he supposed it had been washed away. Now, although many ships have been wrecked upon the reefs and islands of the Indian Ocean few really old wrecks remain, for under the pounding of successive monsoons even the large iron ships soon break up and older wooden vessels have been battered into pulp and scattered abroad long since. Consequently no one was more surprised than I when I stumbled across a sixteenth-century hulk.

Teddy and I were working the submerged spit on the north-west side, across which the tide raced and the current swirled. Because of this we had to work close in along the shore where the going was less difficult and it was there I first came upon a fragment of the old wreck. It was an ancient cannon and lay on a little sand-floored pocket in some fifteen feet of water, completely uncovered and intact, just as though it had been dropped within the last five minutes instead of having lain there for nearly four hundred years. Like any good story-book cannon it was slightly bell-mouthed and had a projecting knob at its breach end. Poking gently at the crusty exterior with a knife I prised off a flake of metal which proved to be iron, not bronze as I had hoped. Measuring it by means of hand-spreads, it worked out as slightly over eight feet in length with a muzzle diameter of ten inches and a bore of about four, although this was difficult to assess, since the barrel was largely blocked with silt and coral. As I was poking about trying to clear it a startled Butterfly fish shot out and hovered anxiously nearby, as I peered down into the recesses of its sanctuary. No sooner had I left this end of the cannon than in it darted again, periodically popping out to peer at me over the muzzle lip in an anxious fashion. The touch hole was completely sealed and the foundry and proof marks which were customarily engraved upon a piece were likewise obscured.

Before very long I came across another cannon and the remains

Astove Island

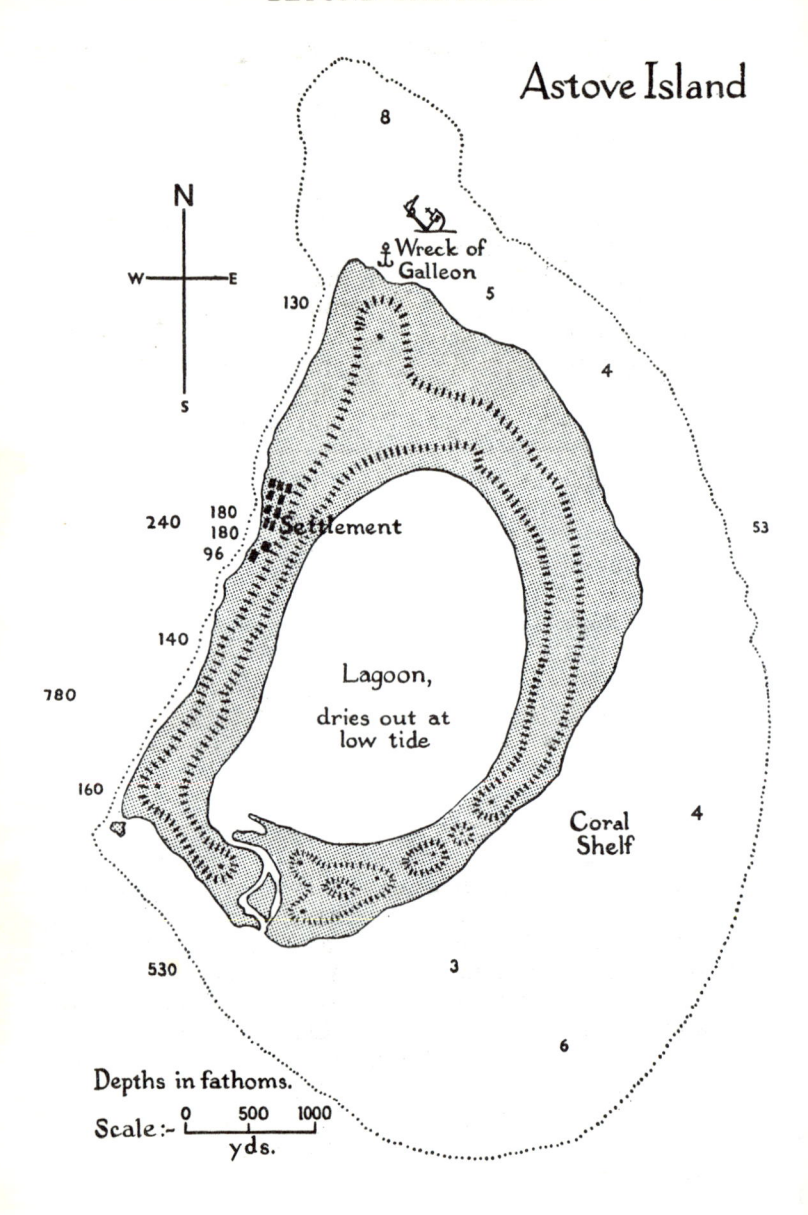

Wreck of Galleon

Settlement

Lagoon, dries out at low tide

Coral Shelf

Depths in fathoms.
Scale:- 0 500 1000 yds.

of a large anchor. The canon was identical with the first, while the anchor was unusual in that its stock appeared to have been stressed with flanking baults of timber, fragments of which still remained bolted to the rusty iron. One of the arms had been torn off and the other had lost its fluke. Through the crown was fastened a massive ring bolt. Presumably this was the anchor that had once lain on the reef itself and which had been dragged back down into the sea by some storm.

A little further on there were two more cannons and near them a beam of timber, wedged between two mounds of coral. Twenty yards away I found another pair of cannon lying one on top of the other in a coral fissure. These were so heavily encrusted that it was difficult to recognize them for what they were and had I not been on the look-out for such remnants I would have passed them by.

By now I was in deeper water and the current was such that I could make no progress against it. Moreover, the wind was rising and scudding black clouds had begun to race across the sky. With few shells and with underwater conditions rapidly becoming impossible I signalled Joseph to collect Teddy and then pick me up. While he was away on this errand I had a further look around the area and discovered the main wreck, a skeletal outline of timbers amongst which were scattered additional cannon. But here I could not dive at all, the current proving far too strong, and so was prevented from making a close examination.

Two days later we were at work along the eastern shore, for by now the wind had swung round to the north-west and our side of the island was therefore relatively sheltered, although there still remained an unpleasant swell and the going was heavy, with only isolated pockets of indifferent shells to show for the labour of our aching limbs. At eleven o'clock we had our customary morning break for tea and biscuits, which I took on the *Argo* so that I might discuss our next move with Captain Calais. Already I had mentally crossed off Astove as unlikely to yield us much and was considering trying the north coast of Cosmoledo again, followed by another sweep along selected spots of Aldabra's southern reef. Then there was St Pierre, an island to the north-east that I wished to take in as well. Sitting there with an open chart on my knees, I did not notice one of the dinghies draw alongside until Ravile called out to me.

BEYOND THE REEFS

'Excuse me, Mr Travis . . . ?' I looked up and saw him sitting there in the little boat along with Sadi, Joseph and Andrea.

'Excuse me, Mr Travis,' he repeated hesitantly. 'We want to go home. We've had enough, we can't go on! We came to tell you. That's all . . .' he finished lamely.

I let the chart fall to the deck and then stood up. Speechless with rage I turned my back and stalked over to the other side of the deck. Who the hell did they think they were? Who was running this show anyway? What gave them the right to dictate to me in this fashion? Going home indeed! Not likely! Not until we'd finished our shell gathering. Damned insolence they had! . . .

I found myself looking out across the sea towards Astove and suddenly I realized that I had not really *seen* the island at all until that moment. I dropped my gaze and saw, far below me, the corals and the lovely fish that swam there. These, too, I knew I had not really seen for many weeks. How long was it since I had entered the water with enjoyment? Christmas morning was the last time I could remember, when I had dived for pleasure and Ti-Royale had come with me and played tag with the fish. Once I had loved the sea and gloried in every minute I had spent beneath it. Now I realized that I should not care if I never swam or dived again.

My eyes dropped still more to take in the sides of the *Argo*, her paintwork scraped bare by countless bags of shells hoisted up over the side from the dinghies. I looked down and saw my feet, the toenails broken by corals, the ankles calloused and swollen from months of continual wearing of swim-fins. Then my knees, criss-crossed with scratches and covered with coral-sore scabs, my hands on the ship's rail, skinned raw in places, the nails worn down to the quick.

All at once I felt the tiredness of many months descend upon my shoulders. I turned and walked back across the deck to look down at those familiar faces in the dinghy. Ravile, for the first time I saw how thin he had got: the stubble on old Joseph's face was nearly all grey, I noticed. Then Sadi, dried up like a cinder with two yellow eyes burning holes in the cavity of his face. My gaze shifted to Andrea, taking in the nervous twitching of his cheek and flickering eyelid, and then back to Ravile.

'You're right, Ravile. It's all over. Finished . . .

ASTOVE

'It's time we went home . . .'

The corals of Assumption, the galleon of Astove, the reefs of St Pierre – those could all wait until another day.

Now we were going home! . . .

Our two schooner sailed into Port Victoria early one morning but already there was a crowd on the quay waiting for us, having recognized the silhouettes of our ships when we were still some miles out. Amongst those standing there I saw friends, vague acquaintances, a few officials and the usual percentage of the professionally curious. As we drew near I wondered if the famous sorceress was present as well. If so, she was due to lose a considerable amount of prestige in the next few minutes for our two ships were heavily laden with shells and all we divers were present without the loss of a single limb.

But there *was* a difference. As I looked them over, those who had dived for shells with me, I saw that these were not the same lads that had set out with me in the beginning. They had been a motley assortment – thin and rather weedy, scared of each other and of the thing to which they were committed.

That group bore no resemblance to these that now returned. These were fit, deep-chested youngsters, confident and talkative. Still too thin, but in a lean, hard way. They were tanned of skin and clear of eye and across their shoulders and down their spines the muscles rippled as they moved. Their coral cuts healed, their tiredness gone (it was mainly due to mental strain), the uncertainties over, they presented a good picture, laughing in the sunlight as they shouted messages across to those who waited for them on the jetty.

Detailing a skeleton crew to guard the ships whilst I was away dealing with the necessary formalities, I told the rest of the crew to do what they liked, but to be back on board in an hour's time to start unloading the shells, for I was not trusting any of our precious sacks to the rough care of the wharf labourers. About mid-day, standing in the hold of the *L. Fred*, stripped to the waist and sweating under the hot sun that poured down through the open hatch as I supervised the hoisting of our cargo, I looked up to see Teddy peering down over the edge at me. Noticing that he was wearing a freshly laundered nylon shirt and an immaculate pair of lovat green shorts, I said irritably, 'Come on, Teddy! Get that shirt off and come down here. We need another person in the hold.'

To which he replied, 'Oh, pardon me, Mr Travis, but now we've come back and have so much money, I don't *have* to do that kind of work any more. You see I've engaged someone, *paid* someone, to do it for me.' So saying he pointed to a grinning young black whom I had not previously noticed but who was laughing up on deck.

I had to laugh. Teddy, the ever-lazy, was certainly beginning to spend the money he had so well earned in a very typical fashion. I could see that this *nouveau riche* class of skin-divers I had created was going to be something of a problem in the future!

Pay-day, the day following, was a shock to us all. Not even I had visualized the sums involved, having left all the final calculations till the shells had been check-weighed in the customs warehouse. Most of the skin-divers and their attendants, after deducting the allotments they had made to their families in their absence, still drew over ninety pounds each. Then there was my share as a diver, which was split up among them again. Then the money for the salted turtle and calipee we had brought back. Lastly, each had a parcel of food stores left over from the voyage.

As each one came up to the deck where I was paying out, I asked him if he knew what he was going to do with this money and whether he would like me to bank any of it for him against hard times. Their answers were interesting.

Teddy was going to buy a bicycle, give a little to his mother and personally keep the rest, so I knew it would all be gone in a month – which was exactly what happened. He then gave me back the ten rupees which he had borrowed prior to setting out and about which I had forgotten. Next was Albert who came with his mother in a taxi, both dressed as if for a wedding, so the least I could do was to pay for the hire of the car! It was she who collected the money on his behalf and then solemnly handed him one hundred and twenty rupees with which to buy a new guitar, the crafty young devil having told her that he had given the old one to Wyn, when in actual fact he had sold it to that individual for sixty rupees. Albert also stopped and repaid me ten rupees which he had also borrowed before setting out. Conrad wanted all his money. He did not know for what purpose but he certainly was not going to let any of it rest with me nor with any savings bank. He had heard of banks going bust, and as for me . . . After counting his money he peeled off the last ten-rupee note and solemnly handed it to me. I looked at it and then at him and asked why he did that. He shuffled his feet and then muttered that he had seen the previous two hand me a similar sum and supposed that he had to as well. This was an interesting sidelight on a Seychelles custom whereby the person who employs a man frequently takes a percentage of his earnings, this being considered just reward for having given the man work in the first place.

Donald only wanted fifty rupees and very surprisingly asked me to bank the rest. This was what I had least expected, for of all the divers he was the one whose character I least liked and such a display of common sense made me feel that perhaps I had misjudged the lad previously. Ti-Royale took some money for his mother, asked me to sell him a set of skin-diving equipment, and to keep the rest for him. I agreed, but in fact made him a present of the gear, which was only fair reward for his having proved the best and hardiest diver of the lot.

Sadi took most of his money and then asked me if I would go with him later to help buy a radio set which would pick up that music from Portuguese East Africa! This I did and afterwards he went on a wonderful binge – on any night for the next month you could tell which bar he was in by the music coming out of it. Somehow the set survived the numerous brawls and drunken falls and on more than one occasion I passed Sadi fast asleep in some alley-way, his head resting on his beloved radio.

Andrea and Joseph took their money together, put down identical sums to be paid by me to their wives (not trusting themselves to do it), and went off quietly and determinedly on a monumental drunk which lasted for about six weeks. During that time I was never able to walk up Market Street without somehow being seen by the pair and hustled into a bar for a drink on them. Since I was English and it was well-known that Englishmen drink whisky, whisky it was, and no amount of protesting on my behalf could convince them that I loathed it. After having been caught a half-dozen times like this, I entered into clandestine arrangement with all the barmen around there that when Andrea and Joseph called for a whisky I was to be served brandy and that in any case it would be put down to my account.

To some it may seem strange and even wicked that such a large proportion of all these earnings should have gone on hard liquor. But it must be remembered that the majority of these men had been out of work, through no fault of their own, for a great deal of their adult lives. Often they had been on the borderline of starvation, with never a penny to call their own. What they earned casually usually went on old grocery bills, overdue rent and such like. Perpetual debt was their normal environment. Suddenly to have 'spending money', cash on which no one had a call but themselves, was too sudden and too great a transition for the majority. And after all, the work of the past months had built up a tremendous thirst in us all.

I did hope that after the next shelling expedition perhaps some of them could be persuaded to save a little – but as long as 'earning power' and 'spending money' were both strange to them, nothing else could be expected. Seen in this light, it is interesting to note that the only member of the crew enjoying security, Ravile, the coxswain and boat-owner, was also the only one to invest his earnings wisely, all of it going on new cordage, sails and a stock of fuel oil for the *L. Fred*.

What old Ton Pierre did with his share I do not know. He took it and, leaving Ravile's employ, emigrated to East Africa where as far as I know he still remains. The young lout Wyn had Albert's guitar broken over his head after a late-night escapade. Subsequently he turned up as a patient in the VD ward of the hospital. That, too, was rather typical.

Viewed from my side the outcome of the expedition seemed both secure and encouraging. A first firm order for seven and a half tons of shells came in right away from Penang at four hundred and ninety pounds sterling per ton. Moreover, it seemed certain that all the rest might be expected to follow at a similar price as soon as we could dispatch them. Confidently I started to plan a similar but improved expedition for the following autumn. Among the innovations were to be motorized underwater sledges for research work, specially built diving dinghies and power-hoists on board the parent ship.

It looked like being a busy summer.

Epilogue

Some six months later, moodily walking along a beach on Mahé I came across a live Green Snail shell. The nacre was poor and the mollusc interested me for only one purpose. With a clasp knife I prised out the snail, wrapped it in a piece of seaweed and set off home. Arriving there I went up the garden to the pig pen, and leaning over the gate proferred my gift to the sow that rooted within and between whose feet scuttled six little piglets. Alice sniffled disgustedly at it, grunted her disapproval and returned to the crushed pawpaw that lay on the ground.

Someone else felt the same way as I did nowadays about Green Snail. We had both changed our views a lot since our days on the *L. Fred*. I did not know the reason for this *volte face* on her part, but I did for my own . . .

The shell merchant in Penang had got our shells all right, but we had not got his money!

Through mischance or trickery he had received the consignment without having made the necessary deposit and once it was in his hands neither word nor cash could be got out of him. For several months we had been trying to get an order for the return of our shells, but the damage was done. Further shipments had been held up, as in accepting his original offer we had declined other slightly lower offers, much to our present regret. Even this would not have proved disastrous and would only have caused an annoying delay in building up fresh contacts, had not something else occurred.

The United Stated synthetics industry finally succeeded in producing an imitation mother-of-pearl that was said to be indistinguishable from the real article, easier to work, of greater durability and of course a fraction of the price of the natural article.

Green Snail went the way of natural tortoiseshell. Consequently the market value of our shells had dropped by late summer to around one hundred pounds per ton, if one was lucky enough to find a buyer. Success is being the right person, in the right place, at the right time. I had had the luck to meet the first two conditions but the third had me beaten!

It was Harvey, though, who had the last word. Provided with an additional team of skin-divers I had managed to train for him he had at last managed to make his long-envisaged shelling expedition to Chagos Archipelago and only came back in late June. Of shell he had not found a trace, but had managed to make good most of his expenses by catching twelve tons of shark which he salted and dried and brought back to Mahé to sell.

After talking over the results of our respective voyages he summed it up thus:

'All I can say is that mine was a shelling trip too, but thank goodness I didn't get a single one! If I'd have struck Green Snail like you I'd have been a financial wreck now, for sure!'

He had something there.

BOOK TWO
SHARK FOR SALE

Preface

Fourteen miles north-west of Mahé, principal island of the Seychelles Group, a massive rampart of granite, 3,000 feet high, rises into the sky.

This craggy islet, called Silhouette, serves as a landmark for ships of all sizes and many nations, for in clear weather it can be seen sixty miles away, long before the steep cliffs of Mahé appear on the horizon. Due to the humidity of the atmosphere and the glare of the tropical sun, it is not generally visible during the day, but it appears as if by magic just before sunset and again at first light, only to fade away in a short while, leaving nothing but the empty horizon . . .

For seven months of the year, the Creole shark-fisherman of the Seychelles lives at sea. Far out on the broad reaches of the Indian Ocean, way out of sight of land, his small and frequently ill-found schooner tacks and turns – a solitary water-beetle on the surface of an immense and desolate pond.

For as many as twenty days at a time he will fish, drifting along invisible current lanes, seeking the elusive sharks that cruise thirty fathoms beneath his keel; he will live on boiled rice and fish, flavoured with curry powder. Each evening he will furl his sails with the setting of the sun and sleep as best he can on the bare deck or, if he has been fortunate, upon the warm carcasses of the sharks he has caught that day. At last, provisions and water nearly finished and his hold filled with salted shark – or not, according to his luck – he will set course for home and a brief twenty-four hours ashore. On this return trip he can relax, resting during the heat of the day, or mending and repairing gear to pass away the long drawn-out hours. Only at dusk and again at dawn is he alert, anxiously scanning the horizon for a familiar

SHARK FOR SALE

outline, a faint shadow upon the world's edge, unmistakable and instantly recognizable. And when at last he does see it from his vantage point at the masthead, he lets the other members of the crew know that all is well and that they are almost home with the traditional, ringing cry . . .

'Silhouette dehors . . .!'

Contents

1. The *Golden Bells* — 223
2. First Trials — 243
3. Fortune Bank and Ishmael — 256
4. Shark Luring — 279
5. The Hunted and the Hunters — 298
6. The Skull on Africa Bar — 318
7. Deep Waters — 335
8. Storm-rack and Sea-birds — 349
9. Lost: The Story of Nelson Toll — 361
10. Leavetaking — 378
    Appendix — 384

ONE

The Golden Bells

*Canst thou draw out leviathan with an hook? . . .
Shall the companions make a banquet of him? Shall
they part him among the merchants?* (Job xli, 1 & 6)

To most people shark-fishing represents a rather exotic and fanciful form of sport – something to indulge in for those in search of a new thrill or else something carried on by the tourist-conscious natives of the Caribbean and Pacific for the benefit of wealthy visitors.

But to the men of Southern Arabia, Somalia, the Malay Archipelago and Ceylon it represents a life-long craft, and for the inland peoples of East Africa and the Far East the efforts of these distant fishermen provide a generally available, cheap and nutritious form of food. Shark-flesh, salted and sun-dried, has a high protein content, requires no specialized processing factory such as a cannery, and does not provide any of the difficulties found in the distribution of frozen or chilled foodstuffs. As such, it has found a ready market throughout these areas for thousands of years. Like most markets of the East, however, the dried shark trade was run on very slipshod lines. The shark was caught, cut up and lightly salted in a variety of fashions, left in the sun for widely differing periods of time, often spoilt by rain or ravaged by flies, and finally sold by weight, size, colour, bundle, bale, basket or piece, seemingly at the whim of the vendor. Once sold, these consignments of shark meat were crammed into the holds of dhows and other native craft where they were left to the mercies of bilge water, cockroaches and rats, and by the time the vessel came to discharge its cargo the flesh had deteriorated into a slimy mound of ammoniated rottenness, fit only for the rankest of

SHARK FOR SALE

palates. It found a ready sale only among the coolie-class of the country where it was taken.

That is how the shark trade was carried on for thousands of years and that is how it would have continued, but for one factor.

Within the last decade the newly-created Asian and African middle-class element has suddenly become aware of its own newly developed needs and tastes, and it is within this period that the demand for a good quality, standard production of salt-shark has arisen.

These people want salt-shark and not the rotten, glutinous residue that goes by that name and is usually found in the holds of the dhows, jahasis and booms trading between Muscat and Dar-es-Salaam, Oman and Penang. They want shark-flesh properly prepared and carefully packed, and are prepared to pay prices far in advance of those asked for the inferior grade.

To cater for this demand shark-fishing has taken on an entirely new commercial aspect in many places throughout the Near East. Not unnaturally, those areas whose style of fishing has been laid down by traditions centuries old have been the least receptive to the new techniques, whilst those countries in which shark-fishing represents a recent innovation are now foremost in this work.

Prominent among the latter group are the Seychelle Islands. Situated in the middle of the Indian Ocean they are ideally suited for such a trade, for not only do cargo ships call there on their way to Africa, India and the Far East, but for many years past their Creole fishermen have been catching sharks for their fins, which are dried and exported to China. Lured on by the new high prices offered in overseas markets for first-grade shark-meat, some Seychellois island and schooner owners started experimenting in the production of salt-shark and it was not long before a standard product, far superior to that of any other area, had found a ready sale in the bazaars and markets of many tropical countries. To meet the increasing demand many others in these tropical islands converted their cargo schooners into fishing vessels, others built new boats or borrowed them, whilst others – like myself – chartered them.

*

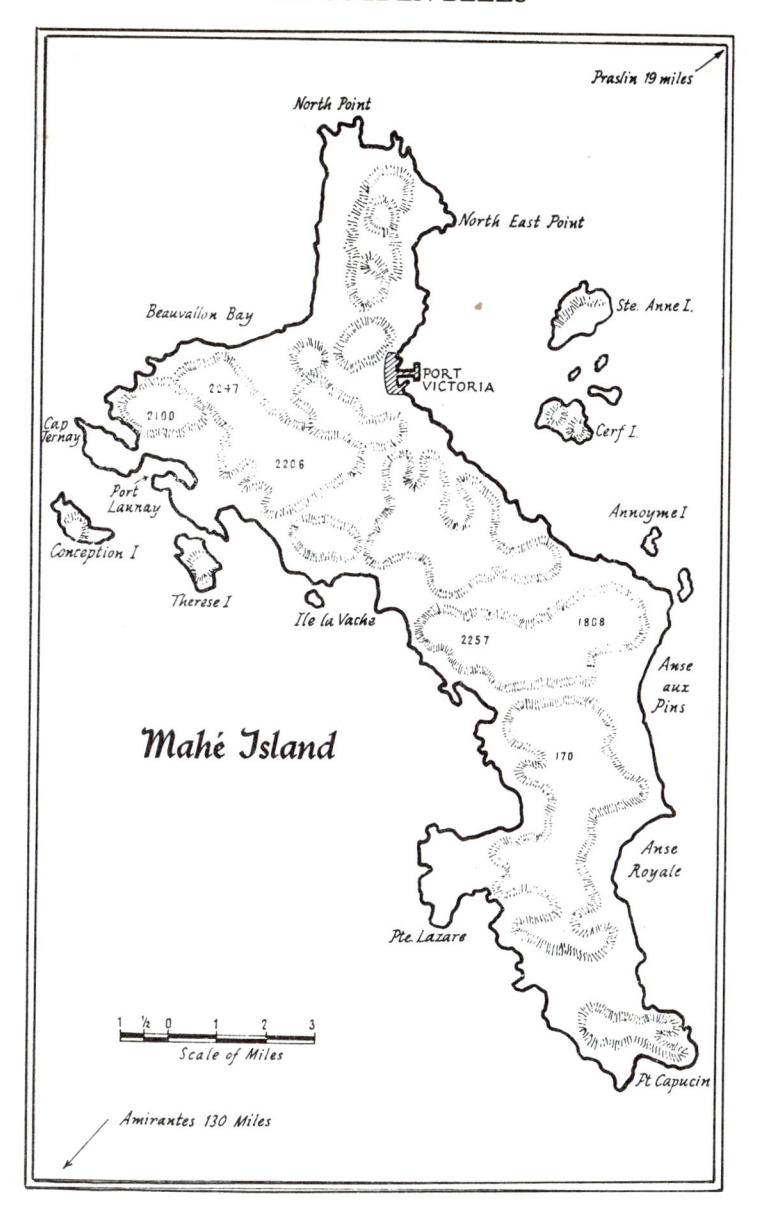

THE GOLDEN BELLS

SHARK FOR SALE

My first introduction to shark-fishing was neither reassuring nor encouraging.

In a rash moment the previous day I had acquired paper-ownership of a six-ton sharking cutter together with its crew, and was now faced with the prospect of seeing what I had let myself in for. I arrived, intentionally, at the Old Quay alongside which the *Golden Bells* was moored at lunch-time knowing that all the crew would be away. Thus I was able to have a good look over the ship, inside and out, without being bothered. So far so good. The cutter, though old, was well built and of solid practical lines. Paint was only remarkable by its absence, but that was usual on a vessel devoted to the rough work that shark-fishing entails. True, the smell of the bilge was awful – a sweet, sickly, rancid odour, compounded of diesel oil and shark residue. I never got over this and it subsequently prevented me from sleeping below deck whatever the weather might be. However, the gear was neatly stowed and the engine was in fair condition. Even the rigging was reasonably kept for a Creole working boat.

Somewhat relieved by what I had found I sat down on the deck to await the arrival of my crew.

Presently, up the rough track that led from the main road to the jetty, there appeared a figure. At first I thought it was a large dog, then a cripple, for it crawled on all fours and its head hung loosely downwards, chin on chest. Twice it fell over and it was only when it drew nearer and I heard a mumbling chant issuing from it that I realized the creature was a normal human being, but drunk, crawling drunk, as gloriously drunk as it possibly could be! On it came. It reached the quayside, fumbled along its edge, arrived at the gang-plank and painfully started to crawl up it, still on hands and knees. This hazard safely negotiated it fell in a heap in the scuppers at my feet. There it stayed for a few seconds, then it roused itself, shook itself like a dog and made its painful way towards the hatch that led down to the cabin. On the edge of the opening it stopped again and turned its head slowly around to look at me over one shoulder. Then for the first time I saw the man's face. It was foxy and pointed, with piercing blue eyes surrounded by a network of red veins. He had a thin, cynical mouth topped by a clipped, tobacco-stained moustache, a long, thin nose and a quizzical expression. It was the face of an Essex poacher.

THE GOLDEN BELLS

The apparition looked me up and down for about five seconds, head nodding slightly, then with a muttered '*Ou capable croire?*' ('Would you believe it?') turned away and fell straight out of sight down the hold in a loose jumble of arms and legs.

Silence followed, and I was just going to see if he had broken his neck when a peaceful and resonant snoring came to my ears. Ton-ton Milot was asleep. Such was my first meeting with the coxswain of the *Golden Bells*.

A few minutes later I saw another man approaching. This time in a normal manner, walking upright. *Homo sapiens erectus*. Coming within a yard or two of the quayside, the newcomer looked up at me from under the brim of his hat, looked down again quickly, shuffled his feet and, his mind made up and the great decision taken, shyly raised his hat and wished me 'Good afternoon' in a hushed voice. Then, the ordeal over, he blushed scarlet and resumed the study of his bare toes, with which he was tracing patterns in the dust. He was a huge man, perhaps forty or forty-two years old, with a fair, pinky-white skin which the tropic sun would never turn anything other than a blotchy, peeling red. Big, square hands that dangled awkwardly at the end of muscular arms. Long, strong legs, knotted and sinewy. His head matched the rest. A long face, with a long, straight Norman nose. A wide mouth, thin lipped. Ears lying flat, close to the skull, and a thatch of unruly mousey-coloured hair, growing a little thin on top. Not a trace of Asiatic or Negroid blood here but pure European peasant stock. One might see his counterpart in any field of northern Europe, striding along behind a plough or heaving hundred-weight sacks of potatoes upon his broad back as though they were full of feathers.

I asked him if he belonged to the *Golden Bells*, and to this he nodded, unable to speak. It was not sullenness nor ill-humour that robbed him of speech, but an overpowering shyness that took possession of him on occasions such as this. This giant, who feared neither man nor beast, would literally take to his heels rather than face the acute agony of having to speak to a stranger. It was causing him such obvious distress to remain there in front of me that to excuse him I asked if he would be good enough to put Ton-ton Milot to bed, since he was taking up floor space down below. Vastly relieved at this suggestion, he came aboard and disappeared down the hatchway. After a few moments I heard Ton-ton Milot's querulous mutter, which was hastily soothed by the other's quiet undertones. From where I sat I could both see and hear all that went on without the big man being aware of it. Ton-ton Milot was picked up, dusted down as though he were a doll and laid gently to rest on a shabby mattress that occupied one corner. After this his nurse loosened his shirt, took off his belt and propped up his head on a coil of rope. Then, using a piece of cotton-waste, he very gently sponged away the dust and sweat that caked the other's face and chest. Like many big men he had an inherent gentleness, and would have made an excellent hospital orderly.

Just then two more of the crew turned up.

One was tall and lean, an obvious mixture of Indian and African strains. The other was shorter, squarer – almost pure negro, with the rather prominent cheekbones and oblique eyes that betrayed a Chinese element somewhere in his family. Both were swaying slightly and had a glassy look in their eyes, but were coherent enough when spoken to. I let them know that we would be sailing with the evening tide and that I was going with them. From the way they nodded I gathered that they had heard this news already through some 'grapevine' of their own. I gave them the list of provisions and gear to collect from the chandlers and asked them if there was anything else. They wanted to know if I was bringing my own food, and seemed surprised when I told them that would not be necessary. Finally, after instructing them to do a few odd jobs around the boat, I left them to their own devices and went in search of Ti-Royale, a young Creole mechanic and skin-diver whom I had employed for the past year and whom I had decided to take shark-fishing with me.

That first trip was not a success.

No sooner were we at sea than the weather deteriorated so much that the familiar mountain peaks of Mahé and the neighbouring islands disappeared completely behind low clouds and rain-squalls. With all their accustomed landmarks hidden from view, the Creole fishermen were plainly at a loss and the *Golden Bells* spent two fruitless days tracking across the empty expanse of leaden ocean, pausing only at infrequent intervals to sound. My crew were also much handicapped by the absence of their coxswain, for Ton-ton Milot hardly put his nose outside the hold. Occasionally a hoarse squawk would proclaim his need for tea,

THE GOLDEN BELLS

which was served him at the double. On the third day out he emerged for a brief spell, glanced up at the driving overcast, muttered *'Ou capable croire?'* and disappeared below again, where he remained for the rest of the voyage. However, though we never so much as cast a line, that first trial served its purpose, for it showed the crew that I was not there to make things difficult for them, nor to interfere in their running of the boat. Soon they had tacitly accepted my presence among them and by the end of the third day the first steps in acquaintanceship had been made, for each ventured to tell his name, and that was important.

In the Seychelles, most Creole people have two or more names. There is their official or 'roll-call' name, and the name by which they are known among themselves. This custom probably dates back to the time when primitive magic and sorcery largely ruled the lives of these descendants of slaves. To possess a person's true name was to possess a part of him and gave one power over his mind and body. In the same way, possession of locks of hair, drops of blood, clippings of finger nails or portions of skin also conferred upon the holder power over, or a magical link with, their owners. You guarded your name as you guarded your body, lest it fall into the hands of someone who wished you ill. Nowadays, though unaware of its origins, this custom still persists but in a broader form. Usually a child is given a nickname (the very derivative of this word in English being a 'Devil's' name, that is, a false name which the devil could know without the person so called coming to harm) as soon as he or she is born, sometimes even beforehand, and it is by this nickname that the person is known amongst themselves.

Unlike European nicknames, which usually contain a direct or obvious reference to the holder (such as 'Fatty', 'Ginger' or 'Lofty'), the Seychellois equivalents are often completely obscure and unsuitable. The intimate names of my crew were no exception.

The huge peasant was known as 'Gandhi', though anyone less Asiatic and ascetic and more European and earthy it would be hard to find. The tall half-African, half-Indian was 'Hassan', though no trace of Arab settlers is to be found within the Seychelles, and the short negroid one was 'Zulu'. This, though more appropriate, could hardly be called a normal name. Ton Milot's real name was Joseph Lablache, the 'Ton' or 'Ton-ton' being the prefix 'Uncle', employed as a mark of respect when speaking to an elderly person. Where the 'Milot' part came from I was never able to find out.

Then there was Ti-Royale, whose real name, which I had known for some time past, was even stranger than his nickname, for it was 'La Moitié Joseph' (literally 'Half-Joseph').

On me, of course, they also bestowed a name, though it was some time before I got to know. At first it was simply 'La Barbe' (The Beard), then later, when someone told them I was once an aviator, it became 'Bouc à l'air' (Billy-goat from the Sky). To my face it was 'M'sieur', or when they wished to flatter me, and usually prior to asking a favour or an advance of pay, it was 'Capitaine'.

On the fourth day it was obvious that the weather would not improve for several more days at least, so we turned back for Port Victoria, our hold empty – except for Ton Milot – and our fishing gear as yet untouched. When we finally moored alongside the quay on our return, Ton Milot was the first ashore, trotting off townwards on his thin legs.

'Hey, Ton-ton,' I yelled at him. 'Where are you off to?'

'To get drunk. *Ou capable croire!*' was his rejoinder.

'But I haven't paid you!' At this he stopped and half-turned.

'You're paying me?'

'Of course!'

'But I haven't worked!'

'I know that, but they tell me you are one of the best coxswains on the island and that you know all the best places on the banks. How can I tell if this is true unless you show me what you can do?'

'You mean you're going to take me on the next trip?'

'Certainly! How else can I find out?'

'*Ou capable croire!*' – and so saying he came back and thus began our long friendship.

Ton Milot was a drunkard. A classic Damon Runyon drunkard, whose drinking bouts were epics and their histories already legendary. He had drunk away whole catches of fish, many seasons' savings and the ownership of several schooners. Home and furniture had all gone to finance this prodigious thirst at one time or another. Some drunkards disgust one, others are boring or morose, but Ton Milot was no ordinary drunkard. A shabby Falstaff, a spindly Toby Belch, a piscine Bacchus. All else might fail, but Ton-ton's ability to convert rupees into liquor, provisions into the contents of pint pots, and fish not yet caught into bar-credit was nothing less than miraculous. Even the alcohol in the compass was not safe from him.

One day, months later, when we were out on the banks and the rest of the crew were already asleep after the day's work, Ton-ton explained to me his behaviour on that first voyage we made together.

'When I heard you were coming with us, what else could I do but go and get drunk? In my fifty years at sea I've never yet had a *patron* who wanted to come shark-fishing. Nobody has. It's unheard of. It's never happened before. I didn't know how to deal with a situation like that. What did you want to come along for, to sleep on a wet deck and eat cold rice and salt-fish, when you could easily stay at home? I had to have a drink to think it out, so I took a pair of sea-boots I happened to have handy – took 'em off a Jap sailor I was drinking with the week before, when he passed out – and the barman at one of the places I go to gave me four rupees on 'em, so I was all right. Well, the more I had, the more certain I was that your coming could mean only one thing. That I was going. Any way I looked at it I got the same answer. Old Ton Milot looking for another ship because of a new *patron* who didn't like him, didn't trust him, and so had to come along himself and catch old Milot out. Well, as it seemed I couldn't do anything about it, I decided I might as well get sacked properly – give this *patron* something to sack me for, see? It seemed like a good idea at the time. *Ou capable croire?* You know the rest – ' He looked at me slyly, one conspirator to another.

'*Ou capable croire?*' That was the key to Ton Milot.

Into that one sentence he could put the dignity of kings, the sorrow of the world, the understanding of a saint. He would stand before you, swaying on his feet, eyes bleary and watery, his breath a pestilence.

'Would you believe it?' he would say softly, and it would be a confession of guilt and an expresion of sorrow.

Again, 'Would *you* believe it?' and it was an outraged demand that you, surely, of all people knew better than to think that he,

SHARK FOR SALE

Ton Milot, could possible be drunk. Good gracious me, what an idea!

Belligerently, '*Would* you believe it?' Did you want to believe that he was drunk? If you did, that was your own affair, and you would get no confirmation from him.

Much of what I learnt of shark-fishing I owe to Ton Milot and still more to his drinking bouts ashore, for when we had been at sea a few days, Ton-ton would begin to feel the effects of his enforced abstinence as, one thing to his credit, he never brought liquor on board. This abstinence would take the form of headaches and insomnia, and to pass away the long night he had to talk to someone. Chiefly it was to me, since I was always willing to sit up with him and listen to his stories. If it were not me, his confidant might be a rat to which he would feed scraps, or a passing cockroach would be beguiled into halting awhile with grains of sugar so that Ton Milot might unburden himself to some living creature and so ease the loneliness of those long dark hours.

A week later, the storm having blown itself out, we set off on our second trip and at last I was able to see exactly how my Creole fishermen went about their work, whilst Ton Milot did his best to explain the reasons that lay behind each move and the general tactics employed in our search for sharks.

Mahé is placed right in the middle of a large submarine plateau, the depth of which is nowhere greater than fifty fathoms, that is 300 feet. At the edge this falls sharply away to 1,500 or 2,000 fathoms, approximately two miles. The plateau, with its sun-warmed shallows, has been used for countless milleniums as a breeding ground and nursery for many types of sharks, and until recently the adults of these species roamed freely over it, both by day and by night. But, with the introduction of extensive shark-fishing, so many large sharks were caught in so short a time, their ranks were depleted so seriously as to make the sight of a full-grown shark in shallow water, by day, a comparative rarity. Those that did survive were the sharks of the *bordage* – the extreme edge of the plateau, where it plunges into the great depths. These sharks only come on to the *sec* – the shallow submarine plateau – at night in order to hunt for food or give birth to their young.

The only ones that now remained on the *sec* during the daytime

THE GOLDEN BELLS

were those youngsters whose mothers had dropped them there, for sharks are viviparous – that is, they give birth to fully formed and live young. These shark 'pups' mill around the *sec*, avoiding any bigger sharks, who would promptly eat them if hungry, until they are sufficiently large to think of braving the dangers of the deep for themselves.

Consequently, the shark-fishermen of Mahé, who had originally been able to catch sizeable sharks all over the *sec* within sight of land, have now been driven far out in search of their prey, right to the *bordage*, which lies many miles beyond the horizon, out of sight of Silhouette and other familiar landmarks. This in itself would not matter, but for one factor. None of these fishermen can *navigate*. These men are never sure of where they are, either in relation to Mahé – long since lost below the horizon – or to their fishing grounds. Each night they must try and anchor wherever they happen to be, lest they drift right off the plateau during the night and so lose their last contact with the land. Since the night is often the best time for shark-fishing, they are once again working under a handicap. In addition, should the weather be rough, they cannot go out at all, since to anchor a small boat in a choppy, open sea puts great strain on all the anchor gear, which might break or suffer damage as a result. This, then, limits their fishing season to seven months of the year, from October to May, the fine weather period of the north-west monsoon.

Once out of sight of land the fishermen's only means of finding out where the *bordage* lies is to sound periodically with a fifty-fathom lead line. The coxswain sounds: thirty fathoms only; so he continues to sail on out for a while. He sounds again: twenty-six fathoms – on he goes. An hour later down goes the lead line once again, and no bottom is struck. The schooner has sailed right over the edge of the plateau and now has two miles of water beneath her keel. Back the coxswain turns and 'feels' his way in again until he strikes bottom again. Then out he sails once more until his vessel is positioned finally on the very edge of the *sec*, on the *bordage* itself. There he fishes and drifts with the current.

In such a fashion did Ton Milot and his crew seek their fishing grounds as usual on our second voyage.

But in spite of this cumbersome and time-wasting method of arriving at their selected grounds, there was no doubt about

SHARK FOR SALE

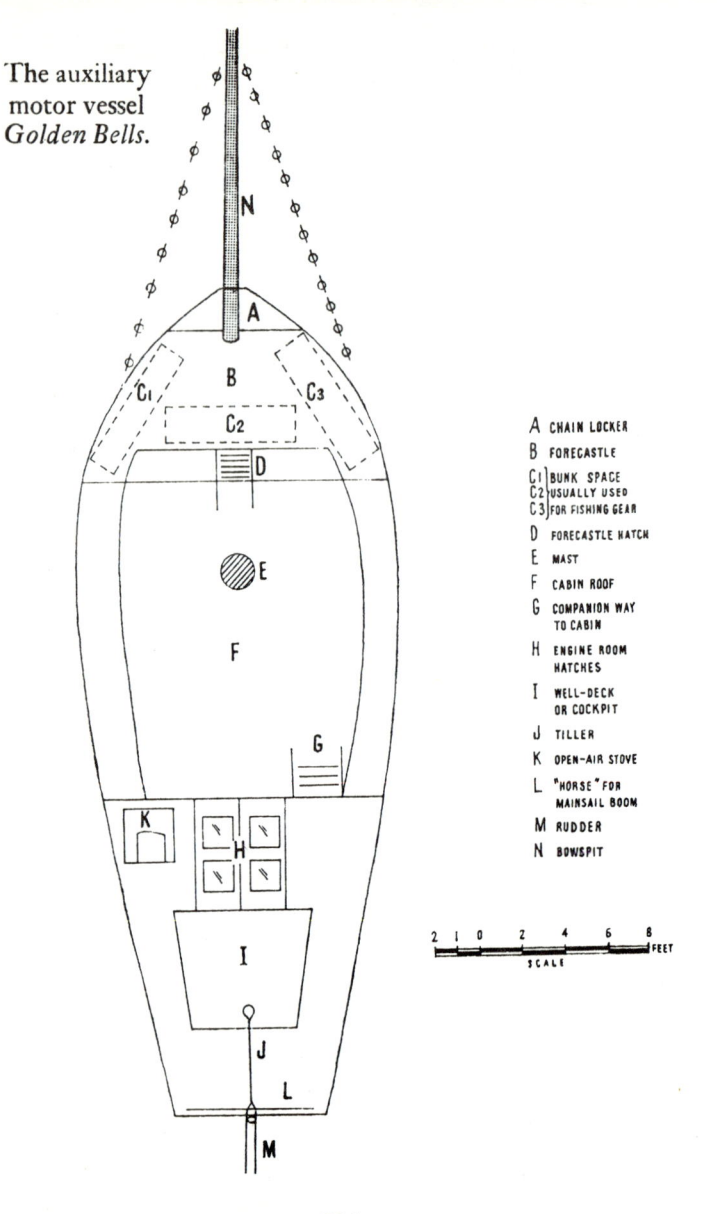

The auxiliary motor vessel *Golden Bells*.

A CHAIN LOCKER
B FORECASTLE
C1 ⎱ BUNK SPACE
C2 ⎬ USUALLY USED
C3 ⎰ FOR FISHING GEAR
D FORECASTLE HATCH
E MAST
F CABIN ROOF
G COMPANION WAY TO CABIN
H ENGINE ROOM HATCHES
I WELL-DECK OR COCKPIT
J TILLER
K OPEN-AIR STOVE
L "HORSE" FOR MAINSAIL BOOM
M RUDDER
N BOWSPIT

THE GOLDEN BELLS

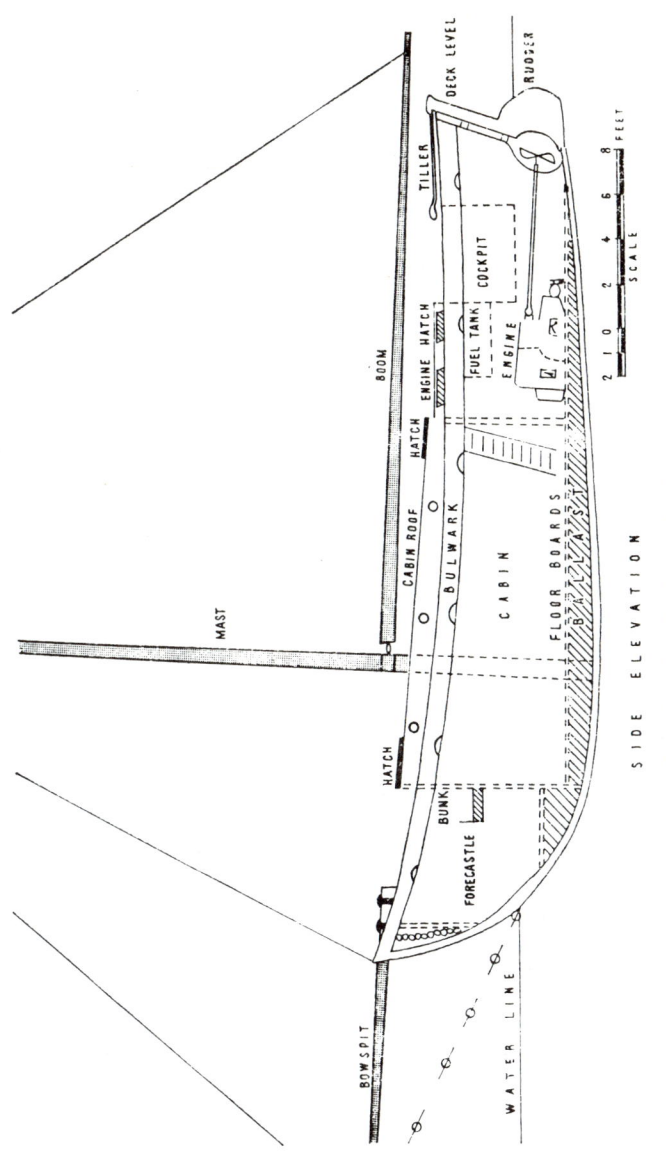

The *Golden Bells*—side elevation.

SHARK FOR SALE

it. Once on the right spot, these Creole fishermen knew their business.

Since there is no commercial refrigeration in the Seychelles, there is no possibility of stocking up with frozen bait prior to setting out. No, the bait must be caught when you get to the fishing grounds, before the real work begins. Sometimes this presents additional problems of its own, as I was now to witness.

Having eventually positioned the *Golden Bells* to his satisfaction, Ton Milot let down into the opaque green water his thin bait-fish line whilst the others busied themselves coiling up ropes, sharpening knives and clearing the deck of all unnecessary gear. To begin with, I peered over the side of the boat trying vainly to see what was happening down there, 180 feet below. Were there fish down there and if so, were there any sharks as well?

Suddenly Ton Milot raised a cautionary finger. Something was nibbling at the line. He struck hard, bearing down on the line so that it was pressed against the low bulwark, giving extra leverage. Satisfied that one fish was securely hooked, he let the weighted line sink back again, until it lightly touched the bottom. Another nibble. Another strike. But this time he shook his head. Missed it! So he continued, until certain that each of the six hooks had either a bait-fish lodged on it, or else the bait itself had gone, eaten by some smaller and more cunning fish. He looked around at the crew who were all standing ready, armed with batons, poles, lance and gaff. Then, with long, swinging arm movements, the gnarled little coxswain began to pull in the line, so that the hooked fish were drawn up rapidly and smoothly. Had he pulled it in jerkily the fish would have responded by fighting back and their violent body movements would have sent urgent shock waves pulsating through the water, announcing to every shark in the vicinity that here were fish and in trouble. An open invitation to an easy lunch.

As it was, we might have been able to get our precious bait unmolested for I could see far below, perhaps ninety feet down, the end of the line with the fish hanging limply from it.

But Hassan, on my left, suddenly shouted '*Requins!*' and pointed to where a sleek bomb-shape was closing in rapidly. Before we could do anything the shark had passed our fish, had executed a quick turn with a flick of its tail, and was coming straight in again. We saw the line jump under Milot's fingers but

THE GOLDEN BELLS

already we had lost one good fish, along with a hook and trace. There still remained four. Ton Milot's back was arched and his sinewy arms moved like pistons in a frantic effort to save the bait. Another shark appeared, way below, climbing vertically upwards with fevered tail thrashings, trying to catch up with his fast-disappearing lunch. Seen from this angle, the shark resembled a jet fighter aircraft – heavy-bodied, short-winged and the supreme master of his element. The line sang in over the bulwark and the rest of the crew hung far out over the side beating the wooden planking of the ship with their batons, or stirring up the water with their poles in an effort to frighten off the thief. With a last desperate heave Ton-ton pulled the fish safely up into the air, where they dangled for an instant before being swung on to the deck in a tangled mess of fish and line. A split second later the whole pointed snout of the shark burst out of the water as he tried vainly, with a last furious wriggle of his tail, to follow his prey.

But no one took any notice of him now. Gandhi stunned the bait-fish, four fat rock cod, with the back of an axe. Ton Milot grabbed each one behind the gills and, with a dexterous twist, rid their mouths of the hooks and then tossed them up to Ti-Royale, who waited forward with another axe. One stroke, and they lost their tails. Two, their heads. Three, and they were split open. Four, five, six and seven, and the carcass was neatly dismembered into eight wedge-shaped segments. Meanwhile, Hassan had been laying out the shark lines, half-inch tarred Japanese line, each one fifty yards in length. One end was left free and to the other was spliced the shark hook, a murderous-looking steel affair six inches or more in length attached to a steel chain some three feet long which, in turn, was joined to the shark line. Ti-Royale then threw four of the eight pieces of bait to Hassan, who quickly skewered them on to the four hooks. Gandhi, meanwhile, had scooped up the heads, guts and tails and lobbed them into the water as ground bait, and Zulu threw a bucket of sea-water over the deck to wash away the slippery mess of scales and blood. Hassan handed each of the others his prepared line and then the four took up their stations along one side of the *Golden Bells*. They tied the free end of the shark lines securely to ring-bolts let into the deck and cast out the baited

SHARK FOR SALE

hooks, which sank rapidly, dragged down by the weight of the chain.

All this time I was sitting on the cabin roof watching closely and wondering how so neat and efficient a working arrangement could result from such apparent pandemonium. Try as I might, I could not trace one wasted movement nor one superfluous action in the whole performance. There and then I realized that given the means to operate all the year round and the certainty of always fishing in the right place and not one they *thought* must be vaguely right, the *Golden Bells* could do well. While I was thinking about this, I saw Hassan stoop and poise his body expectantly. Each man had let his line trail down into the water till only fifteen yards or so remained coiled on deck, between his legs. The line was then held in the right hand, so that it ran between the curled fingers and the palm, coming out over the top of the index finger. Hassan swayed on his feet, balancing his body against each slight heave of the ship for maximum purchase.

He was not looking at the line now, but his ear was cocked towards it as though listening for something. His face was blank and his whole sensory apparatus seemed to be concentrated in that one half-outstretched arm that held the line. Suddenly, I saw the line go taut and at the same instant Hassan swung his body down and around so that the weight of his shoulder came behind the movement of his stiff arm. Then he grabbed the line with both hands and bent down till his knuckles touched the deck and the cord passed up and over the bulwark, which now acted as a brake. The muscles and sinews stood out along his spine like rows of pebbles joined with string. And then suddenly he was forced to let go, relaxing his grip in short bursts, and the line smoked and hissed in running out over the wooden bulwark. He would let it run free for two seconds and then bear down again, braking it to a halt. After a few of these spurts he could hold it. The shark had finished its initial run for freedom.

At the same time as Hassan was fighting with the shark, Zulu and Ti-Royale, the two on either side of him, had hauled in their own lines to prevent it from tangling all three in its wild rushes. Then Ti-Royale went to help Hassan and Zulu made ready the lance and wire noose. Slowly and inexorably the two fishermen drew the shark upwards till its sluggish bulk, no longer agile, wallowed alongside the *Golden Bells* just below the surface. Each

THE GOLDEN BELLS

time its head was lifted out of the water the brute came to life and thrashed wildly until it was once again submerged.

The idea of lifting the shark's head out of the water was to enable Zulu to slip the steel wire noose down over the snout, which he eventually succeeded in doing. Once the noose had fallen back past the shark's eyes it was jerked tight, so that it cut deeply into its hide, just behind the hinge of the jaw-bone. Now the crew had something solid to pull against without fear of it breaking, as might the shark line. Taking up the slack on the noose, they secured its free end to a nearby ring-bolt, and rested for a moment. Then Zulu picked up the long wooden lance with the narrow, spade-shaped iron head and, holding it above his head, thrust straight downward with all his strength. The lance sank in a foot deep, just behind the gill-slots and was immediately wrenched out again. For an instant the shark was motionless then, with a mighty lunge, it reared right up out of the water until its wicked cat's eyes were level with our own and it seemed to stand right up on its tail. At this point the steel wire pulled it up short and it flopped back in a welter of foam now tinged with pink. After struggling a few seconds more, it rolled on its side and again Zulu struck with the lance. Another flurry, but this time not so violent. Several more times this happened until the beast was lying comatose, its life-blood coiling down through the water like smoke. Hassan, Zulu and Ti-Royale pulled its massive head out of the water, right up to the level of the gunwale. No movement now, no fight apparent. But the green cat's eyes still glared balefully at us and the jaw hung obscenely open, revealing row upon row of wicked, triangular teeth.

They did not drag it on board immediately for sharks, though dead in all senses of the word, have a nasty habit of coming to simulated life with spasmodic reflexes.

The fishermen had dealt with the animal's life-force, now they must guard against its post-mortem actions. So two of them held the shark in place, flat against the side of the boat, with its tail dangling in the water, and Ti-Royale rained a shower of blows upon its snout with a heavy wooden mace. This stunned its reflexes, rendering the shark immobile until death had took firm hold of the massive carcass and effectively paralyzed the action of that deadly tail. Only then was the shark pulled on deck. To do this, Ti-Royale took the wire rope and the other two put their

SHARK FOR SALE

hands in through the gill-slots at the back of that grim mouth and grasped the bronchial artery where it joined the gill membranes. With this firm hold they heaved and grunted and groaned till, with a sudden, blubbery rush, the nine-foot length of the shark slid up over the side and settled with a dull thump in the scuppers.

The whole episode had taken perhaps ten minutes from the time Hassan had felt that first heavy, downward pull upon his line. Meanwhile, the others had carried on fishing. Ton-ton for bait – with reasonable success – and Gandhi, up in the bows, for shark – without success.

A little later we caught several more sharks and the same cycle of events led to their being successfully hauled on board. Then we drew a blank for a couple of hours. Eventually, Ton Milot decided we had drifted too far away from the *bordage*, so the engine was started and we had our customary morning meal of fish and rice as we motored out again. For the remainder of the day we cruised back and forth, looking for the edge of the plateau, but it was not until late afternoon that Milot succeeded in placing the *Golden Bells* in its immediate vicinity. By watching closely I was able to see where his navigation had gone astray, but for the present I was there to watch and learn, and it would be pointless to interfere at this stage until I had a complete grasp of the whole undertaking. In this new area we caught several more sharks, mostly small ones of four or five feet, which came on board with little effort. At six o'clock we anchored and the others proceeded to cut up all the sharks we had taken that day, whilst I sat and watched.

I had seen many acts of butchery in the past, ranging from that of cattle in modern abattoirs to various species of buck under the hot East African sun, but no matter how skilfully the job is carried out, I never enjoy these necessary proceedings. I was therefore not looking forward to it this time, but I was agreeably surprised to see how clean and simple this whole operation turned out to be.

Each of the crew selected a shark and, arming himself with a knife, stood astride the carcass. A couple of strokes and the dorsal fin was removed and thrown to one side. Two more slashes and the big pectorals followed. Then a long cut across the upper lobe of the tail and this was removed and thrown overboard (the reason for this being that the upper lobe contains the continuation of the spine and is consequently too boney for preparation as dried shark fins). So far there was no blood at all.

The finless, tail-less body was turned on its side and the knife pushed in through the last gill-slot. A cut was then made up over the top of the head to join the gill-slot on the other side, then on down, underneath, coming up in a complete circle. At that point the entire head, complete with gill-fronds, fell away from the trunk. The head was picked up and dropped overboard and a bucket of sea water was thrown over the stump to wash away the small amount of blood left there. Then the trunk was rolled on its back and slit from vent to stump, whereupon the massive liver, along with the entrails and pancreas, slid gently out and were pushed over the side. Another bucket of sea water and there lay our shark, a great bloodless, odourless and virtually boneless hundredweight of meat. Next this clean, firm, white flesh was carved into neat, flat rectangles – perhaps two feet long, eighteen inches wide and four inches thick. These slabs were then creased longitudinally with a knife and salt was rubbed into the slits thus formed. Finally, all the slabs were collected and stowed down in the main cabin that served as our hold, stacked, one upon another, like bricks. And that was all.

After all the sharks had been disposed of in this fashion we had tea and then Ton Milot and I sat up in the bows talking, whilst the others prepared their gear for the following day. While we were thus occupied I saw a very large shark of eighteen feet or more go swimming sedately by, right on the surface. I jumped to my feet and shouted for a baited shark-line, when Ton-ton interrupted me.

'No good,' he said. 'Supposing you do hook him, what then? He'll pull so hard against the dead weight of the boat that your line will snap. Even if you get him alongside, what then? How will you kill him, without him stoving-in the side of the boat with his tail? It's no good. Leave him alone. We always do,' he added smugly.

So I sat down again.

I asked him about these large sharks and he admitted that there were a lot to be found along the *bordage* and in the deep itself, but that they were just not worth catching. The damage

SHARK FOR SALE

to boat and gear cost far more than they fetched when sold. No, it was no good.

But I was not so sure. After all, one of these sharks, even cut up and salted down, would weight a third of a ton. Maybe half a ton. Two such sharks a day for six days would be a five-ton load, double the normal catch for a ten-day fishing trip. Was it impossible, as Ton Milot had said, or might not some new technique be evolved to deal with these huge beasts?

For the remainder of that trip I examined the problem from all angles and by the time we arrived back in Mahé I had the germ of an idea.

TWO

First Trials

Canst thou fill his skin with barbed irons? Or his head with fish spears? Lay thine hand upon him, remember the battle, do no more. (Job xli, 7 & 8)

Before deciding to take on the *Golden Bells* I had gone into the whole economy of shark-fishing as thoroughly as possible. By and large this local industry was divided into two sections: the catching and salting down of the shark was the work of one group of schooner owners, and the drying-out and marketing was the responsibility of various exporting agencies. A brief study showed where the real profits of the business lay.

Wet-salted shark fetched 300 rupees (£22 10s) per ton, when sold by the fishing boats to the shark-drying concerns. Out of this sum the owner paid his crew ninety rupees as wages to be divided amongst them, and the coxswain received a bonus of an extra twenty rupees on top of this. Then there was salt, fuel, provisions, lines, hooks, upkeep and depreciation of the vessel, all to be taken into consideration. Unless a schooner consistently brought in more than two tons per voyage, the whole undertaking was a financial flop.

On the other hand, the *dried* shark was sold for 1,300 rupees (£100) per ton. Even allowing for a loss in weight of between thirty and thirty-five per cent whilst drying out and fifty rupees per ton for freightage, this still left a very handsome margin of profit for the exporter. Moreover, the dealer in dried shark had little capital at stake in the operation – no ships to lose, no crews to worry about – he simply bought the shark as it arrived. If one boat did not bring in any, another one would. Whatever happened, he was safe.

SHARK FOR SALE

At first glance, then, it would seem that the obvious thing to do would be to combine the two operations under one concern. But there was a serious snag to this. The snag was possessing a piece of land suitable for use as a fish-drying base. In the Seychelles land is at a premium. Not only are prices high but, due to overpopulation, estates seldom come on the market. The price of an indifferent plot is some £80 per acre, but even that would be reasonable if one were ever available. For a shark-drying base one needs three things. Firstly, a coastal strip with good landing facilities; secondly, the area must be free of shady trees and thirdly, and most important, the site must be utterly unapproachable by outsiders. If it were not, then one would be liable to lose one's entire stock of drying fish through petty pilfering.

Such pilfering would not be of an organized nature, but a casual 'lifting' by each and every passer-by. Dried shark-flesh is a comparative luxury to most of the inhabitants, for not only does it nearly all go for export, but the price it commands puts it out of reach of the majority, whose low wages result in a monotonous diet of vegetables, rice and fish. Consequently one cannot really blame those who avail themselves of the opportunity to satisfy a very real hunger, by slipping a nice piece of shark-meat inside their shirts as they happen to stroll by the drying tables.

This 'stealing-to-live' is quite a problem on Mahé. So much so, in fact, that legislation has been introduced ruling that any person carrying more than two coconuts must have a permit. If, in passing a plantation, a Creole helps himself to one or two coconuts, that is legitimate, since presumably he or she intends to eat them, and what authority could morally prevent a hungry person from feeding on so prolific an island? However, a person who collects a sackful of nuts, and does not hold a permit to do so, is a thief, since undoubtedly he intends to sell or barter them for personal gain. A subtle and humane distinction. As regards the drying of salt-fish, it would be useless merely to buy a plot of land, erect a tall fence around it and employ a watchman; fences, apart from being expensive, can be climbed and besides, *who would watch the watchman?*

This problem, then, of having to have one's shark-drying site in an inaccessible place really means that the only satisfactory solution is to own a small island somewhere near Mahé. This is

FIRST TRIALS

precisely what has been done by those engaged in this work, or rather, with the advent of commercial shark-fishing to the Seychelles, those who owned such islands were quick to set aside part of them to serve as a dried-fish base. Since the chance of ever being able to obtain an island of my own was just about nil, it was obvious that, for a start at any rate, I would have to sell my catch to one of the exporters, as did all the other boat-owners. However, I could see from the diminishing catches which the shark-fishermen were now bringing in that the heyday of easy fishing was almost over and that very soon demand would far exceed supply. When that happened, the fishing schooner that continued to bring in consistent catches would be able to dictate terms to the exporter, provided that the owner had sufficient confidence in his fishing technique to sign and maintain a contract to deliver so much wet shark per month. Owing to the haphazardness of the shark-fishing at that moment no boat-owner was in a position to offer such a service.

This meant that I would first have to experiment and train a crew so that a successful and sure technique of shark-catching might be evolved. It was useless merely to sit on shore, as did all the other boat-owners, and send out the *Golden Bells* under the guidance of Ton Milot. Not that he or the crew were not capable of shark-fishing, but if this business were ever to grow into anything, then a new approach to the whole system must be forthcoming. It was quite likely that the difficulties would prove insurmountable and I was prepared to abandon the whole idea should that be the case, but only after I had given it a good try; to this end I gave myself eighteen months in which to achieve success.

The main lesson I had learned on those first two trips was that under the present system the catch of shark depended almost entirely upon the accuracy of navigation. If the boat were positioned and held accurately upon the *bordage*, then a good catch was assured. If one fished elsewhere, it was a mere waste of time. Now it was patently impossible to teach the illiterate coxswains the science of navigation; to use a sextant, to consult mathematical tables, even to read a chart. Put simply, the present fishing method depended upon the fishermen finding the shark. Since they could not be taught to do this, what was the alternative? The only answer I could think of was that if the fishermen could

SHARK FOR SALE

not find the shark, then the shark must find the fishermen. One could not rely on the fishermen; well, then, rely on the shark! And it was no use relying upon the small daytime shark, the pack-shark of the Mahé plateau. These were far too light ever to build up an impressive catch tonnage and besides that they were rapidly being fished out of existence. The answer lay in being able to catch and boat those huge monsters that passed the daytime in the perpetual darkness of the great depths and only ventured on to the plateau at night. To ensure success the *Golden Bells* would have to be placed so that two or three of these giants were taken each and every fishing day, or rather night, since that was their normal feeding time. This meant that we would have to revise our whole timetable. No longer would we fish by day and go to bed with the sun. This in itself would be a radical change and would mean new gear in the form of adequate deck lighting, besides other equipment like lifting tackle for dealing with the heavier carcasses, new killing weapons, fenders to prevent the threshing bodies from damaging the hull, and the many other necessities that sprang to mind. I could see already that the development of a new technique would involve the successful solution of a host of problems and failure to deal with any one of these might mean the collapse of the whole scheme.

With all this to think over and the preparation of the several new gadgets which I hoped would prove useful on this next voyage, it as almost ten days before we were ready to set out again. This time we had with us yet another fisherman, a tall, gaunt, silent man with strange pale-green eyes, like a cat. He was not a stranger but an established member of the crew who, it appeared, had only missed the previous two trips through having gone over to Praslin, a neighbouring island, to visit a sick relative. His name was Ishmael and I wondered whether the bestower of it had ever read Melville's thrilling tale of the great white whale and its human pursuers. Later I had occasion to speculate whether this unusual sobriquet had been bestowed by some prophetic impulse, a premonition of tragedy. I took to him at once, for he had a quiet confidence, an inward reserve that marked him as a man of character. His gauntness was not the result of undernourishment but rather a gypsy leanness that etched his frame with hard, sinewy lines. I was glad to have him with me.

FIRST TRIALS

We weighed anchor in mid-afternoon and, taking advantage of the breeze, sailed up around the northern tip of Mahé and then, altering course, drove between the main island and the humped-up mass of Silhouette towards the distant banks to the west. By daybreak we had lost all sight of land and were well out over the sunken plateau. However, we did not stop there but carried on until evening, by which time we had gained the furthermost edge, about 130 miles from Port Victoria. There we stopped, but in direct contrast to our normal practice, did not anchor. Instead, I had the tiller unshipped and the sails rigged so that the little cutter rode without any way upon her, and drifted gently with the current. Once she had settled down I dropped a heavy line, buoyed at the end with an empty oil drum, over the side. At three points along this rope, thinner shark lines were suspended, weighed down by the heavy metal hooks and trace-chains. I had figured that the most likely method of bringing in any baited hooks in the vicinity of the sharks would be by not remaining in one spot throughout the night but by drifting, willy-nilly, relying on the law of averages to carry the *Golden Bells* and her lines across the path of some night-marauding shark. In this way our vessel would be sweeping an area ten or more miles in length, instead of just that sea-bed beneath her, were she at anchor. To help us further in crossing the tracks of the big fish I had brought along a barrel containing a mulch of turtle guts, crushed crabs, pig's blood and sand. This we would scoop up and toss over the side at intervals throughout the night. The purpose of the sand was to drag fragments and perhaps the scent of the ground-bait down to the bottom, where the sharks we were seeking would cruise. I hoped that this would attract those in the vicinity towards our hooks and also provide a sense-titillating trail in our wake, up which any stray and hungry carnivore might wander unawares.

After we had made these preparations for the night's work, we sat down to a belated meal. Later, the others having all curled upon the bare deck, I found myself chatting away to Milot who was as usual finding it difficult to sleep.

'What do you call those clouds up there, you English?' he said, pointing to the wisp of high cirrus that lay like a veil across the face of the moon. 'Mares' tails,' I replied. 'Some people say that it means strong winds in the offing.'

SHARK FOR SALE

'Hmmmm. Mares' tails, eh? That's an odd name. Which reminds me. Did I ever tell you what happened to me in Durban years ago? No? Well, it was like this. It was my first long voyage abroad and as luck would have it we were held up in port with boiler trouble. I soon ran out of money and got tired of hanging around all day, and as we were due to stay quite a while I decided to nip off and get a job on shore on the quiet. The very first day, *ou capable croire*, I heard that there was a strike of waggon drivers at the breweries and they were taking on temporary help. Now, as you know, there aren't any horses in the Seychelles, but I'd seen pictures of them and their rigging looked quite seaman-like and straightforward, so I thought I'd have a go. Once at the brewery I could scarcely answer the *patron*, who asked me questions about did I know Durban, and was I used to horses, for looking at all the crates of beer lying around. There was beer everywhere, a regular muddle, what with the strike and all. Anyway, I must have looked right or maybe the *patron* was too flustered to care, for the next thing I knew was that I was outside the gates perched up behind the biggest animal I'd ever seen and with a list of streets and stores in my hand. Think of it, Ton Milot in command of a brewer's dray loaded with booze and never seen a horse in his life! Didn't know any of the names of the streets either, for that matter.

'Well, I thought to myself I'd better take things easy and, just to settle my nerves, I reached back and helped myself to a bottle. After I'd drunk that I felt better and since that monstrous beast in front seemed to know where he was going, I just let it go on – after all, he'd been doing the job for years, while this was my first day at it. So I had another bottle of beer to pass the time. After a while I noticed the houses were getting fewer and by the time I'd got things shifted around a bit and got a crate up front with me where it was handy, *ou capable croire*, we were right out in the country. We ambled on for a while and then the old horse turned off down a dirt track, stopped and began to eat some grass. Didn't seem to want to go on, either. So there was Ton Milot in the middle of bloody Africa with a waggon-load of beer and a horse that had joined the rest of the strikers. Must have been a Union horse. It was no good just sitting in the hot sun worrying about it, so I got off and staggered over to a shady tree with two crates of beer. One to sit on and one to help me think.

FIRST TRIALS

Then I went and anchored the horse by putting a couple more crates under the wheels, like hatch-wedges. Like that I was able to go back and think in peace.

'The afternoon came and went and nothing happened except that the horse got restless, so I gave it a beer to steady its nerves, and do-you-know-what, it fair lapped it up. Proper brewery horse that. It made me feel much better somehow, now I'd got someone to drink with. By the time evening came we were proper friendly and I'd figured out how to get him out of the shafts and all. That night I slept under the waggon and the horse under the tree.

'Next morning seemed like being a nice day and I reckoned that the strikers would think it was too nice a day to go back to work, and now that applied to me too. So we spent the day drinking beer and eating grass. Lovely day, that. In the afternoon I went for a little walk and found a small store down the road run by an Indian fellow. After a chat with him I fixed it up to open an account using my beer as credit. When I went back I had blankets, food and tobacco for myself and a bucket for the horse, because I was fed up with him spilling so much beer when I poured it out of the bottle down his gullet. Just because we had a waggon load there was no need to waste it. So there we stayed, the two of us. As things got used up a bit I was able to clear a nice place in the back of the dray and fix up a little cabin for myself. The Indian lent me a chair and sold me a camp bed and a Primus for two crates. Oh, it was a lovely fortnight that! Only trouble was, I'm afraid it ruined that horse. Have you ever seen a drunk horse, m'sieur? My, oh my – what a carry-on! Wouldn't stand up, but just used to roll on the ground making funny noises. Then, when it tried to get up, it used to get its legs all crossed. Once it sat on a crate and I spent the whole day picking splinters of glass out of its backside. One day I thought it had had enough, so I wouldn't give it any more. Got in a terrible temper the thing did. Started kicking and tried to bite me, so I poured it out a bucket-full and then we were friends again. Wonderful drinking partner that horse except when it got the wind. Two whole weeks before we'd drunk or sold all that beer. I gave the last five crates to the Indian and made him promise he'd look after my friend and get a message to the brewery telling them where to find their dray. The Indian got me a lift on a lorry going down to the docks and do you know, *ou capable croire*, that same afternoon I got back, we sailed. I often wondered what became of that horse. Fine animal that. Good friend, too!'

Long before dawn we were all up and eager to see what the night had brought us – if anything. The enthusiasm of the others, I suspected, was largely due to their natural desire to see the 'foreigner' make a fool of himself with all this nonsense of loose lines and buckets of slop. It was therefore doubly reassuring to feel the main line dead and heavy to our pull and to realize that some inert mass was resisting our efforts. While the first shark-line was still some distance away we could make out a pale, leaden, torpedo-shape that swung lazily to and fro way down at the end of the line. A glance showed us that we would not have any trouble with this one, for it hung lifelessly, belly up, having drowned itself in attempting to get rid of the hook. Hoisted on deck it proved something of a disappointment, for this was no giant but a seven or eight foot Soupfin (Carcharinus blekeri), such as we met with frequently near the *bordage*. The crew, too, were unimpressed and it was with some indifference that we returned to our task of hauling in the rest of the line. This attitude soon altered, however, when we felt the rope still unnaturally heavy under our fingers and the strange little tremors that now ran up its taut length. There was still something to come, and something big, too!

All at once the line just stopped coming in and, try as we might, we could not gain another inch. It was as though whatever lay at the end had been asleep and now, on waking, was quietly but determinedly pitting its strength against ours.

The pressure on the line increased relentlessly until we were forced to give way, letting the line out foot by foot in response to this powerful new challenge. Finally, Milot gave it a half turn around a cleat and, momentarily checked, we were able to relieve ourselves of the strain of hauling in the line. Within a few seconds the majestic pull increased still further, the *Golden Bells* swung gently, stern on, to the hidden source of power and gathered speed as she was towed firmly southwards, wavelets slapping protestingly against her square stern at this undignified form of locomotion. We all looked at each other without comment. It was a new experience for us as well as the cutter. After a while,

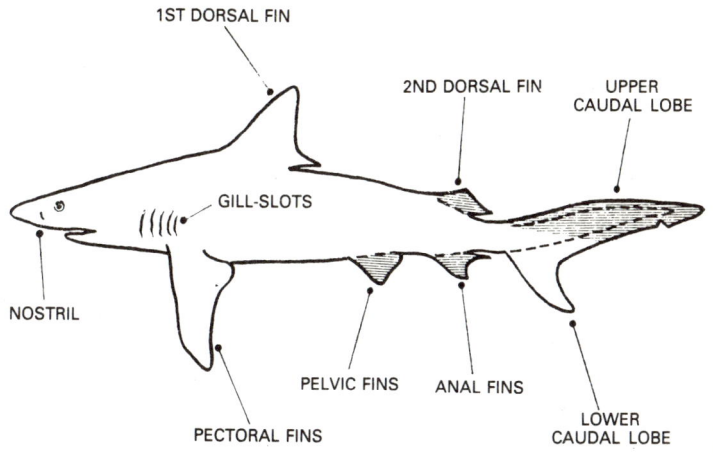

Typical shark – showing fin nomenclature.
Note (i) fins shaded are not used in preparing dried shark-fins;
(ii) continuation of spine shown as dotted line.

when our 'tug' showed no signs of flagging, I started the engine and went full astern in an effort to catch up with whatever-it-was that was towing us and so take in some slack. In this I was only partially successful, for no sooner had we hauled in some fifty yards of line, than the creature – possibly annoyed by the noise of the engine – swung round at right angles and began to zig-zag alarmingly. I cut the motor and at once the pull on the line slackened, for which I was thankful, for while the line had proved capable of holding out against a direct and slowly applied pressure I was doubtful if it could withstand the sudden shocks caused by rapid manoeuvrings. Slowly and gently we continued to take in line until we hung almost above our quarry. All of us leant out over the stern to catch the first glimpse of it. When we did so and the true size of the brute became clear we were, quite honestly, frightened by what we saw. For a start I made out a long, aerofoil object that stirred slightly and showed up lighter than the dark sea-bed surrounding it. It had a vague fishy-shape, though somehow not really shark-like, and moreover though of fair size it could hardly have been big enough to pull the *Golden Bells*. It was only after quite a few seconds that I realized that what I had taken for the entire fish was in fact only its tail-fin and the black mass which I had assumed to be the seabed was in fact the actual shark!

Once again we looked at each other wordlessly; then, like small boys who have looked over a garden wall to find a tribe of real live cannibals camping on the neighbour's lawn, we quietly withdrew to the security of the cockpit and held a whispered conversation. The majority wanted to cut loose from the monster there and then, and I was in two minds to agree with them. Ton Milot, however, was determined to have a try at killing the brute, and in this he was joined by Gandhi, who itched to test his giant strength against this worthy contestant. Finally we decided to make the attempt, but if things got too rough we would abandon the line to the shark.

The first thing was to see how tired the brute was and to determine this we tried hauling the creature up towards the surface, foot by foot. This went off quite well and we were able to raise the shark to within twenty feet of the keel, at which distance it was possible to make a good estimate of its size. As the *Golden Bells* pirouetted slowly with the current we passed right over the giant so that it was possible to effect a direct comparison between our respective lengths. When its snout lay exactly under the rudder I raised my arm so that Ton Milot, who had scurried up to the bows to mark the position of the tail, was able to plumb-bob its nether extremity. At this signal he peered over the side, edged a little further forward and then make a decisive scratch across the bulwark with his knife. The point at which he did so was exactly three feet from the stem of the boat. Our shark measured twenty-nine feet in length.

Once we had established this, I went ahead with identifying the type. It had a broad head, a well-streamlined body and a very large symmetrical tail. In colour it was dark grey above, with pale flanks merging in to the dead-white belly. The fins lacked any tip-markings and immediately in front of the tail the trunk flattened out onto two long horizontal keel surfaces. These points, together with its outstanding size, labelled it clearly as a Great White Shark, sometimes known as 'the white death' – the most dreaded creature of the ocean.

FIRST TRIALS

Professor J. L. B. Smith, in his book, *The Sea Fishes of Southern Africa*, says about this shark '. . . it attains 40 feet and a weight of at least 2 tons. A 12-foot specimen can bite a man in half, a 20-foot specimen can swallow a man whole . . . one of 18 feet, when opened up, contained the foot of a native, half a goat, two pumpkins, a wicker-covered scent bottle, two large fishes, one small shark and unidentifiable remains . . .'

Knowing all this, however, did not help us very much, for the problem still remained as to how to kill the monster and get it on board afterwards. We slackened the line and allowed a greater distance to intervene between us. This not only gave us a feeling of temporary security but allowed us to make our preparations without disturbing the giant.

First of all we got the fenders ready to protect the hull from damage. These consisted of old motor-car tyres, pierced to allow them to be strung on heavy rope and now slung over the side to act as baffles at either end of the ship. Since we anticipated bringing the shark alongside so that its head lay at our stern and its tail at our bows, it was vital to protect these two areas of planking to prevent them being staved in by its frenzied lashings. We then prepared three flexible steel-wire strops to pass around its body and a fourth was shackled to the stand-by anchor. The idea of this last device was that the weight of the anchor when thrown overboard would drag the shark's head down and so lift the tail right out of the water. In this position it would be easy to sever with a blow of the axe the main artery that lay at the base of the tail.

When all was ready and the crew were in their allotted places we began to haul in the line. This time, however, the Great White Shark no longer lay conveniently comatose but began cruising around in a wide arc so that we continually found that the beast was either coming up on the wrong side or else the wrong way round. The tension mounted with each vain attempt and the shark's manoeuvrings became more and more violent until at last Ton Milot yelled at Gandhi to throw over the main anchor and let it drag, so that the *Golden Bells* would, at any rate, stop waltzing around with each fresh movement the shark made. It was a fatal move. No sooner had the anchor bitten into the sand and the cutter began to straighten up, than the huge shark made a determined dash ahead, swung round the anchor chain, baulked as the line caught on it and then, with one savage lunge of its head snapped the rope as if it were a strand of cotton. Five seconds later we on the *Golden Bells* had the ocean to ourselves.

It was then a little past nine o'clock; our efforts of the past three hours had been wasted and all we had to remind us of the incident was a piece of broken line and a knife mark across one bulwark. But the failure had brought us something: *we now knew that at night the giant sharks could be caught on the plateau by this method of drift-fishing*. And this one fact was all I wanted.

After this initial episode of the great white shark we continued with our normal daytime routine to make sure that a fair catch would fill our hold by the end of the voyage. Each evening, however, we set our drift-lines to prove that our first success was not a mere fluke and each morning we had the satisfaction of seeing that we had here the bare bones of a system good enough to open up a new era in shark-fishing. Admittedly there still remained a tremendous amount of experimental work to be done before the technique became reliable, but with each shark we hooked we learnt new facts.

Already we knew that much depended upon the depth at which one trailed the lines and we finally decided that eight fathoms produced the most consistent results. Again, the angle which the vertical bait-lines assumed proved a very critical factor. If they were too light in weight they streamed out to tangle with the main line and if they were too heavy the sharks seemed to have difficulty in swallowing the hook. The right depth depended upon the strength of the current and the weight of chain joining the hook. Obviously, the more hooks one trailed the bigger the area swept and the greater the chances of taking sharks, but there was a practical limit to the length of line it was possible to handle with six men and within a given time. Also, if we strung the hooks too close together then not only did we risk entangling them, but also the catch rate dropped for some reason which we were then at a loss to understand. Another factor which we noticed specially was the length of time we should allow the line to drift. If the line was trailed for too short a period then not only were few sharks taken – sometimes none at all – but those that *were* hooked were far too lively to subdue and because of their size they usually escaped while we were trying to bring

FIRST TRIALS

them on board. On the other hand, if the hooks were left alone all through the night then we usually found that the majority of those caught had been so savaged and mauled by other sharks that they were mostly useless for our purpose. Between these two time limits lay a period in which it was possible to haul in the line and find that the sharks caught were not only, as yet, in good condition but had usually been obliging enough to drown themselves by pulling ineffectively against the spring of the long length of line. All these points and many others we learnt through direct experience before we returned to Mahé.

When we finally did so, it was with a little over two and three quarter tons of wet shark in our hold, of which just over half had been caught by drift-lines. The crew, and Ton Milot in particular, were now entirely 'sold' on this new method of fishing or, as Hassan put it, it was the first time he had been on a ship that obligingly caught sharks for him while he slept! But I knew that many months would pass and much new gear would have to be bought before these trial methods became established day-do-day procedure. From the data we had collected on this trip I had worked out a theoretical and ideal drift-line and now had need of some three-quarters of a mile of special line, fifty or more buoys, dozens of shark hooks, hundreds of yards of suitable chain, rolls of steel trace-wire and other such equipment. But it was also essential that the *Golden Bells* earned the cash to provide all these items by bringing in a record tonnage of shark within the next two months. This, then, was the first, and most important, problem to be tackled.

THREE

Fortune Bank and Ishmael

> *The sword of him that layeth at him cannot hold:*
> *the spear, the dart, nor the habergeon . . . Darts*
> *are counted as stubble: he laugheth at the shaking*
> *of a spear.* (Job xli, 26 & 29)

It was the beginning of our fifth trip. Looking back over the bubbly wake of the *Golden Bells* from where we squatted on the stern, the gaunt skyline of Mahé stood out stark against the lavender sky. The sun was setting and the scene had a certain fixity about it. To the west towering clouds in great masses served as a backcloth to the mountains of the island that lay astern, and overhead a white tropic bird fluttered nervously near the masthead, catching the last rays of the sun with its wings.

For a while we sat on in silence, till the light faded from the sky and the spell was broken.

Ton Milot turned to me. 'Do you know why we Creole fishermen don't swim?' he said.

I shook my head.

'So I never told you the story of Pierrot? No? Then I will now.'

So saying, he settled himself more comfortably on the deck, filled and lit a blackened pipe which he produced from somewhere inside his shirt, puffed a while reflectively and began.

'All this happened before the war, about 1930 or '32. At that time there lived on La Digue,' he named a small island about twenty miles from Mahé, 'a very powerful *Ti-Albert*.[1] One day

---

[1] *Ti-Albert*: A Black Magician (the term originating from Mauritius). *Ti-Albert* (Little Albert) Black Magician. *Grand-Albert* (Big Albert) White Magician. Both derived from Albertus Magnus, a thirteenth-century alchemist, philosopher and wizard. The reason for the differentiation '*Ti*' and '*Grand*' is lost.

this *Ti-Albert* was walking along the beach when he came across a small hammerhead shark trapped by the receding tide in a rock-pool. He saw that it was an evil creature like himself, but that, unlike himself, it was weak-willed and feeble-minded. So he spoke to it and by his art made it his servant, and as a token of its servitude he took it out of the water and with his knife cut certain secret marks and signs upon it here' – he touched his neck – 'and here' – he indicated his flanks. 'In this manner he made it his own and gave it a name, Pierre, in mockery of the disciple who was a fisherman. Then he put it back in the open sea and went on with his walk. Each week, however, he came back to the place and stood at the water's edge and called out in a high voice, "Pierre-oooh!", and each week the young shark came nosing through the sea right to his feet and he would speak to it and see that it was all right and would note its growth and finally give it his dark blessing and dismiss it as one would a servant. At the end of three years the hammerhead was eight feet long and after four it was ten feet or more and the *Ti-Albert* saw that it was now thoroughly nasty and strong enough to start work, so he spoke to it and set it its task in this fashion.

' "Pierrot, now you are big and strong and your mouth can cut a man in half. It's high time you began work and your work is this. You must swim around the shore-lines and the banks of Mahé day and night, in bad weather or calm, never sleeping, never resting, always watchful. When you are doing this you must listen very carefully and every time you hear a fisherman fall into the water out of his canoe or tumble out of his boat, no matter how far away he shall be (for by my magic I shall cause you to hear these sounds the instant they occur), you will straightway transport yourself there with one swish of your tail (and my magic will aid you in this, too), and you will eat up that fisherman and not allow him to escape you. You must do this because here all the fishermen do respect me no longer but laugh at me, and one of them has even run off with my wife! So now you will do this and I shall be pleased. I have no need to call you again, Pierrot. Go now and do your work." The *Ti-Albert* went back to his house and the monster to the depths.

'From then on every fisherman who fell in the water was invariably taken and eaten by Pierrot, so that soon we Creoles were frightened of the sea and would not swim, for Pierrot did not distinguish between those who fell in by accident and those who entered it on purpose.'

Ton Milot finished his story and continued gazing out across the now dark sea.

'And is Pierrot still around nowadays?' I asked.

'No,' he replied. 'The *Ti-Albert* died in '38 and with no one to protect him Pierrot, now grown huge, was mistaken for a submarine during the war and had a depth-charge dropped on him. That finished him off! However, Pierrot was very prolific and peopled these waters with many sons and daughters, and although they have no magical properties they are all still very fierce, so we still don't swim,' he concluded smugly.

'And you believe all this?' I asked.

He turned towards me and I could tell by his voice when he answered that he was grinning to himself in the darkness as he spoke:

'Who? Me? Pouff! I'm Ton Milot! A fine fool I'd be to believe a lot of nonsense like that. Me believe it? *Ou capable croire!* But these do. Don't you, eh? You, Ishmael and you, Gandhi – you'd believe any bloody rubbish, wouldn't you now?'

Silence followed this last remark of his and after a few moments he went on:

'There you are. See. Told you so. What can you do with blokes like that?' He let the sentence hang in the air unanswered.

But it was Gandhi who had the last word. 'Eh, Ton Milot – if it's all foolishness why don't you swim and why do you carry the *Kha* as we do?'

'What's this *Kha*?' I asked.

By way of an answer Ton Milot sucked hard on his pipe until it glowed deep red in the bowl, then quickly removed it and held it aslant beneath his wrist. There on the leathery skin, illuminated by the faint circle of light from the pipe, I saw three small Xs, each separated from the other by a dot. He put the pipe back in his mouth, drew on it again and lit up the other wrist in the same fashion. This time I saw a series of Ks, lying on their sides across his forearm. Moving the pipe further up his arm he showed me a similar series of marks on the inside of the elbow joint.

'Here also,' he said, touching himself on either side of the groin and behind each knee. 'We have them made when we are young men, before we start fishing. Some think it protects us from evil things and happenings at sea. It's probably foolishness, but it is custom.'

'Has it any religious meaning, a Christian origin?' I asked.

'Perhaps. Something to do with Christ maybe. It could be. I don't know . . .' he finished lamely.

None of the others knew either, or if they did they would not tell me. If it was of semi-Christian origin one explanation might be that the Xs represented the Greek *Chi*, the initial letter of Christos. What the Ks stand for remains a mystery. The interesting thing about these marks is that each group is placed at a point on the body where the main arteries are nearest the skin and where the pulse may be felt – perhaps this is significant, perhaps not . . .

For the next two days we sailed on southwards, across the invisible *bordage* and out into the realm of the great ocean itself, for on this voyage our destination was a distant *sec* known as Fortune Bank. My reason for choosing this area was its very remoteness, for I knew the fishing schooners seldom if ever visited it, not daring to leave the main Mahé plateau and sail out over the deep water that separates the two banks. Here I hoped to find sharks in profusion, roaming freely over the shallows during the day as they had once done around Mahé. A quick and successful trip now would go a long way towards providing the new gear needed to continue with the night drift-line experiment.

The morning of the third day found me patently anxious as to whether we would find Fortune Bank, for a high overcast hid the sun and made my sextant, on which we relied to ascertain our position, completely useless. As the morning advanced, however, so did Ton Milot become more and more cheerful, until at length I was forced to ask him the reason.

'Of course I'm happy,' he said. 'We're nearly there! Another hour or two and we'll see sharks enough to fill the boat. How do I know? Easy. Look at that,' he pointed over the side. 'See that strip of seaweed? That's from La Fortune, that is. Look how green it is. It's been floating for less than twelve hours otherwise

SHARK FOR SALE

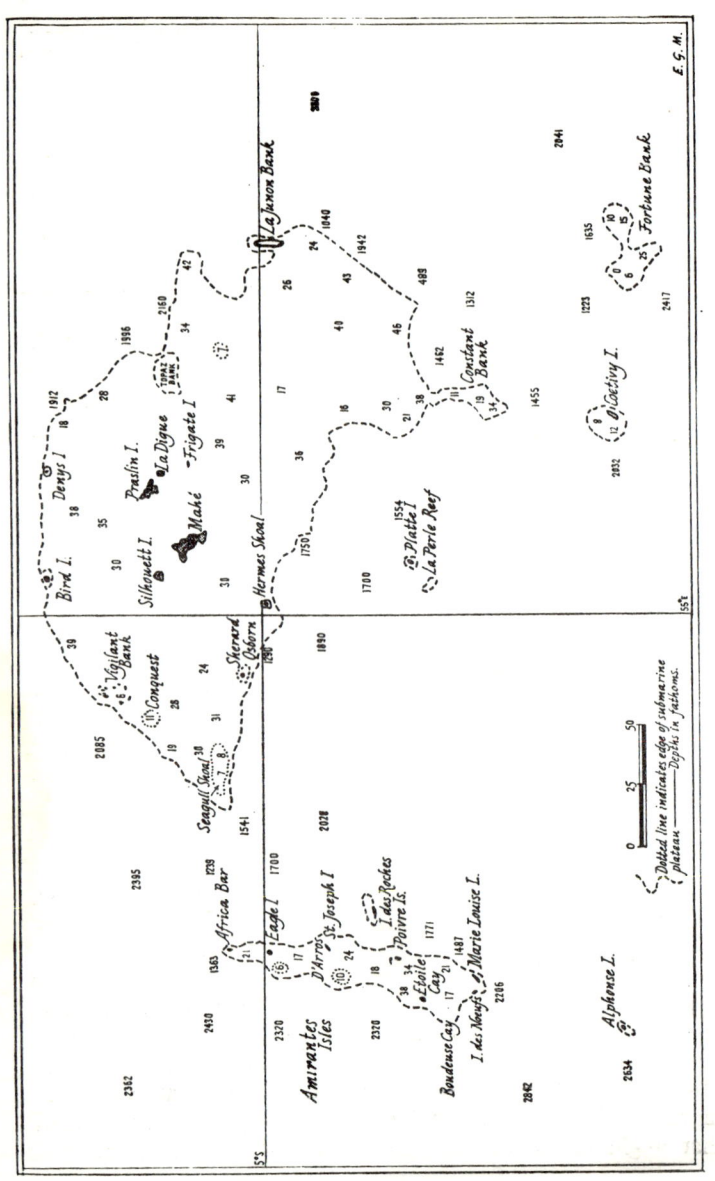

Seychelles Group (Northern portion only)

FORTUNE BANK AND ISHMAEL

it would be brown all round the edges. That means we must be within six or eight miles of the *sec*. Another thing. See the way it lies in the water? It's taken up the lie of the current and we're sailing parallel with it, so La Fortune must be dead ahead. Ton Milot doesn't need a sextant and a pile of complicated books to tell him where he is. He just sniffs the air, cocks an eye at the sea and if he's still none the wiser the seagulls take pity on him and whisper in his ear. *Ou capable croire!*'

Less than an hour later the old man beckoned me forward to where he was lying in the shade of the jib. Without saying a word he pointed ahead. At first I could not see anything, then on the horizon a faint cloud of minute specks became visible, rising and falling like gnats over a pond on a summer's evening. They were sea-birds following a run of fish, and birds in these numbers, far from land, meant fish in considerable quantities. Moreover, such shoals were usually only to be found along the edges of the banks. Sure enough, as we drew nearer the demarcation of a *bordage* became visible: a slow, coiling ribbon of disturbed water whose inner edge was marked by eddies and wavelets.

Such easily visible signs of the presence of a *sec* beneath the surface are to be found only where the drop-off into the abyss is unusually abrupt, causing violent up-wellings along its front. Even then these tell-tale signs are often lost to view in the general movement of the sea's surface, unless the day is unusually calm, as it was then. This time we were fortunate in having both of these factors in our favour, the location of the bank was made easy for us.

An atmosphere of unrest and of anticipation crept over our little ship. We were expecting great things from Fortune Bank and the three-day voyage across the lonely sea had served merely to whet our appetites. Now we were nearly there and the waiting was almost over. Without any of the usual promptings on my part the others had laid out their lines and were making the *Golden Bells* ready for the work that lay ahead. Up in the bows Ishmael was hard at work on a lance-head, honing it to a bright, razor sharpness. Astern, Gandhi had let go two of our heaviest shark-lines, baited with strips of a small tunny caught earlier that morning. These streamed behind us, ready for any cruising shark that might cut across our wake. Ton Milot doused the deck planks with a last bucket of sea water to ensure that no foot would slip.

There was nothing else to do. We were ready and the ripple-marked edge of Fortune Bank was now less than 200 yards away.

'*Aiee-yah! Guette ça!*' It was Hassan at the helm, and before we were able to turn around we felt the deck tilt under our feet as he jammed the rudder hard over. The others, by long experience, knew instinctively what had occurred and immediately swung into action. Ti-Royale cut the throttle and put the motor out of gear, and Ton Milot ran down the jib and foresail in a welter of canvas while Gandhi paid out on the mainsail boom. In a few moments the cutter was brought to a near standstill, lying across the breeze. By this manoeuvre the two lines that had been hanging limply astern were brought onto the beam, but one of them was no longer hanging limp. It was stretched bowstring-taut, dangerously near breaking point. Even as I watched, the other line twitched suddenly and pulled rapidly downwards, drawing off the slack that lay coiled on deck until it, too, was brought up with a jolt by the ringbolt to which it was fastened. Hassan, already trying his hardest to release some of the tension from the first line, was powerless to deal with this second strike. The swarthy Zulu was first to his aid but he, in turn, only served as another human spring, taking the edge of each fresh, savage jerk that threatened to snap the line. After a few moments Gandhi and Ti-Royale arrived and there were two men to each line. Then Ishmael, Ton Milot and myself. Seven of us, and it seemed as though we were trying to drag up the ocean bed itself. A fathom or two would come in and then we would be brought to a halt. The line would grow heavier in our grasp, stretching visibly, and we would be forced to give way, losing perhaps all we had gained. Another heave: another small gain, and so it went on. Our breathing became laboured. Sweat ran slippery down our backs and into our eyes, causing them to smart and sting. But the line was coming in.

Slowly, almost imperceptibly, the downward pull of the two sharks grew weaker. First one man was able to drop out and then another, until there were three of us free to prepare the wire nooses, lances and lifting gear. Leaning far out over the side to see how near the surface the fish were, I discovered that the two lines had become tangled and the sharks, both large *Peau*

FORTUNE BANK AND ISHMAEL

*Claire*s (White-Tipped), now lay side by side, securely trussed and snapping ineffectively. Such a situation could be dangerous, since both beasts would now have to be dealt with at the same time.

Once on the surface the wire nooses were quickly slipped over their snouts, but so completely had these sharks tangled themselves up in the lines in their struggles that very little of their heads remained to be seen, being swathed in coil upon coil of shark-line. To drive the lance in without cutting this and thus freeing the creatures would take the utmost skill. After a short discussion this harpooning was entrusted to Ishmael as being the ablest and most experienced harpooner on board. Under his instructions we brought one shark right alongside, immediately below the spot on deck where the gaunt spearman chose to stand. Ti-Royale handed him his weapon, that same one which he had spent so much time and care in bringing to the exact degree of sharpness. He hefted it in his hand, feeling for the point of balance. Satisfied, he glanced at us ranged on either side of him and with a jerk of his head indicated that we were to stand well clear. With feet braced wide apart and left arm extended palm downward for balance, he raised his other arm – the one holding the lance – until he was one straight line from toe to harpoon butt. At the last moment he baulked, unsure of his stroke. Several times he did this, but Ishmael was taking no risks. He knew his work and the rest of us were silent.

At last he struck, his body curling like a released spring as his whole weight followed behind his arm movement. The lance head bit deep into the beast, burying itself completely within the carcass. As the stroke ended so Ishmael's body began to uncoil again in a swift, sinuous motion designed to pluck the lance from the shark's vitals. But the huge creature came to sudden and unexpected life, writhed grotesquely and tore the haft from the fisherman's clutching fingers. For a second he staggered, thrown off balance by the unexpected jerk. Then his right arm shot out as he sought to regain it.

Meanwhile, driven by pain, the shark lashed itself furiously against the side of the boat and the haft of the lance beat the air wildly above the level of the bulwark. Ishmael, oblivious of the danger, thrust out his arm in the direct path of this gigantic metronome.

SHARK FOR SALE

There was a dry report, like a brittle stick snapping, and his arm was broken just below the elbow. Before the shock had registered, the return stroke caught him on the wrist, smashing this too, the force of the blow swinging Ishmael around to face us.

He stood there woodenly, jaw agape, his right arm held before him like a lop-sided 'Z'. The shark gave a last desperate wriggle; the embedded lance head sliced neatly through the line and then the shark was gone in a tremendous swirl of water. In the moment of stillness that followed my eyes remained fixed on a splintered white end of bone that had broken through the Creole's brown skin and now stuck up in the air at an oblique angle.

'*Ou capable croire?* whispered Ton Milot, and this time the familiar words seemed like a prayer. I raised my eyes to Ishmael's face in time to see the greyness flood into it and great drops of sweat burst out on his forehead.

'What shall I do?' he moaned softly, flapping the useless appendage in front of him as if to shake it off.

'Christ! What a bloody mess!' said Ton Milot in a natural tone and turned away.

The others had gathered in a little group and were whispering among themselves. I pulled myself together and bade Ishmael follow me down into the cabin. Once there I sat him on a box of fishing tackle and took a look at his arm. As Milot had said, it was a mess. Both ends of the radius were pulverized, with jagged splinters of bone slicing through the flesh at various points. Several small bones in the wrist appeared to be smashed as well. While I was examining it I was conscious that there was neither morphine nor splints in the small first aid kit with which I had equipped the boat.

I motioned Ishmael to lie down on Ton Milot's old mattress and then broke up the wooden crate on which he had been sitting. I yelled for Gandhi, as being the strongest, but without result. Sticking my head up through the hatch I saw that the rest of the crew had succeeded in getting the other shark on board and were busy catching more. Gandhi seemed to resent my interrupting his fishing and grumbled as he followed me down into the cabin. Telling him to hold Ishmael tightly under the armpits, I took hold of the mangled forearm and straightened it as much as possible without causing him undue pain. Then, with no indication of my intentions, I transferred my grip to his hand and pulled on the limb with all the strength I could muster. For a second Ishmael's green cat's-eyes opened wide in startled horror, then they glazed over and the yell that was on his lips died in a gurgle as he slumped forward in a dead faint.

His arm was still far from straight but the ugly splinters of bone were no longer exposed to view, nor the nerves left raw to the air. Using the pieces of crate, padded with cotton wool and sail canvas, we managed to fix a reasonable splint, which we lashed in place with fishing-line. The whole process was completed before Ishmael recovered consciousness. Leaving Gandhi to prepare some tea for him, I went on deck to speak to Ton Milot.

'All right, Ton Milot,' I said. 'Let's finish off now. Get the lines in and we'll set course for Mahé.'

'Sweet Mother of God! You mean we're going back?'

'Of course. We've got to get Ishmael to hospital.'

'Hmm. Look, m'sieur. Your business is your business, this is your ship and we're your crew, but Sweet-Jesus-and-All-the-Angels, we can't leave now! Not with all these sharks about. Not because a bloody-fool Creole busts his arm. We can't do it! We've got to stay, begging your pardon. Even if Ishmael's arm drops off we can't go back now. These sharks are money to us and a profit to you. We can't go! To hell with the bastard!'

The rest of the crew, hearing their coxswain's outburst, joined in as well: 'But no. We can't go back . . .'

'. . . first time we've hit sharks like this in ten years.'

'. . . not leave La Fortune. Not now . . .'

'. . . *tant pis*, Ishmael . . .'

They were sullen, vociferous and scared. Scared of having to leave, of not returning to Fortune Bank, of losing the few rupees the sharks meant to them.

In the wake of the silence that followed Ishmael could be heard moaning down in the cabin. '*Aiee-yi-yi. Aiee-yi-yi. Aiee-yi-yi . . .*', over and over again as the pain set in.

Zulu and Hassan looked momentarily startled, then their faces clouded over with sullenness again. The rest pretended not to hear, but nevertheless looked uncomfortable. They waited for me to reply, but I held my tongue for a while in order to let Ishmael's keening sink in. Then I explained that we must go back, that we had no option. But I promised them we would return to La Fortune as soon as possible.

They turned away without saying any more, but by the way they set about their work it was apparent that they resented my decision deeply. Moreover, they did not believe we would ever come back again. For them Fortune Bank was not named after Kerguelen's brave little ship, but because a 'fortune' of sharks lay there. It had always been a near-myth to them, a shark-fishermen's Elysian Fields. Now we were going back and the illusion they had held for a brief while was shattered.

A little later I went down to see Ishmael. He was still crooning to himself: '*Aiee-yi-yi. Aiee-yi-yi,*' over and over again. In my brief absence his condition had worsened considerably. He was running a fever, his eyes were sunken, his head rolled from side to side and his whole body was bathed in sweat. I dosed him with Codeine tablets, gave him a shot of penicillin, loosed the splint bindings for a minute or two and left Gandhi to keep an eye on him. When I went back on deck Ton Milot was alone at the helm, the others having disappeared into the fo'c'sle.

For several minutes we sat in unfriendly silence till the old man raised a scrawny arm and pointed out abeam. At first I could not make out what he had seen. Then an indistinct bubble of whiteness appeared for a moment, only to vanish again over the horizon. Five minutes later it reappeared, and thereafter at more frequent intervals, until by the end of half an hour it had resolved itself into a large full-rigged ship. This vessel was heading in the same direction as we were, but on a slightly converging course, that brought her gradually nearer. Presently she was close enough for us to be able to identify her as one of the rare trading schooners that ply between Mauritius and Mahé, 1,200 miles of deserted ocean, the loneliest trade route in the world.

When the two ships were a mile or so apart I took the tiller from Ton Milot and pointed up at our sails. There was no need to say a word; he had the same idea in mind when he first pointed the vessel out to me. He grinned his old, foxy grin and went forward, pausing only to yell down into the cabin:

'Hey, you. Ishmael! You bloody fool! You're going to sleep in a nice bunk tonight and tomorrow night you'll have a nice little nurse to keep you company and hold your hand. *Ou capable croire!*

FORTUNE BANK AND ISHMAEL

These were the first words spoken to the gaunt fisherman by the other Creole since his accident.

In the next few minutes I brought the *Golden Bells* hard across the newcomer's path and hove to. That the other ship had seen us and was aware of our intention was obvious when she was yet a mile away, for we could see her sails beginning to shake and flutter as the halyards were slackened prior to taking them in.

'What do you want?' yelled a figure from the cabin roof as soon as the large vessel was alongside. 'Food, fuel or a course for Mahé?'

'None of those,' I shouted back. 'Can you take an injured man on to Mahé for us? You're faster than we are and he needs the attention of a doctor badly.'

'Surely,' came the reply. 'What's the trouble?'

While I was explaining, Gandhi and Hassan brought Ishmael up from out of the cabin and between them passed him over the bulwark on to the other ship. As they did so I caught a brief glimpse of the injured man's face. It was fantastic how it had altered in the past hour. Ishmael had always been gaunt, but now he was like a spectre; the flesh had fallen from his cheekbones and his eyes were dull coals in cavernous sockets.

In a matter of minutes the transfer was completed. Ishmael was somewhere below in a decent bunk, the master had been fully informed of the cause of the accident and held in his hand my explanatory letter to the hospital authorities. Neither vessel wished to prolong the rendezvous. The others were eager to get under way towards Mahé and my crew were equally anxious to be off in the opposite direction, back to Fortune Bank. As we cast off and the gap between the two ships widened, none of the Creole fishermen on board the *Golden Bells* bothered to look back. For them the episode was finished, even as was Ishmael's future as a fisherman, which they all knew. *Tant pis*, Ishmael . . .

Due to adverse currents it was mid-afternoon before we struck Fortune Bank again; this time we did not stop at the *bordage*, but sailed on over that area of ripple-marked water until we were well on to the shallows, where the dark blobs of coral outcrops showed clearly on the sea-bed, eight fathoms down. Here we anchored and, after cooking and eating a meal, the first that day, went to bed with the setting sun.

Dawn found us motoring southwards to establish ourselves on

the furthest tip of the bank and there to follow its contours back northwards, fishing as we went. During that day and the four that followed we both saw and caught more shark than ever before or since. Fortune Bank, unfished for years, surpassed even its legends. Each time we looked over the side, it was to see the sinuous, wallowing shapes of at least half a dozen great beasts cruising near at hand. In five days we took on board a dead weight of eighteen tons and lost three times that amount due to snapped lines, mishandling and the rolling overboard of various carcasses that were piled three or four deep upon the deck in a way that threatened at times to capsize us.

At first we began by piling all the sharks head downwards in the sunken cockpit. Thus their deadly jaws were safely out of the way should they momentarily revive, for we had no time to ensure that each and every one was really dead before giving our attention to the next. We soon found, however, that even this procedure was not safe, for in the final death flurry their great tails, raised high above deck level, would thresh wildly, striking down or overboard anyone within range. The first to be struck was Ti-Royale, who received a cuff across the side of the head that sent him right over the stern, almost on top of a large hammerhead that had been drawn alongside prior to lancing! In his desperation to get back on board, the young Creole swung a foot on to the shark's back and, by pushing hard downwards, succeeded in getting himself up out of the water. He was able to grab the rudder stock and was back on deck again within a matter of seconds.

The next victim was myself. This was a comparatively gentle love-tap that caught me across the shoulders, knocked me down, neatly skinned a large portion of one shoulder-blade and left me with a bruise that lasted for several weeks.

Finally, Milot nearly came to grief but ducked just in time and, except for getting his hat knocked off, managed to escape. After this indignity he took upon himself the task of lopping off the tail of each and every shark as soon as it was safely on board. There was only one drawback to this procedure: in the final convulsion gouts of thick blood would spout from the severed ends of the trunks, covering us all with its congealing redness. After a few futile attempts to escape these 'blood-baths', we ignored the heavy spurts which drenched us at each death. The

FORTUNE BANK AND ISHMAEL

blood never had a chance to dry upon our skins, for we were continually showered with fresh drops. But even if we could not keep ourselves clean, we learnt that the decks must at all costs remain spotless. If we allowed a puddle of blood to lie undisturbed on the wooden planks, it would thicken and become as slippery as a layer of heavy oil. Such a hazard could send us sprawling headlong, perhaps within snapping distance of a freshly caught and very lively shark that had that moment been brought on board.

Each day we worked without a thought for food, rest or cleanliness. With the coming of dusk we coiled our lines, dropped the anchor and sought a place to sleep among the high-piled carcasses. Ton Milot showed me how to make a comfortable and secure bed under such conditions. Two large sharks beneath one as a mattress, two more on either side as bolsters to prevent one from rolling overboard and another across the top on which to rest one's head. The hide of a shark does not hold water, nor is it slimy. Their bodies made a firm yet resilient support, not unlike that of an air-mattress. Thus cradled by the bodies of our daytime catch we slept securely. Only once did I wake up in the night and what I saw remained in my memory.

With the onset of death the sharks had developed a startling luminosity which revealed their stark silhouettes and etched in detail their slack down-curving mouths and exposed triangular teeth. These bodies were tumbled all over the deck, covering the entire ship with their inert forms. Half-hidden among them lay the sprawled figures of the sleeping fishermen, visible as darker outlines against the phosphorescent fish-shapes. Here an arm, limp and bent, was thrown up over a monstrous carcass, the body to which it belonged seemingly buried under yet another gigantic form. A human head, jaws agape as if in death, stared sightlessly up towards the stars, the torso blotted out by a dorsal fin which reared up into the night like a nightmarish scimitar. From beneath another pile of violet-gleaming shapes stretched a human foot, apparently severed, for no other portion of the body to which it belonged could be seen. Someone groaned in his sleep and turned over, and a hand was momentarily raised up above the bodies. The fingers flexed and bent, clawed at the empty air, and then the spectral arm sank back out of sight.

Weird noises were caused by the gases that generated in the

sharks' intestines and forced their way up through the gullets, giving rise to pig-like grunts. Pockets of water or even blood would suddenly gurgle and sigh through collapsed gill-slits. The little cutter looked as though some terrifying battle of annihilation between men and monsters had been fought across her deck and now the ship was deserted of all life and only the dead remained. It was a graveyard scene as might have been painted by Bosch, made fantastic by the luminescence of putrefaction and the tangle of bodily components of both human beings and sharks. All around me the grim jaws hung open, with their great teeth bared in lunatic grimaces, while the conical, pointed snouts gave one the inappropriate impression of fools' caps. Here and there the freakish outline of a hammerhead could be seen, the trunk terminating in a hideous anvil-shape at the extremities of which great globular eyes stared out unwinkingly over the heaps of dead.

At one in the morning our ancient alarm clock whirred and buzzed erratically until Milot roused himself sufficiently to shut it off. Afterwards he could be heard groping about in the cabin, muttering to himself, and would eventually emerge carrying three lighted hurricane lanterns. The first of these he would hang out on the end of the boom, the second below the boom near the mast and the third he would string up on the forestay. With this general illumination of the deck the others would also stir themselves, making their way stiffly to the open fireplace, where they would set about splitting kindling and getting a fire going. While the tea was brewing they would set to work sharpening their long knives and honing the axes. Once the tea was made they would take their individual mugs and wander off, still half asleep, to whatever area on the deck took their fancy. The one who happened to pass nearest to where I crouched with my back against the mast, would hand me my cup without a word. It was not a time for talking, anyway. We were all too tired, too freshly risen from sleep, and the flickering lamp-light gave the scene an air of unreality, not unlike that of the dream-world we had too recently quitted. Presently there would be a slithering sound as a carcass was dragged into position. Then the 'thunk' of an axe as the fins were struck off. After that silence would follow as the knives sliced noiselessly through flesh and hide. Finally there would be a series of wet flopping noises as the cut segments were tossed to another cleared area of the deck. Occasionally one of the fishermen would cough and spit, or else mutter a sentence to his neighbour, asking for the sandstone, a bucket, a match for a cigarette.

Through all this I would doze fitfully, vaguely conscious of the mounting piles of prepared shark-meat and the reappearance of order about the deck. Tea would be made again at five and then the work was resumed. Just before sunrise I would wake for good and set about checking the engine and shifting sacks of salt in the cabin to make room for the shark. By eight o'clock the cutting would be finished and the rest of the crew would begin preparing their lines, and checking the gaffs and lances, while Ton Milot personally salted down the mound of flesh and I stacked the fillets, layer upon layer, down in the cabin as he passed them to me. By ten o'clock we would be ready for the day's work to begin all over again.

But before we set about our fishing there was one more chore to do. With the cutting up the tail-fins, backbones, entrails and livers had all been thrown overboard, but not the heads. On that point Ton Milot was adamant. To throw the heads overboard, where they would litter the shallow sea-floor beneath us, would be to drive all the other sharks from the area. Of that he was positive.

So, obedient to his rule, we motored each morning into the deep, a mile or so from the edge of the bank, and there jettisoned the heads. Only then would we be free to start work. At that time I thought this was just another whim of Milot's, a piece of fishery abracadabra, old man's lore, meaningless and without purpose. Later I had the opportunity of seeing how wrong my assumption was.

At noon on the fifth day we had had enough. Not only was the cabin filled to the ceiling with tier upon tier of salted shark flesh, but a further three-quarters of a ton had been crammed into the fo'c'sle, while the sunken cockpit aft was filled to deck level. But it was not the lack of cargo space that caused us to give up; it was ourselves. Incessant work, no proper food and little rest had produced in all of us a state of near-somnambulance. We had become clumsy and slow-witted. Already both Hassan and Gandhi had gashed their hands and forearms badly on the razor-sharp and saw-edged teeth whilst handling the dead

SHARK FOR SALE

bodies. At any moment one of us might be involved in another serious accident. It was time to call a halt.

While the rest of the crew coiled down their lines, Milot unlaced the mainsail and laid it across the boom, making an awning to protect us from the sun. Into this welcome shade we crept and slept until dusk, letting the *Golden Bells* drift as she pleased. Considerably refreshed we set about cleaning ourselves and making ready the little cutter for the long journey home. Only when we were under way, the engine chugging reassuringly and the sails bellying in the light night breeze, did we realize to what extent we were unfit to manage the vessel and how fortunate we were in having fine weather. The trouble was in our hands. Those that were not cut by shark teeth or knives were laid open and raw with line burns. Throughout the previous day, in the excitement of the work, these had been largely ignored. The brief rest we had taken had given the wounds chance to heal a little and now our flesh was suddenly ultra-tender and our hands would no longer obey the brain's commands, shying from the tasks they were called upon to perform. To haul up sail was an agony; to grasp the tiller was impossible, and the most we could do was to tuck it under one arm and steer by leaning on the rudder with a shoulder when necessary.

The evening of the second day brought us within sight of Mahé, but it was two in the morning before we finally came to anchor off St Anne's, one of the several islands lying across the harbour entrance of Port Victoria. It was here we off-loaded our catch at first light, for the island belonged to the concern to whom I had arranged to sell our shark. Following the weighing in of the wet-salted fillets on the end of the jetty, the catch was taken over by a gang of women to whom was entrusted the labour of washing, laying out, drying and subsequently packaging the shark for meat export. The Creole women like this work. The meat is washed in a large circular tank of sea water, around which the women sit and scrub and rub and rinse the excess salt from the fillets. They chat as they wash, recounting scandal or discussing their intimate secrets in a bawdy peasant fashion. They make coarse, earthy jokes with the crews of the unloading schooners who are responsible for bringing the shark to the weighing machine and afterwards carrying it across to the washing tank. Usually the women are under the direction of an old crone who

FORTUNE BANK AND ISHMAEL

rules her charges with harsh authority, particularly those younger, prettier ones who are disposed to flirt with the fishermen.

On the day following our return, all the men assembled again in order to be paid. I had their respective pay packets prepared and, after handing them out, I told them that I was going to the hospital to see Ishmael and to give him his share of the catch money.

Their reaction was immediate. In a second their vociferous gaiety turned into an ugly silence and I became the target for five pairs of suspicious, angry eyes.

'Well?' I asked. 'What now?' For a short while there was no answer until, in response to the others' nudges, Ton Milot spoke out.

'Ahem! You said, *m'sieur*, Ishmael's *share*?' Rank disbelief showed in his voice. I nodded.

'But look, *m'sieur*, Ishmael didn't *do* any fishing. All he did was to get his arm broken and nearly made us leave La Fortune. Why should he have a share?'

I did not know how to answer this. For these Creoles illness or injury was just another hazard. Poverty they had always known and the absence of one crew-member simply meant that the others would receive greater shares. It was no use setting up European ideas of camaraderie and fair-play, sick benefits or 'passing-the-hat'. Such ideas had no place in their lives. Earning a living in the Seychelles was too much of a rat-race to indulge in philanthropic or idealistic gestures. You earned your money or you did not; it was as simple as that. Ishmael had not caught any sharks, therefore he was not entitled to a share. That he had his arm shattered, that he was probably incapacitated for life, had nothing to do with it. That was unfortunate but – *tant pis*, Ishmael!

It was no use arguing with them over this point, which they were prevented by environment from understanding. Risking a possible walkout, I told them as roughly and as abruptly as I could that it was for me to allocate shares as I saw fit. If they did not like my methods they could get off the *Golden Bells* there and then. Because they had been used to harsh treatment from their employers all their lives they accepted my statement and said no more, but mentally classified me as a 'bastard' along with all their previous *patrons*. It was several months before they allowed themselves to forget this episode.

That first catch of ours from Fortune Bank caused quite a stir. It had been many years since a vessel of the size of the *Golden Bells* had brought in such a load. The day after our argument over Ishmael's share brought other fishing schooner crews to my house. These newcomers all wanted to know the same thing. Would I agree to their following the *Golden Bells* on our next trip, so that they might also find Fortune Bank? After a brief talk with Ton Milot to observe his reaction to this scheme, I eventually agreed on the understanding that for every ton of shark which these 'Followers-on' caught they were to pay the *Golden Bells* a royalty of thirty rupees. Of this twenty rupees would go as a direct bonus to my crew and the remaining ten to offset any extra fuel we might burn in zig-zagging around making sure our charges were not lost.

Had I agreed to act as guide free of payment not only would my own crew have been upset at my allowing others to fish on what they considered as 'their bank', but the other crews would have thought me a fool to render them a valuable service for nothing.

In the same way, though I was temporary owner of the *Golden Bells*, nevertheless I counted myself in on all crew payments, allocating myself a share on equal terms. I shared the work and the hardships as a crew member, and I was entitled to a portion of the reward, even though I, as owner, paid this out. Had I not done so, every one of my fishermen would have thought me more than a trifle mad, and madmen have no place on board a shark fishing vessel, nor are they entitled to respect.

Within twenty-four hours of this new arrangement we were at sea again, heading south, back towards Fortune Bank. This time we were not alone, for in our wake followed the other four schooners. During the day our little flotilla spread out over an ocean space of perhaps 10 miles, but with the dusk the others closed in and throughout the night we sailed within hailing distance of one another, keeping station by means of the lanterns we hung from our sterns. Due to the fact that the other ships were not as fast as the *Golden Bells*, it was not until the end of the third day that we arrived at our destination. Positioning ourselves in the middle of the bank, we anchored and then slept for twelve hours in order to begin fishing as fresh as possible.

Once again Fortune Bank surpassed even its legend. We on the *Golden Bells* fished until fatigue brought us to a standstill. Then with a full hold we set off home, leaving the other vessels, with their newer and less hand-skinned crews, to carry on. There was no difficulty about their finding their way back. If they missed Mahé, they must sight Silhouette, La Digue or Praslin. It was only the outward journey that was difficult, and the finding of La Fortune.

For the next six weeks the *Golden Bells* and her four charges made a series of quick successful trips to the bank. Between us we brought back to Mahé a total of fifty-six tons of salted shark representing a 'brought on board' weight of approximately 170 tons of live shark. Towards the end the thinning of the shark ranks was very noticeable and from most areas on the bank we had cleared them entirely. Even so, we could have gone on for a considerable time but for one factor: the other crews, growing greedy and anxious not to waste time unnecessarily (as they thought), took to dumping the shark heads on the bank itself, along with the offal and unwanted fins. At once the remaining sharks began to leave the area, even as Ton Milot had always predicted they would. Still not entirely convinced, I decided on a practical experiment to see whether it was indeed due to this jettisoning of heads or perhaps an unexplained coincidence of current, local sterility of the seabed, or some other factor.

I told Ton Milot to lay up a stock of severed heads in the cockpit and then waited until we were established on a good area where the sharks were taking our baited hooks nicely. Putting on the aqualung, which I always kept on board, I lowered myself over the side, dived down to wedge myself in the propeller arch, legs astride the skeg, and settled down to watch the proceedings.

Tucked away like this I was fairly sure that no shark would notice me, or if it did that it would not venture too close to the drifting ship to investigate the strange white creature that had attached itself to the keel. Still, it was not altogether reassuring to see several large and hungry sharks swimming on the same level as myself and a mere forty or fifty feet away. Consequently, for the first few minutes my entire time was taken up in glancing nervously behind or below to make sure nothing was creeping up on me. However, all the sharks in the vicinity pointedly ignored my presence, and I had soon regained sufficient confidence to set about the experiment.

I banged on the underside of the vessel with my fist and in response to this prearranged signal Milot began dropping the heads overboard. When we began I counted three large *requins de sable* (brown or grey nurse, *carcharinus taurus*), one very large hammerhead, four or five smallish black-tipped sharks and down on the bottom a whole nursery school of three-foot sharklets. All these were within a radius of twenty yards from where I crouched.

As the first head tumbled into the water, the splash caused most of the sharks to whip around and investigate, though the hammerhead continued his stately circlings.

First on the scene were the small and agile black-tipped, who whisked around the head and proceeded to follow as it spun down towards the seabed. The *requins de sable* slanted down at a more majestic angle to intercept the strange new object just as it reached the bottom. Before they reached it two more severed heads came spinning down, and within a minute about ten grisly pates were scattered about the sand. For the most part the heads settled on the bottom, severed base downwards, and in response to the currents swayed sedately from side to side. With their pointed cowl-like snouts and expressionless white masks they gave the impression of an assembly of monks chanting a ghostly underwater litany. Every now and then one of them fell over, revealing the pale pink fronds of gill membrane from which all the blood had long since spilled. This rather spoilt the solemnity of the ritual, as though one of the celebrants was drunk and had fallen from his choir-stall. The next submarine eddy, however, usually righted the fallen heads so that once again they took their appointed places in the ceremony. So intrigued was I by this weird spectacle that I missed the exit of the live members of the group, for when I turned to look it was to discover that all the sharks had unobtrusively left and that this area was deserted.

Annoyed at having allowed myself to be side-tracked from my original purpose, I repeated the experiment in several other localities that day. Each time the same sequence of events took place. With the jettisoning of the heads the sharks in the vicinity showed an interest that lasted only until the debris reached the bottom. Thereafter they made a few cursory circuits and an occasional nosing and then they drew off, and within a matter of minutes they had all left the scene. There was no indication of panic nor of distress; they simply withdrew from the locality. In each case there was not a living shark in the area within six minutes of the moment when the heads were thrown overboard. To conclude my observations, I tried the effect of viscera, fins, livers, corpses without heads and complete bodies. The fins were ignored and produced no effect whatsoever. The viscera were sometimes nuzzled and sometimes left alone, but no sharks seemed to leave on their account. The livers, which floated, produced the same effect as the viscera, with the difference that they seemed to attract the shark pups more than the adults. Headless corpses were investigated more thoroughly and, if opened up, attracted more scavengers. Bodies complete with heads produced the same reaction as heads alone, but after a slightly longer period of time. Whatever it was that upset the living sharks it was obviously connected only with the heads of their dead. No other portion or combination of portions produced this direct and remarkable result.

It does not seem plausible, in view of the remarkably low intelligence of these brutes, that it is from any psychological cause or direct thought-process that this allergy occurs. Rather it might have its origins in a definite chemical or organic emanation from this portion of the animal which acts as a deterrent upon the living members of the species. This idea of a chemical entity has given rise to a host of 'shark repellant' products, prominent among which are compounds of copper acetate which, it has been claimed, approximate to certain substances found in the decomposing bodies of these creatures. So far the effectiveness of these repellants has yet to be proved conclusively, but as a result of my observations I think a chemical analysis of the shark head alone might well yield more valuable results. That dead sharks are a deterrent to other sharks is apparently well-known, for long after this experiment of mine I found out that many whaling stations, to whom the depredations of these creatures means a considerable loss of revenue, effectively clear the area by shooting the surface-cruising sharks with rifles and leaving their bodies to rot on the sea-bed. As far as I know, however, no one has ever isolated the shark-head itself as the repelling

SHARK FOR SALE

agent, and for this discovery I can claim no credit, for Ton Milot knew about it long ago.

By throwing the heads overboard from all the fishing schooners, Fortune Bank was finished. We made one more voyage to the bank, but after two days we gave up; the sharks had gone and the place was deserted.

However, the bank had served its purpose, for now I had sufficient capital reserve to go ahead with the long and expensive process of perfecting our new technique of drift-line fishing. The crew, too, were well pleased, having earned more in this six weeks than they usually did in a whole season.

There was a debit side to all this. On returning from the last trip I learnt that Ishmael would never, as I feared, be able to fish again. His right arm, from the elbow downwards, was finished. He could barely move three fingers of that hand and it was doubted if he would ever regain even the partial use of the limb. It was a heavy price to pay for a few tons of shark-meat.

FOUR

Shark-Luring

Wilt thou play with him (leviathan), as with a bird? . . . (Job xli, 5)

The idea of setting drift-lines for sharks first came to me when watching the big tunny-fishing fleet that the Japanese were operating in the Indian Ocean at that time and which I encountered on previous voyages when cruising around the islands of the Seychelles in search of mother-of-pearl shell. This great armada, which sometimes numbered as many as twenty-seven modern vessels, was remarkable for its efficiency, complexity and outstanding success. The ships -- which included catcher boats, refrigerated floating storerooms and factory canning vessels, all supplied with fuel oil, provisions and gear from a train of transports – had developed their technique to such a degree as to make it possible to fish in areas over a third of the way around the globe from their home port, and still produce high profits in spite of enormous overhead expenses.

This was largely due to the extent to which they had substituted a highly scientific process from mere 'fishing'. Radar, sonic waves, underwater radio transmissions, the partitioning of the ocean beneath their keels into separate search 'bands', depending upon its temperature, salinity and plankton content, all played important parts in their work. Each major vessel had its own laboratory and team of marine research workers who advised as to the overall operation and tactics to be employed.

Their actual methods of catching fish varied from two-man teams of 'pole-fishers', through trolling and electric stunning apparatus, right up to the six-mile 'long-line'. The 'long-line' system, as practised by the Japanese, consisted of an immense length of buoyed line that was laid along a probable tuna 'pathway' and was allowed to drift for periods of up to twelve hours completely free of the ship itself. Strung down from this at short intervals and from every buoy were baited hooks, connected to the main line by means of thin steel wire. At either end floated a radar beacon or reflector, so that the parent ship might keep station on the assembly and neither lose it nor run foul of it during periods of darkness and bad weather. As a further aid, some of the buoys were equipped with blue or yellow electric lanterns so that it could be determined if the line were lying straight in the water and not coiling back on itself due to current eddies or similar causes.

In spite of all these precautions, however, these 'long-lines' were sometimes lost by their owners and it was on one such occasion that I had come across a whole section of this gear drifting haphazardly across an ocean devoid of any Japanese fishing boats. Sharing my Creole's natural acquisitiveness, I was quite as eager as they to get this useful flotsam on board and it was while doing so that the first appreciation of the system as a shark-catching device had occurred to me. That portion of the line which we salvaged had yellowfin tuna on many of its hooks – or in most cases their remains, for sharks had been following the tunny pack and had lost no time in devouring the hooked and helpless fish. In two instances these sharks had engulfed the yellowfin in entirety, much to their own subsequent harm, for now these predators found themselves threaded on to the tuna line and by the time we arrived on the scene they had been dead for many hours, drowned in their efforts to escape. The main point of interest in all this was that these two sharks were large oceanic species, capable of snapping average shark-line as if it were a thread. Yet here they were, lying dead, at the end of a length of comparatively weak tuna line. Had there been any resistance to their flurries they would have broken free in a second or two, but the whole rig, lying slack and unattached to any solid object such as a large boat, had given to their struggles and allowed them to battle as they pleased without throwing any great strain upon the line. Eventually, these two sharks had become exhausted and had drowned. It was this factor of 'strength through non-resistance' which was to be the corner-stone of my scheme for catching the large, night-prowling sharks on the Mahé plateau.

The episode of Fortune Bank once over, I was able to give my attention to the re-equipment of the *Golden Bells* with the necessary new gear, for the successful forays to this distant bank had provided sufficient capital reserve for me to go ahead with the experiment without risking financial ruin should the idea prove impracticable. Moreover, I had now gained the confidence of the crew and it was their enthusiasm and support on which I relied to carry the whole scheme through.

Our first need was for suitable floats with which to buoy the line and after unsuccessful experiments with various combinations of such things as empty oil drums, Ton Milot suggested cutting sections of giant bamboo. These proved ideal, for not only were they fairly easy to come by, but they were immensely strong, easy to tow and very durable. By careful selection we were soon able to collect over a hundred of these floats, identical in size and buoyancy. For the main drift-line we used 400 fathoms of the Japanese tuna-line which I had carefully stored away. Along this, at intervals of twenty fathoms, additional grommets were spliced in and from these points were attached the bamboo floats and the descending eight-fathom lengths of shark-line, complete with hooks. To mark the further end of the rig we had a tall pennant-buoy, and to the near end we spliced in a length of heavier coir rope which we proposed to take on board the *Golden Bells*. Thus equipped, and with our usual shark-lines as a standby, we set off.

To begin with we sailed out as far as we could to the west, until we reached the furthermost edge of the bank, as we had done for the first trials. There we stopped and set about the business of collecting bait. Since we possessed no such refinements as radar or illuminated buoys I dared not risk allowing the long-line to ride entirely on its own, lest we lost it during the night. Such a step might come later when we were more sure of our technique, but for the moment, at any rate, I proposed 'buoying' the nearer end of the assembly with the *Golden Bells* herself and hoped that the little cutter's drag would not resist the flurries of the larger sharks enough to enable them to break free. After three or four nights' fishing, however, I began to have my doubts as to the wisdom of this decision, for although the long-line was indeed bringing in a high average catch of sharks many of these were only medium or small size and, what was more serious, each morning would reveal four or five hooks torn clean away. These, presumably, had been taken by larger or more powerful fish that had managed to escape, carrying off part of the gear with them. My immediate conclusion was that these particular sharks had pitted their strength against the weight of the *Golden Bells* and by the very resistance of its dead weight had been able to snap the line. But there was one very curious feature common to all of these escapes. In every case the line was broken at a point some ten to seventeen feet from the hook-end of the descending line. In no case had the break occurred where the shark-line joined the main-line, nor had the main-line been cut. All the failures were restricted to that one point, two or three fathoms above the hook.

The more I thought about it, the more puzzled I became, until eventually I knew that there was nothing else for it but to enter the water and to watch exactly what went on when a big shark was hooked. To try and find out from the safety of a dinghy, even had the *Golden Bells* possessed one, would have been useless, for what goes on beneath the sea remains a mystery to the man on the surface. Direct submarine observation was the only way and, much as I disliked the idea, I knew it had to be done. To swim around at night would be both stupid and suicidal, for not only would I be unable to see, no matter how bright the moonlight, but I would undoubtedly get taken by those very sharks I was hoping to observe. Similarly, to set the drift-line at dusk as usual and then go and look at the line in the early morning would be equally unprofitable for by then the large sharks would already have made their escape. And if I could not determine how these escapes were being made, I might as well give up all the idea of ever developing the long-line into an effective shark-catching instrument.

After discussing the whole problem with Milot, we agreed upon a plan that seemed to offer the best chance of success. We would lay just half of the long-line (200 fathoms and ten hooks), and that not before three-thirty in the morning. At first light I would go over the side, wearing an aqualung, and would swim up to the line to inspect each hook in turn, while the *Golden*

SHARK-LURING

Bells followed, taking in line, and keeping about 100 yards behind me so as not to disturb the hooked sharks and make them act with unusual frenzy or change their behaviour. It seemed quite simple and straightforward and we hoped by this method to find a large shark that had been hooked and had not yet had time to make good his escape. Then we might also see how the escape was contrived and take steps to eliminate the defect in our gear. It seemed feasible and sounded promising, but when we came to put it into effect I began to find dozens of flaws, particularly in that part which concerned my own safety! For one thing, we had already proved that hooked sharks were an irresistible lure to their own kind, which meant that I would have hungry and free-swimming company down there below the surface. Moreover should I wish to get out of the water quickly, back to the safety of the *Golden Bells*, the bulky aqualung would prevent my doing so. Again, though the surface might be adequately lit by the dawn, the underwater visibility would be very restricted and I might well run into trouble before I realized it.

With these misgivings and with the despondency that comes from having got up long before sunrise, I was in a bad state of jitters when the time came to make the attempt. The sea looked grey and forbidding, the crew went about their work silently and were obviously frightened as to the possible outcome of this latest example of European stupidity – even Ton-ton could find little to say. As I climbed down over the bowsprit the flag-buoy which marked the far end of the long-line, towards which I must go, seemed unbelievably distant. I was cold, miserable and frightened, and wished I had never taken up this ridiculous business of shark-fishing.

Once under the surface and with the relief of physical action I felt better. To try and avoid creating a disturbance in the water with my swim-fins I had decided to swim along some twenty feet down, at which depth I hoped to be able to see the hooks clearly, since they would lie a similar distance below me. In order to maintain this level I had tied a three and a half fathom length of light line to my belt, the other end being attached to the main-line by means of a metal snap-hook. On arriving at each of the buoys and shark-lines that were spaced at twenty-fathom intervals, I was to give a series of jerks upon these which would cause the bamboos to bob about and indicate to Ton Milot that he might bring up the *Golden Bells* and take that particular line in, since this action would signify that the hook held nothing of interest.

The first line I came to was bare, devoid of either bait or shark. The hook glinted dully in the obscurity below and I made a mental note to paint them with diluted Stockholm tar, for sharks – particularly the night-feeding varieties – shun that which is bright and shiny. I was pleased with this observation, for I had already learnt something of value. I swam on to the next marker with more enthusiasm. From a distance I saw that this one held something and I approached very cautiously until I could make out exactly what it was and whether it was still alive. It proved to be a medium-sized *grandes ailes*, bloated and distended with the water it had taken in while drowning. I tugged on the line to signal to Milot and then passed on. As I did so, I was graphically reminded that the sea was even now a hunting ground, for out of the gloom appeared a shark of similar size which, ignoring me completely, closed in on its dead companion and commenced circling it with obvious intent. I did not wait to watch it feed, for I thought it likely that its actions might entice other and bigger sharks in the neighbourhood to draw in as well. The third and fourth hooks were untouched, their baits still hanging limply downwards.

The fifth, sixth and seventh were clean and bare, possibly the work of a pack of small barracuda that could have nibbled the bait away without transfixing themselves. The eighth held an eight-foot hammerhead, still very much alive but very sedate in its movements. This odd-looking creature had managed to foul-hook itself through the side of its horny head and the point of the hook showed plainly, sticking out through its anvil-shaped excresence, just behind the left eye. Hammerheads often get caught in this fashion and I believe it to be due to their habit of circling a bait closely and investigating it closely before biting. To do so, they twist and turn round and round the hook, flinging their weird heads from side to side to aid their manoeuvrings, and it is then that they accidentally impale themselves upon the barb. The young hammerhead in this instance, finding itself securely tethered, contented itself with swimming in slow and sedate circles and did not seem very perturbed. Even my appearance on the scene did not cause it the least alarm, and the only

SHARK-LURING

sign of recognition that I evoked was that a single eye, the one that faced outside, swivelled to keep me in view as long as possible on each and every circuit the fish made.

Having watched this shark for several minutes it seemed there was nothing more to learn from it, I gave the signal for the *Golden Bells* to come up and prepared to move on. In answer to my tugs upon the line, I felt the whole rig pull and jerk as Milot answered back with a series of steady, long heaves. This was the prearranged signal for me to surface at once, an emergency call, and instantly my feeling of security vanished and all my old fears flooded back. Losing no time, I shot up and broke water alongside the buoy, to which I clung while I waited for the cutter to reach me. Most of the crew were up on the bows pointing and gesticulating in my direction, but it was not until they were quite near that I realized that they were pointing not at me, but beyond me, at something in the sea nearby. From my low viewpoint I could not see anything at all unusual, but kept ducking my head under the water to make sure that whatever it was that was causing this excitement was not quietly stealing up on me unobserved. By the time they were alongside, their agitation had transmitted itself to me and I was very relieved to clamber up out of the water on to the bobstay. Here I learnt what was causing all the tumult; not only did I hear about it but, from this higher viewpoint, I could see it!

The tenth buoy, the very last on the line, was behaving like a mad thing. It was rushing across the surface of the sea in a series of zig-zags, turning and twisting as though it were alive. Periodically, it would disappear completely, pulled under by some great force, and would then remain hidden for twenty or thirty seconds when it would bob up again in a different place. Something very large and very active had taken the hook and was now doing its best to escape. By the looks of things it would do so quite quickly, for our long-line could never stand up to such a strain, or so I thought. At any rate, I had wanted to see a large shark at close quarters in the process of smashing up our gear; now was my chance, whether I liked the idea or not.

I told Ton Milot to go on with the line-hauling as rapidly as possible until reaching the ninth float, at which point he was to hold off until I signalled him on again. Then I went back into the water. This time I kept on the surface so that I could pull

SHARK FOR SALE

myself hand-over-hand along the mainline and reach my objective with the least delay. As I drew nearer I felt the rope beneath my fingers quiver and jump continuously as the unknown source of power bore against it. Finally, this movement grew so violent that I was forced to let go and had to dive down several feet to avoid its convulsive and whip-like movements. No sooner had I done so than I became aware of loud shock-waves pulsing and singing through the water with each new flurry. Before I realized how close I was, I caught a glimpse of white in the still-hazy waters ahead and then a massive object came boring out of the obscurity some ten feet below me. It swung upwards in a long arc, passed behind me, paused momentarily to shake its huge head, as might a dog with a rat in its mouth, and then swept on down as though following some invisible contour. At the same instant something cut across my shin and slid down to my ankle, where it caught on the jutting swim-fin, pulling me downwards in the wake of the shark. It was the hook-line running from the shark to the buoy, of which that creature was now attempting to rid itself by a series of savage lunges. Luckily, it had not looped itself around my foot, for then I would never have broken free. As it was, the very force of the pull on my body turned me half-around, my swim-fin was torn off and I was released.

From what had taken place it was obvious that my greatest danger might well be not the captured shark but the possibility of being entangled by the rapidly moving and almost invisible line the shark was towing. Accordingly, I surfaced and chased after the bamboo float that was still bobbing about on the surface. Here, at the hub of all movement, I could scarcely come to harm. This was all very well, but it did not help me in what I was supposed to be doing, for at this far end of the shark-line I could see nothing of the brute and my only indications as to its whereabouts were the direction in which the line moved and the explosive thumps heard underwater with each succession of tail-beats. Once I had regained my breath and recovered from the initial scare, I began hauling myself down the shark-line so that I might see what was going on and by riding with the line avoid the risk of getting caught up in it. As the radius from the buoy increased, so did the relative speed of the line through the water, until I could go no further lest the slipstream tear the mask from off my face. But it was sufficient, for now I could make out –

SHARK-LURING

albeit dimly – the shark that we had hooked. By its heavy, blunt head, short dorsal and general dark colouring I knew it to be a tiger. It was not an outsize specimen, perhaps eleven feet in length and close on 1,000 pounds in weight. It was a male and had not yet reached full maturity, which perhaps accounted for his unusual vivacity, for adult tiger sharks, though extremely powerful, are normally sluggish and heavy-moving.

Through the haze of water I saw that the strain of the battle was already beginning to tell, for the shark's mouth was beginning to gape a little as he fought; this was a certain prelude to his death, for soon he would 'drink water' and drown. Within the space of a few minutes his struggles slowed appreciably and I was able to edge a few feet further down the line. I had become so interested in the spectacle that all my fear had gone and my only regret was that this particular shark might die on the hook before my eyes and we would be no nearer solving the mystery of how the presumably bigger ones were escaping.

Slowly I drew nearer, until I was perhaps eighteen or twenty feet from the dying animal. All of a sudden the tiger shark became aware of me, for it quivered throughout its length, like a cat taken by surprise, turned its head away and downwards and threshed frantically in an effort to escape. The efflux from its tail caught at me and jerked me on the rope like a leaf on a branch. I was sure my mask would give way and closed my eyes in preparation. I was dimly conscious of a series of booming thuds that hurt my eardrums. There was one last thud, the line jerked and twanged, and suddenly I felt free as if I were falling. My eyes opened instinctively and I saw that I was not free nor falling, but still clutching the line. In front of me, however, was a mere eight feet of rope that came to a ragged end. The shark had gone, taking with it about ten feet of line, including the hook and chain trace, in exactly the same way as had all the others.

Once back on board the *Golden Bells* I did my best to reconstruct those movements that had led up to the tiger shark's last convulsions. I drew an outline sketch of the shark upon the deck in chalk, as near to scale as possible, and filled in the relative positions of hook, chain and line as I last saw them, so far as I could remember. When I marked the breaking-point in the line, what must have happened became apparent at once. The tiger shark, when making his bid to get away, had hurled himself straight downwards, so that the trace chain was pulled back alongside his gills and the line lay along his body. The leading edge of his wildly waving tail-fin had probably caught the line and smashed into it with a series of hammer-like blows, and due to the continuing tension had cut it as a blunt sword might have done.

At least that was how it looked to me and it only remained to find out whether a blow from the shark's tail-fin would indeed cut through a rope. I therefore strung a similar shark-line under tension from a ring-bolt in the deck up to a block on the gaff. Gandhi lopped off the upper caudal lobe from the carcass of the *grandes ailes* we had taken that morning and bound it securely to the lance-shaft, to make a flail-like bludgeon. While everyone stood back, he took a swipe at the taut shark-line. At the second blow it parted, revealing the same degree of unravelling at the severed ends as all our previous and unaccountably broken lines. This, then, was the answer to our missing hooks and escaping sharks!

The rest of that day we spent in modifying the long-line in the light of what we had learnt. Amongst the gear I had stowed away on board was a certain quantity of light chain and several dozen heavy steel swivels. This chain was now cut into fourteen-foot lengths, swivels were attached to both ends, and the completed pieces were inserted at the bottom end of the shark-catching lines by means of shackles. Thus each shark-line now consisted of a steel shark hook, to which was attached its own integral three-foot length of heavy chain, followed by a shackle, swivel, shackle, a fourteen-foot length of light chain, shackle, swivel, and finally the eight-fathom shark-line (now shortened to six to make the total length about correct), which ended at the main-line. The whole assembly was then strung up from the rigging and given a coat of Stockholm tar in order to stop reflections from the various shiny metal components. Unfortunately, we did not have sufficient chain to serve for the whole rig, but we managed to prepare ten shark-lines in this fashion which we attached to alternate floats along the twenty-hook long-line.

When this was done it was already mid-afternoon, leaving us barely sufficient time to eat a hasty meal and then set about cutting up the bait-fish that Ton Milot had occupied himself in

SHARK-LURING

catching while the rest of us were preparing the line. As the sun was going down we motored back, out towards the *bordage*, and by 7.30 our new line was laid and we sat back to wait and see what results it brought. At midnight we took in the line and had the satisfaction of bringing on board a twelve-foot *peau claire*, besides the usual collection of eight- and nine-footers of various types. Moreover, though we had lost yet another hook and some trace, this was from one of the unmodified hooks. By 2 a.m. the gear was back in the water again and we settled down to sleep.

Daylight brought us the proof of the system. Not counting half a dozen smaller sharks, we found we had taken two large hammerheads. The bigger one, a female, was over nineteen feet long, and had obligingly drowned herself, thus presenting us with no problem – or so we thought, until we brought her alongside and attempted to haul the carcass on board by means of a block and tackle. Before ten feet of the shark's length was clear of the water the *Golden Bells* had taken on such a list as to make it dangerous to continue. In an attempt to lessen the burden, Gandhi ran a knife up her swollen belly, whereupon well over a barrel of clear sea water gushed out, the cause of death. Even with this respite we were not able to swing the hammerhead clear and were forced to lower the huge corpse back into the water once more. With long knives the crew then cut the trunk in half, just behind the dorsal fin, and each portion was taken on board separately. This cutting up of the shark when secured alongside took considerable time, and I resolved to bring a saw with us in future in order to rip through the cartilaginous vertebrae upon which we broke two knife blades. The second hammerhead was very much alive and gave considerable trouble before we were able to bring his thirteen-foot length near enough to lance. At the final moment, just before Hassan made the stroke, Ti-Royale and Zulu bore down too hard upon the wire noose, lifting the shark's head clean out of the water. Angered by this, the hammerhead opened and shut his jaws with a tremendous snap and sheared clean through the heavy chain next to the hook. At the same time he shook his head violently, forcing Zulu and the mechanic to let go for fear of getting their hands torn to pieces by the steel wire. Completely free, the hammerhead gave an insolent flip to his tail that drenched us all with spume and swam away downwards, trailing behind him the free end of the wire noose and bearing somewhere in his jaw a three-inch hook. After that we were always careful not to infuriate any large shark by pulling its head up out of the sea.

For the next week we set out long-line by night and spent each day in repairing it, catching bait and moving from area to area. At the end of this period we were nowhere as tired as if we had been shark-fishing in the normal manner and we had taken well over twice our usual weight of shark. We were still losing hooks and line, because we had insufficient chain, and eventually, not wishing to risk more gear, I limited the length of the assembly to those ten fully modified hooks. At once our catch-rate decreased, but we ceased to lose hooks, and I decided to carry on in this fashion for another week before returning home, since the weather was good and the crew eager. It was in this second phase of the voyage that we learnt yet another way of catching sharks, and that inadvertently.

It was perhaps our eighth or ninth day out. Unravelling a snarled long-line had taken up most of the early morning and by the time we had it sorted out we had drifted too far in towards the centre of the plateau for it to be worthwhile motoring right out to the *bordage* for a normal day's bait fishing. The area over which we now hung seemed sterile and devoid of fish, and after a few ineffectual casts we gave up all idea of further work until the late afternoon might bring us a cool breeze and some relief from the sweltering sun.

While the others curled up in whatever shade they were able to find, I stripped off and, putting on mask and swim-fins, dropped over the side in an effort to freshen up a little. Since the sea-bed lay about forty fathoms below, it was impossible to discern the bottom, even though the water was crystal clear and the rays of the noon-day sun pierced straight down like the beams of blue searchlights. However, I was very conscious that, for all their apparent emptiness, these were shark-infested waters, so I kept close to the side of the *Golden Bells* whilst I scrubbed at my body in an effort to rid myself of the past weeks' grime. This task completed, I set out in a brisk crawl-stroke to complete a circuit of the little cutter before returning on board by climbing up on the bobstay, beneath the bowsprit, using it as a step from which to reach the deck. Balancing there, removing my flippers, I happened to glance down into the sea just below my feet. To

SHARK-LURING

my amazement I saw four or five all too familiar streamlined shapes, snouts pointed straight at me and tails lashing furiously as the sharks rushed upwards from out of the obscurity of the depths.

With a yell that woke the others out of their stupor, I grabbed the bowsprit and swung myself up on to the deck. A second later the foremost shark, a slim nine-footer, levelled off a few inches below the surface right under the bowsprit and then dashed excitedly hither and thither, around and about the *Golden Bells*. Within a matter of moments he was joined by his companions and the whole school was criss-crossing the area with voracious questings.

Ton Milot was the first to act: *'Déjeuner, mes enfants!'* – and so saying he cast out one of the baited shark-lines that lay to hand. The splash of the hook had barely subsided before the nearest *nez-nez pointe* had taken it. Within the next twenty minutes we took seven of the brutes on board and only gave up when the remaining few went back to the security of the deep whence they had been drawn. Here, no matter how we trailed our baits, they would not bite, neither then nor on any later occasion. On the surface, alert and feverish, they were eager hunters, even at midday. On the bottom, in the comparatively deep 'pools' that lay scattered over the plateau, they were not to be tempted.

Reviewing the incident, it appeared obvious that the vibrations set up by my swim-fins had served to attract them towards the surface and to put them into a 'hunting' frame of mind. There could have been no other explanation for their sudden upward rush. Perhaps my crawl-stroke had produced shock-waves akin to those of shoaling or surface-feeding fish. At any rate, it seemed to stimulate them out of their customary noontide lethargy. The question now was: could such a sequence of events be produced to order?

Now although I was reluctant to tempt providence again, it was essential that each and every possible method of shark-catching be tried if the *Golden Bells* was ever to become for me an efficient source of livelihood. So during the next few days we tried this experiment at every opportunity and the conclusions we reached were as follows. Moderately large sharks of two species (namely *nez-nez pointe* and *grandes ailes*) could be lured in this fashion. Both these types showed a preference for lurking during the heat of the day in the *basins* or 'pools' of deeper water that existed on the main bank itself. Whilst in these retreats they would not take the bait on the bottom nor would they rise to investigate mid-water hooks. But a swimmer (myself), by thrashing around on the surface, particularly if he set up a series of regular pulsations by means of flippers, could ensure an instant and alarming change in their behaviour. The time limit in each and every case was between seventy and ninety seconds from the commencement of the disturbance to the time the sharks first put in an appearance. If an immediate response was not obtained it was useless to continue; either there were no sharks in the area or some unknown factor was missing. For best, almost certain results, a flat calm was necessary, for the shark's response seemed to vary directly with the weather conditions prevailing. Once the sharks had put in an appearance, they could be relied upon to take the proferred baits, but not until they had cruised about the surface for a few seconds to reassure themselves that whatever had attracted them was no longer there.

After a few trials and successes I grew extremely nonchalant about the whole proceedings until two incidents in succession shattered my mounting and foolish confidence. Within a matter of days it had become standard practice for me to try and position the *Golden Bells* over the deep *basins* during the period between 10 a.m. and 2 p.m. and then to try myself out as a lure for any sharks that might be lying-up far down on the bottom.

A leap overboard, a brief splashing, followed by a vigorous crawl right round the little cutter, and then a swing up on to the bobstay. If there were sharks in the vicinity their sleek silhouettes would be visible within seconds of my gaining security. It grew to be a game and I began to feel rather like a ringmaster whose animal charges obeyed his summons.

I was soon disillusioned.

I had almost completed the circuit of the ship with my swim-fins drumming out their urgent call, when a large *nez-nez pointe* shot under the keel of the *Golden Bells* from the far side and passed some four feet below me. In a flash the shark had turned, cut in and luckily checked at the last moment, just as my fingers

SHARK-LURING

closed on the wire of the bobstay and I hauled myself to safety. On thinking it out, it was obvious that this particular marauder had been surface-cruising nearby for some reason and so had closed in far quicker than his brethren lying in the depths. Luckily, my unfamiliar shape had caused him to baulk for a second and so I had escaped; but it was not worth calculating that every hunting shark, on hearing the 'dinner-gong', would have had similar second thoughts.

The very next day, I had safely gained the bobstay and was busy watching the first arrivals cruising back and forth right up on the surface, moving in crisp, decisive bursts of speed. Up and out of their element, witnessing their nervous dashes, I felt vastly superior and had mentally relegated them to the rôle of alley-dogs nosing under a balcony for scraps which might descend from aloft. Suddenly one of these 'dogs', not content with his findings, looked up and, seeing dimly a white but appetizing object close above, launched himself at it. The object was my foot, resting on the bobstay wire, some six inches clear of the surface of the sea! There was a swirl beneath me and I pulled myself up instinctively, to lie on my belly across the bowsprit itself. The upper half of the shark's jaws rose clean out of the water, hung open for a second and then clamped shut, missing my toes by inches but closing on the bobstay, which it worried and shook for a brief second, as a terrier might a rat, before letting go and sinking down into the sea again.

These two experiences frightened me considerably, so I tried various other methods of shark-enticement. Having read of its success among the Polynesian fisherfolk, I strung broken halves of coconut shells together on a thin rattan bow. This I jiggled furiously in the water for hours on end in the apparently mistaken idea that the noise emanating from this contraption again produced shock-waves similar to shoaling fish. The system may work wonders in the Pacific, but in the Seychelles it has little or no effect other than to reduce one's crew to helpless laughter at this new proof of Europeans' willingness to believe any weird and obvious lie. Following one unsuccessful foray in this fashion, Ton Milot approached me on the foredeck where I squatted in the sun to dry while the rest of the crew went about the work of butchering the sharks we had taken the previous night.

SHARK FOR SALE

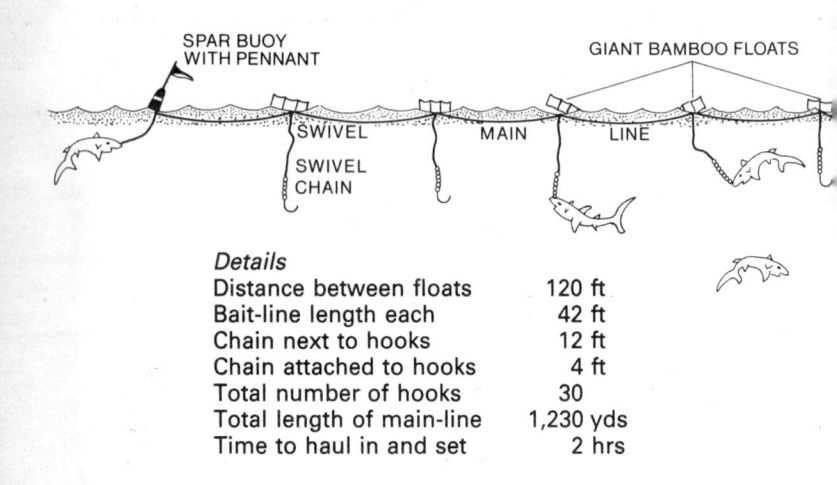

WIND →

SPAR BUOY WITH PENNANT   GIANT BAMBOO FLOATS

SWIVEL   MAIN   LINE
SWIVEL
CHAIN

Details

Distance between floats	120 ft
Bait-line length each	42 ft
Chain next to hooks	12 ft
Chain attached to hooks	4 ft
Total number of hooks	30
Total length of main-line	1,230 yds
Time to haul in and set	2 hrs

'I suppose you'll be trying *gris-gris*[1] next and setting up as a Ti-Albert, eh?'

'Why so?' I asked.

'Well, you seem to be making a business of "shark-calling" these days. Did I ever tell you about Joseph, the Malagash from Agalega? You'd be interested in him. No? *Ou capable croire!* I thought everyone had heard of Joseph. Whatever next, not knowing about Joseph the Malagash. Hmm...' (This was Ton Milot's standard introduction to any subject strange and rare, whereby he would dismiss it as something casual, of common knowledge, and thus make his listener all the more eager to hear about it.)

'Oh well. Old Joseph was a tall, skinny black with a face like a death's head. By day he worked as a labourer and fisherman for the Mauritius company that managed Agalega and by night he made *gris-gris* in a little hut away from the labour lines.

---

[1] *gris-gris*: Black magic.

SHARK-LURING

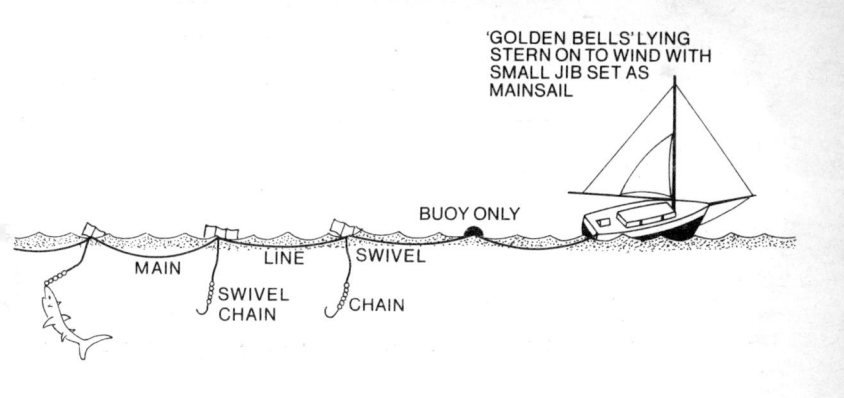

Final form of drift-line fishing as practised by the *Golden Bells*

Nobody took much notice of his medicine-making but everyone took notice of his shark-calling. You couldn't help it. It so happened that at that time, about twenty years ago, I'd just got into a bit of trouble by selling a house that belonged to my wife. She was living in it, you see, and I didn't dare tell her, so I thought I'd better buzz off for a couple of years till she got over the shock. You know how women are, m'sieur, always making a fuss over nothing. Just at that moment the owners of Agalega were recruiting fishermen in Mahé, so I signed on quick as a coxswain and was able to get away before she found out.

'Well, I arrived at Agalega and it wasn't long before old Joseph had me scared out of my wits. There in that island we used to fish from small pirogues, four men to a boat, just out a mile or so from the settlement. Snapper, we used to catch mostly, and small shark. We couldn't take the big ones since our boats were too small. Joseph, the Malagash, was one of my crew and for a while all went well. Then one afternoon we were coming back, having been out since before dawn and having caught very little all day. I was moaning away on my little perch in the stern as I guided the pirogue in towards the pass through the reef – cursing our luck, the fish, the weather, the island and finally my bunch of fishermen. Joseph, the death's head, who was up in the bows, suddenly stopped rowing and called out to me: "It's fish you are after, is it, coxswain? Let old Joseph show you what sort of fish there are at Agalega. Let me show you my children."

'At this the others stopped rowing as well and before I could do anything the Malagash leant over the side and struck the planks of the pirogue first with his fist and then with his knuckles, right down on the water-line. Then he smacked the surface of the sea with the flat of one hand, while he beat a swift tattoo on the hull with the other. Finally, he stood up in the pirogue and drummed on the floorboards with his heels and then stretched his arms high above his head till he looked ten feet tall and let loose the most God-awful wailing.'

'What sort of wailing?' I interrupted.

'Strong and shrill,' he replied, 'and made up of strange words.' I remembered the story of Pierrot and the *Ti-Albert* who called 'in a high voice'.

'What happened?' I asked.

'Nothing for about two minutes, and then slowly there came up out of the sea the biggest fin I'd ever seen. It stood far higher than the side of the pirogue and by its shape I knew it was a hammerhead. It came straight for us quite quietly and passed right alongside. Must have been eighteen feet long, with a body broader than our pirogue. As it came by, Joseph knelt down in the boat and trailed his fingers in the water so that they ran along the creature's back. When he came to the dorsal fin he held it gently until the shark turned lazily round, rocking the boat as it did so. Then the Malagash put his other hand in on the other side of the pirogue and I looked and there was another hammer-head on that side, too. Smaller, this one, maybe twelve feet. By this time all the rest of the crew were lying flat in the bottom of the pirogue, and I joined them. For a few more minutes we heard Joseph crooning and talking and felt the bumping and scratching as the two sharks pressed close alongside. Then there was a silence and I looked up, and saw the old man sitting in the bows and do you know, *m'sieur*, the tears were running down his cheeks. "Have they gone?" I whispered. And he looked down and saw me and said that they had gone, so we all got up and rowed in and never said a word till we were safely on shore.'

'Did Joseph ever do this again?'

'Indeed he did. He became a little more mad after a while and used to do it every time he went fishing.'

'Did the sharks always come?'

'Nearly always, though there were occasions when nothing happened and then he would sit and mope and say that his children no longer cared for their father who loved them. They weren't always hammerheads, either. Twice I saw him do it with tigers and once with a *requin de sable*. But usually it was hammerheads.'

'What happened in the end?'

'Well, things got so bad and all the other fishermen were so scared of him that the manager forbade him to go out and kept him working on shore. But it didn't do any good, for after a few months Joseph went quite mad and laid down the shovel with which he was working and walked down to the beach. Here he removed all his clothes and walked out to the edge of the reef and stood there beating the water with his hands and singing and crying out to his children to come and take him home. Then he held his hands way up on high and walked out until the water covered his head and we saw him no more. Some of the men who were there will tell you that they saw the two great sharks come and carry him away, but that is not true. We never did find his body . . .'

Many months later I checked the records of Agalega. Sure enough, there was the entry:

'Fevrier 7. Joseph, *un vieux laboureur, noyé.
Peut-être suicide ou mangé des requins.*'

Sixteen days after leaving Mahé we returned with five tons of wet salted shark and the knowledge that our long-line was a success. It was all we needed to go ahead with the preparation of a full-sized rig.

FIVE

The Hunted and the Hunters

> . . . *His teeth are terrible round about. His scales are his pride*. . . *He maketh the deep to boil like a pot*. . . *One would think the deep to be hoary. Upon earth there is not his like, who is made without fear.*
> (Job xli. 14, 15, 31, 32 & 33)

The next few months brought about the near-perfection of the long-line as a method of catching sharks. As we became more practised in its use so our catch rate increased until it became customary for the *Golden Bells* to return after a mere eight or nine days at sea, yet with more shark in her hold than we might previously have taken in a three-week cruise. The crew soon caught up on the new routine and with each voyage that passed one or other of them would think up some fresh detail that made for greater efficiency. All this time I was learning too – mainly about the sharks we caught and about my shark-fishermen.

There are well over 100 different species of shark known to science and an equal, if not greater, number of popular misconceptions regarding these creatures. Sharks belong to a very primitive class of fish, coming well before the typical fish families, such as cod, mullet and snapper. They possess no bony structure in their bodies whatsoever. Instead, their skulls and backbones are made up of cartilaginous tissue. They have no scales, but their skin is covered with a protective layer in the form of myriads of tiny overlapping studs, called dermal denticles. It is this which gives shark-skin its roughness and toughness and, incidentally, it is from these very dermal denticles that the human tooth structure has evolved. Unlike most fishes, sharks have no airbladder to enable them to balance freely in the water. Consequently, as soon as a shark stops swimming, it sinks to the bottom. This is the reason why it is not possible to catch sharks by shooting them and then recovering their bodies, unless the water is very shallow. Sharks are viviparous, that is, they give birth to live and fully formed young. Like animals, they reproduce by mating, and the male shark carries two long organs of generation that point rearwards and lie along the stomach, on the inner side of the pelvic fins. These 'claspers', as they are called, are often used by primitive peoples throughout the world as an infallible aphrodisiac, but as with most examples of this commodity any successful results would seem to be due to mental rather than medical causes. As far as I know, the male shark is the only animal to possess two sexual organs, which was always a point of great envy to my fishermen, who considered that in this respect the ways of God were not only weird and strange but grossly unfair to the human race!

The number of young that the female shark carries will vary according to the age of the mother. These fishes become sexually mature at a very early age, and it is not at all unusual to find 'baby' females in an advanced state of pregnancy. To quote an example of this, among other sharks we took one night were two tiger sharks. One was very large, being about fourteen feet long, and the other was scarcely more than a 'pup' of less than four and half feet. Both were females and both proved to be carrying young. The big female had thirty-seven sharklets within her, while the smaller one had on three. These unborn sharks were of an exactly similar foetal development and when placed upon the deck the three from the one shark were undistinguishable from the thirty-seven of the other. Female sharks usually grow to a larger size than the males and, especially when carrying young, are more aggressive and have larger appetites. Of the actual mating habits of sharks little is known. Since many species feed fairly frequently upon smaller members of their own community, it is difficult to understand how the smaller male can go a-courting without risk of ending up as his bride's wedding breakfast. Perhaps that is the reason for the fact that female sharks generally outnumber their male counterparts by seven or eight to one! In all the time that I spent with the *Golden Bells* only once did I come across what may have been the nuptials of these fish. It happened on a calm night at full moon. We had set our long-line and were sitting around the deck drinking tea before turning in. Suddenly we became aware of a distant splashing

SHARK FOR SALE

sound, which we took to be the noise caused by a school of tuna feeding on the surface. This disturbance increased until Ton Milot rose to his feet and went up to the bows to see if he could see anything.

'Sweet-Jesus-and-all-the-Angels! Look at this lot,' he called out. On my joining him, he pointed down into the dark water alongside. There, gyrating and pirouetting, were a dozen or more large sharks, their outlines perfectly visible since they were etched in glowing phosphorescence. As we looked around we saw that the whole sea was alive with these creatures, all engaged in fantastic dance ritual. They weaved in figures of eight, they spun, they rose and slapped the surface with gently waving tails which gave rise to the noise we had heard, and time and again we saw one or other of these sharks do that which we had never seen before, for they rolled lengthwise through the water and sometimes went on swimming upside down. They were not feeding, nor was there any great violence in their movements. Several times we noticed two shapes draw together, head to tail, with the lower fish on its back, inverted. In the light of the moon we could see that this strange gathering of sharks covered a large area, and distant soft splashings could be heard far from our immediate vicinity. One other strange point emphasized their unusual behaviour that night. When we came to haul in the long-line at midnight we found all the baits intact and that we had caught neither shark nor fish of any description. It was the first and only time this happened. Ton Milot in all his years at sea had never seen such a gathering nor similar shark behaviour.

The main offensive weapon of a shark, and quite the most terrifying feature of the animal, are its teeth. These vary from the fused rows of pavement-like crushers possessed by those small sharks that feed upon molluscs, up to the three-inch fangs of the Mako. In fact, so varied and so characteristic are shark teeth that they form the major means of identifying the many species. On the opposite page some typical examples are illustrated. Most of the predatory varieties possess teeth which either penetrate and hold, or else shear away and cut. The long, dagger-like teeth of the Mako and the Grey Nurse are examples of the first kind, while the cockscomb-shaped ones of the tiger and the triangular saw-edged cutters of the great white shark represent the latter type. Most sharks bear their teeth in successive rows,

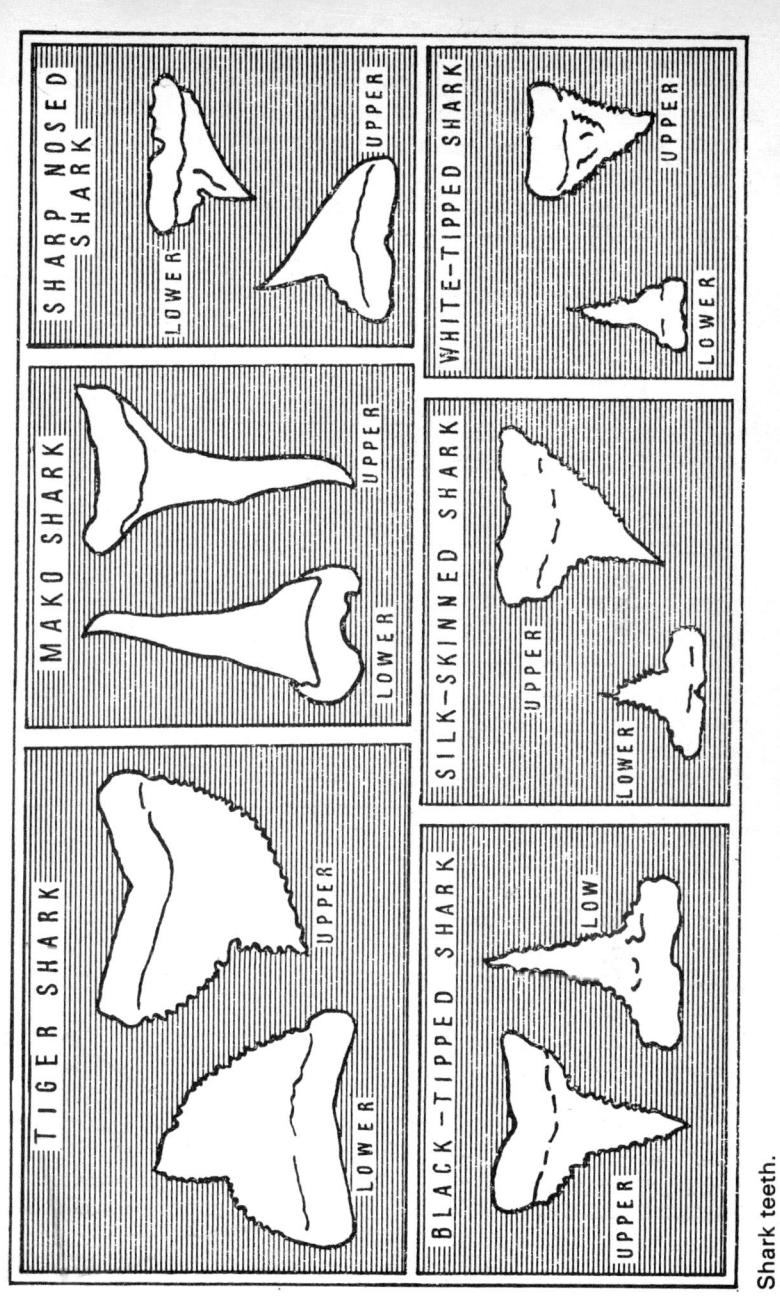

Shark teeth.
Showing how various species may easily be identified.

one behind the other. The number of these rows vary with the type; for example, the great white shark has five or six rows each of twenty-six teeth in the upper jaw and twenty-four in the lower. The first or outer row are normally the only ones that remain firmly erected. However, when the shark opens its jaws, successive rows spring erect and lock behind the first line, so that the mouth now becomes fringed with a thick 'hedge' of triangular blades. It is this feature which makes the bite of such a shark so deadly. With the general wear and tear of a life spent in hunting, the front teeth often become broken or are torn out. When that happens, a tooth from the second row then moves slowly forward to take its place, so that the outer layer of teeth is constantly being renewed and remains always formidable. Contrary to popular belief, sharks do not have to turn on their backs or sides to bite. The fact that their mouths are situated on the underside of their snouts does not matter at all, for their simply override their prey and then bite and worry at it like a dog. This they are able to do on account of their peculiar jaw structure.

The jaw of a shark is hinged in the opposite manner to that of most animals. It is the upper jaw which is free of the skull and is the one that moves, while the lower jaw is fixed. When a shark bites, its whole snout is thrown upwards, presenting an impression, when viewed from in front, that the creature is wearing a huge dunce's cap, for its head is now crowned by the displaced and upward-pointing white cowl of the snout. Thus the shark is unable to see what it is biting, or intending to bite, once the jaws are opened. But a shark does not rely upon its sight alone to secure its prey. Rather it makes use of a number of sensory organs which can be used separately or in conjunction with one another in tracking down and securing food. Patterning the underside and flanks of a shark's snout are a number of deep pores that terminate in sensory nerve endings. These are known as *ampullae*, and there is little doubt that they act as sonic or pressure wave amplifiers, by which the fish can detect and close in on any underwater disturbance over a considerable distance. Most sharks have an acute sense of smell, in consequence of which they are able to track down any bleeding or decomposing object.

There are also strong indications that they have yet another undetected sense, closely allied to radar emanations. By means

THE HUNTED AND THE HUNTERS

of this they are able to swim at speed at night or in murky water without bumping into rocks or other objects. Russian fisheries research workers claim that sharks can be attracted by underwater 'pulsed' radio transmissions of a wavelength of 21 kc/s, which would be in keeping with this theory. There is yet another sense used by sharks in the selection of suitable foods, and that is a tactile one. Time and again one can watch sharks which have been presented with a new form of food 'testing' it by bumping or brushing it with their bodies and especially with their pectoral fins. In an area hitherto unfished it is normal for sharks to experiment in this fashion with the lines and traces to which the hooks are attached, and in clear waters they can be watched closely while they do this until they reach the actual bait and then, by a similar test, decide that the strange dangling morsel is indeed edible.

Thus, the combination of these various sensory systems, together with the brutally efficient jaw structure, makes the shark one of the most deadly hunting and killing creatures imaginable. But although the shark is physically well equipped to deal with either foe or prey, mentally it lags far behind many of the other creatures of the sea, a fact which tends to cancel out these advantages. A shark has little or no memory, no ability to learn or adapt itself and is withal a very foolish creature indeed.

At the beginning of my shark-fishing I amused myself for hours seeing how easy it was to delude the most nimble of these carnivores. I would cast out a baited hook with the deliberate intention of attracting one particular specimen. The shark, seeing the bait, would sweep in to investigate, circle the line a few times, and then come straight in to bite. At the last moment I would give the line a jerk to pull the hook upwards about eighteen inches. The shark's jaws would open and crash shut again on empty sea, while the bait floated safely just above its head. Again the shark would cruise round, again investigate the hook and again come in to take it. Another jerk of the line, the bait would rise upwards, the shark would rush by, and so it went on. This little game could be played for hours until one became bored with it. Never would the shark learn where the bait had disappeared nor how to allow for this last-minute movement. Its form of attack was inflexible and could not be modified.

Actually, what was happening was this: when first circling the hook, the shark was establishing its pattern of approach. By eye, and possibly by sonic or similar emanations, it established the bait's exact distance as it described a circle around it. Then, by similar or allied methods, it decided upon the line or direction of attack. These two factors of direction and distance having been ascertained, it launched itself at the bait along a given path. At a certain point along this path its jaws shot open, hung agape for a second and then slammed shut. The fact that the bait had shifted at the last moment and had thus thrown the whole scheme out of gear did not enter into the calculations. It missed, so it tried again, and this inflexibility of behaviour governs all shark attacks, whether they be carried out against natural prey or even human beings. In every recorded case of shark attacks on humans when there was more than one person in the water, the shark has contented itself with striving after a particular selected victim; and no matter how other humans may have sought to draw or drive the carnivore away, even to the extent of coming between it and the person being attacked, the shark has adhered to its original choice and has never been side-tracked into mauling those who interfered.

The same single-mindedness will cause a shark to return again to a selected food source, even though it suffers grave injury and eventual death in so doing. A shark's purposefulness, once it is under way, is something terrifying to behold, but at the other end of the scale it takes an average shark a very long time indeed to make up its mind to attack at all, particularly if its victim is of an unusual or unknown type. For this very reason, even the larger sharks on those clear and distant banks where we fished, were extremely suspicious and almost pathetically nervous of human beings swimming under the surface. The normal reaction was to void a cloud of excrement in their nervousness, turn tail and disappear from sight. But like all generalizations, this one had its exceptions.

During our voyages I often found it necessary to dive, using an aqualung, either to check the hull, to clear the anchor from coral heads, or else to examine the bottom to see if it was suitable fishing ground. In order to avoid meeting sharks in a feeding frame of mind, I always carried out these chores when the sun was well up, and also at a time when we were not engaged in catching sharks. Consequently, on most occasions I saw little or nothing of these big fish, though there were times when I came across them by accident and it was on these particular forays that I was able to observe their reactions. Most of the large sharks did show both nervousness and an inclination to flight when first they saw me. Two species, however, did not. The first of these were those tiger sharks of eight feet in length or more. Without exception these showed absolutely no fear, but an initial disdain which gradually gave way to curiosity and finally an appraisal and interest that was frightening and would, I am sure, in many cases have led to an extremely dangerous situation had I not withdrawn to the safety of the *Golden Bells*. The other member of the family that refused to be frightened was the hammerhead. These, however, showed immediate but fairly remote interest and usually contented themselves with circling in wide arcs, never sufficiently close to make me apprehensive. Their speed of swimming did not alter nor did they give any other impression than that of keen but well-bred curiosity.

Such behaviour would naturally not apply in many tropical ports, where these creatures have become accustomed to leading the life not of predators but of scavengers. In such localities sharks feed upon carrion, refuse and all manner of things which they would never come across in their proper environment. Under these conditions they might well be prone to attack any object on sight, no matter how strange. Consequently, those who swim in such harbours or estuaries run a very real risk indeed of being taken, for not only will the sharks thereabouts be bold and fearless but the very obscurity of the water will enable them to creep up and reconnoitre their victims unseen. It is from such scavengers that the belief has arisen that the average shark is a dirty and indiscriminate feeder. In actual fact, the true oceanic and bank shark is extremely fussy in its diet, and all bait must be absolutely fresh, otherwise it will be left untouched. True, these creatures will feed upon offal, particularly if there is blood on it, but there again it must be fresh. Bait-fish that is three hours old and has been left in the sun to dry up, or has dangled in the water and become limp and tasteless, will be taken with relish by rock cod, barracuda or snapper, but most sharks will pass it by without a second glance.

In the Seychelles, the most sought-after bait of all is fresh turtle-meat, after which comes porpoise and then fresh fish.

SHARK FOR SALE

Shark-meat for shark-bait is useless, for it will be ignored completely. Conversely, shark-meat forms the finest bait for catching bottom-fish for bait. It is quite true that sharks feed upon each other to a large degree, but for some reason they will not feed upon the flesh of their species when cut up into chunks or strips. This factor of shark preying upon shark gave us trouble at all times, for no sooner was a shark hooked and struggling than all the others in the vicinity would turn upon it in a flash and close in to attack. Presumably, the struggling actions of the hooked specimen released the 'attack pattern' latent in all members of the species. Once the hooked member of the family was brought alongside and lay quiescent in the water, the cannibalistic frenzy of the others diminished to a marked degree and though they would continue to investigate and eventually continue feeding upon their companion, their behaviour lacked the fury of their initial onslaughts. This was so usual that the fishermen, after first striking at a shark to ensure the hook biting in, would allow the creature considerable freedom of movement, if there were others of its kind in the vicinity, seeking to prevent its flurries by allowing it to run, rather than forcing the issue and precipitating certain attack and consequent mutilation of their prize.

When hauling in the long-line it was not at all unusual to find that one shark had taken another on the same hook. This we did not mind, however, for the usual result was that the original and smaller shark upon the hook would have been swallowed by the second and larger shark (all except the head, which would have been merely pushed further up the trace). On opening up the latter we would invariably find the complete trunk of the first victim reposing intact. This we would extract, cut up and salt down, and thus we would have gained two sharks by one hook. Once, inside an eighteen-foot tiger shark we found a nine-foot trunk, inside the nine-foot, one of five, and inside the five-foot the original 'baby' of a mere three. Thus we had taken four sharks on the one line. In view of their prolific nature and rapid growth there is little doubt that the sole reason why sharks are not to be found in swarms in all tropical seas is their own cannibalistic behaviour.

The digestive powers of sharks are not only weird but highly selective. By some latent power they are able to arrest or accelerate this mechanism seemingly at will. Food can pass right through their systems in a matter of very few hours or, conversely, can be 'stored' untouched within the actual stomach for as long as a month at a time. When one considers that the power of a large shark's digestive juices are similar to undiluted hydrochloric acid, this becomes all the more remarkable.

One evening, on Fortune Bank, I watched a particular hammerhead feeding on groups of large snapper that it chased and caught among the corals. This shark was easy to recognize, for it carried a peculiar white scar behind its gill-slots and the top of one pectoral had been bitten in some encounter. As soon as it grew dark, I set a night-line and at ten o'clock this was taken by this very hammerhead, as we saw when we brought it on deck. On butchering it we found that the stomach and guts were entirely empty and devoid of all trace of food. In one 'pocket' within the stomach, however, we found sixty-eight large gill-plate bones, all that were left of thirty-four red snapper, presumably those I had watched the hammerhead catch and eat not five hours earlier. These bones were absolutely free of all traces of flesh and might well have been within its stomach for months, judging from their condition, and I would indeed have assumed so had I not witnessed it feeding upon those fish early that evening.

At the other end of the scale there have been recorded incidents of sharks keeping whole dolphins untouched in their stomachs for a period of thirty days and a human arm for slightly over two weeks! Both these instances have taken place in aquaria and are well authenticated. Incidentally, there are strong reasons for believing that human flesh proves both unpalatable and indigestible to many 'dangerous' sharks, for there have been numerous occasions on which the attacker has regurgitated part or whole of his victim some hours after engulfing the poor wretch. Several times we on board the *Golden Bells* retrieved the most curious objects from within our catches, but on no occasion did we have any indication as to how long they had lain there. Amongst other items, I remember a large cat – its fur bedraggled but undamaged – a giant clam, the head of a dugong and a small but whole hawksbill turtle. It was more usual, however, for us to find that bout ninety per cent of the sharks taken were entirely empty. This did not necessarily mean that they were ravenous or near starvation. Though sharks can and do feed with frenzied appetite upon occasion, their metabolism is such that they can do without food for extremely long periods and are not normally heavy eaters. Specimens kept in captivity have refused food for as long as two months at a time without loss in weight, health or vitality. An eleven-foot specimen in Taronga Park Zoo, Sydney, ate a total weight of only twenty-one pounds of fish over a period of four months, yet continued to thrive. During a complete twelve-month period this particular shark consumed a bare 178 pounds of foodstuffs. This hardly fits in with the popular conception of a ravening monster with an insatiable appetite.

In common with many of the lower orders, the vitality of sharks is both horrifying and mystifying. Ton Milot showed me how sharks, hauled on board alive, gutted completely and then thrown into the sea devoid of all entrails, liver and heart, would swim steadily off again as though nothing had happened. In such a state they could even be made to show interest in or even bite a baited hook if it were thrown to them. I have seen specimens, their heads completely transfixed by a lance which had passed through the brain, break away and escape, only to be seen again hours later (and in one particular case, the next day) milling around with the rest of their comrades below our keel, seemingly in perfect health. Their small hearts, cut out and left in a bucket of sea water, will continue to pump unaided for four or five hours, and their headless bodies will flip and quiver for a similar length of time.

The backbone of a shark consists of a series of cartilaginous discs, of a thickness of about half their diameter and joined one to the other by thin gristle. The fishermen sometimes collect these backbones and make them into ornamental walking-sticks for sale to the tourists who visit Mahé. To make one is quite simple. Firstly, the limp and flesh-tatty spine is trailed behind the boat for several days, which cleans and bleaches it thoroughly. It is then strung up in the rigging or lashed to a shroud in order to dry. After five days one has a bone-dry and dead-straight cane to which a ferrule and handle of wood or shell can then be attached and your walking-stick is ready.

Most people have heard of shark-fin soup, but few know the whys and wherefores of this Eastern delicacy. The four main fins of a shark (two pectoral, one dorsal and the lower lobe of the caudal or tail) are cut from the body, trimmed of any flesh, and left in the sun to dry. A week of such treatment and the fin has lost all moisture and much of its original thickness. It is now wrinkled, with the edges possibly curling and presenting a parchment-like appearance. In this state it is easy to see the individual 'rays' or ligaments that form the main ingredient for shark-fin soup. After further treatment, brought about by boiling over a long period, it is possible to extract these fibres with tweezers. They look like strands of uncooked vermicelli and have much the same texture. These shark-fin fibres are then carefully dried and stored until the day they are used as the basis of the 'stock' from which the soup is made. Real shark-fin soup can take as long as five days to prepare and in its more usual form is presented as a clear broth very similar to thin chicken soup. Like many exotic dishes it may serve to titillate the jaded palate, but most people of healthy appetite might well find it disappointing and over-rated. In common with other sea-food, such as *bêche-de-mer* (sea slugs) it owes much of its popularity in the East to its reputed aphrodisiac qualities, and as such always commands a high price.

The flesh of sharks on the other hand is undoubtedly of very great food value. Its protein content is higher than that of most fishes and it is rich in phosphorous. The meat is clean, bloodless and heavy. Being boneless and of similar texture throughout the body it is good value for money for the buyer. It is entirely 'unfishy' and has a flavour far removed from that of other fishes. One either likes it or one does not. It is a food about which it is difficult to be indifferent. I loathed it, though on many occasions I was forced to eat it owing to lack of an alternative. The least unpleasant form in which it could be eaten was, to my mind, as a kedgeree and then only when unborn baby sharks were used. These small creatures are highly esteemed by the Creoles and it is quite true that their flesh is more tender and the flavour more delicate and less distinctive than that of their elders. There is little doubt that shark-flesh, suitably tinted and packed in brine or oil, finds its way into many tins labelled 'Tuna', 'Tunny-fish', and even 'Salmon'. This does not detract in any way from its nutritive excellence.

Shark-liver oil forms yet another valuable commodity which this creature surrenders to its captor. For comparison with other fishes the livers of these carnivores are immense and may make up almost one-third of their total bulk. After putting these organs through a hand-mincer and then boiling the residue in water (to which a small amount of caustic soda has been added to break down the fatty tissues), the oil can be extracted and poured off. The greatest quantity of oil we were able to extract from the liver of one shark was forty-two gallons. This was a female tiger shark about seventeen feet long. Unfortunately, the livers of those sharks that inhabit the equatorial zone of the Indian Ocean seem very low in Vitamin A content, and it is on this factor that one relies to market the commodity. A 'good' Seychelles shark might provide oil of 15,000 international units per fluid ounce, but general market requirements were of the order of 27,000 units. It appeared that the better oil in this respect was usually taken from the livers of those sharks that inhabited colder seas, where the fishes' metabolism had need of richer fuel. As it was, shark-liver oil of the type we were able to produce fetched only a low price as 'fish oil', and after a few attempts I gave up even trying to market it. We still extracted the oil upon occasion, but this was used for dressing the mast and as a general lubricant on board; we stored all hooks and chains in a great vat of it in order to prevent corrosion. One point of interest was that later, when we began taking sharks from the great depths (and presumably cold water) we found that their liver yield in Vitamin A was often three times what we had come to expect as normal from the sharks of the *bordage* and plateau.

There was little of the shark that we did not utilize for some purpose or other – flesh, fins, back-bones, livers and even the teeth. If we had taken a large shark the head would be reserved for our attention at a later date. Then, when we had some time to spare, the entire jaw-structure would be cut clear of the skull, cleaned of all meat and left in the sun to dry. When ready, this mask would be sold to decorate someone's verandah, as are the horns of antelope, paws of otters, and similar trophies in other lands. Or else the whole jaw would be boiled in water and caustic soda until all the teeth dropped out. The largest and best of these would then be dried and sold either separately as curios and good-luck charms or else be made up into sharks'-teeth bracelets and beach jewellery.

It did not take me long to learn that just as the habits of the

THE HUNTED AND THE HUNTERS

sharks we sought were governed by strict and inflexible rules, so too were the lives of my fishermen. Partly on account of their insular environment and partly through the demands of their trade, they had developed through the years a code of conduct entirely suited to their needs, but none the less unique. This way of living set them apart from the other Creoles, for they had long since given up trying to explain their hopes and fears to either *patrons* or friends. On shore and in port their *patron* was their employer, a person to be propitated and circumvented. At sea, this august being faded into the obscurity that surrounded all those who were left behind. Out on the banks the men, and they alone, were responsible, not merely for their own safety and livelihood, but their employer's investment as well. He was in their hands, not they in his. As such they were men, not underlings, *pêcheurs des requins*, and they acted accordingly. They made the rules, not the others.

These rules of theirs made themselves felt with the start of each fresh voyage. Friday, they would not sail. Conveniently, it was a day of fasting. Sunday, similarly, was the day of rest. Saturday – well, that was sandwiched between the two, and might be unlucky, so no shark-fishermen set out from port on that day either. If one tried to press the point a thousand unforeseen difficulties would suddenly arise. Someone would 'go sick', the coxswain would discover that the salt was wet and needed drying out, the mechanic would find that the engine needed retiming, and so on. In the end one waited until Monday, as was normal, and all would be well.

Then there was the question of *D'av*. These were the advances to which the crew were entitled by custom before setting out: five rupees for each crew-member and eight or ten for the coxswain. Again, the fishermen were accustomed to return to their homes after having made the ship ready, there to wash and change, spend a little time with their wives or girl-friends and then saunter back down to the quayside, stopping *en route* at their favourite bar for a little something. To a newcomer, these delays were infuriating, but after a while I began to see the independent spirit that lay behind it all and grew to value their conventions.

Finally, when the agreed time of departure arrived the crew would turn up, one by one, each carrying a little basket. Though

SHARK FOR SALE

they were dressed in clean, pressed clothes and were freshly shaven as though for a holiday, they were unaccompanied by any of their families, for this was all part of their work ritual and not a Sunday outing. On board, they would hang up their precious baskets on hooks in the fo'c'sle and then quickly set about the business of getting the ship out of the harbour. Once away, they would take it in turn to go below, where they stripped off their clean and near-best clothes and put on ragged shorts and sometimes singlets that would remain on their bodies till the voyage was over. Their clean clothes, carefully folded and wrapped in newspaper, would go into their baskets, along with the little bundle of pillow-cases that they had brought with them. These pillow-cases were a source of great amusement to me at first. Each fisherman might possess a dozen of these, half of which he would bring on a voyage. They would be hand-made, often with beautiful lace edges or fanciful embroidery in coloured cottons. Some might carry the owner's initials, worked as a monogram; others, a religious verse or symbol. All, without exception, were spotlessly laundered and smelt of thyme, lavender or other herbs. It was Ton Milot who first noticed my interest in these. 'It's all right for you to smile, *m'sieur*. You wait. Wait until we've been out two, three weeks and you stink of shark, your skin is all scaly, the decks are powdered with salt and the only thing you have to lay your head on, come nightfall, is the flank of a shark. Just you try to sleep then! Ha! But with one of these against your cheek, no matter if the decks are awash and the rest of you is soaked, you'll sleep as sound as if you were in your own bed, just you see.'

As usual Ton Milot was right. Nursing a little kapok pillow, with one's nose buried deep into the comforting sweetness of its fragrance, once could forget the dirt and dross of one's surroundings and find all the rest one wished. To protect these pillow-cases as far as possible, the fishermen used first to lay a clean piece of sacking upon the deck or shark carcass on which they proposed to lie. Even so, three nights or so was sufficient to befoul them and to destroy their somnolent effect. Hence the reason for bringing so many of them on each trip.

Equal to their ritual of departure was the dogma which surrounded the labour of heaving up the anchor. Shark-fishing schooners were accustomed to anchoring each night in depths of

THE HUNTED AND THE HUNTERS

up to thirty fathoms and accordingly carried anything up to seventy fathoms of anchor chain. None of them were equipped with power or even hand-operated winches and consequently it was no small task to take in the major portion of this length each morning. Moreover, should the chain have coiled around coral-heads on the bottom, considerable skill was necessary on the part of the man at the helm in order to position the vessel so that the rest of the crew might be able to pull freely. For this reason, it was usual for the coxswain to be at the tiller and to appoint one of the crew as head of the anchor gang. On the *Golden Bells* this task fell to Gandhi. In order to synchronize the efforts of the rest of the crew, each anchor bo'sun himself composed a litany, usually inveigling half the more obscure female saints of the Catholic calendar and all the local and popular whores of the town to help the crews in their efforts. Gandhi's particular refrain went like this:

> 'Ho-yo! Up the chain, for the bread of my children. Ugh!
> Ho-yo! Pull, for the sweet love of Christ. Ugh!
> Ho-yo! Aid us, St Cecilia. Hi-yah!
> Hi-yup! Pull, my children!
>
> Ho-yo! I'll see you Thursday night, Violette! Ugh!
> Ho-yo! Aid us poor mortals, St Columbia. Ugh!
> Ho-yo! I dream of your sweet breasts, Paulette!
> Hi-yup! By the sweet of your brows, pull!
>
> Ho-yo! She rises. Up, up! Ugh!
> Ho-yo! Give us strength, St Eugenie, Ugh!
> Ho-yo! I rejoice in your beauty, Marie-Therese. Ugh!
> Hi-yup! Long pull together. And again, my children.
>   There! It is done!'

– and it usually was!

There was nothing intentionally sacrilegous about the mixing of the names of ladies-of-the-veil and ladies-of-the-town in their pleas. All my fishermen were not so much immoral as amoral, and had no more idea of fidelity in their dealings with the female sex than a collection of tom-cats. The islands of the Seychelles offer few relaxations to the poor majority of its population but it does enjoy (or suffer, according to how one looks at it) a great surplus of available women. These islands were, until very recently, entirely Victorian in their attitude of female subjugation. It was only in 1941 that a Bill was passed allowing women the right to separate passports from their husbands. Women were the chattels of men. They were taught to sew, to cook and to keep house. They were expected to marry and bear their husband's children. Those that did not marry were usually forced through economic necessity to form the most permanent liaison possible with any admirer, whether married or not. A Seychelles girl, on being invited out for an evening stroll by a young man, knew that her acceptance would mean a direct assault on her virtue, for such was the normal practice. In the circumstances all she could hope for was to make herself sufficiently attractive and pleasing on the chance that her friend might even think of marrying her. If he did not, it was too bad, but illegitimacy is accepted as normal, nor is there any stigma attached to the rank of bastard.

Among the crew of the *Golden Bells* Ton Milot alone enjoyed the distinction of having a lawful, wedded wife. She, long-suffering woman that she was, lived in a little house on Praslin, the sister isle to Mahé. Milot used to visit her only during the off-season, when he was near starvation, or else when rumour had it that she had collected together a few hard-earned rupees by some means or other. On such occasions he would descend unheralded, wheedle as much cash as he could from her, lay in a stock of booze and invite his friends in to help him dispose of it. Nonetheless, his wife always saw him off again with a clean shirt or two and a new pair of socks. He was a drunk, a nuisance, but he was Ton Milot and had once been gracious enough to confer his name upon her; because of that she would be forever in his debt and he, the old rascal, knew it.

None of the rest of my fishermen were, strictly speaking, married. Hassan, however, had two common-law wives. One on Praslin and one on La Digue. Whilst he was with me he acquired yet another, this time the island of St Anne, where we went to discharge our shark after each voyage. Big Gandhi, as strong as an ox and as docile as a St Bernard, had inevitably got himself into a liaison with a tiny shrew of a woman, who had beaten him regularly for the past nine years. He once confided in me that somehow this made him feel much better, just as though she were really his wife and had a right to do so. Since this woman was neither young nor pretty she must have been very sure of herself, for there were dozens of teen-aged girls who would have welcomed the permanent caresses of the big fisherman, had he ever felt so inclined. As it was, Gandhi was never unfaithful to his 'wife' more than once or twice a month, which established a near-record of constancy, judging from the behaviour of the rest. Zulu and Ti-Royale leapt from one amatory success to another with the speed and agility of buck-rabbits and I soon gave up trying to keep up with their *petites amies* of the moment. In all their love affairs they were good-natured and amicable and never displayed the least jealousy when some other fisherman took up with their girl of the moment whilst they were away. To them the whole thing was sport – good fun, but never to be taken seriously. After all, the loss of one pretty girl or another was nothing, there were always half a dozen more or equal attractions just round the corner.

Only once was the equanimity of the *Golden Bells* shattered by female intrusion and that was when a very pretty young negress, about fifteen years old, laid claim to the entire crew! She even approached me with the idea that I would give my official sanction to the arrangement, for would it not be – she said – a good idea if all my fishermen spent their nights ashore under one roof, for then I would know just where to find them if need be? No, she had no sister, but could manage them all quite well herself, thank you. She was young and strong and liked fishermen because they had strong arms and tasted of salt. Her name was 'Killing-Baby'. 'Baby' on account of her years and the other epithet as token of her ability to 'kill' the most virile of men. After this revelation I hastily passed her on to Ton Milot before she included me in with the rest of the crew. After a few weeks it came to my ears that my fishermen had indeed taken her up on her offer and those few months that followed, during which time she took polygamous care of them all, remained notable for the absence of extreme drunkenness amongst them and also for the excellence of her laundry and needlework, plainly visible in their outward appearance.

With regard to their religious practices the fishermen were once again bound by the life they led and had adapted their Roman Catholic creed to suit their own requirements. Though they would not leave port on a Friday or a Sunday, once at sea each day became a working day and no exceptions were made. If they said their prayers, which was not very often, it was when they lay down to sleep at night and they did not kneel to do so. Before each meal they crossed themselves, and also in moments of anxiety or distress. Most of them carried a coloured postcard of one of the many saints, which they pinned above the nail on which they hung their baskets. A few carried St Christophers or similar medallions and the older ones wore protective tattooing, as described in an earlier chapter. That was as far as it went. Never once did I hear religion discussed between them, nor did they display much interest in the supernatural, with the exception of a general and sincere belief in witchcraft, sorcerers and *gris-gris*.[1] The Powers of Darkness were far more real to these Creoles than the Heavenly Host.

One evening, beating back towards Port Victoria, we were delayed by an adverse wind and sought anchorage in one of the many inlets on the north-west coast of Mahé. It so happened that we had run short of firewood and I dropped Zulu and Hassan on shore to search for driftwood along the beach. Before many minutes had passed we heard them calling frantically for us to come in and take them on board again. Not knowing what had happened we did so and found them empty-handed but both a dirty grey with fear. For a while they could not talk, but pointed shaking hands towards the groves of casuarina trees which fringed the dark shore. On looking carefully I could see a little green light bobbing about between the trunks of the trees, apparently some five feet off the ground. It moved in and out, sometimes resting in one place and then darting on again. Sometimes it waned and at other moments it glowed quite brightly. Eventually, it moved up to higher ground and then disappeared from view. About half an hour later it reappeared, a mile or more up the overhanging mountainside, still hopping and skipping through the night, and though so far away it was still as plainly visible as when it ran along the beach. The crew knew what it was, or so they insisted. It was a particularly evil spirit that haunted lonely pathways and guided travellers to their deaths in chasms or over precipices. Should it describe a circle around a person,

[1]*Gris-gris*: black magic.

he or she would be compelled to follow, knowing full well that this must result in destruction. It was quite a well-known phenomenon, apparently, and there was even an untranslatable Creole name for it. It was one of the many 'night-walkers' that exist to carry out the Evil One's work, or so my Creoles thought. Whatever it was, nothing would make any of the crew return to the shore again that night and they were all so visibly upset that I moved the *Golden Bells* out 150 yards from shore before anchoring again. To my mind this flickering emanation seemed similar to that caused by marsh gas, a 'will-o'-the-wisp', but the soil there was not marshy, nor had I heard of such a light climbing up mountain slopes. My fishermen were much amused at my various explanations. Why go to all that trouble to compound theories that did not fit? they asked. The thing was plainly a 'night-walker', and if I could not recognize it as such, more fool I!

They had other superstitions as well. Like sailors in many parts of the world, they believed that the little wave-dappling bird, the stormy petrel, heralded bad weather and that porpoises leaping clean out of the water meant the same. Catching a tiger shark brought on high winds. All these had an element of truth about them in many cases and were general rules compiled from a mass of separate instances. Others were more fanciful and less credible. Among these was the belief that dead men haunted those reefs upon which they were drowned and that they might be seen at very low spring tides, by day or by night, walking about on them. It is interesting to note that this conviction is widely held by the Polynesians as well.

But for all their primitive convictions, basically they were active, hard-working men, clean in their personal habits and independent of spirit. As such, they were fit opponents for the beasts they hunted.

SIX

The Skull on Africa Bar

Yet man is born unto trouble, as the sparks fly upward. (Job v, 7)

Though our catch rate was steadily improving I was still very conscious of the fact that the business of shark-fishing with the *Golden Bells* could never be placed on a firm financial footing until I had my own fish-drying base and was able to market my own produce. To this end I was continuously searching for a suitable site or to come to an arrangement with someone who possessed such a thing. Eventually, some fourteen months after I had taken over the little cutter, an opportunity for this came about.

At that time there lived in the Seychelles a retired tea-planter with whom I had had previous business dealings in my search for mother-of-pearl shell amongst the outer islands. Since then, along with other commitments, Bentley-Buckle had taken on the lease of several islands in the Amirantes group. These, unfortunately, had brought him little profit, being too small for copra production on any scale, and had proved expensive to supply and maintain. Knowing that I was looking for a base from which to operate and on which I might prepare dried shark, he now offered me the use of these islets together with certain facilities, in return for which I would be responsible for running a shuttle-service on my outward and return trips carrying such working personnel, supplies and produce as might be required. I was also to pay him a royalty on all dried shark prepared on his islands. Such an agreement suited me well and I gladly accepted.

Bentley-Buckle's major holding in the Amirantes was a circular islet, some third of a mile in diameter, by name Remire or Eagle Island. On this there were some dozen families, plantation labourers and fishermen, with a manager. Some eighty miles to the south lay the lozenge-shaped cay known as Marie Louise, upon which some eight Creole families were similarly employed and within visual distance of Marie Louise were two tiny sand-bars, Ile des Noeufs and Boudeuse Cay. Both of these came under the jurisdiction of Marie Louise and were uninhabited for all but two months of the year when temporary camps were set up on them for the labourers who came to collect the sea-birds' eggs, for these formed one of the group's major financial assets. Fifteen miles north of Remire, on the extreme northern tip of the Amirantes Bank, there is a similar bird's-egg islet, known as Africa Bar, but owing to poachers this had become unproductive and was almost valueless. I chose Remire as my base on account of the good anchorage, rather than Marie Louise which, though nearer to the good 'sharking' areas, was extremely steep-to and suffered from a heavy ground-swell.

Our first voyage there proved highly entertaining. Along with our fishing gear, provisions and fuel for a three-week trip, we carried food for Marie Louise and Remire for the next two months, plus thirteen Creole passengers in the form of island labourers and their families, together with all their luggage. To crown it all we also transported a sixteen-stone Australian, a personal friend of both Bentley-Buckle and myself, who was going to live on Remire and supervise things in general. Like many other white men who have come to settle in the Seychelles, Harry Benson was a personality of singular uniqueness. Then in his late fifties, Harry had passed his life wandering about the world engaged in the most unlikely pursuits: as a veterinary surgeon and abbatoir official in South America; as a cattle buyer for the British Government in Somalia and Abyssinia; in transporting his own livestock from Australia to Madagascar and East Africa and in other such occupations. Periodically, he would experience a brief attack of homesickness and scurry back to Queensland, only to find that he disliked his fellow-countrymen even more than those 'pommy-bastards' (the British) he was forced to put up with when abroad. Like many of his race he was generous, quick-tempered, unpredictable, loud, outspoken and entirely genuine. Always 'agin' the Government and particu-

SHARK FOR SALE

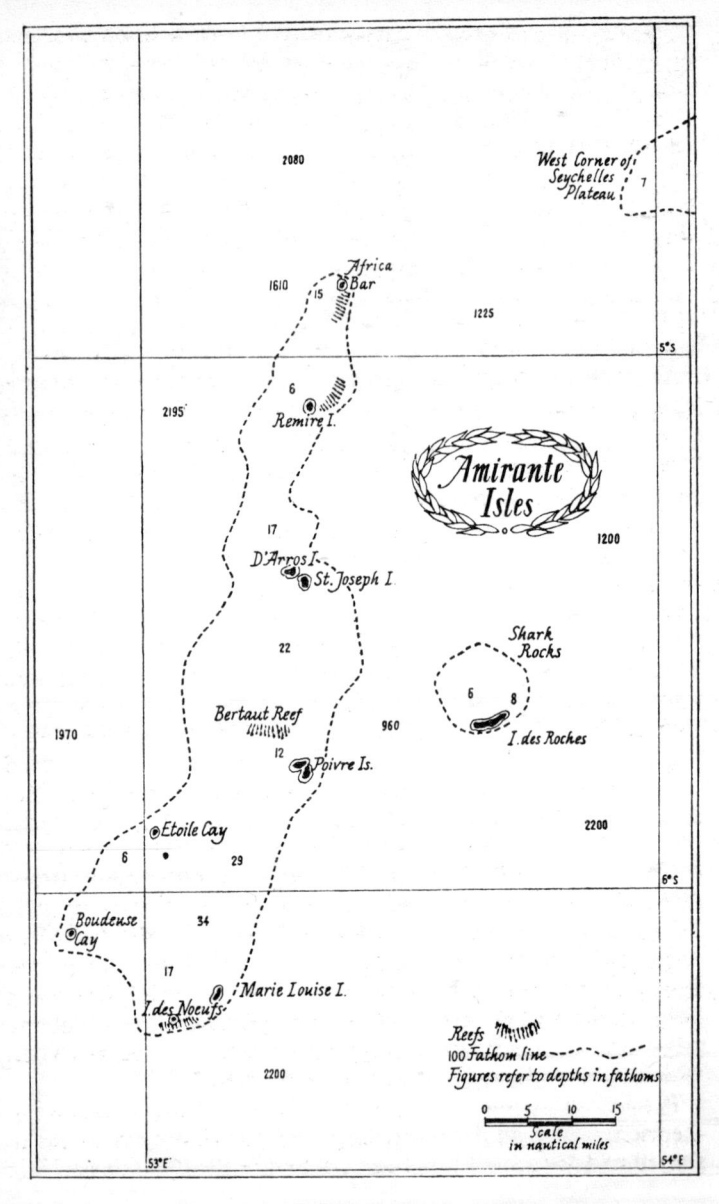

larly the Colonial Office, he had nevertheless joined the Australian Expeditionary Force at the age of sixteen in the First World War and had immediately volunteered on the outbreak of the Second. He had made enough money to live comfortably anywhere in the world, yet he had sought out the Seychelles as being remote and unsophisticated, a place where he might live simply and enjoy his one passion in life, sea fishing. Not content with that, he had now offered to maroon himself on Remire for six months to look after Bentley-Buckle's labourers and to help establish the fish-drying base. He was under no obligation to do either of these things; he stood to gain nothing by such an action. It was typical of Harry Benson, and that was all there was to it.

Once on board, Harry took one look in the hold, jammed with various shades of sweating humanity, muttered profanely under his breath and then established himself along with his sleeping-bag in a place of eminence on the cabin roof with his back to the mast, and there he remained throughout the voyage. His reason for not joining those other passengers below was very understandable. The Seychellois possess an entirely Victorian attitude to the concept of travel. Women are creatures of the home; unfit for any other activity. On a journey, then, they would be useless and get in the way as much as possible. Moreover, they should be sick, or at least try to be, in order to satisfy convention. Consequently our female passengers had to be more or less carried on board, as though they had lost the use of their legs, and then hurried down into the cabin, where they had busied themselves in sorting out their belongings and laying claim to as much space as they might reasonably occupy. This they did by unrolling large feather mattresses, surrounding these with a defensive wall of packages and boxes and then prostrating themselves in the middle of it all. This was made more difficult by the fact that each and every one was wearing a large and formidable black straw hat, another concession to local etiquette. Owing to the stores that the *Golden Bells* now carried, headroom below decks was reduced to some four feet; nevertheless, not one straw hat was removed, though most were knocked askew in their owners' efforts to get installed satisfactorily.

Before getting under way these ladies passed the time fanning themselves idly and chit-chatting. No sooner was the engine started and the anchor weighed than there was a further scuffling as the entire group rummaged through their respective paper parcels and brought to light four further items necessary to their status as female travellers. These were, in order of importance: a huge ornate, Victorian chamber-pot; a beautifully embroidered lace pillow; a bottle of cheap lavender or violet water; and a delicate lace handkerchief. Custom decreed that they were to be sick; very well, then, they were going to be sick in style. In point of fact, not one of them showed the least signs of indisposition on this or any subsequent voyage, but they tried very hard. They groaned, they mopped their brows with toilet water, they hid their heads for hours upon end within the confines of their chamber-pots, all of which remained unsullied and dazzling white. Periodically, in order to call attention to their Victorian femininity, they would lift their faces and call piteously to their menfolk on deck or to any passing member of the crew, asking for a drink of water, a cup of herbal tea, to be fanned awhile, to be reassured that this torment was not going to last indefinitely, that they were not in mortal danger from storm or shipwreck, and that the *Golden Bells* was not due to sink within the next few minutes.

All these demands were met most gallantly by the men, both crew and labourers alike. On deck the business of running the ship was left almost entirely to Ton Milot and myself whilst the others bustled to and fro, getting in each other's way and generally causing complete chaos in their efforts to satisfy the Creole ladies' incessant demands. As the journey went on so did the situation become more farcical, as each female passenger thought up new ways of calling attention to her dreadful plight, so emphasizing her gentility and good-breeding. The more they groaned and moaned, the more impossible their requests, the more ludicrous their fears, the higher their prestige mounted. Gandhi, whose natural kindliness blossomed under such conditions and who neither ate nor slept for the thirty hours that it took to reach Remire, once paused for a moment in his ministrations to tell me that 'the old cow' who occupied the corner of the cabin and who had been one of the most vociferous of our seraglio had asked him if he could remove all the brass portholes, complete with frames, and replace them with something else, as the smell of that metal always upset her and gave her a migraine. 'Whatever will she think up next!' he concluded, his voice expressing the most sincere admiration.

THE SKULL ON AFRICA BAR

Amid all this turmoil Harry Benson squatted on his sleeping-bag, as heavy-bellied and immovable as a Chinese deity, doing his best to appear inscrutable and aloof from such goings-on. Occasionally, however, things would become too much for him to bear and his harsh voice would blare out in strident protestation against some trespass or other. This had no effect whatsoever on the Creoles, for Harry had disdained to learn the patois (though he had mastered many more difficult languages during his life), and the Seychellois always remains supremely indifferent to other forms of speech which he just pretends not to hear.

It was with some relief therefore that we anchored just off the beach at Remire and were able to lighten the *Golden Bells* of her burden of human and other freight. In fact, we rested there a day before departing on the next stage of the voyage, which was to transport Harry down to Marie Louise, eighty miles to the south, where we were to drop him before setting off shark-fishing. On our return we were to call in again to pick him up, by which time he would have finished what administrative and planning work he had in mind there and would sail back with us to Remire. Here we would deposit our load, replenish our stores and refuel before setting off on another fishing trip, whilst Harry supervised the setting up of drying tables and the preparation of our shark.

The journey down to Marie Louise was uneventful. We left in the late afternoon, taking advantage of a full moon to allow us to weave between the many islets and reefs that dotted our path. In this way we were able to take advantage of the coolness of the night and the light breeze that accompanied it. Arriving off Marie Louise at ten in the morning we were more than surprised to see what was apparently the entire islet's harbour force coming out to meet us in a pirogue. Even before the usual greetings had been passed most of its occupants had clambered up on board the *Golden Bells* and with one voice announced that there they were and neither God nor Devil would move them – back to Mahé they must go, for never would they set foot on Marie Louise again. It was not for some little while, when the tumult had died down, that I was able to ask the reason for all this hubbub. To my questions the answers came but slowly and most vaguely: the (working) conditions were not good, provisions were low, there was much *traca* (trouble), they had been there too long, the island was bad, and so on. It was very obvious that all this was getting us nowhere and eventually I persuaded some of them, with Ton Milot's assistance, to row back to shore on the pretext of getting hold of some firewood. Privately, I told the little coxswain to have a look round, to try and locate the missing manager, and to worm out of those that accompanied him the reason behind this odd reception. We then sat back and waited for his return. During all this Harry had been ominously quiet, most unlike his usual self, and I erroneously put this down to his disgust with the Creole and with the singularly Latin display of temperament that had greeted us.

After an hour or so Ton Milot reappeared and was able to explain the mystery of the absent manager and the mutinous labourers. The fault lay, as might have been expected, in a woman. Not the manager's middle-aged wife, but a slim and hungry-eyed quadroon who was the consort of one of the labourers and who had lost no time since her arrival on the islet some eight months ago in establishing herself as the manager's mistress. Once in this position she had elevated her man to the position of foreman, had taken over the issue of rations and the allocation of work tasks, and had imposed her rule upon the island in no uncertain manner. The manager had begun to regret his hasty amour (after a few weeks), but being weak was dominated by the young virago and was unable to do anything about it. His wife, a heavy lymphatic creature, also submitted to this new tyranny and had become more or less a servant in her own house. In a modern world such a situation seems almost unbelievable, but the Seychelles are not modern and the setting for this little drama must be taken into consideration. Here was a tiny speck of land, completely cut off from the outside world for periods of four or five months at a time. On it were housed fourteen people under the jurisdiction of a manager who possessed over them the powers of magistrate, doctor and priest, and who kept both food supplies and water under lock and key. Moreover, since the labourers were illiterate, their daily living was in his hands since he controlled the computation of wages, their debit for purchases at the little shop, deductions for this, credits for that. On him depended the whole economic structure of their livelihood, whether they would go back to Mahé after their two- or three-year contract with a hundred rupees in their

THE SKULL ON AFRICA BAR

pockets or one thousand. Throughout their lives as island workers they had grown accustomed to knowing no law but his, and obedience to such an authority was deep-rooted in them all. The fact that their law-giver had taken the woman of one of their companions and had in consequence promoted him over them, was not important. It was unjust but something to be accepted. Even the fact that it was this woman herself who now issued the orders, albeit through the person of the manager, did not disturb them unduly for such things had happened in the past and doubtless would again. No, it was only when the woman herself seized and took over the distribution of the rations, withholding some from this family, giving more to this favourite, that the trouble started. It was fear that caused it. Fear that the food stocks would be exhausted before the supply schooner arrived on her next routine visit; for the island was not self-supporting nor did it possess any boats capable of making the journey to Mahé or any of the other populated centres. Fear that this woman's stupidity and greed would be the destruction of them all.

Once the labourers realized that not only did we carry the new stock of provisions for the island but that Harry would be staying with them awhile as the owner's representative, the panic dissolved and some order was established. Their confidence was further restored when they learnt that when the *Golden Bells* returned to pick up Harry, she would also be taking off those whose work contracts had expired, for the craven manager, who was still skulking somewhere out of sight ashore, fell into this category.

By the time Harry, his belongings and the various inhabitants of Marie Louise had all been rowed in, it was late afternoon, too late for us to think of fishing that night. Thankful of the opportunity for a quiet swim, I lowered myself over the side and set out to have a pleasant hour's goggling. I had not been in the water for more than ten minutes when I heard first the sound of our anchor chain being hauled in and then the noise of the engine starting up. Thinking that Ton Milot had decided to change our mooring point for some reason or other I paid no attention until the *Golden Bells* came right up alongside me and I saw Milot gesticulating for me to climb on board. When I had done so he gave me the reason. Marie Louise, and this particular locality

SHARK FOR SALE

just off-shore, was renowned for the number of the size of tiger sharks that lurked there, for the islet lay on a spur of the main Amirantes Bank and there was deep water within half a mile of it on three sides. What had really caused him to come and get me was the fact that he had been witness of a shark-attack in this very spot and not very long ago and the incident had made a deep impression upon him.

'What happened?' I asked.

'Well, m'sieur, it was like this. We had come to Marie Louise to discharge stores, just as we have been doing today. It was not easy though, for there was a heavy *raz marée* (ground swell), and the pirogues had great difficulty in riding the surf. Eventually, one of them capsized and all the provisions went to the bottom. As for the men in it, they all went with the waves and made the beach except for one who was frightened of the breakers. He turned round and swam out to our schooner, which was anchored just as we are now, a bare fifty yards from the shore. He had got to within five yards of us, and already we were reaching down to help him out of the water, when we saw a great black shadow come up beneath him. I caught a glimpse of white as the shark's snout came upwards; then it opened its jaws and the fellow in the water gave a terrible scream and was drawn down and backwards. In a moment he was back on the surface again with both hands outstretched towards us, his mouth wide open but no sound coming from it. From below his armpits we could see nothing, for all was obscured in a great cloud of blood. Then his neck went limp, his head rolled on his shoulders, and he sank down into the darkness of his blood and disappeared. We could follow the black cloud downwards as it sank, but could not see what was happening for some minutes until there was no more blood and the water became clear. Then we saw what was left, a half-man with everything missing below the waist, rolling about on the sand beneath our keel. As far as I could judge there had been just one attack, the first, which had chopped him in two as neat as you like, and the lower portion had been swallowed. Do you know, m'sieur, all the afternoon that poor remnant of a man rolled about on the sand there, right under us. It was a full moon that night and he was still there until three in the morning. I know, because I could not sleep, neither could I prevent myself peering over the side periodically to look at him. Then he disappeared and I saw him no more. Thank God! We finished discharging the rest of the cargo after sunrise and left as soon as we could. One of the islanders suggested laying out a set-line for the shark that had taken Aristide, but nothing was done about it, mainly because no one liked the idea of opening up the brute afterwards and finding the missing half. Both before and since I've seen many big tigers here. Usually they travel in pairs or alone, never in groups. If you keep on watching the water between here and the shore, I bet you'll see some before we leave.'

Sure enough, just before sunset two long, heavy shadows slid silently past the *Golden Bells*, hugging the bottom. Blunt heads, short dorsals – tiger sharks! I thought of the labourer Aristide and shivered.

Six days later we were back at Marie Louise, eager to embark Harry and his islanders and to return northwards. When the heavily-built Australian climbed on board he appeared somewhat morose and I concluded that he had not enjoyed his spell ashore nor the company there. When the rest of the passengers were ferried out to us and clambered up on deck, I noticed two tough and ugly young labourers who, quite unlike the usual well-mannered Creoles, did nothing to assist any of the women nor help with loading the baggage, which was their task. I asked the pasty-faced manager to tell them to do something for their passage, but that individual had lost all interest in the proceedings once his two precious pigs were safely tethered to the mast, and he declined to do anything about it. It was the last straw when these two surly youths kicked Harry's sleeping bag and other belongings to one side and insolently planted themselves in the space thus made available. With a bellow of rage Harry lumbered to his feet, strode across the deck and thrust his scowling face close to that of the labourer.

'So, my lads, not content with pushing women around, you now think you can do the same to me, eh?'

'*Pas connais* (don't understand),' said one of them and spat deliberately over Harry's shoulder.

'It's a fight then you want, is it? Try that, you young swine!' – and for all his near sixty years the Australian gave the Creole

SHARK FOR SALE

a cuff over the ear that sent him spinning across the deck. Normally, the Seychellois is far from being a pugnacious character – in fact he will usually go to great lengths to avoid physical violence. On this occasion, however, the labourer recovered his balance, spat like a cat, and then launched himself at Harry with all the muscular power of a lifetime of hard manual labour. Given more room and a firm stance, the older man would have been more than a match for him, for Harry, like most of his countrymen, was well accustomed to using his fists. But on this occasion he had no chance, for in trying to sidestep he tripped on a coil of rope and in throwing out an arm to prevent himself from falling left himself wide open. The Creole grabbed him by the throat while his friend seized Harry's arms and pinned them behind him. The other then proceeded systematically to throttle Harry. To aid him in this, the one who held his arms reached down, grabbed up an empty bottle that was on the deck and swung it up with the intention of breaking it on the back of the Australian's skull. It was at this point that I came on deck, for I had been in the cabin arranging the baggage and all that went on up to this moment was only related to me afterwards. Before I could size up the situation effectively, I heard a roar of anger from behind me and Gandhi leapt past me to catch the bottle-swinger's arm in mid-air. His shoulder thudded into that of the other, toppling him off balance so that he stumbled down into the scuppers, caught his shins on the bulwarks and fell over the side.

The original attacker, surprised at this new assault, loosened his stranglehold and turned round to see what was going on. It was a fatal mistake. Harry half turned, his knee came up into the other's groin and as the fellow doubled up Harry caught him under the chin with the heel of his hand. The labourer's head snapped back, a look of dazed surprise came over his face and he too disappeared into the sea. For a while there was further confusion as the two Creoles splashed and struggled alongside, not daring to try and climb up because Harry, who was now thoroughly enraged, had seized a shark-club from the cockpit and was intent on braining the first one that tried it. The chaos was completed when the Australian turned on Gandhi, who was trying to quieten him, under the mistaken impression that the latter was trying to grapple with him as well. At this point the

THE SKULL ON AFRICA BAR

two in the water turned and struck out for the islet, yelling as they did so that they never wanted to go on the *Golden Bells* anyway! They added a string of obscenities directed against Harry and what they would do to him on a dark night if they ever caught up with him, but their bravado was soon cut short by Ton Milot, who cried out '*Requins! Requins demoiselles!*' This had an instant and sobering effect on everyone and within seconds it was Harry himself who was leaning over the side to haul the nearest one (albeit roughly) up on deck and to safety. Both on board again, I turned to Ton Milot to ask him the whereabouts of the tiger sharks he had seen, to which he replied with a sly grin:

'Why, *m'sieur*, I never said I *saw* sharks. I just cried out "tiger sharks" for the hell of it, just as I might exclaim "*vive le rhum*", "*à votre santé*", or even "*ou capable croire*"!'

On hearing this I was momentarily worried lest Harry should try to toss the two troublemakers over the side again, but the Australian had already lost interest in the affair and now sat in the shade of the awning examining himself for possible damage. I went over and joined him, leaving Milot to get both crew and passengers sorted out again. Harry apologized for losing his temper, which I had thought he was quite justified in doing, explaining that for the past ten days he had been suffering first from an attack of enteric fever, and then from a severe bout of malaria to which he was prone. He was indeed far from well and was still running a high temperature, which accounted for the unusual reticence and moroseness which I had noticed earlier.

Back at Remire Island all our passengers disembarked, leaving the *Golden Bells* free to search for sharks once more. This we then did, after having told Harry that we would be back in a week or so to discharge our catch. In the meantime he was going to supervise the erection of the drying tables on the islet and see to it that the shark we had already taken was properly processed.

After a comparatively successful eight days' fishing we were making our way back to our new base when I decided to call in at Africa Bar, the uninhabited sand-pit close by Remire. My main reason was that it possessed an excellent bad-weather anchorage with which I wished to familiarize myself. Ton Milot's reason for encouraging me in this idea was the fact that the sooty terns and noddies that nested there were in the middle of their laying and after our fish-and-shark diet of the past three weeks he felt badly in need of an omelette. After we had examined the anchorage, he put this suggestion forward and found me equally enthusiastic. Accordingly, we brought the cutter in through the reef on the north-west side and thence to within twenty yards of a picture-postcard beach, where clear blue water ran in with barely a ripple to lap the golden sand. Above the beach lay a sandy hillock, tufted with marram grass, while the crest of the islet was crowned with a few coconut palms whose stiff fronds rattled gently in the morning breeze. On such a day Africa Bar was all that one might imagine a tropic island to be. To add the final touch to this 'Treasure Island' setting, the first thing I saw on wading ashore was a human skull grinning at me from the sand a few feet above the tide-line. Further up the slope, among the first clumps of grass, several rib bones stuck up out of the ground.

'Hey, Ton Milot! Look at this!'

'Huh, what? Oh, *that*! That's old Ping-Pong. Don't you know about him? Sweet Mother of God, I thought everyone did. We'll get the eggs and then I'll tell you about it after breakfast' – and with that I had to be satisfied.

After we had had our omelette and were sailing on towards Remire, Milot told me the story of the skull on Africa Bar.

In 1951, or thereabouts, a ship belonging to an international cable company was in the vicinity of the Seychelles carrying out inspection and repair to the submarine cable link which joins East Africa to the Far Eastern network. Whilst engaged in this work a Chinese steward on board fell ill and died. On examination of his papers the dead man was found to be a Methodist, so arrangements were made for the necessary funeral service. That particular morning the cable ship was passing close to Africa Bar and, seeing such a locality near at hand, it was decided to conduct the service on shore rather than bury this ex-steward at sea. Such an arrangement would be simple and would also serve as an admirable excuse for some of the crew to stretch their legs ashore. The idea was eagerly accepted by all concerned – the Chinaman having no say in the matter.

On arrival, however, the burial party soon found that what had looked like a cool and delightful beach when viewed from the cable-ship was, in fact, a furnace of scorching sand from

THE SKULL ON AFRICA BAR

which the sun's glare was reflected in blinding intensity. Moreover, the 'cool green vegetation' proved to be leg-scratching marram grass, and the coral rock foundation of the island stoutly resisted their attempts to dig deeper than a scant few inches – only just through the thin layer of guano that had accumulated on its surface and which effectively hid its true nature. Finally, there was no shade and, what with the heat, the stubborn rock, the burning sand and the acrid-smelling bird droppings, the burial party certainly lost no time in returning to their ship after having uncermoniously bundled the Chinaman into the shallow niche which was all they were able to provide by way of a grave.

Hardly was the cable-vessel hull down on the horizon when into the anchorage sailed a local shark-fishing schooner, whose crew had watched these goings-on with curiosity from a mile or so away and were now bent on finding out what it was all about. Once ashore they had not far to look, for the burial party had left one pathetic foot sticking up out of the sand. The coxswain circled the barely concealed body a few times, eyeing it with wonder. Finally, coming back to the exposed extremity, he looked at it speculatively, noting its size and the neat white tennis shoe that adorned it. He glanced down at his own bare toes and then, without more ado, bent down, undid the laces, and transferred it to his own foot. Finding it a good fit, he unearthed the other leg and took off the remaining shoe. Just then the rest of his crew turned up and before very long the Chinaman was reduced to his underpants, which they left for the sake of decency. Having no spade, they made an even poorer job of covering 'Ping Pong', as the coxswain had named the corpse, than had the original burial party. However, they made up for this by emplanting a rough wooden cross at the Chinaman's head, a gesture which the cable-ship's crew had omitted in their haste. The Creoles then collected some birds' eggs and set off on their shark-fishing again.

Two weeks later they returned. The weather had been bad, sharks few to find, lines and gear had been lost, and their store of precious salt spoilt by sea water. For the coxswain this was a major disaster, since this one voyage would put him in debt for the rest of the season. He needed some money – he needed it badly – and he had remembered something. The dead Chinaman, like many of his race, had apparently invested a great deal of his wages in dental display, for his gaping jaw had exposed to view many gold teeth and several gold inlays. These now went the way of the tennis shoes and sailed with their new owner back to Mahé. There, in the confines of his house and under cover of darkness, they were melted down into a rough ingot with the aid of a blowlamp. There was no problem as to the disposal of this form of currency. That same night the small bar of precious metal was traded in for hard cash to a Chinese merchant, who did a back-door business in such things and who was never known to ask awkward questions about the origin of the objects people brought to him. But though this trader was as bland and as seemingly unconcerned as usual when he took the ingot from the fisherman, his curiosity was aroused. No sooner had the Creole left than the Chinaman dispatched one of his many touts to the little bar where the coxswain was accustomed to go each evening when ashore. There, acting on his master's instructions, the tout proceeded to worm his way into the fisherman's confidence through the simple expedient of buying him drinks. Later that night – considerably later, in fact, for the fisherman had not only a good thirst to assuage but a strong head as well – the hireling crept back with the news that the gold had come from Africa Bar, but more than that he had been unable to find out. That it had come from such a remote and uninhabited islet meant but one thing to the merchant. Treasure! Buried treasure! Furthermore, knowing the canniness of the Seychellois, the trader was reasonably sure that the coxswain would never have lifted it all at once, but would have cached the major portion of the hoard, probably somewhere quite near the original hiding place on the islet itself. Thinking himself secure with his secret, the fisherman would probably return there at intervals to unearth more gold, which he would doubtless bring to the Chinaman's back door to exchange for rupees as and when he was in need of cash. That way, he would not give rise to any suspicion of sudden wealth – or so the Chinaman reasoned. Now although the profit from these future transactions would be very welcome, what was to stop him himself from taking the treasure now that he knew its whereabouts? After all, Africa Bar was a tiny place, a mere sandbank, and there could not be many worthwhile hiding places upon it.

The very next day the merchant chartered a schooner and

THE SKULL ON AFRICA BAR

manned it with a crew he scraped together from amongst the dockside loafers. He then went back to his store to gloat over the march he had stolen on the shark-fisherman. He would not have felt so happy had he known what went on down at the port after he left, for his hireling, seeing the opportunity of making some money on the side, had already sold the 'exclusive' secret to several other Indian and Chinese businessmen, who were even then making preparations to send their own working parties off to Africa Bar as quickly as possible.

That same week more than half a dozen chartered schooners and motor vessels converged on the little sandbank. Within ten days these labour gangs had scoured the 200 yards from end to end, all to no avail. The presence of the other treasure-seekers merely served to egg each party on, making them more certain than ever that there must be an ancient chest, *plein d'or*, somewhere on the sandbar. They dug and they probed, they searched along the reef at low tide, they drove away the nesting birds and the turtles that were accustomed to mount the beaches to lay their eggs. On top of it all, the corpse of poor Ping-Pong was picked up and moved a dozen times by the eager searchers, who were far too incensed by thoughts of gold and too unwilling to leave a square foot of ground unexamined, to think of leaving him in peace. Eventually, like a piece of discarded rubbish, he was pushed right out to the periphery, to the shore-line where I saw him, and from where through empty eyes he watched the disgruntled treasure-seekers leave. At long last he had rest and maybe a quiet chuckle or two. . .

Back at Remire we found everything going well. Under Harry's guidance the shark-drying was making good progress, with drying tables, washing tubs and storage racks all erected and in use. The only note of discord was due to those labourers we had picked up from Marie Louise who were constantly bickering as to when they would be taken on to Mahé and whose influence might have had a bad effect upon the regular Remire workers if they were left there for long in enforced idleness. Having finished their contracts on the other island, these labourers could not now take part in any work until they had been officially discharged at Mahé and then re-engaged. As we should soon be needing more salt and fuel oil, I decided to sail back to the main island at once and collect a fresh load of these necessities. At the same time we would be able to rid Harry of his troublesome charges, and also take along a load of Remire's coconuts for Bentley-Buckle. There was no trouble this time over the embarkation of the labourers, who were only too pleased to be on their way to Mahé at last. I was wrong, however, in thinking that the two young trouble-makers had forgotten their enmity towards Harry, myself and the *Golden Bells* in general.

All the way back they gave no cause for complaint and did what they were told without murmur. Once we were tied up alongside the old jetty in Port Victoria they even helped unload a few bits of baggage. At the last moment, their own belongings safely on shore, one whipped out a knife and ripped a long gash in the mainsail which Gandhi was rigging as an awning, while the other picked up Gandhi's basket containing his clean clothes and pillow cases and threw it into the harbour. They then spat on the deck and jumped ashore as nimbly as a pair of alley-cats. The big fisherman let out a roar of anger and dived over the side after his precious pillow cases, while the two louts stood giggling on the quayside. On board, Ton Milot was the first to react. Enraged beyond discretion by the business of the sail and the affront to the deck of the *Golden Bells*, he seized a brand of firewood and raced after them. Not waiting for the diminutive coxswain to reach them, the miscreants turned and ran, though they were both more than a match for the old man. Ton Milot pursued them for about twenty yards and then, seeing no hope of catching them, stopped and let fly with his piece of wood. It caught one of them clean across the back of his neck and he went down in his stride. For a moment I thought his neck was broken, but after a few seconds he got to his knees and crawled painfully away. His companion had never stopped running. Ton Milot turned back to the cutter.

'Not Seychellois, that pair. Scum, that's what! *Ou capable croire.*'

SEVEN

Deep Waters

> *Hast thou entered into the springs of the sea? Or hast thou walked in the search of the depth?* (Job xxxviii, 16)

As our experience and skill in using the long-line increased, so did our dissatisfaction with the more conventional forms of shark-fishing, until the stage was reached where, apart from collecting bait, little or no work was done at sea during the hours of daylight.

This was quite understandable, for the effort involved in seeking out the small bank sharks was almost equal to that of taking the large night-feeding ones. Moreover, each voyage that passed saw fewer and smaller 'packs' of the blackfin and white-tipped that made up these smaller species, for within the past year the total number of vessels engaged in this work had almost doubled and the main Mahé plateau was scoured from end to end by all these new fishing boats.

Being left with time on our hands was all very well, but we were out on the banks for one purpose only, namely to catch sharks. If now, by reason of our new technique, we were limited to fishing only during the night, then we were scarcely better off than when we were restricted to daytime fishing. My goal was still not achieved.

My first attempt to solve the problem was by sailing across the *bordage*, way off the bank, and out over the two-mile deep abyss. Here I thought that we might be able to pick up the migratory routes along which the wandering tuna cruised, for in their wake followed the true oceanic sharks. If we were lucky enough to find a run of tuna feeding near the surface, by trailing our lines across their wake we should be sure to make contact with their pursuers, or so I thought. Now I knew that these tuna often cruised along localized ocean currents, whose presence was sometimes revealed by a coiling 'slick' of glassy water that had a leaden appearance to the eye and could be easily located in calm weather. It was in search of such current streaks that we now sailed. Before long we were able to position ourselves on such a 'slick' and with it we patiently drifted, our lines hanging hopefully into its translucent depths throughout the midday hours that followed.

By late afternoon we were still waiting for something to happen, something to break the blue monotony of the gently heaving ocean. But on every side spread the same vacant infinity of waters without sign of life – no hesitant sea-birds whose distant flutterings would mark the unseen fish below them, no broaching porpoises, no solitary whale-spout, no surface flurry as shoaling fish moved across the wide expanse. Not even a cloud nor breath of wind served to break the lifelessness of the scene. Time hung suspended and the day seemed interminable. Under the spell of such stillness we on the *Golden Bells* became torpid, slack lines held in limp hands, heads nodding under hat-brims. We no longer even felt the disappointment of a wasted day, but by common, unvoiced consent awaited the onset of dusk so that we might stream out the long-line and continue with our aimless drifting throughout the gentle night. Not one of us wished to start the engine and motor back to the shallow bank, there to set about the bustle of a normal night's fishing. The halcyon calm had stolen our senses and its opiate had lulled our beings into forgetfulness of all outside things. We were as one with the sea, a part of its tranquillity.

Came evening and the same lethargy hung upon us. Half-heartedly we baited and set the long-line, not really caring whether we caught anything or not. We ate our evening meal in silence and then curled up in our cotton blankets and stared up at the stars until sleep came stealing upon us. About midnight I awakened, but not to the peace which I had expected. Instead, the whole ocean was alive with noise and motion. Deep grunts there were and heavy splashings, wallowing noises and soft, sibilant sighs. The sea was bespeckled with artificial wave crests that glistened momentarily as plashes of white against the overall darkness. Right beside the *Golden Bells* I could descry strange stirrings in the water as lumpy bodies passed close under the surface. On all sides was bustle and commotion and the noise grew until it was sufficient to wake the heaviest slumberer.

A great stream of tuna, such as we had sought so unsuccessfully all day, had come upon us while we slept and the fish were now feeding all around us. Porpoises were there too, their dark silhouettes leaping clear of the water as they hurried by. Invisible above us, great clouds of sea-birds hung, adding their thin, incessant screamings to the uproar. The long-line beneath our questioning hands jumped and quivered with odd shocks, now hanging slack and unresponsive and then again stretched tight and vibrant. This mass of fish must have covered an area of many square miles and it took more than an hour for them to pass us. While they were passing it was impossible to take in our line for fear of tangling it with the rush of bodies. Finally, when we did, it was too late, for though nearly every hook held tunny, all of these had been so badly mauled by sharks, with crescent wounds criss-crossing their bodies, as to be virtually useless. Moreover, so plentiful had been their prey that not one shark had paused to stop and engulf the hooked tuna in entirety, for then they themselves would have been threaded upon the line. They had merely slashed away a mouthful of the rich, dark flesh in passing and then swept on to other victims.

Later that same night another shoal passed us, this time a smaller one. Once again all that we brought on board were mutilated fish and I realized that trying to catch the shark that followed the tuna streams was hopeless, for they would never take our limp baits while live fish, rich in blood, were to be had for the taking.

My calculations of our position at dawn showed that we were now more than eighty miles from the shallow plateau. Since there was nothing to be gained from staying where we were, I decided to work our way back again, fishing those areas that appeared worthwhile as we went. For this, however, we required bait, of which we had none, having used up all our supply during the night. True, we had a few torn and mutilated tuna, but these would not go far. Much as I disliked the idea, I could see no alternative to harpooning several porpoises, those small beaked whales of the tropics, often erroneously referred to as 'dolphins'.

SHARK FOR SALE

On countless occasions in the past my crew had begged to be allowed to spear these creatures as they played around our bows, and I had always refused. They were such friendly animals, always seeking out the company of ships on their perennial wanderings. But now we needed both bait and food, so reluctantly I told Ton Milot to make ready the massive swivel-headed harpoon.

Sure enough, before long a cluster of black hump-backed shapes were seen out to starboard, cutting in towards the *Golden Bells*. Within a few minutes the familiar cavalcade of leaping, darting bodies were everywhere around us and Gandhi, in the bows, had difficulty in selecting a target, so many there were that offered themselves at point-blank range. Suddenly he struck and by the way in which the coiled line was pulled off downwards I knew that his barb had sunk home. After a minute's pause the wretched porpoise came to the surface, a dark tendril of blood growing from out of its back where the harpoon had penetrated. From then on the animal remained on the surface, its blowhole opening and shutting with strange wheezings as it sought to drag itself away. Initially the rest of the school had sounded, but now they all reappeared beside the stricken one, nuzzling it closely as though to help it on, shortening their tail strokes to keep their progress through the water as slow as was their companion's. Meanwhile Gandhi, with savage ululations, heaved in on the line, shortening the gap between his victim and the *Golden Bells*. Even when the poor brute was close alongside the other porpoises would not draw off but vainly sought to corral the tethered one away from the ship. One in particular kept pushing its way between the ship's side and the one which we had harpooned. As this particular specimen rolled I saw that it was a male and when, a moment later, Zulu sought to gaff the wounded creature it turned in a flurry of desperation and revealed itself as a female. Even after we had hoisted her on deck and the work of butchery was over, the solitary male hung around, though all the rest had vanished. In answer to my questions, Ton Milot said he thought that these animals mated for life, and added that should we harpoon a male his female consort would promptly flee the scene, whereas the male would remain at considerable risk, offering his sadly useless aid, if the female was taken. This was quite true, as I subsequently saw for myself.

DEEP WATERS

When cooked the meat was dark and oily, with a fishy pork-flavour. Gandhi offered me the brains, which my Creoles considered a special delicacy and which he had reserved for himself. However, I had watched him dismember the animal and the internal structure of its head was so human in form and layout that I could not accept his offer. In particular the size and convolutions of the brain had attracted my attention, revealing as it did that the porpoise was a creature of a high degree of intelligence and mental development.

On regaining the bank we set about our normal routine and in a few days had made up for the time we had wasted out over the deep water. But it was not long before our paltry daytime catches again set us seeking some other method of shark fishing and we tried now to track down those night-prowling sharks in their daytime haunts. That with the coming of the dawn they left the shallows and took to the depths we well knew, but what we did not know was at what depth they cruised throughout the daylight hours and at what distance from the *bordage*. Even if we struck the right combination there was no telling whether the creatures would take our baited hooks, for we had had previous experience in the behaviour of shark which spent the noon period in those deep pools upon the *sec* and which categorically refused all bait whilst at those levels. Still, it was something we could only find out by trial and to this end we now applied ourselves.

Throughout half a dozen voyages we set deep lines at various points just off the bank and in steps of twenty-five fathoms from 100 fathoms downwards. For a long time we appeared to be wasting our time, for nothing ever happened and all our bait remained untouched. Twice we experienced the excitement of seeing the marker buoys bob and sway, finally to be pulled below the surface in their entirety. On each occasion we rushed to the line, only to find that the deep-set hooks had fouled on some submarine projection of the bank and that it was the action of the current upon the line that had caused the buoy to be drawn under. Finally we reached the stage where we were setting our hooks at over 200 fathoms, which was about the extreme limit with the gear we had. By now we no longer expected any results and were continuing with the attempt largely because we could think of no other possible method worth trying. This, as it turned out, was just as well.

SHARK FOR SALE

We had sat around the deck all morning watching the bamboo float that marked the line floating serenely and undisturbed upon an ocean that was unruffled and placid. Dazed with boredom and with eyes sore from the reflected glare, we sought respite in cooking and eating a monumental fish stew. Halfway through this meal Hassan gestured with his spoon out across the bulwarks and said: 'Look at that! There go those sea-rabbits,[1] playing about with the gear, trying to make fools out of us poor fishermen again.' Sure enough, the buoy was bobbing up and down exactly as it had done on the previous occasions when it had caught on the edge of the plateau. After about a minute it disappeared from sight completely, in much the same manner as before. Since it had already gone I decided that there was not much to be gained by manoeuvring over the spot in the *Golden Bells* in an effort to dislodge it right away. We might just as well finish our meal in peace and then get on with the chore of trying to regain the line.

About five minutes later another exclamation from Hassan caused us to look up, and there was the buoy back on the surface. Before any of us could even begin to theorize as to wheth r the line had snapped under the strain or a change in current had caused this reappearance, the bamboo float set off with quiet determination in a westerly direction. This was no ocean-bed we had hooked, but something large and strong and active! Enamel plates were flung aside, mugs of water kicked over, and spoons were dropped as though red hot. Ti-Royale fell down the engine-room hatch in a jumble of legs and arms but somehow managed to get the engine started at the same instant. Ton Milot, despairing to wait for the tiller which we had stowed below decks, thrust the haft of a lance into the slot in the rudder and threw all his weight upon it to bring the cutter round on to the line of the bamboo float. Gandhi rushed up to the bows, from where he shouted steering directions, Hassan undid the spare lance from its lashings in the shrouds, whilst Zulu and I made clear the decks as best we could. Within the space of a couple of minutes we had caught up with the buoy and were able to take the surface end of the line on board. Once we laid our hands on it we could tell from the strain and the decisive way it cut steadily and calmly

---

[1]'Sea-rabbits' – Creole term for any mysterious marine happening that cannot be explained through obvious and natural causes.

through the water that we were in for a long struggle, as indeed it turned out to be.

Three hours later we had succeeded in raising whatever it was that had taken our hook a bare twenty fathoms nearer the surface and that was all. Already I was debating our next move, whether to continue with the fight, losing our chance of catching bait that day and thus also losing a whole night's fishing, or to cut loose and return to the bank. I decided to put off the decision for a further thirty minutes, more in the hope that something unexpected might occur to solve the problem than in the belief that the issue would be decided within that time. With a bare ten minutes to go to this new deadline, Ton Milot – who had left his position at the tiller to take over the task of controlling the men on the line – suddenly exclaimed:

'He's coming up! No, he isn't, he's sounding! Pull, you men, pull. Give it to him slowly now. Make him pay for every inch of line. Sweet-Jesus-and-all-the-angels, what a weight! Now he shakes it. I can feel him rolling, and again! It's the end, for sure he dies! Feel him die! Die then! There, now it is over. It is finished. Pull now, easy. See how the line comes. Up with him. Let us see you now, my beauty.'

Three minutes later our first catch from the great depths was wallowing alongside. Even in death it was a beautiful sight. This shark, unlike any other I had seen previously, was of deep blue colouring, metallic in its brightness. The under-surfaces, instead of the customary greyish or creamy white, were as dazzling as porcelain. In shape it was perfectly streamlined, with a slender pointed snout and powerful crescent tail. The eyes were large, far larger than normal, and had not yet lost the luminosity of life. Seen in the water, it was a creature of elegance, a dandy of the submarine world. Only when we had hauled it on deck and rolled its sixteen-foot length over did we begin to realize that besides being beautiful it was, or had been but recently, a highly efficient and deadly mechanism of death. In place of the customary U-shaped slot that outlines a shark's mouth and behind which are concealed the creature's teeth, this specimen had its armament ready and bared, for the mouth, though shut, was outlined by a fringe of protruding three-inch fangs, which gave the creature an appearance of unbelievable ferocity. On pulling up the snout, these stuck out like so many clawing fingers, curving predatorily inwards. Such a feature instantly labelled it as a mako, a creature of the great ocean. The crew did not know what it was, but called it a *gros bébête*, for there is no name for the mako in the Creole tongue. Ton Milot had heard vague rumours of such but had never seen one. Hassan thought it a kind of *montant bleu* (blue whaler), which, though rare, are occasionally met with by the shark-fishing schooners. That such creatures existed outside their ken was a profound shock to these fishermen, who thought that in the ways and types of sharks they knew all that was to be known. Indeed, it was only the fact that their interest had been aroused which prevented them from sulking, which was their normal reaction to anything which hurt their pride, as had this incident. For a while they salved their egos by considering the capture of the mako as a once-in-a-lifetime fluke. This attitude of theirs made me all the more determined to prove that fishing the deeper layers was not a matter of chance but a technique that might be developed, as our long-line technique had been.

During the week that followed I concentrated upon working the 200-fathom band at a similar distance from the edge of the bank and at various points along it. Invariably we hooked large shark, though many were not brought on board, as they succeeded in smashing the tackle and escaping. Without exception, all those that we did bring up were of two species hitherto unknown to us, big makos and even larger blue whalers (*Carcharinus glaucus*). But in spite of having at last tracked down these deep-cruising fish, in one sense we had failed, for never did we catch a single one of those types that hunted across the shallows by night, and this had been our original intention. Whether these did indeed pass the hours of daylight around this 200-fathom mark but did not feed during this period, we had no way of knowing. They might have been there, the tigers and the great white sharks, swimming side by side in the inky darkness along with the makos and blue whalers, or they might have been deeper yet and far from the near-edge of the *bordage* where we now fished.

One fact which we did establish was that besides the usual strong current that encircled the whole of the Mahé plateau and which followed along its edge, there also existed a similar but deeper-lying stream of water that flowed in the opposite direction

DEEP WATERS

and which lay about three miles out from the *bordage*. It was here that our deep-swimming sharks were to be found, along the edges of this counter-current. That there were other predatory fish in these areas were soon made obvious to us, for on many occasions our baits were taken and the line broken in a manner entirely alien to the behaviour pattern of a shark. In an effort to find out what creatures these might be I tried heavier tackle and used as bait whole, but small, tuna. On the second attempt this lure was taken and the buoy disappeared peremptorily from our sight. Try as we might, we could not arrest the downward surge of whatever it was that lay at the other end and before three minutes were up we had 600 fathoms of line out and the near vertical pull showed no signs of abating. Suddenly the whole rig went slack in our hands and, thinking the line had snapped, once again we began hauling in. Much to our surprise we found that the trace, hook and bait were intact – or rather not intact, but still there. The tuna, however, had been squeezed flat across the middle by some great toothless mouth that had taken the fish as a dog might take a bone. The crescent-shaped imprint of this mandible was clearly etched in the bruised flesh, but to what giant creature it belonged we had no means of telling. Possibly the attacker was a marlin, but if so it was of a size hitherto undreamt of in the Indian Ocean.

The makos and blue whalers that we took with our deep lines were remarkable for one other characteristic, and that was the number and size of the remoras that they carried with them. Most ocean-cruising sharks carry two types of parasitic fish along with them on their travels. Firstly there are the pilot fish, with vivid yellow bodies transversed by broad bands of black. These little fellows tuck themselves away below the belly, under the chin or sometimes upon the very snout of the shark. In these positions they get caught up in the eddy vortices of the shark as it swims along and are kept there, without effort, in the same way as a cyclist who places himself close behind a moving truck. When the shark slows down or rests the pilot fish move away from the sanctuary of their host and browse around, searching for food or other amenable predators. It is this way of investigating objects nearby that has given them their name, for in the past sharks were supposed to have very poor sight and the pilot fish were believed to guide them to suitable prey.

SHARK FOR SALE

Along with the pilot fish go the remoras, but these creatures have extended the art of parasitic living to yet a further stage. On the upper surface of their flat heads lies a slotted disc, for all the world like the sole of a tennis shoe. By this, through suction, they are able to cling firmly to any smooth surface and they attach themselves to the belly or under-chin of such carnivores as they find. In this position they are able to feed on the 'crumbs' that may fall from their host's mouth, or fragments of foodstuffs that drift past his flanks. When a large shark is caught and taken on board, the pilot fish that accompany him swim off in search of a new benefactor. The remoras, however, usually attach themselves at once to the keel of the ship that has taken their patron. To a shark-fishing vessel they represent a serious annoyance when they do so, for they then proceed to swim after every hook that is cast over the side and nibble away the bait before any sharks can get to it. Since their mouths are small they cannot be caught by the hook itself and some other means must be employed to get rid of them. On the *Golden Bells* we used to mix up rat poison with grains of rice, dropping the mixture over the side, close to the hull, where the ever-hungry remoras would snatch it up. Even if one caught them on very small hooks, it was wasted labour, for their flesh is rank and slimy and their eel-like bodies are slippery and unpleasant to handle.

Consequently, I was more than surprised when, after a successful day's deep fishing, I noticed Gandhi painstakingly fishing for those that had taken refuge under the planks of our cutter. When he saw me watching him, the big, clumsy fisherman blushed beetroot-red, hastily gathered up his miniature line and pretended to be engaged in something else. I likewise pretended to take no notice and passed on. The next evening I caught him at it again, and yet again on the third night. By now my curiosity was thoroughly aroused and I asked him why he was wasting his time on these wretched fish. To this he mumbled some excuse or other and quickly changed the subject. Later that evening I asked Ton Milot what it was all about. 'Ha! That bloody fool Gandhi! Ask him to show you what he's got hidden in his box and if he shows you, I'll tell you.' Intrigued, I went in search of the huge Creole and then badgered and bullied him until he gave in and unearthed a small cardboard box from within the basket that held his clean linen. Inside it lay, one upon the other, some dozen dried sucker-discs cut from the heads of remoras. By now Gandhi was so embarrassed that not a word could be got out of him, so back I went to Milot.

'Well, it's like this,' said Ton Milot by way of explanation. 'That fool Gandhi thinks he's in love with little Rose Monique – you know, the slim, sixteen-year-old half-Indian girl. He's been pestering her now for the past three months and she won't have none of him. Won't even let him hold her hand. And he a big shark-fisherman at that. *Ou capable croire?* Anyway, he got so desperate about it that he went to see a *gris-gris* woman about it, old fat —— who lives at Forêt Noire. Before she would help him she wanted half his catch-money for the next six voyages. Bloody fool agreed, too! And do you know what she told him, m'sieur? She said to him, "Gandhi," she said, "you're a shark-fisherman and know all about the sea. Tell me, do you know what a 'scuccer' (*remora*, Creole) is?" "Yes, ma'am," says Gandhi, polite as you please to the old witch. "And you know what the 'scuccer' does?" "Why yes, ma'am. It sticks onto sharks." "Just so, Gandhi. Now next time you go out fishing you catch yourself some 'scuccers'. Cut off their suckers in secret and dry them well. Bring them back to Mahé with you and wait for the full moon. Then go out by yourself, somewhere near midnight, and find yourself a lonely place where there are some big rocks. Lay the dried suckers on a big rock in the direct light of the moon and pound them into dust with a small piece of stone taken from the same place. Gather up the dust and put it in this little cloth bag which I will give you now. The next day, buy a nice little cake from the baker. Fill it full of good jam, into which you must mix as much of this sucker-powder as will go without giving it a taste. Then get your little girl to accept it, or give it to her mother with a suitable present, but be sure that this girl that you want eats a portion of it. Once she has done that there is no help for it but she must cling to you and attach herself to you even as the "scuccer" sticks and clings to her master, the shark. Should you neglect to pay me, the spell will not work, by the way, so don't get any funny ideas, my son."

'There, m'sieur, what do you think of that for a lot of nonsense? And Gandhi believes it all! *Ou capable croire!*'

It was, surprising enough, Gandhi who had the last laugh. The very next trip, when we all met together at the quayside before

SHARK FOR SALE

setting off, our big fisherman turned up with his little brown minx clinging on to his arm quite as tightly as any sucker-fish! When asked the reason for her change of heart, he swore to us privately that it was the love-potion that had undoubtedly accomplished the miracle, for there was nothing else to account for it. He added, moreover, that he had never spent the proceeds of half a dozen voyages so profitably! Later, Ton Milot told me that he had heard that the real truth of the matter was that the old *gris-gris* woman had promised the girl's mother a half-share in the transaction if she could persuade her daughter to accept Gandhi's advances. Neither of us had the heart to shatter Gandhi's childlike faith with this mercenary truth. After all, he was happy, the girl was happy and so were both the old women, apparently.

There was, however, one serious disadvantage to this daylight deep fishing. Whereas at night we were able to lay out a line of nearly a mile in length from which streamed thirty or more shark-hooks, our daytime 200-fathom technique did not allow us to use more than two descending lines and consequently only two baited hooks. We soon learnt that to attempt to set more only resulted in one getting wrapped around the other and the whole rig being rendered useless. As it was, the only way in which we could safely deal with two was by lowering one to its full depth, securing the free end to a buoy and afterwards attaching a floating line to this marker as we motored carefully away from it. Having gone about half a mile we would then lower the second hook, attach this to a buoy which in turn was made fast to another floating line and then return slowly towards the first, taking in its line as we did so and paying out the second. In this way we would take up station mid-way between the two markers and then drift with them, using the engine as necessary to maintain our position.

When one hook was taken we would throw off the line attaching us to the other and hope that this freed shark-line would not be pulled under by another heavy shark whilst we were dealing with the first. Usually we were lucky in this respect, though there were times when we had the chagrin not only of losing the battle with one giant, but of seeing our other buoy gaily waltzing off across the ocean and ourselves too much engaged to do anything

DEEP WATERS

other than curse the fates. But in spite of our losses in gear and the numerous days on which our deep-set hooks remained untouched, this new method did indeed prove to be the long-sought complement to our nocturnal long-line. Now we were able to relax under an awning for most of the day whilst our deep-set hooks drifted silently through the regions of eternal night, those gloomy wastes through which the great sharks endlessly cruised.

For every two days that we fished in this way we averaged but one shark – but each shark was well over 1,000 pounds in weight. Had we continued seeking out the diminishing packs of small 'bank' sharks, not only would the men have become exhausted under the continual strain of working by night and holding individual shark-lines in their hands throughout the day, but our catch in terms of weight would have been far less, for these 'sharklets' of the shallows, when cut up and salted down, often weighed less than thirty pounds apiece.

So at last our various trials and experiments in shark-fishing crystallized into two set techniques, and with this standardization the *Golden Bells* entered into the heyday of her career as a 'sharking' vessel.

One further problem continued to bother us until the very last, and that was the subject of bait. There was an answer to that too, but my Creole fishermen would have none of it. As it was, each afternoon's drift-fishing was cut short by our having to return to the plateau in order to catch bait for the night's work. My situation was simple and, I thought, reasonable. We would take along with us a small dinghy which would remain lashed on deck until we reached our chosen area. Here in the shallows each morning we would deposit the dinghy loaded with rations, fresh water, fishing tackle and the two crew members. The *Golden Bells*, with the rest of us, would then sail off about five miles to sweep the abyssal waters with her deep lines. Towards evening we would return, pick up the dinghy, its occupants and the fish that they had caught, and set about the night's work. In theory it seemed simple and reasonable – but not to the eyes of my Creoles! Not one of them, not even Ton Milot, could be persuaded to set foot in the dinghy and be thus cast adrift to collect bait. In vain did I point out that on the Newfoundland cod banks most of the fishing was done in this way, from small dory dropped by a mother-ship and subsequently collected again. No, it was no good. To them the ocean was no place for men in rowing boats. Too often had their companions been lost at sea whilst sailing in full-sized fishing craft for them to contemplate such foolhardy action. They were not cowards, but they had respect for the loneliness of this great ocean over whose surface they worked and well they knew the insignificance of one tiny dinghy and the ease with which it might be lost and never found again.

Perhaps they were right in their refusal.

EIGHT

Storm-Rack and Sea-birds

> ... *When shall I arise, and the night be gone? And I am full of tossings to and fro unto the dawning of the day.* (Job vii, 4)

Although the shark-fishing season in the Seychelles ran from late September until the end of April – that is, during the fine weather period of the north-west monsoon – this did not mean that every day at sea was one of calm waters and gentle breezes. Only too often line-squalls, thunderstorms or rough and ragged seas would make our work difficult and living conditions upon such small craft as the *Golden Bells* hard to bear.

If rain fell during the day we enjoyed it, for it enabled us to wash the salt crust from off our skins; whatever chores were going on would be abandoned at the first onset as we hastily grabbed the soap and stripped off the rags we were wearing in order not to miss the least drop of such a shower. Frequently the little cutter would pass out from under the cloud shadow too soon, leaving us all still covered in suds, which we would then be unable to rinse from our bodies. When this happened we would set off in hot pursuit of the disappearing rain-squall in order to finish our ablutions.

But when the same wet conditions occurred in the late afternoon they merely left us dispirited and miserable, for the deck-planks – our bed-boards – would not have time to dry and we would be condemned to spend a damp and wretched night.

As for rain during the night itself, that was the very devil. Tucked away under a blanket or morsel of sail, the first drops upon my face would wake me instantly. Glancing up at the black shadow that obliterated most of the stars overhead, I would try

SHARK FOR SALE

to assess what was coming. All too recently jerked out of sleep and pleasantly conscious of the body's warmth and well-being, my usual reaction was to will the evil umbra to pass on without shedding any more of its moisture. Usually, within a matter of seconds the quickening patter of raindrops upon the deck proclaimed the abject failure of my will, but by the time I had acknowledged the situation as hopeless and stirred myself it would be too late, for by then my bedding would be sodden and all hope gone of further sleep that night. Crouching in the smoky confines of the engine-room I would try and dry out against the exhaust manifolds which, with luck, would still be warm. To seek the shelter of the cabin was usually impossible, for the layers upon layers of shark-flesh gave no room and the acrid fumes of ammonia from the wet meat made the atmosphere not only unendurable but also highly dangerous if inhaled for any length of time.

For rainstorms at night, each member of the crew had his own particular 'bunk-hole' to which he would retire. Hassan and Zulu shared the chain-locker; Ti-Royale lay across the engine; Gandhi somehow wormed his great bulk into a little cupboard in the cockpit, in which he kept the firewood; whilst I would crawl back past the engine to stretch out along the exhaust pipe. As for Ton Milot, fair weather or foul, he slept in the cabin on top of what shark or fish there might be. How he survived this I do not know, for many times have I been driven out by the acrid gas and Gandhi was once completely overcome and lost consciousness whilst restacking our catch. But the old coxswain claimed that the effluvium merely helped to clear his head and dull the insomnia that otherwise claimed his nights. True, he coughed a lot, but he did that anyway.

Besides the interruptions of rain or bad weather there were the normal night-time disturbances due to the nature of our work. If we were on passage, then there would be a three-hour spell at the helm for each of us. Additionally, we could anticipate being roused at least three times to trim or alter the set of the sails as the capricious wind changed. Moreover, once a night on the average we might expect to be soaked right through by some irregular wavecrest which, curling high above the gunwale, would hang suspended for an instant before descending abruptly and exactly upon the sleeper in the scuppers. On the actual fishing

STORM-RACK AND SEA-BIRDS

grounds our sleeping habits became more settled, for our usual timetable called for the long-line to be laid at dusk, hauled in shortly before midnight, relaid again before 2 a.m. and recovered finally at seven. This gave us two periods of three hours each during which we might sleep without disturbance and, once we became accustomed to it, proved quite sufficient.

But it was not only we, the crew of the *Golden Bells*, that sought rest in sleep each night upon her deck-planks; there were the birds as well. Where we fished, far out on the banks, there accompanied us throughout each voyage a host of small birds, mostly various species of terns and noddies. For the most part these creatures did not alight upon the sea at all, but flew above its surface with flickering wings and plaintive cries for days on end, returning but seldom to the distant sandbars and islets where they had their nests. For these small wanderers the *Golden Bells* and other similar craft provided a welcome resting place and they would centre their activities around the vessel, following her day after day as she fished and drifted across the ocean. With the coming of twilight our little flock would wing in from all points of the compass, until by the time darkness was upon us the air around us was thick with fluttering wings. These birds would circle close above the masthead until all activity on deck was over and we had ranged ourselves in our accustomed sleeping places. Then in ones and twos they would drift lower and lower until, with a final whirring of wings, they would land wherever they might find a suitable space and be sound asleep within seconds. They chose the deck rather than the mast or rigging, because of the lesser movement there, for even on the calmest night the topmast would dip and roll in such a fashion as to unseat any bird, no matter how close it clung.

But the deck had for them several great disadvantages. It was flat, offered too poor a foothold for their narrow feet, and with their long thin wings and short legs it proved difficult for them to take off satisfactorily. They therefore preferred something that was raised a little, had definite protrusions which their small claws might grip, and which yet offered some protection against the elements. Our sleeping, sail-wrapped or blanket-wrapped bodies provided just those conditions. In the last moments of wakefulness one became dimly aware of faint flutterings and soft cheepings within a few inches of one's face. These would be followed by a series of tiny impacts usually beginning at the feet and working their way steadily upwards as bird after bird settled down gently on its human perch. Because of their slightly elevated positions the toes, knees, chin, nose and forehead were the most popular and crowded areas or, if one slept upon one's side, then the ankle, hip, elbow or shoulder. To move in an effort to dislodge one's uninvited guests was not only unkind but useless for, after taking wing in great agitation, one's personal colony would merely complete a few circuits of the darkened deck before realighting in the same place. More than that, if one did disturb them, in the excitement and confusion that went on whilst they took off, several of them would so far forget themselves as to bespatter one's body or face with the fishy tokens of their displeasure. Since this was bound to happen at odd occasions throughout the night, as one turned or rolled over inadvertently, one learnt to cover one's head with a corner of the sail or blanket and thus avoid the more unpleasant consequences.

When the old alarm clock set up its jangling clamour, summoning us to our midnight work, the birds would rise from our bodies with shrill pipings of fear that would pierce the depths of our slumbers more effectively than the alarm itself. Whilst we laboured over the long-line they swept low over our heads, complaining peevishly. Occasionally, one that was bolder than the rest would settle on a bamboo float and remain there until that portion of the line was heaved on deck, whereupon the occupant would join its companions aloft in the night sky. No sooner was the work completed and we were once more within our blankets than they would return to their resting places upon us, but this time they took longer to settle down and would cheep and scold amongst themselves for many minutes before sleep claimed them. Long before sunrise, they would leave, mounting up into the still dark air in wide arcs. From this moment till evening came we would see them but rarely and only at a distance, crisscrossing the ocean in ones and twos, in their never-ending search for food.

Normally, the *Golden Bells* was for them a convenience rather than a necessity. It was only during extended periods of bad weather that we became a vital sanctuary. At such times, when vicious waves made their food-gathering difficult and incessant winds and driving rain tired their wing muscles to the point of

STORM-RACK AND SEA-BIRDS

exhaustion, they would plummet down upon our wet decks in desperation, there to slide about, miserable and bedraggled bundles of wet feathers, but at least able to rest after a fashion. Under these conditions they could be picked up and handled with very little apparent distress on their part. In an attempt to help them and also to get them out from under our feet, I installed some planks under the deck-beams in the roof of the engine-room. Here I would place them in solemn rows, like toy soldiers, to dry out and recover. Strangely enough, the noise of the diesel motor, within a few feet of their perch, seemed not to worry them at all. At first they tended to fall off with each lurch of the ship, but I put up a small guard rail on which they could rest their chests and buffer themselves against the pitching and rolling. Here they would nod and sway, like old men asleep in railway carriages, until the weather moderated sufficiently for them to leave. I tried feeding them on fish scraps and gruel, but they would have none of it; neither would they drink. Occasionally one would die – from exhaustion, shock, exposure, who could say? Then the pathetic little body would join the other flotsam and storm-wrack that was scattered across the surface of the ugly sea.

Besides sea-birds our cutter was a home for other creatures less pleasant. Foremost among these and the most unpleasant were the cockroaches that boarded us by night when we lay alongside the jetty in Port Victoria. They were the three-inch, fluttery sort, and for the most part they preferred to scuttle around in dark corners, eating our food supplies, our clothes and even upon occasion the skin from the soles of our feet as we slept. For the first week of each new voyage these revolting insects plagued us considerably, but their greed proved their own destruction and by the time we returned to harbour few if any were left. This state of affairs was brought about by our catch. No sooner had we begun to pile shark-fillets in the cabin than the roaches would congregate beneath the floorboards within easy scuttling-distance of this mound of food. As the weight of payload increased the pressure upon the mounting tiers served to squeeze out the moisture in it and it was this liquid that carried off most of the ammonia content of the meat. Trickling down into the bilges it impregnated the floor-boards to such a degree and gave off such fumes as to kill all the insects that lurked there. Nevertheless, the cockroaches would not leave the cabin, but stayed, grew fat and died in consequence of their cupidity.

Along with the wharfside roaches came rats. At night, in the harbour, one could both hear and see the cockroaches fly in, but the rats came on board stealthily and unseen, surmounting the inverted tin cones we threaded on the mooring ropes and which were supposed to prevent their entry. Usually we did not discover their presence for some time, for they lay low and fed initially upon the cockroaches in dark corners of the ship. When this source of food was killed off by ammonia fumes, they became bolder and hungrier and we would hear their thin squeakings as they ran beneath the floorboards. Since they would not touch the salted shark they would go for our provisions and we would be forced to trap them. We did not altogether relish this job for they were proper seafaring rats – not unduly scared by us, but treating us as fellow ship-dwellers, sharers in the small wooden hull that comprised our mutual universe. On calm nights they would roam freely about the deck, scurrying and squeaking from shadow to shadow, between the sleeping bodies and across the legs of the helmsman. For the man at the tiller their antics formed a welcome diversion and served to make the long-drawn-out watch-hours pass more rapidly. For a long while there was one that used to clamber up from the bulwark to the rudder post and thence along the tiller to the helmsman's hand, upon which it would scramble and there rest, seeming to keep a look-out from this vantage point.

One night, while it was thus engaged during my watch, the rat suddenly took it into its head to run up my bare arm and seek what went on under my shirt. Surprised at this unexpected movement I let go of the tiller and tried to shake it off. I did so and it vanished overboard. The *Golden Bells* had not continued on her way for more than a few yards when a frantic chattering made me look round. In the light of the moon our wake was plainly visible, a broad V upon the gently heaving surface. In the centre of this could be discerned a second, miniature V, the wake created by the rat as he swam after us desperately. Even as I watched, the distance between us increased and the little creature fell steadily behind. As it did so, its squeakings grew fainter but more desperate. I realized that in another minute the gap would be twenty-five yards, then fifty, then even more until

STORM-RACK AND SEA-BIRDS

at last there would be just one small rat, ploughing a tiny wake in an otherwise empty ocean. How long before it tired and sank? For how many hours might its shrill twitterings echo across the unhearing sea? I picked up a coil of rope that lay near at hand and, standing up, cast it out astern. The propellor-wash caught it and streamed it back towards the little animal. With teeth or claws or both the rat took grasp hold and crawled along it. In the meantime I secured the inboard end of the rope to the port bulwark and left it at that. I did no more, for this was a true nautical rat, well able to climb up a rope by itself. Sure enough, within a couple of minutes a bedraggled little figure came up over the side, shook itself, swore at me and then hurried away down to the engine-room to get dry.

However, like fishermen the world over, our main adversary was neither rat nor cockroach, hunger nor thirst, but the sea itself. Though a whole voyage might pass as one long calm, yet we always watched for signs of impending storms, taking note of each sunset and sunrise, reading the messages carried by the clouds and borne on the winds, so that our attention was divided, half being taken up with that which went on beneath our keel and the rest in the happenings aloft. We had good reasons to fear these things. Our fishing grounds were sometimes hundreds of miles from the nearest shelter and we had no place to hide should we be caught out. Should we be dismasted or crippled we had no means of informing anyone of our plight, and we carried no lifeboat, nor even a raft. The near-equatorial latitudes that we sailed had a reputation for sudden, treacherous changes of weather, made the more deadly by the fine periods that usually preceded them and which lulled the complacent fisherman into a feeling of false security. The Indian Ocean permitted us to work over its lonely savannahs on sufferance only, and well we knew it.

On the average I suppose we met with four or five severe tropical storms per season, out of which one at least would be sufficiently violent for us to consider ourselves lucky to have survived. Each season brought with it a bill for damage in the shape of sails blown out, topmasts and bowsprits smashed, rudders carried away, anchors lost and fishing gear abandoned. The voyages on which such mishaps occurred were doubly feared, for we would usually return with an empty hold as well as expensive repairs to be done before we set out again.

Apart from the physical damage there was the loss of confidence in our own abilities that followed each encounter. Time after time it was proved to us that it was not the ship that had failed, but we, the crew. We could fight through twenty-four hours of storm unscathed: thirty-six was bearable, but anything over two complete days was too much, and it was then that we made mistakes and the *Golden Bells* suffered accordingly. It was not a question of not being able to eat or anything under such conditions, nor of suffering physical injury; it was a matter of sleep, or rather the lack of it. So violent would be the motion that rest was impossible regardless of how we wedged ourselves against or lashed ourselves to parts of the vessel's framework. For the first day one wondered how long it would continue: on the second day, how much longer we could stand it, and after forty-eight hours we no longer cared and the accidents began. At that point, the only solution was to try to rig and hold some small storm canvas aloft, stream out a sea-anchor, close up everything, and stay below and let the ship ride it out until the storm abated – praying meanwhile that we were not being driven on to one of the many islands or reefs. It was this final surrender to inaction, the acceptance of our inadequacy, that destroyed our confidence and broke our spirits. It was not a pleasant experience.

Of course, not all storms were like this. There were those which, through their limit in time or force, merely made us exult at proving ourselves masters of the situation. Great seas might hiss by, cresting the gunwhale: overhead, black scudding clouds appear but dimly through the driving rain, seemingly little higher than the mast. Yet out beyond the prancing bowsprit a lightening of the gloom ahead would give evidence that the worst was over and wet, cold and hungry though we might be, the endeavour would then seem worthwhile and the triumph sweet to the senses. One such occasion will always remain in my memory.

Against our better judgment and in face of unfavourable weather forecasts, we had set out for Mahé to fish the Amirantes and off-load our catch on Remire. No sooner had we rounded the north-east point of the island than our folly became apparent. Away to the west and north-west, directly across our track, a series of line-squalls, arched and threatening, masked the horizon. But because we thought it likely that once through this dark barrier conditions would become more favourable, and also because our pride as shark-fishermen made us reluctant to turn back without having made the attempt, we shortened our sails, made clear the deck and kept our course.

By the time we drew level with Cap Ternay, the north-westernmost promontory of Mahé, the first vicious spats of rain were already reaching out towards us. Ton Milot threw the *Golden Bells* on to a north-westerly tack in order to clear the land and thus avoid the sudden spiteful eddies and down-draughts that might be expected sailing that close under these towering cliffs. No sooner had he done so than the first buffet of wind struck us, so that the cutter heeled alarmingly, the lee gunwhale being buried in the sea that hissed past under this new impetus. With the wind came the rain, and with the rain came near-darkness. Plunging and rearing, her tall mast visibly bending under the strain, the *Golden Bells* staggered away northwards, the power transmitted by her canvas causing her to smash into the steep and violent sea, scattering spume and spray in sheets with each fresh impact.

Two hours later, conditions being exactly the same, and worried lest we drive right on to the island of Silhouette, we came about and took up a southerly tack. After three hours of this, Cap Ternay loomed out of the murk a bare fifty yards away, so back we bore to the north-west again. By now we knew that we were in for a bad time for, due to the current that swept through the bottleneck between Mahé and Silhouette and which was now even fiercer because of the following wind, we had made no headway whatsoever. This time we stuck to our course until Silhouette appeared, its granite slopes apparent as vague outlines more sombre than the swirling clouds about us. Again we turned and by the time evening fell we had the satisfaction of seeing Cap Ternay pass on our port hand perhaps half a mile off, as onward to the south we drove. At nine we came about once more, for I did not wish to be driven too far south and thus be unable to make the Amirantes. But it was no good. By midnight, though the rain came now in isolated showers instead of a steady downpour, the wind had if anything increased, and holding the small ship to her course became increasingly difficult, as each wave that thumped heavily into us caused her to give way and

SHARK FOR SALE

fall off. Moreover, the compass light had failed, leaving the helmsman to steer by the feel of the wind on his face with only occasional checks of the wildly gyrating needle. Also, we were all becoming tired, though real exhaustion was still a long way off. Crouched in the cockpit, shouting into each other's ears to make ourselves heard above the roaring wind, Ton Milot and I hurled question and answer at each other as we dipped into each wave-trough where the noise was momentarily a little less. To go on was futile: sooner or later something – topmast, stay or sail – would give, and in the darkness we might well come to grief before we could rectify it. To return to Port Victoria was equally impossible, for the coast was unlighted and, driving with the wind, we might well pile up on Cap Ternay or North Point in our attempts to clear them. To heave-to under stay sail or sea anchor would be extremely foolish, for we would certainly be swept on to the island by the wind and current.

'Have . . . one idea,' came Milot's voice as from a distance.

'What then?' I asked.

'Could try for Port Launay . . . sheltered . . . might make it . . . done it before . . . possible . . . eh?'

Now Port Launay was no port at all, but a tiny cove to the south of Cap Ternay, shielded on three sides by high mountains and guarded from the sea by Conception Isle that lay astride the entrance. Within the cove lay deep water and a safe anchorage, but to reach it, even in daylight, was not easy. Here was Ton Milot proposing to attempt the passage in a full gale in the middle of the night.

'. . . head in on easterly slant . . . too far south, cut north to pass inside Ile Therese . . . north . . . weather Ternay or Conception . . . if we miss Mahé . . . land Praslin in morning . . . perhaps . . .'

Finally it was arranged. Ton Milot was in the bows, flat on the deck as look-out. He would signal by banging on the planks with a mallet. One for steer to port: two, starboard; three, imminent collision. Gandhi would crouch by the mast with Zulu to help him, ready to let fall the sails. Ti-Royale in the engine room, with me lying on the hatch on deck to shout down instructions, and Hassan at the helm. Having taken up these positions we swung slowly around and then, as the wind and sea caught us, we careered wildly back towards the dark coast that was hidden

STORM-RACK AND SEA-BIRDS

by the night and the storm, but which lay, we hoped, somewhere ahead.

The sensation now was exhilarating in the extreme. Instead of labouring under the bludgeoning of the waves, the cutter sped with them, stern raised high and bowsprit almost touching the water. Because of our speed the rollers remained with us, seeming stationary, and the noise of the wind in the stays seemed lost astern. In twenty minutes we covered as much distance as it had taken us six hours to make. I was sure that such a mad, headlong dash was bound to finish with our being smashed to pieces against some wall of rock or else the bottom would be ripped out as we drove across an off-shore reef. But I did not care, and neither did any of the crew. We were like madmen, possessed by and borne up by the fury of the wild night. Long since we had discarded all our clothing, for those wet rags served only to chill us further. Naked we pranced and hurled defiant invectives against the night. In the engine-room Ti-Royale laughed and sang and beat swift tattoos upon the crankcase cover with a spanner. Gandhi and Zulu, the latter almost invisible against the darkness, now stood with feet apart and bodies braced against the mast, chanting some strange duet of which no word reached my ears. Ton Milot lay across the foredeck, legs straddling the bits, waving us on with wild swingings of his mallet. All this I saw under the fitful gleams of moonlight that appeared intermittently between the scudding clouds.

Suddenly I felt the deck-planks beneath my feet echo with two heavy reverberations and thought for an instant that we had struck, until a shaft of moonlight revealed Ton Milot gesticulating furiously to starboard; then I remembered our arrangement for signalling. I reached back until my heel came in contact with the tiller and kicked it over to the left. Hassan followed my meaning and bore down upon the rope bridle with which he held the rudder steady and the *Golden Bells* slewed to starboard. Immediately I saw a sheer wall of land close to port, and white surf twenty or thirty yards off, now lying parallel to our track. Hassan's hand grasped my ankle and in response to a jerk of his chin I looked out on the other side. There, a little further off and therefore less discernible, towered another dark land mass. It was impossible to tell whether the *Golden Bells* was racing between two islands or else headed straight in towards land in

SHARK FOR SALE

some windswept bay. Whatever the answer there could be no drawing back and this we both knew. Yet it made no difference to our exhilaration, only serving to heighten the tension and make the experience more vivid. Even when a furious blast of rain burst upon us, obliterating in an instant all sign of land or breakers, so that we plunged on in darkness, it did not curb the madness that possessed us. In the comparative lull of a trough I heard Hassan's shrill laugh, as weird as a jackal's rising above the roar of the storm. On we sped.

Again I felt a shock upon the deck, a single one this time, but before I had time to react I felt the deck tilt under me as Hassan swung the ship to port. A second later, there followed another blow, and again we pivoted so that now the wind smote us from just abaft the beam and we heeled hard over as Gandhi and Zulu hauled in on the sheet. I had no time to consider whether old Milot's directions were to be trusted, or whether we were indeed hurling ourselves onto those rocks that we had seen so close abeam less than five minutes ago. The thought flashed into my head that if we did run aground it would be in the most spectacular way imaginable but then, in an instant, our whole conception of the world underwent a complete change. At one moment the *Golden Bells* was tearing through the black night in a sheet of blinding rain and spume, whilst on her decks we, her naked crew, were driven to hysteria by the fury of the storm and the strain upon our nerves. The next second the little cutter had shot into an area of completely calm water, had righted herself and was coasting along under her own impetus, with sails flapping idly in the still air. In the silence Hassan's paean of wild laughter echoed back from steep cliffs that now surrounded us on three sides. Somewhere high above us, lost in the darkness, the wind sighed distantly over the lofty mountain tops. Ahead a strip of sand gleamed whitely and beyond it a lamp burned steadily in the window of a cottage. Under our bows the water gurgled and whispered as we glided on towards the shore. A fine soft mist began to fall. No sooner was the way off the ship than we let go the anchor. Suddenly sober and feeling inexpressively tired, we lay down to sleep without a word. Twice during the remainder of that night I was woken by one of the others crying out in their sleep.

Such was my introduction to Port Launay to which, in some miraculous fashion, Ton Milot had safely brought us.

NINE

Lost: The Story of Nelson Toll

*Have the gates of death been opened unto thee? Or
hast thou seen the doors of the shadow of death?*
(Job xxxviii, 17)

In the middle of October it became necessary for me to travel to East Africa on business. Not wishing to leave the *Golden Bells* in the hands of a stranger, I arranged for certain repairs to be carried out on her during my absence by the local shipyard; I paid the crew for a month in advance and, after telling them the day on which I would be back, set off.

On my return five weeks later, I was greeted at the quayside by Milot, from whom I enquired all the latest local news. This he gave me, saying that the *Golden Bells* was ready for sea, her rudder repaired, cordage renewed and crew assembled. The *Pelor*, another shark-fishing schooner, had rammed a whale-shark at night and had damaged her hull; that Gandhi's wife had taken to beating him again; that the Chinese trader known as 'Dirty Paws' (*Pattes Sales*), was paying less for green turtles this year; that Violette had left Big Harry and was now living with Moustache, and other such tit-bits of information. Finally, the whole of Mahé's population having been dealt with, the wizened coxswain paused for a moment, cocked a bird-like eye up at me and then went on:

'And there's one other thing. Nelson Toll's lost.'

'Lost? What do you mean? Where?'

'Out there,' he waved a sinewy arm in the direction of the open sea. 'Hasn't come back. Drifted off the bank, I guess. Long overdue now . . .'

'How long exactly?'

SHARK FOR SALE

'Nearly four weeks. He had food and water for twelve, maybe fourteen days.'

At that there crept into my mind the image of the *St Antoine*, that shabby little sailing vessel, drifting helplessly somewhere out there on the Indian Ocean. Dismasted perhaps, certainly with her engine out of order, or else with no fuel. The crew by now would be suffering intensely and soon they would become too weak to take advantage of any fair wind that might spring up. Then, one by one, they would go mad and die, but their little ship would still drift across the desolate expanse of sea, caught in the remorseless, slow merry-go-round of the doldrums, now travelling north, then perhaps west, then back south again, still bearing its cargo of black and bloated cadavers. Eventually the hulk might run aground somewhere on the barren Somalia coast, or else be pounded into driftwood on the reefs of the distant Maldives. Whatever its ultimate end, it seemed reasonable to suppose that Nelson and his crew would never again be seen along the waterfront of Mahé.

As to their being rescued, their chances were slight.

For one thing there were no facilities in the Seychelles, neither coastguard vessel, patrol aircraft nor rescue launch to search for an overdue fishing craft. Even had there been, the problem would have been well-nigh insurmountable, for the Seychelles banks and their adjoining waters cover almost 500,000 square miles of ocean. In addition, no one would know in which direction to look first, for the shark-fishermen of Mahé keep silent as to their fishing areas and do not usually decide their route until after leaving port. As to the possibility of being sighted by a merchant ship, this again was extremely unlikely, for the Seychelles lie well off the main Indian Ocean shipping routes.

No, to be overdue at sea in these waters – to have gone past the safe period as governed by fuel, food and water – meant that the chances of survival were very small. It was as simple as that. But their deaths would serve to keep fresh in the minds of the other fishermen their greatest danger, that of drifting off the Mahé plateau and thus losing their bearings and themselves. For the rest of that season, at any rate, few if any of the coxswains would risk fishing the extreme limits of the bank. But by next year the incident would have become dimmed in their minds and again they would venture far out in search of better catches until

LOST: THE STORY OF NELSON TOLL

another vessel was lost in the same way, and so the cycle of disaster, fear, prudence, forgetfulness, risk and then loss again, would continue. Nelson Toll's fate was nothing new. Many had been lost in the same way before and would be lost in the future. But this did not lessen the impact of each fresh occurrence.

The next day I was on my way down to the *Golden Bells* when I noticed a crowd gathering around the Port Office. Thinking that this was for some routine matter, such as the hiring of casual wharf labour, I would have passed by had I not heard the word 'Nelson' run through the throng in a hot, excited whisper. Pushing my way to the front I saw the following message pinned to the notice board:

FROM MASTER SS SALWEEN TO HARBOUR MASTER SEYCHELLES. POSITION AT 0700 0512S 5853E HAVE CONTACTED FISHING CRAFT ST ANTOINE HAVE SUPPLIED FOOD WATER OIL SKIPPER IS GOING TO STEER COURSE WEST BY NORTH REQUEST ASSISTANCE BE SENT ALL WELL WEATHER WIND WSW FORCE 4 SEA ROUGH SIGNED MASTER.

Nelson Toll had been reprieved! And with this realization there came flooding into my mind a host of mental images of the little fisherman who, even now, was headed back towards Mahé and a new lease of life.

I had first come across Nelson some two years previously, when he had been serving as bo'sun on a trading schooner on which I was travelling. He was a short, stocky man with long, sloping shoulders and blunt, squared-off hands. His skin was as fair as any Lofoten islander's and his eyes were of that pale yet piercing blue so often seen among those Norse sailors. Yet he was as Creole as the blackest of them, born of typical Seychellois fisherfolk.

At that time he was perhaps fifty-four years old and was already beginning to give way to middle age. He no longer led the crew by example, but preferred to supervise from a comfortable position – such as a bale of soft merchandise on which he would squat at ease. He was already, one felt, practising for the day when he would give up the sea entirely and join the rest of the old men who passed their time sitting on the sea wall sunning themselves. When off watch he could usually be found up in the bows, perched on the windlass smoking a crooked, black-stemmed pipe, hands clasped across á plump little paunch, the

SHARK FOR SALE

legacy of his recent laziness. Nelson was a contemporary of Milot's and like that individual had led an eventful and much-travelled life. However, he lacked the sparkle and fire of Tonton, being of a quiet and thoughtful disposition. Even when he got drunk it was in a steady, unobtrusive sort of a way. So much so that it was quite usual for the proprietors of the Market Street bars to find old Nelson fast asleep under a table long after everyone had thought he had gone home. He was a man born to be overlooked.

Later I had heard that he had given up his berth as bosun and had retired, but poverty had driven him back to sea again, this time in the rougher world of the shark-fishermen. As a killer of sharks he was useless, lacking both the drive and that insatiable 'fish-hunger' which is the hall-mark of the professional fisherman. However, he knew the islands and the currents that coiled between as few others did, and the men respected his weatherlore and seamanship. Consequently, after a very few trips as deckhand he had been appointed coxswain on one of the smaller schooners. Thus it was that Nelson Toll came to be beating back towards the safety of Mahé on that November morning.

That afternoon, while loading provisions on to the *Golden Bells*, we watched the departure of the schooner which the harbour authorities had chartered to go and meet the *St Antoine* and escort her back to Mahé. For a while I toyed with the idea of going along to help bring Nelson in as well, but the crew were anxious to begin shark-fishing again and since at that time we were working an area lying at the opposite end of the bank from the direction in which the *St Antoine* lay, I decided against it.

On our return nine days later, we saw no sign of the *St Antoine* lying alongside the jetty nor within the basin of the Old Port. One of the crew suggested that Nelson might have come in, refuelled and then gone off again, but this was unlikely and we all knew it. Before we had tied up to the wharf the news had been shouted across to us: Nelson had not returned nor had the Government vessel found any trace of the fishing schooner. For five days they had beat and tacked across the eastern edge of the main Seychelles bank, covering and re-covering the *St Antoine*'s proposed track, all without success. The *St Antoine* had disappeared for the second time.

At first people did not take this very seriously. It was too

LOST: THE STORY OF NELSON TOLL

ridiculous. Nelson must have slipped by the searching vessel in the night and must have put in at one of the smaller neighbouring islands for some reason. But I was not too sure and remained worried. I knew only too well the conflicting and often violent currents that swept around the periphery of the Seychelles bank and which are capable of driving a little fishing vessel far off its course in a matter of hours. To my mind it seemed likely that the *St Antoine* had been carried far to the north, up around the edge of the bank and thus into the empty regions of the doldrums. Here he might wander without sighting anything until first fuel, then food and finally water were exhausted once more.

As the days went by and all enquiries at these distant anchorages met with negative answers it became all too apparent that the *St Antoine* and her crew had indeed met with some new misfortune. Throughout the weeks that followed all ships in the neighbourhood kept a special watch for any sign of wreckage or debris that might explain the disappearance, but without result. The few passing cargo boats were requested to give what aid they could, but the central Indian Ocean is one of the loneliest and most unfrequented of all seas, and nothing fresh was added to the mystery.

A month passed and it was tacitly accepted that Nelson Toll was now dead – lost at sea as had been so many of his kind. After six weeks the subject was no longer mentioned and the *St Antoine* was struck off the Fishing Boat Registry. This set the official seal to her loss. In church the families of her crew now prayed each Sunday, not for the return of their menfolk, but for the peace of their souls.

Then came the second wireless message. An Italian tanker on its way to the Persian Gulf had run down a drifting hulk on which lay five men near to death. The survivors were now in the ship's sick-bay and it was believed that they would all live. No one on board the tanker could understand the language these men spoke but it was believed that they had come from the Seychelles, 800 miles to the south. If so, would the Seychelles authorities arrange for their repatriation on arrival at Bahrein.

For the second time on that voyage Nelson had the unprecedented luck of being sighted by a merchant ship.

Three months later the crew of the *St Antoine* arrived back in

SHARK FOR SALE

Mahé, having been returned by way of Bombay. As usual, it was Ton Milot who brought me the news.

'Where is Nelson now?' I asked.

'On the end of the jetty, sitting down, as always. But, *m'sieur*, be gentle. Nelson's an old man now. Also he isn't himself anymore. His spirit is broken. All his life at sea, and now the sea does this to him. *Ou capable croire?*'

I went on down to the jetty to where I could see a solitary figure right at the far end. Nelson sat, legs dangling over the parapet, shoulders hunched, gazing out across the harbour towards the empty horizon. He was such a small insignificant man and even at a distance you could sense his isolation. He had his back to the town, to Mahé and the world of men in general. He was apart and near the sea and that was what he wanted.

I walked up quietly to a point near him but a few yards to one side. He neither noticed my arrival nor gave any sign of awareness of my presence. Covertly, I studied his face. The Nelson I had known had been plump and red-cheeked, a man strong and still in his middle years. This could have been his father, gaunt, stooped, haggard with age and almost senile. An old man near to death, one would have thought.

'Hello, Nelson. Glad to see you back,' I said quietly.

For perhaps fifteen seconds there was no response and then slowly, reluctantly, the scrawny old head turned in my direction and I looked into his eyes. Nelson's eyes were as blue and as child-like as ever, only now they seemed not to focus properly. You could see comprehension begin to stir beneath their surfaces and then slowly displace the sea-emptiness that clouded them. His lips trembled and moved and then an old man's voice, reed-like and thin, issued like a whisper.

'Hello, *m'sieur*. Thank you. It's good to be home again. And I like it up here. It's quiet and peaceful and no one bothers me.'

He didn't mean it as a rebuke. It was just a flat statement of fact. I sat on with him in silence for another ten minutes and then got up to go. He did not answer my leave-taking, nor did he notice my departure. Nelson Toll, the real Nelson Toll, was already far away, somewhere beyond the thin line of the horizon, out in the great ocean that was as blue and empty as his gaze.

Gradually, throughout the months that followed, Nelson got slowly well again in his mind. But he still remained an old man.

LOST: THE STORY OF NELSON TOLL

Equally gradually, in meeting after meeting I was able to put together the story of his last voyage. This came out in scattered fragments of talk, for in his brain it had assumed the quality of a terrible and yet fascinating dream, which he strove to forget, but which kept bubbling continually to the surface of his consciousness.

This is the story of Nelson Toll:

The *St Antoine*, with her crew of five, had left Victoria late one October afternoon. There were to have been six on board, for Ton Milot had arranged to go with them 'for the ride', but just as they were casting off a message came calling him back on some other business. As it turned out, his leaving them had a decisive effect on subsequent events, for now, though their numbers were reduced to five, they carried extra water, Ton Milot's ration.

Once away from the land Nelson was able to decide in which direction they would strike first. The sea was calm, the sky cloudless except for a few streaks of 'fair weather' cirrus, and what breeze there was came from the south. Now was the 'in-between' monsoon period, the best and most reliable fishing weather of the year. Reassured, Nelson decided to make his way slowly out of the south-east corner of the bank, fishing as he went. Since he had joined the *St Antoine* he had learned to be extra cautious in his decisions, for this little fishing craft had a very bad name as a sea-boat. Her patron was a plantation-owner who knew little or nothing about the design of ships, nor did he care for them. The *St Antoine* was to be a means of making money in the new shark-fishing boom and that was all. The result of all this was a slab-sided ship about twenty-eight feet long, too fine below the water-line and having too sharp a bow, too square a stern and an ill-placed mast. Consequently, the *St Antoine*'s performance under sail was very poor and it was with the greatest difficulty that she could be coaxed to move in any direction other than sideways if the wind were forward of the beam. In a steep sea she had a nasty habit of burying her nose right into each successive wave. Altogether she was not the sort of craft in which one would choose to go far away from port if one could help it. Two previous coxswains had already left because of those bad qualities. Nelson Toll, too much in need of work and getting old now, could not afford to do likewise. Instead, he gambled on his seamanship and local knowledge to help him succeed where others had failed.

For the next three days they sailed and fished alternately and without much success until they arrived at the edge of the sunken plateau on which Mahé and the other islands stand. Here they worked their way along until they came to a narrow neck of the bank that ran out into deep water. This 'tongue' was known as Constance Bank and across it prowled large oceanic sharks that came from the deeper water on one side to seek the deeper water on the other. Because of its formation, Constance was an area of turbulent and conflicting currents and few of the shark-fishermen worked it. It says much for Nelson's seamanship that he was able to remain on this difficult patch for three days and two nights, particularly in view of the boat he was in. At the end of that time they had to return to the main bank, for the continual tossing caused by the various tide-rips and current eddies had prevented them from sleeping and also brought a great strain upon their anchor gear. Besides, though they had caught a few big sharks, the area had not lived up to its repute. Once in calmer waters Nelson Toll decided to try the eastern edge of the bank for a few days before setting course for home, so having rested for twenty-four hours they continued with their work. The ninth night following their departure they anchored about half a mile in from the edge of the bank and went to sleep. They were in sixteen fathoms of water and had let out some forty-five fathoms of chain. The sea was calm.

Some hours later Nelson was awakened by an unfamiliar motion of the ship. Walking up to the bows he felt the anchor chain with the sole of his bare foot. As the boat swung he felt none of the grating he should have done as the cable moved across the sea-bed; moreover, the chain hung too steeply. The *St Antoine* had dragged and was now in deep water, her anchor and all her chain hanging down uselessly into the 2,000-fathom gulf beneath them. Not seriously perturbed the plump little coxswain roused the rest of the crew and told the mechanic to start the auxiliary engine while the others were hauling in the cable.

His intention was to motor west until they struck the bank

LOST: THE STORY OF NELSON TOLL

again and then to anchor further in, where the current would not drag them out again into the deep. When the chain was nearly all in Nelson shouted to the mechanic to hurry up and get the motor going and put her in gear. To this there was no reply. Grumbling to himself, he went aft to find out what was causing the delay, for each minute wasted meant a further 50 yards drift from the bank, already perhaps several miles to westward. Down below the afterdeck, in the tiny compartment that served to house the diesel motor, he found young Georges sweating and grunting freely as he strove to make the engine fire, but to no avail. It would not start. Leaving the boy to go on trying, Nelson climbed back on deck and tested the breeze with a moistened finger. What little there was came in occasional puffs from the west, insufficient to belly the sails, even had they been coming from a favourable direction.

There was nothing to do but repair whatever was wrong with the engine. In the meantime he could try to arrest their drift away from the bank and safety, and he ordered the rest of the crew to lower the anchor again with all the chain available.

This weight hanging down from the bows might conceiveably enter into a deeper and contrary current to the one on the surface. If so, it would act as a drag to their progress. Also there was the slight chance that they might drift over a projecting 'neck' of the bank, in which case the anchor might bite in and hold them. This done, they sat back to watch through the long hours of darkness, alert lest the wind freshen and change so that they might hoist sail and claw their way westwards.

Down below the mechanic worked as best as he could in the flickering light of the hurricane lantern that Nelson held for him.

At daybreak they were able to review their position. Some seabirds had roosted for the night upon the rigging of the *St Antoine*, and with the coming of the light they left. Nelson watched them go and continued to do so until they were almost out of sight, when his perseverance was rewarded; for the little covey suddenly changed direction and flew northwards, dipping low over the sea until they were lost to view. From their actions he was confident that the *bordage* still lay quite near, within a mile at any rate, for such sea-birds seek their food along the edge of banks and their sudden turn indicated that they had positioned themselves there to begin the day's hunting. Cheered by this thought he went to

SHARK FOR SALE

see how Georges was getting on with the engine. The trouble, it appeared, lay partly in a dirty injector. It had already been removed and was now taken down to its smallest components, cleaned and reassembled.

Time passed and it was nine o'clock before the engine was ready to be tested once again. After a few preliminary coughs it began to work normally, or apparently so, but not wishing to waste fuel Nelson ordered it to be stopped while the anchor was hauled up. This done and everything made ready, Georges was told to start up. A further delay was then caused by the mechanic announcing that the sump was low in oil and that he would have to top up. Eventually, the *St Antoine* started to plough her slow way back to the bank, and all the crew relaxed, feeling sure that their little misadventure was now over.

They had not gone half a mile when there was a frantic yell from Georges, who, on going back to check, had found hot oil spraying from the crankcase all over the engine room and the engine temperature rising to beyond its safe limits. There was nothing to do but stop it. When the engine was cool enough to touch, the mess was cleaned up and the damage evaluated. From all appearances it seemed that either the crankcase was cracked or the gasket had 'blown' but when the engine was running so much oil was spurting out that it was impossible to tell which. Nelson fully realized the gravity of this new situation. Unless they could get an hour's running out of the motor now, they might very soon drift a long way out and really lose the bank. It was imperative that they reach the shallows at once. There they could anchor and effect repairs, or just hang on and wait for a favourable wind. Out here they could do nothing except drift further away, out into the deep where no fishing boats came, no fish were to be caught and where they would be truly lost.

He stationed two men beside the engine: Georges to supervise things in general and another of the crew to hold a pad of cloth over the point of leakage and thus try to plug it temporarily. Another fisherman lay on the engine room hatch, a four gallon tin of lubricating oil in his hands. This he was to pour down a funnel held by Georges and leading into the oil filler. Thus set, he gave the order and again they started off.

This time they were able to run for barely ten minutes before having to give up, with the engine on the point of siezing, the

LOST: THE STORY OF NELSON TOLL

lubricating oil finished and the two Creoles who were below the deck burnt by hot oil and by contact with the crankcase. Meanwhile, all the available oil was now swilling about in the bilges.

This was then pumped out, collected, filtered after a fashion and poured back into the sump. Again they tried, again with the same results.

They went on like this until mid-afternoon, by which time they were all covered in oil and blisters and were so tired that they could hardly move. And they were still no nearer the bank; if anything, they had drifted further away. Realizing that they could do no more that day, Nelson had the anchor and all its chain paid out again, told the mechanic to strip the engine as far as he could with the tools available, and then proceeded to check their water and food supplies himself. For the night he instituted a watch system, so that no helpful breeze might pass unnoticed while they slept, nor any ship slip by under cover of darkness.

Throughout the next day and for the following week their routine was the same. Each morning Georges would try some new method of making the engine run without spewing out its oil in the space of a few minutes. They tried bolstering the gasket with sail canvas and with paper. They tried minute wooden wedges and pads bound on with fishing line. They used sea-bird feathers and caulking mixture prised up from the deck seams. All with no success.

Five or six times each day they hauled in the anchor in anticipation of a breeze that might help them, only to lower all the chain again when it did not materialize. They tried crude oars, made out of the lance hafts with blades of packing-case wood and for hours upon end they laboured, four men at a time, in an effort to make a little headway or at least to arrest their drift. On the fifth day Nelson jettisoned all the sacks of salt that lay in the hold and from his provisions threw out the curry powder and pepper as likely to promote thirst.

By the end of a week they had to give up the business of the anchor chain, for by now they were on very short rations and were beginning to lose their strength. Several times the wind started to rise, but on each occasion only from the western quarter, which meant that with such a boat as theirs they could only skate along in a northerly or southerly direction, without ever

SHARK FOR SALE

gaining a yard towards Mahé. At night, they spread the sail as an awning in the hope of collecting a little dew to supplement their water supply.

The beginning of the fourth week at sea found the crew of the *St Antoine* surprisingly cheerful. Their water was now almost gone, but they were confident that they could last out until a consistent wind, from a direction other than westerly, would enable them to make the main bank again.

This confidence of theirs was so great that when a 4,000-ton cargo vessel came over the horizon and tracked majestically across their bows they took it with extraordinary calmness and not as the miraculous event which it indeed was. This attitude considerably surprised the captain of the merchant ship when they were brought on deck. Adrift like this in the middle of the ocean, out of food and nearly out of water, he expected the coxswain to abandon his wretched little craft and ask to be taken to wherever the ss *Salween* was bound (which in this case was Sydney, Australia). But no, the little man with the blue eyes merely asked for water, some food, a few gallons of lubricating oil and the assistance of an engineer to try and patch up his engine.

With the proper tools and materials, a fresh gasket was soon produced and within four hours the *St Antoine*, declining all further aid other than a course to steer, had set off on the long haul back. The master of the *Salween*, still not entirely easy in his mind as regards the future welfare of these fishermen, sent a radio message to Mahé explaining the position and asking for an escort to be sent out to meet the boat. Unaware of this, Nelson and his crew continued merrily on their way.

Although the wind was blowing strongly from the west-southwest they were now able to hoist the jib, thanks to the impetus of the engine, and this considerably reduced the buffeting which the head-seas would otherwise have given them. They knew that they had about 240 miles to cover before reaching Mahé and were not unduly surprised at not sighting land after two days. On the third day, however, with still no sign of any familiar landmark on the horizon and still not being able to reach the bottom with a sounding line, Nelson began to worry.

After some deliberation, he came to the conclusion that the same currents that had caused him to drift off the bank in the first place were now preventing him from making the progress

LOST: THE STORY OF NELSON TOLL

he had anticipated, and he decided to carry on for another thirty-six hours before taking action. Actually, what had happened was that the *St Antoine* had entered a region of strong north-going oceanic drift which, combined with her bad sailing qualities, had caused the fishing craft to be swept up far to the north without ever crossing the Mahé plateau.

On the fifth day following their meeting with the *Salween* Nelson altered course to the west and that evening he struck off first to south-west and finally south. The wind still lay in the south-west quarter, which meant that he had to reef his sails and plough into the heavy sea under engine alone. The *St Antoine* made poor progress, burying her bows deep into each wave in turn until Nelson was obliged to reduce speed to prevent the inrush of water.

By now he fully realized he must be to the north of Mahé, for had he been to the south he would have struck Coetivy, Platte, the Amirantes or Alphonse, all of which lie to the south of the main island. For the next four days he kept going but the wind and the seas were against him. There were no sea-birds to guide him back to land, nor shoals of fish nor current streaks to mark the edge of the bank. Three days later they ran out of fuel and then the wind and sea eased and finally there came a great calm, for now, unknowingly, they had drifted into the doldrums.

Perhaps a week later they ran out of food. For a while they staved off severe hunger by catching those few pilot fish and remoras that had taken refuge under the *St Antoine* when their original shark-hosts had been caught and taken on board at the beginning of the voyage. When these were finished they sought the tiny crabs and other minute marine organisms that inhabited the thin growth of weed that grew beneath the water-line. Later they tried drawing a handkerchief through the water to catch the drifting plankton, but this brought little result. Each night they hung out all available sail and clothing to trap any dew that might fall and each dawn they tested with their tongues to see if they might draw any moisture and thus save their fast dwindling water supply.

At night they placed a hurricane lantern against the mainsail in order to catch flying fish which, attracted by the light, might skim over the water to hit the sail and drop on to the deck. But there were no flying fish in these waters, nor any other visible living creature. Finally they scraped the weed off the hull itself and ate that.

After five weeks their water gave out and with it their hopes. They were not angry with fate for having protracted their lives in this fashion. They did not curse their luck, nor the weather, nor even the bad qualities of the *St Antoine* that had brought them to this pass. They had all lived with this hazard far too long to rant against it. The most one of them ever said was: '*La mer est comme les femmes. Ou jamais connais qui faire*' (The sea is like all women. You can never tell what she'll do next).

Then they lay down under their awning and prepared to die. One day without water. Two days. Three days.

By day the blazing sun and its reflection that pierced their sunken eyes whenever they were opened.

Heat and no wind. The furnace of mid-day. Silence and heat. Heat . . .

In the evening a coolness that all too soon gave way to an intense cold that ate into their bones and left them shivering and numb, the result of their starvation.

On the fourth night one of them dreamt that he had spoken with his father, dead now for fifteen years. His father told him: 'It's all right. It will soon be over. Have no fear, you.'

In the morning he recounted this to the others. It took him a long time, for he could barely speak.

When he had finished they thought about it and all came to the same conclusion: that their sufferings were nearly over and very soon they would die. None of them doubted but that it was the fisherman's father who had visited the *St Antoine*.

It was no mere dream but a visitation. Comforted, they lay back and waited for death.

Some hours later the one who had dreamt the dream became aware of a steady pulsating noise that was being transmitted to his ears through the deck planks on which his head was resting. For several minutes he lay on there, too far gone even to puzzle over this intrusion into the quietude that had surrounded them for so long. Eventually, he roused himself sufficiently to roll over in an effort to move away from the noise. In doing so he glanced casually out over the stern. There, bearing fast down on them,

LOST: THE STORY OF NELSON TOLL

was a large tanker. For long seconds he stared incredulously at the ship until he awoke sufficiently to lean over and prod young Georges, who lay next to him. His efforts might have been useless if the tanker, at that moment, had not sounded a blast from her siren. This tremendous noise caused them all to jerk upright, but they were too weak to do other than wave feebly as the great ship came on.

For some moments it looked as though their rescuer might also be their destroyer, for so close were they when first seen that the other vessel had no chance to alter course, but had put her engines at full astern in an effort to avoid crushing the *St Antoine* like matchwood beneath her bows.

As it was the tanker had very little way when she struck the little fishing craft, and her steel bows sheered into the wooden hull with sufficient force to carry the schooner under. At the same instant, ropes fell heavily on the deck among the crouching fishermen but they were too weak and too stupefied to take hold. Seconds later several deckhands scrambled down onto the splintered, battered *St Antoine* and succeeded in making her fast to the tanker which now wallowed gently at a dead stop.

Slings were passed down, the fishermen hoisted on board and rushed into the sick-bay. After one look at the damage already done to the fishing boat the captain of the tanker saw that it would be impossible to bring her in too and, rather than leave her as a menace to other shipping, decided to sink her. Accordingly he drew off and then ran down the little derelict once more. There was a splintering noise, a slight shock of impact and then all that remained of the *St Antoine* was a conglomeration of timbers, cordage and sail that lay scattered in the tanker's wake. The Indian Ocean had claimed the *St Antoine* at last, but Nelson Toll and his crew were safe!

There is one other person who figures indirectly, but prominently, in this story: the owner of the *St Antoine*. When his ship first became overdue he neither reported this fact nor took any other action. Much later, when Nelson Toll and his companions eventually arrived back in Mahé, several of them had to be sent to hospital for further convalescence. Whilst there, their *patron* neither visited them nor sent any word of condolence. Nelson only saw him once again in connection with the *St Antoine* and that was when he went to ask for those few rupees back pay due to himself as coxswain and also for that due to the mechanic. He came away empty-handed.

There is nothing unusual about the experience of Nelson Toll, other than that he survived. The other shark-fishing crews of the Seychelles risk their lives in similar fashion each day during the season. The fear of drifting off the bank, of engine failure and an ill-placed wind, of storm and cyclone are threats with which they live constantly. To combat these they have only their skill, initiative and courage, for their boats are frequently shabby, patched-up old vessels with unreliable and badly-maintained engines. Nor are their rewards large. Should a boat bring in consistently good catches the shark-fishermen on board might average about five or six pounds per month from October to April. For the rest of the year they live as best they can on what little they have saved, aided by what casual labour they can pick up. In many instances these men could earn more money in other employment, but to do so would be considered a breach of faith, for their professional self-respect is considerable. *Un pêcheur des requins* looks down upon the plantation worker, the labourer, the clerk and the shopkeeper as, quite rightly, inferior beings. For they are, too.

The shark-fisherman must always be an individualist, standing apart from most other members of his society. Whilst others sleep secure in their beds he knows the wildness of the night, the stinging slap of driving spray, bitter cold, discomfort, fear and danger.

He knows that he will never become rich and that all too soon he will join the ranks of those shabby and rheumy old men who sun themselves along the harbour wall and talk of past voyages. All this the shark-fisherman of Mahé knows, yet he is willing to trade his chances in other walks of life for that one thing he values: the ability to act as an independent human being; to make decisions and to be bound by them. For these are men.

AUTHOR'S NOTE

To show that the story of Nelson Toll does not represent an isolated and rare incident, the following newspaper report is quoted from the *Mombasa Times* of 27 February 1960. '. . . Another tragic reminder of the Seychellois fishing indus-

LOST: THE STORY OF NELSON TOLL

try's need for assistance is contained in the news of yet another fishing boat missing, and despite searches nothing has been heard of the crew of five. Recently, one crippled vessel was found by a Japanese tunny-fishing boat 300 miles out after having been adrift for 50 days. The five-man crew had been without food or water for six days . . .'

TEN

Leavetaking

When a few years are come, then I shall go the way whence I shall not return. (Job xvi, 22)

Two years came and went and with it the realization that shark-fishing in the Seychelles would never assume the commercial proportions that I had once hoped.

There were two reasons for this. Though the advent of the long-line had made it possible for the *Golden Bells* still to bring in good catches as compared with the other schooners, yet even we were being forced further and further afield in search of new grounds, for the very success of our technique had cleared the more accessible areas of all the large night-prowling sharks. By cruising far out off the distant banks, such as Saya de Malha, Nazareth or even Chagos – still as yet untouched – it would be possible to fill our hold on every trip, but the *Golden Bells* was too small a craft for the great distances involved. To make such voyages worthwhile one would need a vessel of at least fifty tons burthen. Such a ship would need more crew, a skilled engineer, would consume five times as much fuel oil, would require considerable upkeep and, in short, the larger catch would only serve to cover the higher operating expenses. Financially, it was a vicious circle.

As for continuing with the *Golden Bells* at her present level of production, that I would not do. In that small sphere I had learnt all I could of this work and my body that had taken the discomforts and hardships of a shark-fisherman's life without too much complaint now rebelled at the prospect of further toil. I did not mind working as a native as long as I was learning and the interest held, but having absorbed all I could I was not tempted to continue just for the fun of it. But I could not quit overnight. For one thing I had acquired a crew, lived with them and trained them – or more accurately they had trained me, for that was how the fishermen saw it, and they were probably right. Then there were other Creoles, deckhands and coxswains of various schooners whom I knew to be hard-working and decent men. They, too, were affected by the declining catches and it was generally felt that within a year most of the larger power-driven vessels would be laid up and their crews out of work.

But while commercial fishing in the Seychelles was fast dying, that in East Africa was fast expanding. The main reason for this was the recent installation of cold storage units throughout the smaller towns and distribution centres there, which meant that fresh sea-fish, locally caught, might now become available to the general population. The demand was there, the capital to build ships and set up refrigeration was available, but trained fishermen were scarce. Making use of this I was able, after several months of correspondence, to offer definite contracts to twenty chosen fishermen on behalf of a fishing enterprise based at Mombasa. Moreover, if these first crews were successful the way might be open to many more. For this reason it was essential for those selected in the first batch to be the most reliable and conscientious of the Creole fishermen available.

The crew of the *Golden Bells* qualified, that went without saying, with the exception, however, of Ton Milot. I had awful visions of what might happen to him over there and myself not on the spot to curb him. Brewery drays waylaid, fuel-oil given in exchange for ship's rum, voyages delayed because of his absence on a 'drunk'. Yet I could not find it in me to leave him out and for many weeks this was my greatest worry.

As it transpired, Ton Milot himself solved my dilemma. Almost before I had made the first obvious selections and had the chosen men vaccinated and issued with identity papers, the news of this recruitment was being bandied about the bars and the market-place. Men I did not know and had never seen on board a fishing vessel accosted me asking for jobs. The bolder ones asserted or exaggerated their abilities, the more honest and therefore the hardest to turn away admitted their lack of skill but simply asked, 'if there was, perhaps, a chance'. It was 'Capitaine' all the time now, no longer 'M'sieur'. To these men the thought of regular employment was like the scent of fresh meat to hungry dogs, and like dogs they fought among themselves for the prize. To the average Seychellois East Africa has always had the aspect of an El Dorado. It is here that those fortunate few in each generation are able to emigrate, whence they usually return many years later in comparative wealth to visit their relatives and to strike envy into the hearts of those who were compelled to remain behind. Hitherto only those families which could afford the passage money, the Immigration Bond and the many other expenses had been able to consider such a step, but here was a chance for the poorest to get away from those islands which, though they love, they feel to be accursed and which offer them so little in return for their labours. No wonder, then, that the competition to be selected ran so fierce.

Under these conditions it did not take Ton Milot long to work out a successful racket for himself. Everyone knew him as my coxswain and as such he might therefore be expected to have some influence with me. A good word from him, and who knew but that a borderline candidate for one of these precious vacancies might become a certainty. He began to drop hints of this around the town (as I heard later), and since everyone knew the way to Ton Milot's heart it was not long before the free drinks started coming in. Once the snowball began to roll, the rest was easy. The buyer of Tuesday's liquor had only to be told that Wednesday's sponsor was now slightly in favour to make the individual concerned redouble his efforts and his spending to make up the lost ground. Ton Milot had found yet another way of getting liquor and one that seemed likely to surpass all his previous schemes in its effectiveness . . .

Busy as I was with all the preparations for the move to Africa, I did not realize what was going on, though I remembered wondering where Ton Milot spent most of his days ashore, for now he was seldom seen sitting, as was customary, on the jetty wall alongside the *Golden Bells* with the rest of the crew. Even the increasing number of applicants who remarked that 'they knew Ton Milot', or that Milot would vouch for them, or again '. . . but had not Milot mentioned their name?', failed to arouse my suspicion as it should have done.

When it came to setting off on each fresh sharking cruise Ton

LEAVETAKING

Milot became increasingly reluctant to leave port. First his wife was ill, then his rheumatism was troubling him, his laundry was not ready, the weather looked bad, and so it went on with each new excuse becoming more and more feeble as his desperation increased and his inventiveness ran out. None of these appeals having had any effect upon me whatsoever, the little coxswain finally announced that he wished to stay behind for one voyage in order to get drunk. This so obviously rang true and took me so much by surprise that I let him go, for the trip in question was mainly an island-supplying run and we had no need of a full crew. On our return, however, I arranged for a quick turn-around and laid on the necessary stores for a full two-week fishing expedition in order to make up for this. Came the morning scheduled for our departure and in the wake of the rest of the crew came Ton Milot, plaintively asking for an hour's delay in order that he might attend some urgent business. I said that he could have thirty minutes and with that he trotted off townwards. On the dot of the deadline I saw his sinewy figure marching back up the jetty. Arriving at the gangplank, he looked up at me and said:

'*M'sieur*, I can't come with you. Someone is buying me drinks and you know how it is with me. I can't go. Not now.'

'You're sure?' I asked.

He nodded and turned away. I signalled to Gandhi to take the helm, told Ti-Royale to start up and we pulled away from the quay wall and headed out to sea.

We did well on that voyage. It was sixteen days before we returned, but when we did so it was with the satisfaction of having unloaded a good tonnage of shark on to the drying tables at Remire Island. By this time I had found out the reason for Ton Milot's strange behaviour of late, his miraculous source of ready liquor and his reasons for not wishing to go fishing. When we motored into Port Victoria I saw his solitary figure waiting for us at the usual tying-up place. He helped us bring the *Golden Bells* alongside without speaking. He seemed his customary self – perhaps a little subdued, but not penitent. He was Ton Milot and either you accepted him along with all his faults or not. Either way it was up to you.

Finally he looked directly at me and spoke:

'I'm through, aren't I?' he said.

SHARK FOR SALE

'Yes,' I answered.

'Thought so,' came the reply. 'Well, I'll just collect my things and then I'll be off. We're still friends, aren't we?'

'Yes, Ton Milot. It doesn't alter that.'

'That's all right then . . .' A pause. '*Captaine*, don't be too soft with those Seychellois you take to Africa with you. Ride them hard or they'll take you.'

'I know that, Ton Milot.'

Then, after he had collected the grubby beret, the wooden beer box of fishing oddments, the three torn socks and the old sail that was his bedding, he went ashore. Standing on the quayside there, his worldly belongings at his feet, he scratched his rough chin with a scrawny hand, cocked an eye up at the sky and remarked to no one in particular:

'Sweet Mother of God, but I'm thirsty!'

He was Ton Milot, he did not beg. Either you took the hint or you did not. It was up to you.

'Any use?' I held up a rupee between my fingers. He nodded and I flipped the coin across the water to him. He caught it deftly, grinned his sly, foxy grin, turned away and ambled off down the quay. Halfway along it he turned back.

'*Captaine*?' he yelled.

'Yes. What is it?'

'*Captaine*. Don't forget Milot Lablache. I'm Milot Lablache! No one else is. Only me. Don't forget that, ever. *Moi Milot, moi . . . ! Ou capable croire?*' This last, defiantly.

It was a typical Ton Milot statement. Weird, unworldly and one that set you thinking. I puzzled over it as he went on again, away down the long pier, a ragged cock-sparrow figure with a hesitant walk. I was still puzzling over it as he turned the corner at the far end and disappeared from sight.

Some weeks later I left the Seychelles on board one of the infrequent passenger ships that call there. The *Golden Bells* had been returned to her owner, the stocks of shark from Remire baled, brought back to Mahé and exported to East Africa. Though my active shark-fishing days were over and the whole enterprise had come to nought, there yet remained something worthwhile, for along with me there travelled three full crews of

LEAVETAKING

shark-fishermen. These were the first batch of what I hoped might eventually become a regular traffic and thus alleviate the unemployment amongst the Creole fisher-folk that I felt sure would otherwise occur.

We sailed at ten in the morning and by late afternoon had left the familiar peaks and cliffs of Mahé far astern, so that even the unmistakable outline of Silhouette was lost to view. Just before sundown we crossed the *bordage*, made visible by current ripples across it. So intent was I upon this last link with that part of my life which was now past that I failed to notice the little fishing vessel that had appeared, as if from nowhere, and which passed within a stone's throw. Then Gandhi at my side nudged me and drew my attention to it.

It was a Praslin craft – small, single-masted and without an engine. It was a long way out for its type and I speculated idly as to whose it might be before my eyes were attracted by a figure crouching in the stern, and I realized why it was that Gandhi had nudged me. A small, thin little man, squatting on his hams. On his head a flat and rakishly tilted straw boater of ancient design. His head was turned towards us and though in shadow he was obviously staring up at us even as we gazed down at him.

It was Ton Milot, far out on the banks that he loved. He saw us and we saw him. Neither side gave any sign of recognition – we did not need to. We had lived and worked side by side too long for such superfluous gestures. We looked and saw and then he turned away and went on unravelling the bait-fish line with old but nimble fingers.

And so we left him there, rocking in our wake.

Appendix

Types of sharks found around the Seychelles

COMMON NAME	CREOLE EQUIVALENT	SCIENTIFIC
Lesser white-tipped	Peau claire or Requin hoareau	Carcharinus albimarginatus
Black-tipped shark	Requin bar	" melanopterus
Soupfin shark	Requin grandes ailes	" longimanus
Tiger shark	Demoiselle	Galeocerdo cuvier
Pointed-nosed shark	Requin nez-nez pointe	Carcharinus sorrah
White death or Great white shark	Requin gros blanc	Carcharodon carcharias
Greater white-tipped	Requin canal	Eulamia longimanus
Sharp-nosed shark	Requin bordage	Scoliodon dumerilii
Bull shark	Requin gros la tête	Eulamia leucas
Blue whaler	Montant bleu	Carcharinus glaucus
Hammerhead	Marteau	Sphyrna
Brown, Sand or Grey nurse shark	Requin de sable	Carcharinus taurus
Mako shark	Montant bleu (incorrectly)	Isurus glaucus
Whale shark	Chagrin	Rhinodon typicus
Nurse shark	Endormi	Ginglymostoma cirratus
Rat or Cat shark	Endormi requin	Trianodon obesus
White shark	Requin blanc	Carcharinus bleckeri